Lecture Notes in Computer Science 2362

Edited by G. Goos, J. Hartmanis and J. van Leeuwen

T0230294

Springer
Berlin
Heidelberg
New York
Barcelona
Hong Kong
London
Milan
Paris
Tokyo

Makoto Tanabe Peter van den Besselaar
Toru Ishida (Eds.)

Digital Cities II

Computational and Sociological Approaches

Second Kyoto Workshop on Digital Cities
Kyoto, Japan, October 18-20, 2001
Revised Papers

 Springer

Volume Editors

Makoto Tanabe
Ube National College of Technology
Tokiwadai, Ube City
Yamaguchi Pref., 755-8555, Japan
E-mail: tanabe@ube-k.ac.jp

Peter van den Besselaar
Department of Social Sciences
Netherlands Institute of Scientific Information NIWI
Royal Netherlands Academy of Arts and Sciences
Joan Muyskenweg 25, PO Box 95110
1090 HC Amsterdam, The Netherlands
and
University of Amsterdam
Social Informatics Program, Faculty of Social and Behavioral Sciences
Amsterdam, The Netherlands
E-mail: peter.van.den.besselaar@niwi.knaw.nl

Toru Ishida
Kyoto University, Department of Social Informatics
Laboratory for Global Information Network
Yoshida-honmachi, Sakyo-ku
606-8501 Kyoto, Japan
E-mail: ishida@i.kyoto-u.ac.jp

Cataloging-in-Publication Data applied for

Die Deutsche Bibliothek - CIP-Einheitsaufnahme

Digital cities II : revised papers / Second Kyoto Workshop on Digital
Cities, Kyoto, Japan, October 19 - 20, 2001. Makoto Tanabe ... (ed.). -
Berlin ; Heidelberg ; New York ; Barcelona ; Hong Kong ; London ; Milan ;
Paris ; Tokyo : Springer, 2002
    (Lecture notes in computer science ; 2362)
    ISBN 3-540-43963-3

CR Subject Classification (1998): K.4, C.2, H.4, H.5.2-3, K.8, I.2, J.4

ISSN 0302-9743
ISBN 3-540-43963-3 Springer-Verlag Berlin Heidelberg New York

Springer-Verlag Berlin Heidelberg New York,
a member of BertelsmannSpringer Science+Business Media GmbH
© Springer-Verlag Berlin Heidelberg 2002
Printed in Germany

Typesetting: Camera-ready by author, data-conversion by PTP-Berlin, Stefan Sossna e.K.
Printed on acid-free paper   SPIN: 10870287   06/3142   5 4 3 2 1 0

Preface

This book contains the papers presented at the *second Kyoto Workshop on Digital Cities* that took place in October 2001. This was the third in a series of three related conferences. The previous conferences were the *Kyoto Workshop on Communityware and Social Interaction* in 1998, and the *first Kyoto Workshop on Digital Cities*, in September 1999. Together they have contributed to the advancement of the research on digital cities, one of the research topics within the emerging field of 'social informatics'.

The meeting aimed at improving our understanding of the current status and future of those classes of systems that can be subsumed under the heading of digital city. What are feasible models for digital cities? What do experiments with digital cities teach us? What new technologies for digital cities emerge? The meeting aimed at encouraging research and practical activities in this field, and enabled the interaction between computer scientists, social scientists, and enlightened practitioners, engaged with digital cities. Topics of discussion were design and analysis, theoretical perspectives on digital cities, experiments with digital cities and with community networks, applications of digital cities, user studies, visualization, (mobile) technologies for digital cities, social interaction and communityware, user involvement in digital cities and community networks, and organizational and business models for digital cities.

The symposium which took place on the first day of the meeting was attended by more than 300 participants. The two other days of the meeting were open for invited participants only, and were attended by about 60 researchers from 13 countries from all over the world: Austria, Brazil, Canada, China, Finland, Germany, Greece, Ireland, Japan, The Netherlands, Sweden, UK, and the US. More than 30 papers were presented together with demonstrations of developed software, giving a good overview of the state of the art of the field. The meeting concluded with a special *panel on the future of collaboration*, which was organized by the NTT Communication Laboratory as a celebration of its 10th anniversary. This volume consists of most of the papers presented during the meeting.

The volume is organized as follows. In the introduction, we discuss the concept of the digital city and we give an overview of the content of this volume. We also present the issues in digital cities research, development, and practice that emerged from the discussions held during the meeting. Part 1 of the book contains theoretical chapters offering several perspectives on digital cities. In part 2, three chapters are collected that describe the digital cities movement from various techno-political perspectives. In part 3, examples of and experiments with digital cities and related systems are described and analyzed. The five examples come from various parts of the world: Ireland, US, Germany, and Japan. The five chapters of part 4 present evaluations of various aspects of digital cities. In the next parts, the focus shifts from the social and organizational dimension to the technical dimension. In part 5, architectures for digital cities are discussed, and part 6 presents technologies for several services digital cities may provide.

Despite the fact that the workshop took place shortly after the drama of 11 September, almost all participants were able to come to Kyoto. However, as digital cities are related to real cities, the reflection on digital cities was influenced by the attacks on the World Trade Center in New York and its aftermath. This is clearly visible in several of the papers included is this book.

Last but not least we would like to acknowledge the very generous support from various sides. The Japan Science and Technology Corporation (JST), the Department of Social Informatics, Kyoto University, and the NTT Communication Science Laboratories sponsored the meeting in various ways. We would like to thank the members of the International Program Committee for their work in the review process. Finally, the local organizers and especially Shoko Toda did a great job, and through their hard work the workshop turned into a successful and pleasant event.

May 2002

Makoto Tanabe
Peter van den Besselaar
Toru Ishida

Organization

Committee

Symposium Chair:	Toru Ishida (Kyoto University, Japan)
Workshop Chairs:	Peter van den Besselaar (University of Amsterdam, The Netherlands)
	Makoto Tanabe (JST Digital City Research Center, Japan)
Panel Chair:	Kiyoshi Kogure (NTT Communication Science Laboratories, Japan)
Exhibition Chair:	Hiroshi Ishiguro (Wakayama University, Japan)
Secretariat:	Shoko Toda (JST Digital City Research Center, Japan)

Workshop Program Committee

M. Antonietta	H. Ishiguro	E. Osawa
N. Arai	K. Kogure	P. Resnic
S. Azechi	F. Kusunoki	H. Schlichter
L. Bannon	K. Kuutti	A. Serra
A. Bianchi	K.J. Lee	H. Sheng
G.C. Bowker	B.D. Loader	H. Shimazu
J-P. Briot	P. Luff	S. Shimojo
A. Cardon	P. Mambrey	Y. Sumi
L. Cheng	P. Marti	T. Terano
N.S. Contractor	K. Matsuda	H. Tsuji
M. Gurstein	H. Nakanishi	M. Tsukamoto
K. Hanson	K. Nakata	A. Yoshida
H. Isahara	Y. Nakatani	
K.C. Isbister	I. Noda	

Sponsoring Institutions

Japan Science and Technology Corporation (JST), Japan
Department of Social Informatics, Kyoto University, Japan
NTT Communication Science Laboratories, NTT Corporation, Japan

Table of Contents

Evaluations

Architectures for Digital Cities

Technologies for Digital Cities

Introduction: Digital Cities Research and Open Issues

Peter van den Besselaar[1], Makoto Tanabe[2], and Toru Ishida[3]

[1]Social Sciences Department, Netherlands Institute of Scientific Information
Royal Netherlands Academy of Arts and Sciences
PO Box 95110, 1090 HC Amsterdam, The Netherlands
Peter.van.den.besselaar@niwi.knaw.nl
[2]Ube National College of Technology
Tokiwadai, Ube, Yamaguchi, 755- 8555, Japan
tanabe@ube-k.ac.jp
[3]Department of Social Informatics, Kyoto University,
Kyoto, 606-8501, Japan
ishida@i.kyoto-u.ac.jp

Modern information and communication technologies are leaving the company and the work place, and are entering everyday life in a fast pace [1, 2, 4]. As a consequence, new research fields emerge focusing on the design, evaluation, and implications of ICT based systems for social and urban life, the field of digital cities research being one of those. This volume gives a broad and up to date overview of the research done in this field.[1]

1   What Is a Digital City?

Information and communication spaces using the *city metaphor* are being developed worldwide: Seattle, Blacksburg, Amsterdam, Helsinki, Shanghai, and Kyoto, to name only some well-known examples [8]. However, despite the common terminology digital cities have different goals, offer different services, use different system architectures, and have developed different organizational forms and business models. This variety is related to the different social contexts in which digital cities have developed. At the same time digital cities are a dynamic phenomenon, and it is expected that digital cities will change as computer and network technologies develop, and as the social and economic environment in which they operate is changing. Evaluations of some of the earlier experiments have already illustrated this [10].

The diversity of the digital cities phenomenon is also visible in this volume. The digital cities analyzed here are very heterogeneous, even if one restricts a comparison to the aims of the projects only. Some are aiming at empowering local citizens in general (Seattle), or more specific low income communities (Cramfield). Other projects are aiming at local or regional development and on educating and training people in using ICT (Gelsenkirchen, Ennis) or try to develop modern ICT

---

[1] For an earlier overview of digital city research: [7]. For an extensive description and analysis of six digital cities: [8]

M. Tanabe, P. van den Besselaar, T. Ishida (Eds.): Digital Cities, LNCS 2362, pp. 1-9, 2002.
© Springer-Verlag Berlin Heidelberg 2002

infrastructures to support E-government (Vienna). Other aims are the development of a public virtual communication space (Amsterdam) and the development of models for building and maintaining a website for a town (Westfield). Finally, digital city projects are engaged in developing next generation community networks (Urban-net), or social information infrastructures for the 21st century (Kyoto). Apart from the diverging aims, the digital city projects differ in size and numbers of users, in organizational format, in funding opportunities, in ownership and involvement of local organizations and citizens, in technology used (from low-tech to very advanced ICT), and so on. This variety leads to the question whether all these digital city projects belong to a single category of systems? If so, what are the general characteristics, and what does this imply for research?

The concept of digital city is used in three different but related ways. First of all, a digital city is a *representation of a real city*, town or village on the Internet, offering citizens all kinds of information about the real city, as well as possibilities for communication and social interaction. Second, a digital city can be defined as a city with an *advanced information and communication infrastructure* needed to catch up with the global economic dynamics, or to revitalize the local or regional economic structure. Third, the concept of a digital city can refer to *systems that use the city metaphor*, like virtual communities for collaboration or for playing games. Examples in this volume of the first category are - despite many differences - Digital City Kyoto, Seattle Community Network, Westfield Directory, and Amsterdam Digital City. Examples of the second category are Urban-net NY, Project Gelsenkirchen/ Rheinisch-Bergische Kreis, Ennis Information Age Town, and the City of Vienna. The Cramfield Estate-MIT Community Connections Project belongs also to this category, although the focus of this project is on supporting a small low-income community, more that on revitalizing the techno-economic structure of a town. Examples in this volume of the third category are virtual environments like 'Twin Worlds', 'V-Chat', and the virtual learning environments 'DigitalEE'.

What perspectives on digital cities kind can be discerned, and which theories can be used to study digital cities? One approach is to place the phenomenon of digital cities in the larger socio-economic developments of the network society [2]. A second approach is to study a digital city from the perspective of urban studies, focusing on how advanced ICT's interact with urban structures and dynamics [3, 9]. A third 'micro' approach studies digital cities as a resource for individual persons in their social networks [11]. Finally, one can look at the digital city from a 'webometrics' point of view, that is applying the 'laws of the web' on the development of digital cities [5].

2   Digital Cities Research: An Overview of This Volume

In *part one* of this volume, some of these theoretical approaches are discussed. Barry Wellman, using a social network analysis point of view, discusses the changes that have taken place in personal networks and communities, from little boxes via glocalization to what he calls networked individualism. The changing nature of social networks is linked to the development of the new communication media, and implications for designing digital cities are suggested.

In the next chapter, Gary Gumpert and Susan Drucker argue how communication theory can inform the study of digital cities. In their view cities are communication systems, and ICT creates a new urban communication infrastructure that will change urban life. As these changes also create new risks (for example surveillance), there is an urgent need for new regulatory frameworks.

A third theoretical perspective is introduced by Stelios Lelis et al and by Victor Kryssanov et al; both chapters suggest to apply theories of self-organization to understand the dynamics, the emerging structure and the identity of digital cities.

Digital cities are not only subjects of academic research but also embedded in policy contexts. In the chapters of *part two* of this volume, different political visions on digital cities are developed. The chair of the European TeleCities consortium, Ingrid Götzl, places the digital city in a technological-economic perspective. In her view, cities should develop policies to introduce ICT's in fast pace, in order to adapt to the dynamics of technological and economic change.

Doug Schuler develops a techno-activist perspective, in which digital cities are seen as community networks to empower ordinary citizens. The difference with the TeleCities perspective is considerable, as in Götzl's approach government and (large) companies are the main actors involved, where Schuler stresses the role of non-profit organizations, NGO's, and individual citizens.

Peter Day, adopting a point of view similar to that of Doug Schuler, analyses previous experiences with community networks. From this, he develops normative guidelines for democratic design of community ICT initiatives. He stresses the need to embed these initiatives in the local community, and to stimulate community ownership of the systems.

In *part three*, five digital city projects are analyzed. Randal Pinkett describes an ongoing project where computers are introduced in a low-income community for the purpose of community building and economic development. His paper describes the theoretical approach, the methodology adopted, and the first research results. The project improves the relations between residents, local businesses and local institutions and organizations, and increases the awareness of the assets available to the community.

Karrie Hanson and Gerald Karam describe the development of a local information and communication network in a small town. Many municipalities do have community websites but it is well known that the information on these websites is often outdated and badly maintained. Their project aimed at the development of technical tools and organizational structures to solve these maintenance problems.

One of the lessons is that the selection of sponsors is crucial, as specific interests of sponsors may interfere with the development and the results of the project.

Helen McQuillan describes a heavily funded project to introduce advanced ICT in a small Irish town. She discusses the aims and organization, the participation of various partners in the project, and the building blocks: access to the communication infrastructure, developing skills, public sector projects, and the local community website. Successes are summarized, as well as remaining problems around uneven participation and the digital divide.

Kikuko Harada and Hiroshi Hoshino analyze a project of virtual enterprise networks aiming at the development of entrepreneurial skills. The project did create virtual communities of students, teachers, and business people to simulate enterprises, in interaction with real communities and real enterprises. In the evaluation, the participants were rather positive about what they had learned from the experiment. Their entrepreneurial skills had increased, and the projects created a useful overview of the resources available within the community.

In the last chapter in this part, Dieter Rehfeld and Ileana Hamburg present the goals and set-up of a recently started project which uses ICT for the revitalization of the economic structure of a region that suffered from the decline of traditional manufacturing industries. The project will focus on the development of a digital infrastructure supporting knowledge-based services and on the use of ICT's to create advanced learning environments.

In *part four* several aspects of digital cities are evaluated. Murali Venkatesh and Donghee Shin analyze the dilemma's emerging in large-scale projects aiming at advanced local community infrastructures. Despite the social goals formulated at the start of the project, the large investors in Urban-net focused on the resource-rich and profitable customers, while neglecting the resource-poor groups. This resulted in a strong tension between the economic interests and the social interests of the project. The authors remain rather pessimistic about the possibilities to realize the social goals under these circumstances.

Agneta Ranerup analyzes a similar situation in Sweden. She also shows the contradictory interests of the parties involved. However, as the funding was partly obtained from EU research programs, and as a powerful social organization (the Swedish trade union) was involved in the project, it proved to be possible to realize also the social goals and not only the commercial ones.

Lili Cheng and her co-workers studied social interaction within virtual environments in order to learn about the design of digital cities. They focus on the factors that create sustainability of on-line communities. The lessons learned refer to various levels: the individual, the social dynamics, and the environment. One of the interesting lessons is that communication tools have to be highly efficient. Therefore, the advanced 3-D graphical interfaces and tools for synchronous communication were not very popular, as they are difficult to handle in coordinating interaction.

Els Rommes evaluates the interface of the Amsterdam Digital City (DDS). The designers of the DDS wanted to create an interface which was easy to understand, and which one could learn to use by 'playing around'. However, Els Rommes' experiments show that the interface is not easy at all for several categories of users, especially for novices, and that learning by 'playing around' may be attractive for advanced computer users – like the designers of the system – but not for novices.

In the last chapter, Kaoru Hiramatsu evaluates the map-based search engine of the Digital City Kyoto, using log-files covering a 16 months period. He found that users visit sites on entertainment, sports, and computers and the Internet much more frequently than sites with more serious content such as education, health, politics and science. Another result he found is that the presence of geographical maps does influence the search process. Areas with dense supply of content do attract many more visitors to the websites belonging to that geographical area.

After part four, the focus shifts from the sociological to the technological dimensions of digital cities, and in *part five* several architectures for digital cities are presented. In the first chapter, Toru Ishida and his colleagues describe the approach adopted in Digital City Kyoto project. The architecture of this project consists of basic technologies for representing geographical information, for receiving and sending information, and for participation. As a goal for the future, Toru Ishida suggests the extension of the architecture with technologies for real time translation, in order to support cross-cultural communication in digital cities.

Katy Börner presents her Twin Worlds, a 3-D architecture for navigating in information spaces. The system does not only visualize the shared information space, but also the interaction of the users with the information in that space. She argues that this type of advanced visualization techniques are needed in the digital cities of tomorrow.

In the third chapter, Tomohiro Fukuhara and his colleagues outline the Public Opinion Channel, an architecture enabling informal communication within digital cities. Experiments indicate that this type of systems may help newcomers to integrate more easily in the local discussions.

In the next chapter, Jun-ichi Akahani and his co-workers introduce an agent based system for coordinating regional information services. In their view, such systems are needed to cope with the heterogeneous and distributed nature of local and regional information systems and services.

The last chapter describes a digital learning environment. Masaya Okada and his colleagues have developed DigitalEE, an architecture for public participation and for education within dynamically changing virtual environments.

The chapters collected in *part six* present a variety of systems for digital cities. Hiroya Tanaka and her collaborators have developed a tool, which enables people without special computing skills to create 'pseudo 3-D environments' using digital photos. The usability of the tool was demonstrated in an experiment, as the participants were able to create a 3-D representation of a street within an hour.

Koichi Goto and Yahiko Kambayashi have developed a mobile passenger support system for public transport, as an example of an ICT based service in a digital city. The prototype they have developed supports visual handicapped people to find their way in train stations.

If digital cities are a virtual representation of the real city to inform citizens and visitors, the updating and use of the information should not be restricted to those sitting behind their computer. An obvious possibility to avoid this restriction is using mobile telephones. Hiroshi Tsuji and his co-workers have developed a concept of a mobile phone based system for sharing spatial information.

In the fourth chapter, Bernard Burg discusses the need for standardizing 'active web-based services', in relation to the semantic web and agent technologies. The Agentcities project is presented, a testbed environment, open for anybody who wants to participate.

Satoshi Koizumi, Guiming Dai and Hiroshi Ishiguro propose a system for creating image based virtual reality applications. Cameras are used to create the digital images of a real space, and by interpolating the system creates a smooth, continuous view, which enables users to navigate through the virtual representation of the real space.

The next chapter describes a system for simulating disasters and rescue activities. Itsuki Noda and co-workers propose a model for simulating communication between civilian agents and rescue agents during disasters. The ultimate system may be used for evaluating emergency plans, for training rescue teams, and for supporting real time planning of rescue activities.

In the final chapter, Aradhana Goel investigates the use of handheld mobile devices for navigation in cities that goes beyond static maps and directories. The proposed dynamic system reflects the volatile and unpredictable nature of urban life. It aims at mapping personal and collective experiences, using social networks for sharing those experiences.

3   Issues for Further Research

As last part of this introduction, we briefly summarize the discussions that took place during the workshop. Of course, this is not an exhaustive overview, but we hope to have covered the most important issues. First of all, digital city development and research are a *multidisciplinary* activity, including practitioners, technologists, and social researchers, and they do not necessarily share the same goals and perspectives. Practitioners, like community builders, civil servants and citizens often want to create useful things for now. Technologist, on the other hand, often look forward and ask what new and advanced things we may be able to make in the future. As soon as technologists have developed something, they want to go further. New 'hot' technical questions are often asked even before the answers on previous questions have been evaluated. Social researchers generally want to look back and do research on real life experiences with the use of the technological systems. How does technology interact with urban life, with social networks, and with organizations an institutions? Consequently there is a need for improving the communication between these three groups involved. How can practitioners and social researchers inform the technological research agenda? And how can social researchers and technologists inform practitioners, without eliminating the room for practitioners to specify their aims, needs and experiences. How can we bring about that the various disciplines unite, and join forces to improve digital cities design, research, and practice?

As the chapters in this volume indicate, a lot of development work is done to create architectures for digital cities, to create tools for building digital cities, and to create relevant applications of digital cities. At the same time, there is a need for more *experimenting and testing*. Especially real-life, large-scale, and long-term tests are needed to investigate the usability but also the second-order and unforeseen effects of the technologies, as well as the way the technologies are used and domesticated by the users. And not only testing, but also *theoretical understanding* may help the improvement of digital city design. The chapters in the first part of this volume suggest some directions to follow, but a lot of work is still needed.

An important issue is the increasing use of monitoring and feedback tools in the systems developed, and the risks this brings for *privacy and autonomy*. To improve communication, navigation and awareness in digital cities, information on behavior is needed: log-files, cameras, tracking, profiling and user feedback systems. Technologists like this type of information to monitor and improve their systems; business people operating the system want this type of information as it creates opportunities for earning money; politicians want it for control and surveillance; and sociologists love this information as it is a rich data source for analyzing use and users behavior, and for analyzing the implications of technical systems on social processes. Even the users may want this kind of information to navigate and to find and do things they want. However, the dangerous part is that privacy and autonomy are under thread, and the trade off between opportunities and risks of monitoring and feedback systems urgently needs further thought and reflection.

A fourth issue is the tension between *commercial and social aims* of digital cities. Digital infrastructures and services require investments, and therefore resource-rich customers. This may increase the digital divide, despite the social goals the projects may initially have had. On the other hand, if community networks and digital cities aim at improving the opportunities and access to resources for low-income groups, then private companies should be part of the partnership, as they bring in resources (jobs, subsidies, etc.), however without being able to take over the whole project for commercialization. Related to this is *the problem of organizational forms* for digital cities. Relevant questions to be answered are: What parties should be involved, how should user involvement and representation be organized, what funding mechanisms may work? Existing digital cities show a large variety of organizational forms, but what models are sustainable is still an open question.

Digital cities and community networks are often described as tools to support *social development and empowerment*. But what are the benefits of introducing ICT's for social development? Offering people the possibility to use advanced ICT's does not necessarily imply that these possibilities are used, and when they are used, it is still the question for what. More fundamentally, even if the technological possibilities are used, why should we expect that they form a relevant resource for social development, for creating a better life (e.g. finding a job)? The question to be answered is *under which conditions* new technologies can be used for social development and empowerment.

Finally, quite some *design issues* were discussed, such as the question whether to use low-tech or high-tech solutions. Should we go for high-tech solutions, as we are often told that within a couple of years all problems with software and bandwidth are solved? Or does the advancement of the technology always re-create those problems on a higher level? And, do users want the high-tech solutions? Increasing technical possibilities may not be used, as people have only limited capacities for communication and information processing. This dilemma cannot be really 'solved', and it reflects the different views in a multidisciplinary environment already discussed above. Of course, from a users point of view, low-tech solutions may often fit better in ongoing practices. And high-tech solutions may decrease the number of people who have access, resulting in a deepening of the digital divide. However, one should not forget that today's low-tech is yesterdays high-tech. And some high-tech is diffusing very quickly, as for example cellular phones. Other examples of today's high-tech (like 3-D interfaces) may become generally available and used somewhere in the near future. In other words, the boundary between high-tech and low-tech moves with technological development and with the processes of social learning in the user communities. Therefore, the dilemma is how to stimulate processes of co-evolution between use and development of digital city technologies in a fruitful way, keeping in mind the danger of a persisting or even increasing digital divide

The chapters in this volume give a broad and up to date overview of digital cities research and development, and digital cities social research. It has resulted in interesting systems, experiments and lessons. At the same time, we still face many open questions that ask for further work. We hope that this volume stimulates further work in this scientifically challenging and socially useful field of *social informatics*.

References

[1]   American Behavioral Scientist 45, 3, November 2001.
[2]   M. Castells, The internet galaxy. Oxford, Oxford University Press, 2001.
[3]   S. Graham and S. Marvin Telecommunications and the city, London, Routledge, 1996.

[4] P. Howard, L. Rainie and S. Jones "Days and nights on the internet: the impact of a diffusing technology," American Behavioral Scientist 45, 3 pp. 363-382, 2001.

[5] A. Huberman, Laws of the web. Cambridge, MIT Press, 2001.

[6] T. Ishida (Ed.), Community Computing and Support Systems, Lecture Notes in Computer Science, Vol. 1519, Springer-Verlag, 1998.

[7] T. Ishida, and K. Isbister (Eds.), Digital cities, experiences, trends, and perspectives, Lecture Notes in Computer Science 1765, Springer-Verlag, 2000.

[8] T. Ishida, World digital cities. Forthcoming

[9] W.J. Mitchell, E-topia; It's urban life Jim, but not as we know it. Cambridge, MIT Press, 1999.

[10] P. Van den Besselaar, "E-community versus E-commerce: the rise and decline of the Amsterdam Digital City," AI & Society 15, pp. 280-288, 2001.

[11] B. Wellman, Networks in the global village. Boulder: Westview Press,1999.

Little Boxes, Glocalization, and Networked Individualism

Barry Wellman

Centre for Urban & Community Studies, University of Toronto,
455 Spadina Avenue, Toronto Canada M5S 1A1
wellman@chass.utoronto.ca
http://www.chass.utoronto.ca/~wellman

Abstract. Much thinking about digital cities is in terms of community groups. Yet, the world is composed of social networks and not of groups. This paper traces how communities have changed from densely-knit "Little Boxes" (densely-knit, linking people door-to-door) to "Glocalized" networks (sparsely-knit but with clusters, linking households both locally and globally) to "Networked Individualism" (sparsely-knit, linking individuals with little regard to space). The transformation affects design considerations for computer systems that would support digital cities.

1   From Little Boxes to Social Networks

The developed world is in the midst of a paradigm shift both in the ways in which people and institutions are actually connected. It is a shift from being bound up in homogenous "little boxes" to surfing life through diffuse, variegated social networks. Although the transformation began in the pre-Internet 1960s, the proliferation of the Internet both reflects and facilitates the shift.

The "little boxes" metaphor (from Malvena Reynolds' 1963 song) connotes people socially and cognitively encapsulated by homogeneous, broadly-embracing groups. Members of traditional little-box societies deal principally with fellow members of the few groups to which they belong: at home, in the neighborhood, at work, or in voluntary organizations. They work in a discrete work group within a single organization; they live in a household in a neighborhood; they are members of one or two kinship groups; and they participate in structured voluntary organizations: churches, bowling leagues, the ACM, and the like. These groups often have boundaries for inclusion and structured, hierarchical, organization: supervisors and employees, parents and children, pastors and churchgoers, organizational executives and members. In such a society, each interaction is in its place: one group at a time.

Much social organization no longer fits the little-boxes model. Work, community and domesticity have moved from hierarchically arranged, densely knit, bounded groups ("little boxes") to social networks. (Formally, a group is a special type of social network, but it is cognitively easier to compare the "group" metaphor with the "network" metaphor.) In networked societies, boundaries are more permeable, interactions are with diverse others, linkages switch between multiple networks, and hierarchies are both flatter and more complexly structured.

M. Tanabe, P. van den Besselaar, T. Ishida (Eds.): Digital Cities, LNCS 2362, pp. 10-25, 2002.

The change from groups to networks can be seen in many milieus and at many levels. Trading and political blocs have lost their monolithic character in the world system. Organizations form complex networks of alliance and exchange, often in transient virtual or networked organizations. Workers (especially professionals, technical workers, and managers) report to multiple peers and superiors. Work relations spill over their nominal work group's boundaries, and may even connect them to outside organizations. In virtual and networked organizations, management by network has people reporting to shifting sets of supervisors, peers, and even nominal subordinates.

Rather than fitting into the same group as those around them, each person has her own personal network. Household members keep separate schedules, with family get-togethers – even common meals – on the decline. Instead of belonging to two stable kinship groups, people often have complex household relations, with stepchildren, ex-marital partners (and their progeny), and multiple sets of in-laws. Communities – in the flesh as well as in the ether – are far-flung, loosely-bounded, sparsely-knit and fragmentary. Most people operate in multiple, partial communities as they deal with shifting, amorphous networks of kin, neighbors, friends, workmates, and organizational ties. Their activities and relationships are informal rather than organizationally structured. If they go bowling, they rarely join formal leagues [7]. Only a minority of network members are directly connected with each another. Most friends and relatives live in different neighborhoods; many live in different metropolitan areas. At work, people often work *with* distant others and not those sitting near them [8].

This is a time for individuals and their networks, and not for groups. The proliferation of computer-supported social networks fosters changes in *"network capital"*: how people contact, interact, and obtain resources from each other. The broadly-embracing collectivity, nurturing and controlling, has become a fragmented, variegated and personalized social network. Autonomy, opportunity, and uncertainty are the rule.

Complex social networks have always existed, but recent technological developments have afforded their emergence as a dominant form of social organization. Just as computer networks link machines, social networks link people. When computer-mediated communication networks link people, institutions and knowledge, they are *computer-supported social networks.* Often computer networks and social networks work conjointly, with computer networks linking people in social networks, and with people bringing their offline situations to bear when they use computer networks to communicate.

The technological development of computer-communications networks and the societal flourish of social networks are now affording the rise of *"networked individualism"* in a positive feedback loop. Just as the flexibility of less-bounded, spatially dispersed, social networks creates demand for collaborative communication and information sharing, the rapid development of computer-communications networks nourishes societal transitions from little boxes to social networks [1].

How has this transition come about? What implications does it have for computing, humanity and society? To address these questions, I build this article around a tripartite typology:

> Groups

> Glocalization

> Networked Individualism

This typology, illustrated in Fig. 1, reflects our NetLab's cumulative work. More details are in Table 1 and in the references. I offer it provisionally as a heuristic. In so doing, I invoke three escape clauses.

1. The typology is over-generalized: what sociologists call "ideal types". In practice, groups have cleavages and links to the outside; networks are lumpy like the universe, with regions of high and low density, coupling and decoupling.

2. The three ideal types are not mutually exclusive in societies or in people. In practice, societies and people's lives are often mixtures of groups and networks.

3. This is an attempt to highlight interpersonal phenomena relevant to computer scientists. It does not attempt to be an exhaustive list of such phenomena. There are overlapping phenomena and debatable fit into broader organizing categories. I have tried to be useful rather than produce a comprehensive account. This is a start, and hopefully, a helpful start.

Little Boxes   **Glocalization**

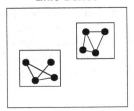   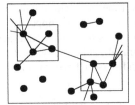

Networked Individualism

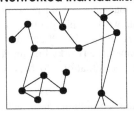

Fig. 1. Three Models of Community and Work Social Networks

2 Towards Glocalization

2.1 Little Boxes

The jump from traditional group solidarities to the evolving networked individualism has not been instantaneous. One transition was the twentieth century move from group to glocalized relationships at work and in the community. ("Glocalization" is a neologism meaning the combination of intense local and extensive global interaction.) This transition was driven by revolutionary developments in both transportation and communication. It was a move away from a solidary group in a single locale to contact between people in different places and multiple social networks. Households and worksites became important centers for networking; neighborhoods became less important. This shift has been afforded both by social changes – such as liberalized divorce laws – and technological changes – such as the proliferation of expressways and affordable air transportation [9].

Pre-industrial social relationships were based on itinerant bands, agrarian villages, trading towns, and urban neighborhoods. People walked door-to-door to visit each other in spatially compact and densely-knit milieus. If most settlements or neighborhoods contained less than a thousand people, then almost everybody would know each other. Communities were bounded, so that most relationships happened within their gates rather than across them. Much interaction stayed within neighborhoods, even in big cities and trading towns. When people visited someone, most neighbors knew who was going to see whom and what their interaction was about. Contact was essentially between households, with the awareness, sanction and control of the settlement.

This is the world that much CSCW "groupware" has been developed for, including videoconferencing, collaborative writing, and workflow. Groupware assumes a defined, fully visible population; focused on aspects of a single joint task; with all directly accessible to all. These are viable solutions, but incomplete solutions and possibly minority solutions in their assumption that the small group is all-encompassing and all-important.

2.2 Glocalized Networks

The transition from group to networked connectivity meant a shift from the settlement to the household and workgroup as the primary units of activity. If "community" is defined socially rather than spatially, then it is clear that contemporary communities rarely are limited to neighborhoods. They are communities of shared interest rather than communities of shared kinship or locality. People usually obtain support, companionship, information and a sense of belonging from those who do not live within the same neighborhood or even within the same metropolitan area. Many people's work involves contact with shifting sets of people in other units, workplaces, and even other organizations. People maintain these ties through phoning, emailing, writing, driving, railroading, transiting, and flying [9].

Neighborhoods and large work units have become more residual: variably safe and salubrious milieus from which people sally forth from their households and workplaces in their cars, telephone from their kitchens and offices, or email from their dens and desktops. Most North Americans have little interpersonal connection with their neighborhoods; they are only lightly subject to the social control of neighborhood groups. Community interactions have moved inside the private home — where most entertaining, phone-calling and emailing take place — and away from chatting with patrons in public spaces such as bars, street corners and coffee shops. The percentage of North Americans regularly socializing with neighbors has been steadily declining for three decades [7]. Few neighbors are known, and those known are rarely known well.

Glocalized networks operate more independently of their surrounding environment than little-box groups. This is not social disintegration. People and places are connected. Yet there is little social or physical intersection with the intervening spaces between households. It is place-to-place connectivity, and not door-to-door. People often get on an expressway near their home and get off near their friend or colleague's home with little sense of what is in-between. Airplane travel and email are even more context-less.

Place – in the form of households and work units does remain important – even if neighborhood or village does not. People go from some*where* to some*where* to meet some*one*, usually inside their homes. Or people telephone some*where* to talk to some*one*. The household or work unit is what is visited, telephoned or emailed. Relations within the household or work unit continue to be somewhat communal, supportive and controlling. They are the home bases from which people reach out in-person and ethereally, to engage with their networks. Yet home and office often function in private spaces that do not involve surrounding local areas. Social closeness does not mean physical closeness.

Home and office have become bases for privatized relationships that are more voluntary and selective than those that functioned in the public spaces of the past. Only a minority of ties in the developed world operate in the public contexts of neighborhood, formal organizations, or work. By contrast to traditional meetings in village squares or pubs, friends and relatives get together in private as small sets of singles or couples, but rarely as communal groups. Relationships are more selective. Networks now contain high proportions of people who enjoy one other. They contain low proportions of people who are forced to interact with each other because they are juxtaposed in the same neighborhood, kinship group, organization, or workplace.

Many characteristics of the Internet reinforce glocalized, place-to-place connectivity. Although an Internet account is usually for a person and not for a place, Internet communications are usually sent and received from a fixed place: home or office. People usually have a good idea of the sociophysical places in which the people they know are reading their messages. If they send messages to their mothers, they have a high expectancy that others at home will also read it.

The Internet both provides a ramp onto the global information highway and strengthens local links within neighborhoods and households. For all its global access, the Internet reinforces stay-at-homes. Glocalization occurs, both because the Internet makes it easy to contact many neighbors, and because fixed, wired Internet connections tether users to home and office desks.

At work or at home, many emails are local and refer to local arrangements. For example, 57% of the email messages received by computer-intensive students in my Berkeley graduate course came from within Berkeley, with another 15% coming from within the Bay area. Both friendship and involvement in joint tasks drive the frequency of emailing and face-to-face meetings, at work as well as at home. Rather than being exclusively online or in-person, many relationships are complex dances of face-to-face encounters, scheduled meetings, two-person telephone calls, emails to one or more persons, and online discussions among those sharing interests. Thus, the glocalized type is a mixed model: containing elements similar to both the little boxes and the networked individualism types (see Appendix: Table 1).

At work or in the community, glocalized connectivity affords fluid systems for using ramified networks to access resources at work and in the community: material, cognitive, and influential. No more are people identified as members of a single group; they can switch among multiple networks. Switching and maneuvering among networks, people can use ties to one network to bring resources to another. Indeed, the very fact of their ties to other networks will be a resource, creating the possibility of linkage, trade and cooperation. Knowing how to network (on and offline) becomes a human capital resource, and having a supportive network becomes a social capital resource [2]. The cost is the loss of a palpably present and visible local group at work and in the community that could provide social identity and a sense of belonging. The gain is the increased diversity of opportunity, greater scope for individual agency, and the freedom from a single group's constrictive control.

3 The Rise of Networked Individualism

3.1   From Place-To-Place to Person-To-Person

When someone calls to a telephone that is hardwired into the telephone network, the phone rings at the *place*, no matter which *person* is being called. Indeed, many place-to-place ties have connected workgroups and households as much as individuals. The Internet is changing this: People have individual Internet accounts accessible from any place.

We are now experiencing another transition, from place-to-place to person-to-person connectivity. Moving around with a mobile phone, pager, or wireless Internet makes people less dependent on place. Because connections are to people and not to places, the technology affords shifting of work and community ties from linking people-in-places to linking people wherever they are. It is I-alone that is reachable wherever I am: at a house, hotel, office, freeway or mall. The person has become the portal [9].

Where high speed place-to-place communication supports the dispersal and fragmentation of organizations and community, high speed person-to-person communication supports the dispersal and role-fragmentation of workgroups and households. The shift to a personalized, wireless world affords *networked individualism*, with each person switching between ties and networks. People remain connected, but as individuals rather than being rooted in the home bases of work unit and household. Individuals switch rapidly between their social networks. Each person separately operates his networks to obtain information, collaboration, orders, support, sociability, and a sense of belonging (see Table 1).

The organization of information-based work, manipulating bits instead of atoms, is shifting to networked individualism. By contrast to traditional organizational structures, employees in *networked organizations* have (a) multiple and shifting work partners, and (b) partial involvements with shifting sets of workgroups. Work relations are dispersed, with ties often extending across cities, provinces, nations, and even continents. Structurally, these ties extend to multiple units within the organization and, at times, to organizations elsewhere. Workers have discretion about whom they deal with, how they interact, and the time and place of their interactions.

Virtual organizations go one step further, cutting across the home organization's structure to link people from multiple organizations in temporary networks to deal with tasks. Participants inherently have multiple loyalties and partial commitments. They have other projects and task groups in which they are involved, and within-organizational careers to nurture.

Networkware affords needed flexibility to interactions in networked and virtual organizations as well as in networked communities [2, 6]. With portable communication or its flipside — ubiquitous connectivity to computer networks — physical context becomes less important. Supportive work and community convoys travel with people ethereally. They can link what they are doing at the moment to their far-flung networks, as when Bell Canada technicians climb telephone poles while wear their computers or when a lover uses her mobile phone to describe a Rembrandt exhibition to a distant partner. Physical surroundings must be described, rather than assumed because people have uncertain knowledge about the immediate whereabouts and social contexts of their mobile network members. Often, the sociophysical context is ignored, as when people talk loudly on their mobile phones in public. They are not being anti-social: the very fact of their conversation means they are socially connected. Rather, people's awareness and behavior are in private cyberspace even though their bodies are in public space.

3.2   Specialized Roles

Many interpersonal relationships are based on the specialized roles that people play. Such specialized relationships are abundant in work and community situations where people cycle through multiple social networks. At times, people prefer specialized relationships. For example, scholarly collaborators often prefer the autonomy of emailing others at a distance to the more compelling, less specialized, face-to-face relationships. They balance a desire to function according to their own independent rhythms and a desire to obtain the intellectual, material and social rewards of membership in scholarly communities. Shifting from face-to-face contact to disembodied email contact is a possible means of obtaining autonomy: Isolation is achieved without effort. These scholars can interact in narrow roles without being constrained to deal with the whole person.

At times, the Internet's lack of communicative richness can foster contact with more diverse others. The lack of social and physical cues on-line makes it difficult to find out if another online community member has similar social characteristics or attractive physical characteristics. Asynchronous communication gives participants more control over the timing and content of their self-disclosures. This allows specialized relationships to develop from shared interests rather than be stunted at the onset by differences in social status. This focus on shared interests rather than on similar characteristics can be especially empowering for members of lower-status and disenfranchised groups.

Specialized social networks consist of either like-minded people — BMW 325ix drivers or collaborating web designers — or people with complementary roles — violinists and cellists, supervisors and employees. Although such networks predate the Internet, they are flourishing as the Internet's capabilities develop and groups give way to personalized connectivity. People participate in many ways. They work almost concurrently on multiple projects that come across their computer desktop. They subscribe to multiple discussion lists and newsgroups, letting others organize the membership and course of the communities. Discussion lists and newsgroups provide permeable, shifting sets of participants, with more intense relationships continued by private email.

People vary in their involvements in different networks, participating actively in some, occasionally in others, and being silent "lurkers" in still others. Friends forward communications to third parties. In so doing, they provide indirect contact between previously-disconnected people who can then make direct contact. The proliferation of computer-supported specialized relationships provides a basis for interest-based structures that provide support, partial solidarity, and vehicles for aggregating and articulating interests. This is an Internet *cum* Tocquevillean substitute for the decline of organized community groups in America [7].

When strong ties are unable to provide information, people are likely to seek it from weak ties. Because people with strong ties are more likely to be socially similar and to know the same persons, they are more likely to possess the same information. By contrast, new information is more apt to come through weaker ties better connected with other, more diverse social circles. Hence, computer-supported solutions are developing for working through trusted interpersonal relationships to identify, locate, and receive information within and between organizations.

Will networked individualism deconstruct holistic individual identities? A person would become the sum of her roles, and need to present multiple personas to the world. This compartmentalization of personal life—within the household, at work, and in communities — may create insecure milieus where people do not fully know each other.

4 Implications for Computer Supported Social Networks

If Novell had not gotten there first, computer users might be saying "netware"™ instead of "groupware". Why is groupware a misleading term? For one thing, a group is only one special type of a social network. We need to think about the broader social processes that occur outside of groups. What is more important, "group" inaccurately describes how people interact today in the developed world, at work, in the community, and even at home. Designers need to know how the world actually functions rather than trying to force their interactions into misspecified templates. People live and work in networks, not in groups. Realizing this can aid the design and use of the right computer tools for our times.

As networked individualism develops, computer systems are being increasingly used to support person-to-person and role-to-role relationships at work, in the community and at home. To be sure, some people continue to function in traditional groups most of the time; many people function in traditional groups some of the time. Hence, groupware remains useful, but only as one part of a differentiated tool-kit to support a variety of interaction modalities. Issues of shifting connectivity, trust, knowledge management, and privacy become important as networkware evolves to support glocalization and networked individualism. A decade of research has dispelled fears that computer-mediated communication would destroy community and hinder work [3, 5, 9]. Abundant questions remain:

1. Is the online-offline dichotomy overdone? The cyberspace-physical space comparison is a false dichotomy. Many ties operate in both cyberspace and physical space. They do not exist only online but use online contact to fill the gaps between in-person meetings. Computer mediated communications supplements, arranges and amplifies in-person and telephone communications rather than replacing them. The Internet provides ease and flexibility in who communicates with whom, what means they use to communicate, what they communicate, and when they communicate. Most people communicate with their friends, relatives, neighbors and workmates, using whatever online or offline means is available, convenient, and appropriate at the moment. The stronger the tie, the more media are used.

2. Are online relationships as good as face-to-face relationships where people can see, hear, smell and touch someone, usually in a social context? Probably not, but the question has an utopian assumption that if people were not online, they would be engaged in stimulating community, household, or personal activities. In reality, online relationships often fill empty spots in people's lives now that residential dispersal and dual careers mean that they no longer wander to the local pub or café to engage with their community members. Participating in online community substitutes for television watching. As the networked individual substitutes for the lonely crowd, online relationships may be increasing the frequency and intensity of community ties, although at the potential cost of strained household ties. At times, online relationships and social networks develop their own strength and dynamics. Participants can develop interpersonal feelings of belonging, being wanted, obtaining important resources, and having a shared identity. Yet our survey of 40,000 visitors to the *National Geographic* website finds that the *more* people are online, the *less* their sense of belonging to an online community [10]. Is this a result of overload, routinization, or greater exposure to dismaying online communications?

3. What are the organizing criteria of interaction? To what extent does the Internet reduce the importance of traditional social organizing criteria such as: gender, social class, ethnicity, language, life-cycle stage, and physical location. Are these residues of little boxes, or do they reflect continuing interests? There appears to be much involvement in teams and communities of shared interest and practice. Moreover, the supplanting of little boxes by networks means more cross-cutting social ties interweaving formerly disconnected social groups and categories. With fuzzy network boundaries, individual autonomy and agency become more important, as each person becomes the responsible operator of her own personal network. Yet the traditional social organizing criteria continue to command continual attention.

4. Is the map of the world disappearing? Proximity continues to matter, but is losing its dominance. Although the work unit and the household are important bases from which to sally forth, they are only two of the multiple networks in which people are engaged. Teams and communities are more spatially and temporally dispersed. Interactions beyond the immediate work unit and household home bases are losing their privileged positions. Spatial and social peripheries have come closer to the center. Yet, glocalization expands local interactions as well as global reach. Although the Internet has its unique affordances, people continue to value the in-person experiences the proximity affords. Moreover, people, including CSCW researchers, travel long distances to hold frequent get-togethers *in-person.*

5. Does the Internet increase, decrease or supplement other forms of interaction? The evidence is mixed. At work, those who use email a lot also see each other a lot. Both working together on a task and being friends are the independent drivers. Indeed, friendship has a slightly more powerful effect than working together. In the community, those residents of "Netville" who are connected to a very high speed network know and visit more neighbors than the less-wired residents of this suburb. For example, wired residents know twenty-five neighbors, while the unwired know eight. Nor is this just local connectivity: wired families maintain more social contact and supportive exchanges with friends and relatives living outside of Netville [4]. Similarly, our *National Geographic* study reveals that people who are involved with organizations offline are also involved with them online [10]. Yet this same study shows that Internet use supplements — rather than increases — in-person and telephone contact with friends and relatives, both near and far.

6. Will the use of computer-mediated communication become more transparent as people get more experienced, and as such communication develops more verisimilitude through the use of video, et al? Is the comparison with face-to-face relationships always a rigged game in which online relationships can never be quite equal? Or would it be wiser to ask if online interaction is developing its own strengths and creating its own norms and dynamics? There already are unique Internet dynamics: folding-in two disconnected friends into the same conversation, asking personal messages of posters to online discussion groups, developing personal relationships in these groups, typographical conventions of embedding interleaved responses inside original messages, and responding to messages at the top of the message exchange rather than on the bottom. Online communication also extends the reach of networks: allowing more ties to be maintained and fostering specialized relationships in networks. Unlike face-to-face ties, the Internet simultaneously affords: (a) *personal communications* between one or multiple friends, (b) within-network *broadcasts*; and (c) *public addresses* to strangers.

7. Does the Internet promote two-person interactions at the expense of interactions happening in group or social network contexts? Such a situation emphasizes "individualism" over "networked". On the one hand, it is easy to include others in a computer-mediated conversation by sending a message to multiple others or forwarding an already-received message. On the other hand, these are always deliberate choices. By contrast, happenstance as well as deliberate choice leads people to public, in-person interactions. Such public interactions are observable and afford opportunities for others to join in.

8. As connectivity becomes person-to-person (and not door-to-door or even place-to-place), do people feel responsible for their strong relationships but not for the many acquaintances and strangers with whom they rub shoulders but are not connected? Private contact with familiar friends and workmates is replacing public gregariousness so that people pass each other unsmiling on streets, highways and hallways. Such privatization may be responsible for the lack of informal help given to strangers in public spaces. It may also explain the paradox of well-connected people feeling lonely because of the lack of physically present members of their social networks.

9. Does glocalization and networked individualism create new social needs? The good and bad thing about traditional little boxes is that they are always there. The membership and their resources are known and potentially available, whether wanted or not. The costs of this are high social control and resources limited to what is available within the group. By contrast, it is more difficult to locate and access resources in socially and spatially dispersed networks. Hence the move to a networked society places an increased importance of network capital in the fund of desirable resources, along with financial capital, human capital, organizational capital, and cultural capital. Such network capital includes the fund of others who provide tangible and intangible resources: information, knowledge, material aid, financial aid, alliances, emotional support, and a sense of being connected. It includes knowing who such people are, what resources they possess and would make available, and the indirect ties they provide to resourceful others. For example, networked individuals need to know how to maintain a networked computer; search for information on the Internet and use the knowledge gained; create and sustain online relationships; and use these relationships to obtain needed resources, including ties to friends of friends.

10. Can groupware be networkware? Networkware is not just a larger form of groupware. They serve fundamentally different social models (see Appendix: Table 1). Groupware assumes that all participants are known and largely trusted, while the essence of networkware is (a) shifting sets of interactors, and (b) the search for information and the selective disclosure of one's own information. Yet, reality rarely contains pure ideal types: Most people's lives are mixtures of groups and networks. The real question is: can groupware and networkware co-exist in the same or conjoint computer systems? Or do their disparate social characteristics inherently foster incompatible design implications?

Acknowledgements. Research underlying this article has been supported by the Bell University Laboratories, Communications and Information Technology Ontario, Mitel Networks, the Office of Learning Technologies (Human Resources and Development Canada), and the Social Science and Humanities Research Council of Canada. Kristine Klement and Uyen Quach provided valuable assistance.

References

1. Castells, M. *The Rise of the Network Society*. Blackwell, Malden, MA, 1996.
2. Cohen, D. and Prusak, L. *In Good Company: How Social Capital Makes Organizations Work*. Harvard Business School Press, Boston, MA, 2001.
3. DiMaggio, P., Hargittai, E., Neuman, W.R., and Robinson, J. Social Implications of the Internet. *Annual Review of Sociology*. 27, 2001. 307-336.
4. Hampton, K. and Wellman, B. Long Distance Community in the Network Society: Contact and Support Beyond Netville. *American Behavioral Scientist*, 45 (November), 2001, 477-496.
5. Haythornthwaite, C. and Wellman, B. Eds. *The Internet in Everyday Life*. Special issue of the *American Behavioral Scientist*, 45 (November), 2001.
6. Nardi, B.A., Whittaker, S. and Schwartz, H. It's Not What You Know, It's Who You Know: Work in the Information Age. *First Monday*, 5, 2000: http://www.firstmonday.org/issues/issue5_5/nardi/index.html
7. Putnam, R.D. *Bowling Alone*. Simon & Schuster, New York, 2000.
8. Wellman, B. The Network Community. in Wellman, B. ed. *Networks in the Global Village*, Westview, Boulder, CO, 1999, 1-48.
9. Wellman, B. Physical Place and Cyber-Place: The Rise of Networked Individualism. *International Journal for Urban and Regional Research*, 25, 2001, 227-52.
10. Wellman, B., Quan Haase, A., Witte, J. and Hampton, K. Does the Internet Increase, Decrease, or Supplement Social Capital? Social Networks, Participation, and Community Commitment. *American Behavioral Scientist*, 45 (November), 2001, 437-56.

Appendix -Table 1. Three Modes of Interaction

A. Boundaries

Phenomenon	Little Boxes	Glocalization	Networked Individualism
Physical Context	Dominance of Immediate Context	Relevance of Immediate Context	Ignorance of Immediate Context
Modality	Door-to-Door	Place-to-Place	Person-to-Person
Predominant Mode of Communication	Face-to-Face	Wired Phone Internet	Mobile Phone Wireless Modem
Spatial Range	Local	GloCal = Local + Global	Global
Locale	All in Common Household Work Space	Common Household Workspace for Core + External Periphery	External
Awareness and Availability	All Visible & Audible to All High Awareness of Availability	Core Members are Immediately Visible, Audible Little Awareness of Others' Availability Must be Contacted	Little Awareness of Availability Must be Contacted Visibility & Audibility Must be Negotiated
Access Control	Doors Wide Open to In-Group Members; Walled Off from Others External Gate Guarded	Doors Ajar Within and Between Networks Look, Knock & Ask	Doors Closed Access to Others by Request Knock & Ask
Physical Access	All Have Immediate Access to All	Core Have Immediate Access. Contacting Others Requires a Journey or Telecommunications	Contact Requires a Journey or Telecommunications
Permeability	Impermeable Wall Around Unit	Household & Workgroup have Strong to Weak Outside Connections	Individual Has Strong to Weak Connections
Interruptibility	High (Open Door): Norm of Interruption	Mixed: Core Interruptible. Others Require Deliberate Requests: Answering Machine; Knocking on Door that May be Ajar or Closed. Norm of Interruption Within Immediate Network Only	Low: Contact Must be Requested; May be Avoided or Refused: Prioritizing Voice Mail Internet Filter Knocking on Door that May be Ajar or Closed Norm of Interruption within Immediate Network Only
Observability	High: All Can See When Other Group Members are Interacting	Mixed: Core Can Observe Core. Periphery Cannot Observe Core or Interactions with Other Network Members	Low: Interactions with Other Network Members Rarely Visible
Privacy	Low Information Control: Few Secrets Status-Position are Important Capital	Low Information Control Few Secrets for Core Variable Information Control for Periphery Material Resources & Network Connections are Important Capital	High Information Control: Many Secrets Information & Ties Become Important Capital
Joining In	Anyone Can Observe Interactions Anyone Can Join Interactions	Interactions Outside the Core Rarely Observable Difficult to Join	Interactions Rarely Observable Difficult to Join
Alerts	Little Awareness of Others Approaching Open, Unlocked Doors	High Prior Awareness of Periphery's Desire to Interact. Telephone Ring Knock on Door	High Prior Awareness of Others' Desire to Interact. Formal Requests

B. Social Structure

Phenomenon	Little Boxes	Glocalization	Networked Individualism
Metaphor	Fishbowl	Core-Periphery	Switchboard
Unit of Analysis	Village Band Shop Office	Household Work Unit Multiple Networks	Networked Individual.
Social Organization	Groups	Home Bases Network of Networks	Networked Individualism
Social Structure	Hierarchically-Organized Workgroups Discrete Neighborhoods	Work Unit in Soft Hierarchy; Otherwise Amorphous	Amorphous Individual Status Determines
Era	Traditional	Contemporary	Emerging

C. Interpersonal Interactions

Phenomenon	Little Boxes	Glocalization	Networked Individualism
Predominant Basis of Interaction	Ascription (What You are Born Into): e.g., Gender, Ethnicity	Mixed Ascription & Achievement	Achievement (What You Make of Yourself): e.g., Social Class
Personal Style	Conformity	"Protect Your Base Before You Attack" (attributed to Mao)	Free Agent
Frequency of Contact	High Within Group	Moderate Within Core; Low to Moderate Outside of Core	Low with Most Others; Moderate Overall
Recurrency	Recurrent Interactions Within Group	Recurrent Interactions Within Core Intermittent with Each Network Member	Intermittent Interactions with Each Network Member
Duration	Long-Duration Ties (Cradle-to-Grave, Employed for Life)	Long Duration for Household Core (Except for Divorce) Short Duration Otherwise	Short Duration Ties
Domesticity	Cradle-to-Grave Mom & Dad: Dick (9) & Jane (6)	Long-Term Partners Serial Monogamy Dick Lives with Divorced Spouse	Changing Partners; Living Together, Singles, Single Parents Nanny cares for Jane
Scheduling	Drop-In Anytime	Drop-In Within Household & Work Core Appointments Otherwise	Scheduled Appointments
Transaction Speed	Slow	Variable in Core Fast in Periphery	Fast
Autonomy & Proactivity	Low Autonomy High Reactivity	Mixed Reactivity & Autonomy Within Household & Work Cores High Proactivity & Autonomy with Others	High Autonomy High Proactivity

Tie Maintenance	Group Maintains Ties	Core Groups Maintain Internal Ties Other Ties Must Be Actively Maintained	Ties Must Be Actively Maintained, One-By-One
Predictability	Predictability, Certainty & Security Within Group Interactions	Moderate Predictability, Certainty & Security Within Core Interactions with Others Less Predictable, Certain & Secure	Unpredictability Uncertainty Insecurity Contingency Opportunity
Latency	Leaving is Betrayal Re-Entry Difficult	Ability to Re-Establish Relationships Quickly with Network Members Not Seen in Years	Ability to Re-Establish Relationships Quickly with Network Members Not Seen in Years

D. Social Networks

Phenomenon	Little Boxes	Glocalization	Networked Individualism
Number of Social Circles	Few: Household-Kin, Work	Multiple: Core Household, Work Unit + Multiple Sets of Friends, Kin, Work Associates, Neighbors	Multiple: Dyadic or Network Ties with Household, Work Unit, Friends, Kin, Work Associates, Neighbors
Maneuverability	Little Choice of Social Circles	Choice of Core & Other Social Circles	Choice of Social Circles
Trust Building	Enforced by Group Betrayal of One is a Betrayal of All	Core Enforces Trust Network Members Depend on Cumulative Reciprocal Exchanges & Ties with Mutual Others	Dependant on Cumulative Reciprocal Exchanges & Ties with Mutual Others
Social Support	Broad ("Multistranded")	Broad Household & Work Core Specialized Kin, Friends, Other Work	Specialized
Social Integration	Within Group Only	Cross-Cutting Ties Between Networks Integrate Society Core is the Common Hub	Cross-Cutting Ties Between Networks Integrate Society
Cooperation	Cooperation & Joint Activity for Clear, Collective Purposes	Core Cooperation; Otherwise, Short-Term Alliances Tentatively Reinforced by Trust Building & Ties with Mutual Others	Independent Schedules Transient Alliances with Shifting Sets of Others
Knowledge	All Aware of Most Information Information Open to All Within Unit Secret to Outsiders	Core Knows Most Things Variable Awareness of – and Access to – What Periphery Knows	Variable Awareness of – and Access to – What Periphery Knows
Social Control	Superiors & Group Exercise Tight Control	Moderate Control by Core Household & Workgroup, with Some Spillover to Interactions with Periphery Fragmented Control Within Specialized Networks Adherence to Norms Must Be Internalized by Individuals	Subgroups, Cleavages Partial, Fragmented Control Within Specialized Networks Adherence to Norms Must Be Internalized by Individuals
Resources	Conserves Resources	Acquires Resources for Core Units	Acquires Resources for Self
Basis of Success	Getting Along Position Within Group	Getting Along & Position Within Core Networking	Networking Filling Structural Holes Between Networks

E. Norms and Perceptions

Phenomenon	Little Boxes	Glocalization	Networked Individualism
Socialization	Obey Group Elders	Obey Your Parents, Cherish Your Spouse, Nurture Your Children Defer to Your Boss Work & Play Well with Colleagues & Friends	Develop Strategies & Tactics for Self-Advancement
Sense of Solidarity	High Group Solidarity Collective Name & Identity.	Moderate Solidarity within Core Household & Workgroup Vitiated by Many Individual Ties to Different Peripheries.	Sense of Being an Autonomous Individual. Fuzzily Identifiable Networks
Loyalty	*Particularistic:* High Group Loyalty	*Public & Private Spheres:* Moderate Loyalty to Home Base Takes Precedence over Weak Loyalty Elsewhere	*Self and Global:* Weak, Divided Loyalties
Conflict Handling	Revolt Coup Irrevocable Departure	Back-Biting Keeping Distance	Avoidance Exit
Commitment to Network Members	High Within Groups	High Within Core Variable Elsewhere	Variable
Zeitgeist	Communitarian	Conflicted	Existential

Privacy, Predictability or Serendipity and Digital Cities

"...sociability is a large part of why cities exist
and streets are a major if not the only
public place for that sociability to develop"[1].

Gary Gumpert[1] and Susan Drucker[2]

[1]Communication Landscapers
6 Fourth Road
Great Neck, New York, 11021 USA
listra@optonline.net

[2]School of Communication
Hofstra University
Hempstead, New York 11549, USA
sujie@optonline.net

Abstract. This paper explores the relationship of unplanned social interaction and the fear associated with current attitudes about cities, both place-based and digital. The symbiotic relationship of the physical and digital city is considered. Specifically, the chapter addresses the three types of infrastructures supporting both physical and digital cities: a) physical infrastructure; b) psycho-social infrastructure and c) regulatory infrastructure. The argument is made that the technology of communication, while extending the ability to transcend locality, accepts and demands control of the environment through surveillance. But in order for the physical and digital city to co-exist, and to offer a choice and quality of life, a degree of *controlled unpredictability* is required.

1 Preface

For some time we have been researching and writing about the relationship of communication technology and urban development. The body of this manuscript was written prior to the catastrophic events of September 11, 2001. But there is a sense of hollowness that envelops these observations now, because it is impossible to discuss the social nature of the city without reflecting upon the implications of a world changed. While many individuals seek refuge from cities in general because they are potential targets for terrorists, our belief in the values and importance of urban centers has been strengthened by the recent devastating events. More than *ever* cities and suburbs ought not be constructed, altered, modified, or regulated solely by the threat of neighbors, strangers, immigrants, crime or terrorism.

There is a body of literature on the landscape of fear that could be introduced into this discussion, but our introductory comments are quite simple. The smell of panic ought not reconfigure our conception of the vibrant, stimulating, and cultural city. One can never adjust to terror and horror of such unimaginable dimension, but at the

M. Tanabe, P. van den Besselaar, T. Ishida (Eds.): Digital Cities, LNCS 2362, pp. 26-40, 2002.
© Springer-Verlag Berlin Heidelberg 2002

same time one cannot suspend normal daily activity and civility for safety and security. We need to be careful that the digital city does not evolve into the easy answer to sociability, economics, and culture threatened by terror and apprehension. We must guard against the rise of the virtual existence and the fall of the social city.

2 The City of Social Relationships

Cities are constructed and exist for human relationships. The city is never static but evolves, changing form and social function as seen by the development of the suburb. The suburb, an outgrowth of technological developments in communication and transportation is a forerunner of the digital city offering a technological based social alternative. In *The City in History* [2]), Lewis Mumford wrote "[f]rom the thirteen century on, the dread of plague prompted a periodic exodus from the city; and in that sense, one may say that the modern suburb began as a sort of rural isolation ward"[2]. But, can the same be said for the digital city? The convergence of the physical and virtual technologies of transportation and communication define cities, suburbs, and rural area, and the relationship between them. The technology of communication, while extending our ability to transcend locality also accepts and demands control of the environment. The social city is being reformulated by the technologies that permit communication through connection rather than through more traditional face-to-face contact. The social life once offered by the urban environment, one replete with busy streets, markets, parks, promenades, and squares is being re-channeled and transformed through the infrastructure of the digital city.

What is a digital city? The digital city is a conception of urban space that emphasizes the electronic transmission of public information and interaction. It represents the intersection of information technology and urban life. The process bringing about the greatest change in communication technology is digitalization permitting the integration of different channels of communication once separate and discrete. Digitalization facilitates multi-functional terminals and multi-media networks, a development best characterized as *media convergence* [3].

So when dealing with "digital cities" it is the form of the media environment, the communication skeletal frame of the city, that constitutes an infrastructure central to the changing relationship of individual to city. Quite clearly, the social, informational, and cultural identity of the city has and is being reformulated through digitalization. Digitalization takes all prior media and imposes a new unseen structure upon the city.

Cities have always been communication environments so there is nothing new in recognizing the power of communication technologies and practices as forces transforming cities. Every media innovation has its prognosticators of doom and gloom and prophets of salvation. With the introduction of the printing press, the role of architecture as a mode of expression was threatened. Back in 1831 Victor Hugo gave voice to reactions to the impact of a new communication technology (the printing press) on physical spaces and social institutions. In the *Hunchback of Notre Dame* [4] the character of the Archdeacon proclaims with alarm "the book will kill the building" [4]. From the vantage point of history, perhaps it is not unexpected that future media innovations would lead to cries that the city would 'dissolve' in the face of new technologies. However, the dire warnings and expectations have waned and instead some critics now maintain that the "urban areas across the world" will be globally interconnected into a planetary metropolitan system [5].

The omnipresent forces of computerization and media convergence shape any city which functions within the contemporary media landscape, even without a thought out plan of digitalization. But the digital city is more than a simple electronic connection because as the media environment of the digital city is technologically reconfigured, so too is the fabric and quality of life of those that inhabit that space.

The relationship of the city to individual humans beings is often neglected in the rush to give meaning to the vast structural, design and technological changes that abound. The optimists and pessimists examining the changing city have missed the point. The nature of social interaction and the use of cities will change and the city, physical or digital must be reevaluated from the perspective of a smaller unit of analysis—that of human needs and communication in cities within the larger media landscape. The range of communicative options, the lack of choices, access, resources, or the perception of alternatives serves as a critical factor in describing, explaining and predicting the causal relationship of technology and acts of communication. *We argue the need to connect the influence of the physical, social/psychological, and regulatory infrastructure, that is to say, the concealed frame giving shape to the physical and digital city alike, in order to understand the impact of digitalization upon the variations of old and new relational patterns.* Our specific concern addresses the changing relationship between individual and city, the displacement of individuals from traditional patterns of place and the ways in which the human need for community, inclusion and variety confront the needs for control, predictability, privacy and the safety provided by surveillance.

3 The City, the Digital City, the Individual, and Place

One view of the digital city assumes the referent as the built environment. As suburbs are linked to cities, so too is the digital city linked to the physical city. The anticipated result is a renaissance of urbanism, localism enhanced, a reconnection of once fragmented social, economic and cultural segments of society into a renewed civic culture with social cohesion. It is envisioned that economic development of the city is therefore linked to the globalized context in which the digital city operates. This conceptualization of the digital city is represented in the work of members of Telecities that undertook the InfoCities project.

The objective of InfoCities is to evaluate the application of information and communication technologies (ICT) to deliver integrated public services, moving towards a 'one-stop' point of service delivery. The service areas chosen for the feasibility phase were education, health, transport, culture, electronic commerce and public information. InfoCities also aims to improve access to public and city services for residents, and to offer value added services to businesses and professionals. Among those using InfoCities applications and services have been: residents, visitors and tourists using public access points (such as street kiosks and public library Internet access points), schools and other educational bodies, businesses and professional organizations (from SMEs to hospitals), households and community organizations [6].

But "one-stop" public access to local information in a globalized world is not the only conceptualization of the digital city. In another version, the Teleport serves as the centerpiece for urban development or redevelopment with new offices, industrial and high-status housing used as a marketing device to attract investment and global businesses. "Teleports aim to emerge as centers for the diffusion of innovations into the wider urban economy, through the creation of 'hot spots' of telematics" [7]. Such sites may be city building or nation building devices such as Malaysia's multi-media super corridor rooted in the digital city of Cyberjaya and Cyberport currently being developed in Hong Kong. Cyberport is being advertised for its " low-density, campus-style environment optimizes a unique oceanfront location close to Hong Kong's central business and financial district, providing a first class living and working environment"[8].

In a third version, virtual space acts as metaphor for integrated networks constituting virtual communities or digital towns created so that their identity and existence are defined purely by the online environment. Like a suburb without a city, a symbol without a site-specific referent, the virtual community achieves identity and provides services to its inhabitants through digital connection without the necessity of physical contact. Searching the Internet reveals many diverse examples of such virtual cities including AlphaWorld, a multi-user virtual world where people, represented as avatars, can meet and interact in a world is rendered in fully three-dimensional graphics. Other sites include "City4ALL" a high-speed 3D system offering interaction, information and shopping [9]. Cybertown offers an illusion of city life that can be shared over the Net [10].

3.1   Dis-placement , Connection, Disconnection and the City

Parables of Connection. The following story appeared in the New York Times on May 31,2001.

> On May 14, Kaycee Nicole Swenson, an effervescent 19-year-old, died from complications surrounding leukemia, which she had bee years. From her home in Kansas, Kaycee, an unyieldingly optimistic high school basketball star, had chronicled her remissions and relapses in her online n battling for nearly two diary, or Weblog, which she had dubbed "Living Colours."

> For nearly a year, thousands of people went to the site to follow her travails. Many came to feel as if they knew her, and a few talked with her regularly on the phone. Some sent her gifts. Others with cancer spoke of her as an inspiration. On May 15, when Kaycee's online followers went to her Weblog, they found a small image of a rose, accompanied by an announcement of her death:

> "Thank you for the love, the joy, the laughter and the tears. We shall love you always and forever." [11].

The sad story turns out to be a fabrication created by a 40-year-old mother of two teenagers who lives in the state of Kansas. The shock waves of anger and disbelief swept through the Internet world when the truth of the deception emerged.

The second story explores how corporate call centers for businesses including General Electric and British Airways use phone banks for customer inquiries located in India where labor costs are lower and employees are trained to sound American. "Hi, my name is Susan Sanders, and I'm from Chicago," said C.R. Suman, 22, who is in fact a native of Bangalore and fields calls from customers of a telecommunications company in the United States... In case her callers ask personal questions, Ms. Suman has conjured up a fictional American life with parents Bob and Ann, brother Mark and a made up business degree from the University of Illinois"[12].

Now it is not the matter of deception that is at the heart of the matter, but rather the creation and need for relationships in a digital climate of connection. The concern for a critically ill young girl is understandable, but needs to be understood within the nature of daily urban life in which those concerned may be unaware of their neighbors' lives. The fictionalized life of an Indian operator physically located half way around the world from those who required attention and service simply is a testament that individuals require relationships in their digital transactions and that the model of all transactions is essentially a human interpersonal one.

Both stories are indications as to how the awareness of communication technology changes the way one perceives of oneself within an environment. The channels of communication available and the degree to which they connect one individual with another or others define the scope and boundary of that setting. The intimate world we acknowledge as ours is expanded as we link with another through a medium of communication. The nature of connection is, however, always two-sided, since while a medium links one site with another, it also implicitly liberates and disconnects the individual from the site of location. Thus, the telephone extends relationship and transaction through time and space, while it simultaneously pulls sites apart. The very act of co-existence includes separate, but interdependent expectations, values and attitudes. As the borders or the perimeters of site (place) are transcended by communication technology, the dependence upon that place for relationship and sustenance are attenuated and sometimes severed.

This reciprocal and defining interdependence of place modified by communication technology can perhaps be described as "*dis-place-ment*." To understand one of the fundamental aspects of changing place we borrow a notion from the field of physics where displacement refers to the "weight of the volume of fluid displaced by a floating or submerged body." [13]. The time available for the purpose of communication is finite, and the shifting of activity from one or more other channels affects prior channels and situations. Even with the talent of multi-tasking, the attention spent with one communication opportunity has an impact upon the other. One occasion replaces or *dis-places* the other. Mediated place (the connection of one site with another) reallocates some portion of time shared with the other.

From a slightly different definition borrowed from the field of psychoanalysis "displacement" refers to "the transfer of an emotion from the object about which it originally was experienced to another object or a person." In that respect the emotional or affective attachment of person to place (and to those that inhabit those places) also shifts with the mediation of location). Suggested by the tales of Bangalore and death of Kaycee Nicole Swenson, is that time and place are dis-placed.

Displacement also describes the conversion of *place* into *space* in which connection rather than location is stressed and defines the experience. Strangely, displacement is rooted in connection. Stephen Graham has suggested that an aim of telecities "is to construct telematics applications which help 'reconnect' the economic, social, geographic and cultural fragments that increasingly characterize contemporary cities" [7]. This suggests developments grounded in telecommunication can reconnect people to cities by recreating urban life through the virtual city or by revitalizing the connection through to the physical city. But it must be emphasized that that relationship, that connection has been changed. The infrastructure has changed the relationship of individual to his/her immediate environment (both physical and virtual).

4 The Physical Infrastructure and Communication

Cities have been about *connection* since the beginning. Cities exist to connect people who live in communities. Infrastructures have always provided the web of connections needed for community life. The original infrastructure of cities was the physical environment: paths, roads, street, market places, meeting places, and city walls. The streets and patterns of expansion tell the story of development and growth. From ancient Athens to medieval European cities the infrastructure for connection can be found. "Being beyond the metropolitan limits came to mean being past the reach of the trolley car lines, the water supply system, and the sewers. These networks tended to thin out gradually, rather than disappear suddenly, with increasingly distance from urban centers" [14]. To the degree that cities and their infrastructure are about connecting people, the physical environment has long served as a medium of communication.

The infrastructure supplied by media technology is not new either. In what has been called "the Victorian Internet" [15], the telegraph led to the first wiring of cities. "A worldwide communications network whose cables spanned continents and oceans, it revolutionized business practice, gave rise to new forms of crime, and inundated its users with a deluge of information[1] [15].

The bowels of cities were employed for communication well before current efforts to pull "fiberoptic cable" or "glass" below city streets today. Congestion of telegraph offices led to the installation of a steam-powered pneumatic tube system to carry telegraph forms to the main telegraph office. Such pneumatic tubes were installed in London by 1854. By 1865 the tube network was installed in Liverpool, Birmingham, Manchester, and Berlin. This was followed by pneumatic tube networks in Vienna, Prague, Munich, Rio de Janeiro, Dublin, Rome, Naples, Milan and Marseilles [15]. In 1866 the device was introduced in Paris and remains extant. By 1897 the United States postal service was making use of a similar system in New York, Boston,

---

[1] According to Standage, "Romances blossomed over the wires. Secret codes were devised by some users and cracked by others. The benefits of the network were relentlessly hyped by its advocates and dismissed by the skeptics. Governments and regulators tried and failed to control the new medium. Attitudes toward everything from newsgathering to diplomacy had to be completely rethought. Meanwhile, out on the wires, a technological subculture with its own customs and vocabulary was establishing itself" [15].

Philadelphia, Chicago and St. Louis in which tubes snaked under city streets. There were more than 56 miles of mail tubes on the East Coast delivering as many as 200,000 letters per tube every hour. In New York, such tubes wide enough to accommodate small packages linked post offices of Manhattan and Brooklyn[2]. At the time the subterranean network fueled by pressurized air to move a mail canister through an underground eight-inch cast-iron pipe was considered high-tech. Service continued in most cities until 1918 but in New York the tubes remained in use until 1953 [16]. Currently the feasibility of recycling and reviving this network is being explored as a cost-saving way of bringing fiber optic cables into buildings to connect with existing telecommunications conduits [16].

The lines providing electricity and then telephone systems expanded the wired system. Some digital telecommunications infrastructure is using existing copper wiring but more significantly, the wireless age (terrestrial and satellite), microwave links and wireless cellular systems are increasingly becoming capable of providing a new communications infrastructure.

So networked cities are not new. "Intra-urban digital networking furthers the long evolution of human settlements from loose collections of more or less independent dwellings to highly integrated, networked cities in which multiple infrastructures of tracks, pipes, and wires deliver centrally supplied services to buildings..." [14]. Real-world and virtual communities are inhabited by the same people whose underlying interests, needs and motivations are common to both environments [17]. The relationship between virtual cities and understanding the infrastructure of the physical city has been recognized as vital in designing effective online sites. William Mitchell has underscored that understanding the social function of physically based qualities of cities will help evaluate and design for the on-line world. Judith S. Donath, also of MIT, exploring the design of social environments for electronic communities, argues:

> ... in order to foster the development of vibrant and viable online communities, the environment - i.e. the technical infrastructure and user interface - must provide the means to communicate social cues and information: the participants must be able to perceive the social patterns of activity and affiliation and the community must be able to evolve a fluid and subtle cultural vocabulary. [18]

These scholars note that keys to a vital urban physical environment are likely to hold true for electronic communities as well.

5   The Psycho-Social Infrastructure: Digital Cities and Human Needs

There are fundamental human needs associated with connection and disconnection. A popular social scientific concept embodied in the work of William Schutz [19]

---

[2] In New York the tube system extended 27 miles from the old Custom House in Battery Park to Harlem and back through Times Square and Grand Central Terminal to the main post office by Pennsylvania Station [16].

identifies social needs that motivate individuals to form and maintain relationships. Specifically, the three interpersonal needs are: inclusion, affection and control. *Inclusion* represents the need to include others in activities or to be included by others; *control*, the need to make decisions and take responsibility or the willingness to abrogate such responsibility and accede to the decisions of others: *affection* represents the need to be loved and accepted by others or the willingness to love and offer acceptance to others.

It is asserted that there are individualized levels associated with each social need, so the degree and influence of a particular need as a force affecting associational patterns differs from person to person. The level of each need changes over time. A considerable body of literature suggests the existence and significance of these needs, with some going so far as to assert that most interpersonal behavior can be directly tied to these three social needs.   Further, social exchange theory suggests that relationships are sustained when they are relatively rewarding and discontinued when they are relatively costly [20]. The search for the fulfillment of needs occurs in both physical and virtual environments. "P[p]eople on the net should be thought of not only as solitary information processors but also as social beings. People are not only looking for information; they are also looking for affiliation, support and affirmation..." [21].

Engagement in community and the ability to connect arguably both emerge in response to an individual's social need for inclusion. People construct their lives to include others and be included in the activities of others. Sometimes this goal is achieved by sharing a social environment.

Inclusion and social affiliation, is at the heart of community engagement. The need for inclusion manifests itself in group affiliation. The concepts of "common," "communication," and "community" are intertwined. The Middle English root is *commun* and the Latin root is *communis*. The meanings range from *belonging equally to more than one*, to *generally accessible*, to *share and participate with others*. The explicit connection between "common", and "communication" is "community." Social exchange theory suggests a cost-benefit analysis can explain the degree of engagement in community (physical or virtual, face-to-face or digital).

Control, the degree a person feels the need to be in charge of a situation leads to the need to connect or sometimes the need to disconnect. Control strategies are triggered by fear or insecurity that results when one cannot control a situation in which the individual's needs for control is strong. Media technology provides individuals with the ability to control connection while at home and work while offering the tools for insulating oneself when in public. Mobile public privacy meets the needs of a public alienated, disconnected and distrusting of public spaces. The jogger encapsulated by a walkman, the bicycle rider with a small radio attached, pedestrians talking intently on their cellular phones, and commuters wearing headphones, all reflect increased control over their communication environment.

But lack of control, fear and insecurity may result in avoidance of the situation or the disconnection from other people and social environments associated with the uncomfortable level of control. Control fuels disconnection.

> The more we extend our connection, the more insular we become. The more we control our communication environment, the less is surprise or chance a daily expectation. The more we connect, the more we seek to

control the connection. The more we detach from our immediate surroundings, the more we rely upon surveillance of the environment. The more communication choice offered, the less we trust the information we receive. The more information and data available, the more we need. The more individuality we achieve, the more communities we seek. The more we extend our senses, the less we depend upon our sensorium [22].

5.1   Control, Surveillance, Privacy, and Cities

Surveillance cameras placed in public places by security forces and police departments, and cameras linked for transmission via the Internet, represent variations on a theme of control. Extending control over the street is not new and has not been limited to media technologically based methods. Walls surrounded medieval towns for protection. Surveillance zones are part of the attraction of the omnipresent-gated communities becoming increasingly popular in the growing suburbs around metropolitan areas.

The cult of surveillance arises from the need for control as well as a need for safety, a particularly strong need, an assertion supported by A.H. Maslow's five general categories of needs which reveals the high priority given to safety. Safety is ranked second behind physiological needs and before the need for love, esteem or self-actualization. So according to Maslow, [23] once biological needs related to self-preservation have been satisfied, the desire for a sense of security and avoidance of personal harm, disease and violence are of greatest concern. A strong preference exists for a safe, predictable environment accompanied by a drive to avoid those sites and circumstances perceived as potentially dangerous or beyond control.

Control of the communication environment is at the heart of the incongruous public/private nature in the use of communication technology. At the start of the 21st century, we see the rise of privacy as a social value with the accompanying shift of life from the uncontrollable exterior to the controllable interior. In this process the more we seek safety, the more we deny the security provided by human interdependence. Denial of obligation is linked to risk and chance taking. We avoid others because of potential dangers and embrace technology to reduce risk. On the other hand, technology may provide a sense of control, however, illusory that sense might be.

Theoretically, the awareness of cameras is thought to foster a sense of safety and therefore to serve as a means of revitalizing public spaces, making them more inviting as sites of safe social life and political activism. Public officials like New York City's Mayor Rudolph Guiliani argue, "It's all about balancing a sense of security" [24]. In 1997 it was estimated that the average New Yorker appears on camera 20 times per day [25] and this figure has risen since that time. *USA Today* reported that in the United States in the year 2000, a million closed-circuit cameras, most with videotape recorders, were used by the private sector in offices, apartment buildings, garages, stores, banks and restaurants [26]. Most, if not all, urban centers in the United States utilize closed-circuit television in public places for surveillance purposes. The proliferation of surveillance cameras trained on public spaces has received extensive examination in New York City where the New York Civil Liberties Union has undertaken the Surveillance Camera Project. 2,397 visible surveillance cameras were found in Manhattan alone, not accounting for the unknown numbers hidden from view [27]. Cameras were distinguished as either public or private based upon the assumed ownership of the structure to which they were affixed. Surveillance cameras are placed in the public streets by government agencies, (often police), by private companies (outside of storefronts and buildings), and by television stations and traffic services [28]. Digital cameras were placed at the entrances to the Super Bowl, where photographs were taken of all entering fans. The images were fed into the FBI's database, to search for matches with known criminals. Entry into this public place was viewed as consent to surveillance.

The United Kingdom is the largest user of closed-circuit television (CCTV) in the world [29]. Clive Norris, a criminologist at Hull University estimated a million cameras in use there. On an average day in London more than 300 cameras from 30 different CCTV networks film an individual [30].

Simultaneously, as activity shifts online, each mouse click results in a data trail which traces transactions and interactions. Increasingly, surveillance is associated not only with the visual or auditory observation of public behavior and interaction but of informational surveillance and online interaction. After September 11th we find people increasingly accepting, even looking to surveillance, as an anti-terrorism tool and source of comfort – bargaining away privacy in exchange for security. Technological and cultural changes have undermined the ability to control personal information [31]. Electronic surveillance devices, computerized data collection and computer-mediated communication have fueled concerns for privacy. Data collection, storage, and control, informational and associational privacy are monitored. Cookies provide a unique identifier that a web server places on a computer. Using any major search engine results in that action being logged by organizations having access to an individual's seemingly private search for data and interaction. Data access and communicative interactions are traceable and observable. Software enables web site operators or the sponsor of a message board to scan the board for key terms and then target an advertiser's ad to the user who posted the particular message. All e-mails sent over AOL are stored at headquarters in Virginia. Surveillance of online chat-room and e-mail environments raise new issues of control. Who has information about an individual? Is such information accurate? What is going to be done with it? Can information obtained be sold to telemarketers or shared with potential employers or law enforcement? The US does not currently have a law that requires websites to have a privacy policy. Many other countries including Canada and some EU countries do have such laws.

Privacy policies may lead to the creation of digital cities prohibited from trading with each other. The European Union adopted a directive that prohibits the transfer of personal data on the Internet (European Parliament and European Council Directive 1995). The directive took effect in October 1998 but differing privacy policies throughout the world could make trade throughout the world problematic as evidenced by the fact that U.S. policy on privacy laws conflicts with this E.U. directive currently leaving the parties at an impasse [32].

Technology of communication, while extending our ability to transcend locality, also accepts and demands control of the environment. While we seek safe serendipity "online", the accidental and unplanned is designed out of urban and suburban environments. Human beings need a degree of stimulation and uncertainty along with a degree of predictability. The city, potentially a place of social interaction and auditory/visual stimulation, is composed of architectural elements (commercial buildings, homes, construction etc.), urban environmental factors (streets, stores, restaurants, cafes, advertising etc.), transportation settings (public and private) and people. The social life of the digital city is composed of nodes, servers, links, websites, chat rooms, MUDs, etc., providing diverse options and possible encounters. But the traditional sites, whether they be public or private, are guarded and surprise eliminated whenever possible. Currently, surprise and unpredictability is more accepted, welcomed and even sought in virtual spaces. Ideally both the physical and digital environments ought to include a balance of order and disorder, of balance and unpredictability.

6 Regulatory Infrastructure

A regulatory infrastructure shapes the social environment of the physical and digital cities -- a set of rules, codes, laws, legal precedents, all of which shape social interaction. But for the digital city, this element of the infrastructure is often neglected. According to Stephen Graham:

> Most policy-makers have a crude understanding of the technological and regulatory shifts that are under way in telecommunications. And because urban politicians and planners still remain firmly wedded to the tangible world of salient aspects of cities, the arcane, mysterious and intangible world of telecommunications presents major problems as a focus of intervention [7].

Graham further notes a fundamental truth with regard to the regulation of telecommunication media: Regulations are generally at the national level in marked contrast to the heavily local regulatory schema of cities and municipalities. Traditionally the technologies of telecommunications, broadcasting, satellite and computing operated independently while the industries associated with each were regulated independently, along the same lines. The result may be that "the concept of an urban communication infrastructure was not expressed in local institutions ...... communication is not usually treated as part of the local technical infrastructure of urban life" [7].

A complex regulatory web shapes behavior in the traditional environment of face-to-face communication primarily through diverse local laws and codes [33]. On a local level the regulatory infrastructure ranges from zoning laws (which address signage, facade, parking, display windows, take-out and delivery service, and vending machines, the segregation of functions, design districts), to penal codes, minimum drinking and driving ages, and the regulation of smoking in public places. Technological convergence challenges the vertical regulatory models of broadcasting, telecommunications and computer services while simultaneously testing the traditional approach to regulation by nation-states. The result is moving communication regulatory activity further from the local while turning to the international and global. The current path reflected by communication regulations shifts the emphasis from communities of place to virtual communities where technological convergence leads to regulatory convergence ever more divorced from local control.

Traditionally the welfare of the community was a dominating reason for regulation. It was assumed that there was to be a strong link between a specific location and the media that served that site. Thus, the assignment of radio frequencies was made on the premise that community was to be served by a radio station directly connected to a geographical site. But from a regulatory perspective, community or city as a geographically contiguous site is irrelevant to the technology of the Internet. The specific reasons, areas of regulation and motivation behind regulation are debatable, but un-debatable is that the responsibility and legal parameters of jurisdiction are shifted from the proximate local to *any* local site, no matter where that "local" might be geographically situated. Does site of transmission or site of reception determine jurisdiction? Regulatory power and jurisdiction, geographically/territorially based terms, are undermined when borders become transparent, easily permeable and often imperceptible. Diverse suggestions with regard to regulation have led to some legal thinkers advocating that cyberspace be conceptualized as a "place" rather than a medium with its own constitution on which to base a developing body of applicable law and self-regulatory systems. To date, the regulatory infrastructure remains a force without clear rules affecting the digital dimensions of physical cities and virtual cities.

7 Conclusions

There is growing awareness that understanding the physical city can be applied to designing digital cities, which either link the physical with virtual or create virtual cities for online populations [14]. It has been recognized that an infrastructure designed for the physical population is of course different from an infrastructure designed for linking data. It has been recognized that an infrastructure designed for the physical population is of course different than that of an infrastructure designed for linking data, yet there is a relationship between the two. A vital function of both infrastructures is to create and foster community engagement and encourage, shape, and constrain communication among people. The fascination with technology, the new challenges presented by the digital city should not obscure the importance of the symbiotic relationship of physical and digital cities. The creation of one affects the other; the decay of one ought not to be accepted because of the promise of the other.

The late 20th century saw the ascending value of privacy and the decline in public obligation along with the acceptance of disconnection. Simultaneously, social interaction has moved from the public realm into protected and controlled homes, offices, and laptops. The digital city offers the binary choice of turning a real or virtual community on and off. This alternative to the demands of the traditional city can be liberating. Physical communities can be obligation intensive, over-social and uncontrollable but can be turned "off" to the extent one retreats into a private realm in which to meet social needs. Now the physical community can be turned on and off in both the physical *and* digital realms. The presence of options alters both physical and virtual places. Not only does communication technology connect one physical site to another, but also the possibility of connection changes each site and also creates a new site. Every medium acts both centrifugally and centripetally.

In *The Politics* [34] Aristotle argued that humans belong in the city. "Cities are by nature places that men and women have created out of need or affection, so that they become the home of creativity itself" [35]. But cities cannot stagnate, "the city is always marked by forces of change" [35].

Lewis Mumford concludes his monumental history of the city stating:

> As we have seen, the city has undergone many changes during the last five thousand years; and further changes are doubtless in store. But the innovations that beckon urgently are not in the extension and perfection of physical equipment: still less in multiplying automatic electronic devices for dispersing into formless sub-urban dust the remaining organs of culture. Just the contrary: significant improvements will come only through applying art and thought to the city's central human concerns, with a fresh dedication to the cosmic and ecological processes that enfold all being. We must restore to the city the maternal, life-nurturing functions, the autonomous activities, the symbiotic associations that have long been neglected or suppressed. [2].

We believe there is a need to enliven the physical city as it competes and interacts with the digital city. A vital city embraces safety and control but also allows for the activity of the unplanned. It is the electricity of potential, the sense of possibility of the unplanned, the insertion of a pleasing degree of risk that energizes the performance of the city. We would characterize this ideal balance as *controlled unpredictability*.

8 Epilogue

On Oct. 26, 2001 President George W. Bush signed a new antiterrorism law expanding the government's ability to conduct electronic surveillance as one of several measures designed to thwart terrorism. The measure relaxes the rules under which intelligence wiretaps may be issued, allows for the authorization of roving wiretaps and provides for expanded surveillance of computers and telephones. Data collection is enhanced by widening the ability to obtain business records, and lowers the standard to obtain pen registers that provide detailed information on telephone records. The new law called the USA Patriot Act extends the pen register and so-called trap and trace statute to Internet covering data on dialing, routing, addressing and signal information. Many of these provisions will expire after four years. This authorization of increased surveillance far surpassing previously permitted incursions on personal privacy, was passed in near record time, with only one public hearing and little debate. The acceptance of such sweeping changes in personal privacy protections evidences the metamorphosis of safety issues into security concerns, and the public fervor for control and security.

References

1. Jacobs, A. B. Great Streets. MIT Press, Cambridge, MA (1993) 4.
2. Mumford, L. The City in History: Its origins, its transformations, and its prospects. New York: MJF Books (1989) 487.
3. Holznagel, B. New Challenges: Convergence of Markets, Divergence of Law? Questions Regarding the Future of Communications Regulation, International Journal of Communications Law and Policy, (1998/1999 winter). http://www.digital-law.net/IJCLP/1_1998/ijclp_webdoc_6_1_1998.html.
4. Hugo, V. The Hunchback of Notre Dame, New American Library, New York (1964).
5. Graham, S. & Marvin, S. Telecommunications and the City: Electronic Spaces, Urban Places. Routledge, London (1996).
6. Infocities Project http://www.infocities.eu.int/html/whatis.html. (2001).
7. Graham, S. Towards Urban Cyberspace Planning: Grounding the Global through Urban Telematics Policy and Planning. In J. Downey & J. McGuigan, Technocities, Sage Publications, London (1999) 9-33.
8. Cyberport http://www.cyberport.com.hk/home.htm (2001).
9. City4All http://www.city4all.com/2000/index_e.html (2001).
10. Cybertown http://www.cybertown.com/main_ie.(2001).
11. Hafner, K. (2001, May 31). A beautiful life, an early death, a fraud exposed. The New York Times, (2001, May 31) G1 & G 5.
12. Landler, M.. Hi, I'm in Bangalore (but I Can't say so). The New York Times, (2001, March 21). D 1.
13. Random House Dictionary of the English Language Random House, New York (1966).
14. Mitchell, W. J. E-topia: "urban life, Jim-but not as we know it." MIT Press, Cambridge, MA (1999).
15. Standage, T. The Victorian Internet: The Remarkable Story of the Telegraph and the Nineteenth Century's On-Line Pioneers, Walker and Company, New York (1998).
16. Pogrebin, R. Underground mail road: Modern plans for all-but-forgotten delivery system. The New York Times, (2001, May 7) B1.
17. Wellman and Gulia. Net surfers don't ride alone: virtual communities as communities. Forthcoming in (P. Kollock and M. Smith, eds.) Communities in Cyberspace, University of California Press, Berkeley. (1996).
18. Donath, J.S. Inhabiting the virtual city: The design of social environments for electronic communities. http://smg.media.mit.edu/people/Judith/Thesis/Conclusion.frame.html, (2001)
19. Schutz, Wm. C. FIRO: A Three –Dimensional theory of Interpersonal Behavior, New York, Holt, Rinehart and Winston (1958).
20. Thibaut, J.W. & Kelley, H. The Social Psychology of Groups, Wiley Co., New York (1959).
21. Sproull, Lee and Faraj, Samer.. Atheism, sex and databases: the net as a social technology. in (B. Kahin and J. Keller, eds.) Public Access to the Internet. Prentice-Hall (1993).
22. Gumpert, G. Communications and Our Sense of Community: a Planning Agenda, Inter/Media, August/September 1996, Vol.24., No.4.,.41-44 (1996).
23. Maslow, A.H. A theory of human motivation. Psychological Review, 50 (1943) 370-396.
24. Boal, M. The Surveillance Society: Parts One, Two and Three. The Village Voice, http://www.villagevoice.com/features/9840/boal.shtml/(1998, Sept. 30-Oct. 6).
25. WCBS Radio, New York. Newsbroadcast. (1997, Nov. 17).
26. Zuckerman, M.J. Chances are, somebody's watching you. USA Today, http://www.usa today.com /life/cyber/tech/cti856.htm._(2001, Nov. 30).
27. New York City Surveillance Camera Project, http://NYCLUmediaeater.com/cameras /breakdown/html. (1999).

28. Halbfinger, D.M. As Surveillance cameras peer, some wonder if they also pry. The New York Times, (1998, Feb. 22). A1 & 32.

29. Bulos, M. & Chaker, W. Changing the home environment: The Case of Closed Circuit Television (CCTV) Surveillance, paper delivered at the International Association of People Environment Studies conference, Eindhoven, The Netherlands,(July, 1998).

30. Gadher, D. Smile, you are on 300 candid cameras.
    http://www.mediaeater.com/cameras/news/02098.htm. (1999, Feb. 14).

31. Rosen, J. The Unwanted Gaze: The Destruction of Privacy in America, Random House, New York (2000).

32. Thibodeau, P. Bush rejects EU privacy plan. Computerworld, Vol 35, No.14, (2001, April 2). 1 & 12.

33. Drucker, S. & Gumpert, G.. The Regulation of public social life: Communication law revisited, Communication Quarterly, Vol (1996) 9, 7-32.

34. Aristotle. The Politics (T.A. Sinclair, Tans. & T.J. Suandes, Ed.). Penguin Classics, London. (1988).

35. Ackroyd, P. "The Life of the City," The Observer Century City, The Tate Modern, (2001, February-April) 4-5.

Regularities in the Formation and Evolution of Information Cities[1]

Stelios Lelis[1], Petros Kavassalis[2], Jakka Sairamesh[3], Seif Haridi[4],
Fredrik Holmgren[4], Mahmoud Rafea[4], and Antonis Hatzistamatiou[1]

[1] Institute for Computer Science, Foundation of Research and Technology - Hellas, ICS-FORTH, Science and Technology Park of Crete, P.O.Box 1385, GR 711 10 Heraklion, Crete, Greece
{slelis, hatzist}@ics.forth.gr
[2] (Person to contact) Institute for Computer Science, Foundation of Research and Technology - Hellas, ICS-FORTH, Science and Technology Park of Crete, P.O.Box 1385, GR 711 10 Heraklion, Crete, Greece
petros@rpcp.mit.edu
http://atlantis.uoc.gr
[3] IBM Institute for Advanced Commerce, IBM Thomas J. Watson Research Center, P.O. Box 704, Yorktown Heights, NY 10598
jramesh@us.ibm.com
[4] Swedish Institute of Computer Science, SICS, Box 1263, SE-16429 Kista, Sweden
{seif, fredrikh, mahmoud}@sics.se

Abstract. In the real world, cities exist because of external economies associated with the geographic concentration of firms within a city. Of course, such a geographic proximity with input providers and consumers, would at first reduce transportation costs. But why cities, information cities, i.e. large agglomerations of people and economic activity emerge in the virtual world? In the Internet, transportation costs are zero. Web sites can easily be reached from anybody and everywhere with no particular cost. In these conditions of equal access distance, one would rather expect a smooth web geography with a relatively even distribution of visitors per site. However, the web economy illustrates strong agglomeration trends with a very small number of web sites capturing a large segment of the web population and the most of virtual economic activity. This paper attempts to provide a sound basis for the dynamics of population concentration in the web under increasing returns.

1 Introduction

Just like physical cities, "information cities" are envisioned to emerge in the future, where each information city will be inhabited by millions (virtual inhabitants) of participants (human or software agents) involved in one or more activities in these cities -- such as buying, selling, chatting, discussing, socializing and collaborating. Evidence of this, is already clear with web portals such as Yahoo!, AOL, Amazon and

---

[1] This paper summarizes some of the findings of *iCities project*, funded by European Commission (Future and Emerging Technologies, IST-1999-11337), on which we will publish more extensively elsewhere.

M. Tanabe, P. van den Besselaar, T. Ishida (Eds.): Digital Cities, LNCS 2362, pp. 41-55, 2002.
© Springer-Verlag Berlin Heidelberg 2002

others popular web locations (information and/or commercial sites, business-to-business hubs, aggregations of virtual communities) that attract millions of users everyday to conduct one or more activities. Internet industry observers and academics expect many more to emerge in various industrial sectors, regions and so on [1, 2].

However, what Internet observers understand as an increasing trend, i.e. a web geography with disparities between densely populated areas with complex organization (big portals and B2C popular web sites, large B2B marketplaces, virtual communities etc.) and desolate web servers, may appear as a paradox. In the real world, cities exist – according to urban economists and geographers – because of the presence of external economies associated with the geographic concentration of industry within a city [3]. Transportation costs further reinforce the aggregation of firms and workers within large agglomerations. Transportation costs, as commuting costs (i.e. diseconomies of scale) define also the optimal size of the city, thus creating natural limits in cities' growth process. In the Internet, transportation costs are zero. Why, then, cities would emerge in the virtual world? Given the Internet architecture (no *king* networks, full interoperability) [4], all web sites can be easily reached from everywhere and anybody, with no transportation cost, just at the click of a button. In these conditions of equal access distance, one should rather expect a sort of smooth web geography with a relatively even distribution of the number of visitors per site, across the Internet landscape. Locational dispersion would be easier to understand than concentration and cities' formation. There would, admittedly, be some irregularities in the density of cyber-population due to the particular attractiveness of certain web sites. It is easy to understand why Disney, CNN, Sony, or Yahoo!, Amazon, e-bay, brand names of the "brick-and-mortar" world or glory pioneers of the "new economy" are able to attract Internet users' attention. But how did we go from there to large population agglomerations and information cities? Undoubtedly, this is an issue that needs to be elucidated. Especially because it appears that the agglomeration of population over the web illustrates an intriguing empirical regularity.

It is easy to observe that web sites come not only in a large diversity of categories but also in a wide variety of *sizes* (here, the size is defined as a function of the number of visitors). It is probably more difficult to understand why these sizes exhibit a sustained empirical regularity, a power law. In fact, research performed at Xerox Parc with data provided by AOL [5], reveals that the distribution of visitors per Internet site surprisingly follows a universal power law similar to what found in distribution of larger cities in US (and elsewhere) or in income distribution. More precisely, it appears that a small number of sites (about 10%) capture a very large segment of the web population (almost 80%), clear signature of a Zipf-like distribution of the web audience. Very likely, not only audience but also advertising, transactions, e-commerce, all web economic activity are going to be similarly, i.e. non-evenly, distributed across the web. In short, the economic geography of the web space is dramatically bumpy. What may cause concentration in the web and how can we explain these striking empirical data? In this paper we explore potential reasons behind the formation of web agglomeration. We model web population concentration using an agent-based computational model in which aggregate outcomes arise from the bottom-up, through the repeated interaction of autonomous agents. Drawing analogies from Fujita, Krugman and Venables work on the formation of physical cities [6], we especially investigate the contribution of *increasing returns* in the concentration of virtual social and economic activity in particular places and the emergence of a spatial ordering.

The structure of the article is as follows. In section 2, we document the formation of agglomeration in the web and discuss the striking empirical success of a power law in describing *size* distribution of web sites. We also provide a theoretical approach to deal with this empirical regularity, assuming the presence of some form of increasing returns, with population concentration being self-reinforced. Section 3 introduces this approach in the context of a specific agent-base computational model in which heterogeneous, boundedly rational agents, choose sites to visit (and "stay") in an environment of increasing returns and positive feedbacks. The model reproduces the power law character of the empirical data and provides a simple explanation of this phenomenon mostly based on the mechanisms through which information is transmitted in the Internet. In fact, our results demonstrate that web sites' growth is not only the result of the inherent differences between web sites (crystallized in that might be the "competitive advantage" of a web site), but also a result of some set of cumulative processes, involving *informational increasing returns, i.e. word-of-mouth positive feedbacks* and *web surfing path-generated linkages.*

2 The Spatial Order of the Web Economy

The exponential growth of the World Wide Web (W^3) has been accompanied by a global increase in the number of web locations where Internet users (more than 200 millions active Internet users in July 2001 according to Nielsen/NetRatings) spend personal time to get valuable information, socialize and, to a less extent, make transactions and conduct product purchases. Whereas in 1998 there were 2 million of web sites globally, at the end of 2000, the number web sites has increased to 8 million. In addition to this remarkable growth, the diversity of web sites has been considerably reinforced. As a result, Internet users profit from a wider set of location choices, and most likely of a wider range of product versions (and bundles), than those available in the real economy.

However, albeit this extraordinary diversity of web sites, the distribution of visitors across the Internet landscape, illustrates a dramatic unevenness. According to AOL data collected and interpreted by Xerox Internet Ecologies Project, the distribution of larger web sites is surprisingly well described by a power law [5] – the pattern is so universal that applies both in the case of all sites and sites in specific categories (adult sites, educational sites). As Adamic and Huberman [ibid.] explain and Fig. 1 and Table 1 prove, the existence of a power law implies that a small number of sites command the traffic of a large segment of the web population[2].

---

[2] Formally speaking, the number of web sites whose visits is exactly P, is proportional to P to some negative power (P^{-p}). We consider that for a particular site, the number of (unique) visitors it receives in one day, week or month, illustrates site's popularity and, of course, relates to its *size*.

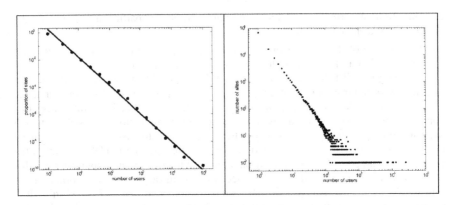

Fig. 1. Occurrence of sites by popularity according to Xerox Internet Ecologies Project (vertical axis: proportion of sites/number of sites, horizontal axe: number of users)

Table 1. Distribution of user volume among web sites according to Xerox Internet Ecologies Project

	% users volume		
% sites	all sites	adult sites	educational sites
0.1	32.36	1.4	2.81
1	55.63	15.83	23.76
5	74.81	41.75	59.50
10	82.26	59.29	74.48
50	94.92	90.76	96.88

We reached exactly the same conclusion by examining a different set of data provided to us by PC Data Online[3]. In this sample as well, distribution of unique visits among web sites is fairly described by a power law where the top 10% sites capture almost the 60% of the attention of the sampled users. More interesting, web sites ranked in top-high positions remain relatively stable in their rank in a percentage that approaches, during the examined period, the 50%. While relative ranking stability is a clear characteristic of the sample, data provide also clear indications for new sites succeeding to reach high-top ranking positions. To give an example, the panel of 1000 top-high positions is constantly renewed (i.e. weekly) in a percentage close to 15%. However, falls from the high-top positions and rises in top ranks of new sites are

---

[3] PC Data Online (now at http://www.netscoreonline.com) had monitored the behavior of a sample of 10,000 Internet users, in both free of access web sites and proprietary content online providers. Data we have used refer to the period February to September 2000. Adamic and Huberman [5] obtained the distribution of web users among web sites from access logs of a subset of AOL users active December 1, 1997. The subset comprised 60,000 web users accessing 120,000 web sites.

rarely dramatic. They happen rather incrementally, and certainly within a longer period of time.

What is interesting in observing this parameter, the number of visitors or the popularity of a site? Of course, the number of unique visitors has *de facto* become an indicator for the market success of a web site (a short of an index for observing aggregate demand). But it also captures how spatial population accumulation happens across the web. That signification we retain here. At least, except for *eyes-balls* advertisers, the number of visitors does not say so much about the profitability and the competitive positioning of a particular web site in its industry segment. Surely, it is more valuable for urban planners of the virtual space who want to understand the population aggregation/segregation trends and for web designers who design the appropriate infrastructure allowing a web site to serve its customers. In short, we perceive the number of visitors for a web site as the equivalent of the *city size* in the physical world. Likewise, the city metaphor has some relevance to the matter in hand. Exactly as in the urban ecology paradigm [7], the size of web sites, as they evolve towards information cities, together with density and population heterogeneity, might become important to study: i) the nature of these cities, ii) the features of social and economic relationships found in them and, iii) the social norms that will emerge in virtual urban environments[4].

Furthermore, exactly as in the size distribution of physical cities [8][5], we can see in the power law describing web sites' *sizes* distribution the existence of some hidden principle at work, proof of order arising from self-organization. It is likely that the Internet exhibits sustained empirical regularities that are as striking and consistent as those of the urban and regional economy. Maybe, one can learn a lot by studying models of economic geography in which there is concentration of activity in particular locations. What economic geography does principally have to say to the Internet? The response holds in just a word: *increasing returns* [9]. In a spatial economy with increasing returns, competition between locations to attract industries, involves mechanisms of positive feedback systematically working to reinforce the winner-places (by amplifying an initial advantage) and challenge less quickly growing locations. Arthur [10], Fujita, Krugman and Venables [6] and Krugman [8], all see geographical concentration in the real world as the result not necessarily of

---

[4] There is an essential difference in the notion of size in the real and the virtual world. Physical cities' habitants live only in one location while *infohabitants* may easily live different "lives" in many virtual spaces. However, in reality, the number of these "lives" is rather limited or, putting it in another way, the *portfolio of choice of an infohabitant* is not very large in size. What is a portfolio of choice? The unique sites an Internet user visits during a specific time period (usually companies that collect these statistics work on weekly or monthly basis) is often referred as repertoire or portfolio. An Internet user may visit a certain web site several times during a week/month but it would count only once in its portfolio. According to Nielsen/NetRatings, the average portfolio size of European Internet users in April 2001 ranged from 13 (Sweden) to 26 (Germany), while the average portfolio size of US Internet users has been 20.

[5] A rank size rule applies to the distribution of physical cities sizes (i.e. the population of a city is inversely proportional to its rank), which comes to approach a Zipf-distribution. More precisely, there seems to be something close to a log-linear relationship between rank and population (i.e. a straight line) with the slope of this approximately linear relationship to be almost -1.

inherent (quality-based) differences among locations, "but of some set of cumulative processes, necessarily involving some form of increasing returns, whereby geographical concentration can be self-reinforcing" [6]. In a similar manner, if the web locational system generates so much agglomeration (i.e. population accumulation) in particular places (portals, auction sites, specialized content providers), it is reasonable to suppose that something is working behind the surface to prevent dispersion and keep Internet consumers more and more congregated in a few places. Something that shapes the dynamics of competition and produces imperfect competition-like results[6] in an economy with certainly lower transactions, compared with the real world economies, and low market friction [11]. We would argue that, exactly as in the spatial economy, a credible story about web spatial development should focus on the role of increasing returns. Our sense is that increasing returns in the virtual space mostly arise from *informational feedbacks:* interactions among economic agents in the virtual space are found on information flows, generated through information dissemination, information collection and processing, and information exchange processes. To give an example, in a chaotic space such as the web, information gathering and much of individual learning about web sites can be viewed as a sampling or "polling" process of the experience of other Internet users, i.e. previous visitors in these web sites (*i.e. increasing returns from word-of-mouth feedbacks*)[7].

To proceed further we need to model informational increasing returns as emerging from the behaviour of individual agents. We need, in other words, to design a robust model able to give deeper insights to web concentration phenomenon while integrating some of the above mentioned informational increasing returns. The other point is that the model should also generate something that looks as a power law. One way to model power law phenomena would be to assume a stochastic process of growth that can produce a large range of sizes whose upper part will follow a power law distribution[8]. However in this paper, following Krugman's suggestion, we are more tempted to explore a model *involving random networks of interaction among agents* rather than random growth. "The randomness", Krugman explains, "that creates the power law may not involve random growth but random 'connections' in space. For example, imagine port cities that serve the interior along a transport network formed with random connections among transport nodes, with the direction of the preferred connections reflecting accidents either of history or geography. Alternatively, we could suppose that the connections lie in some abstract space of industry linkages..."[6]. In the next section, we will describe a computational agent-based model that relies on two "random" networks: one network transmits *word-of-mouth information* among Internet consumers; another one *(the underlying network)* defines relational paths between web sites that make navigation very hierarchical. Both structures are allowing for *random connections* to be generating and both "carry" increasing returns.

---

[6] As Adamic and Huberman notice, "sites are rewarded by relative performance than absolute performance" [5].

[7] Not strangely, word-of-mouth or *viral marketing* in the professional jargon, is largely recognized as a powerful arm for efficient web marketing.

[8] This is the approach taken by Simon [12] to model real cities' rank-size rule and by Adamic and Huberman [5] to model web markets.

3   Power Law-Based Competitive Dynamics of Web Sites under Informational Increasing Returns: A Computational Model with Agents

A model in which heterogeneous agents select web sites to visit and "stay"[9] is described in this section. Their behavior is quite complex. To effectively navigate in the web, they may explore by their own means, opportunities offered by this immense space (i.e. web sites that can satisfy their tastes). Sometimes, given the high uncertainty of that environment, they collect information that may help them to better navigate from asking advice from previous visitors, sampling their experience – which sites they have visited and appreciated. Apparently, the central cognitive issues raised in this model are these of *exploration along a transport network* and *information contagion* within local social networks. The goal of this modeling work is to understand how an aggregate distribution of web sites as a function of their size may emerge from the behavior of individual agents.

3.1   Behavioral Foundations

We start with two stylized facts. First, suppose an Internet user surfing on the Net. Which sites will he visit? He may start from interesting sites that he has visited in the past, one or more times (bookmarks file). Or, he may discover new ones, through media information and advertising or by using a search engine to help him. Alternatively, he may ask advice from friends; or a friend of him will show up and tell him, "Oh, have you seen this site, it's really good!". Obviously, which sites an Internet user will decide to visit merely depends on which sites other Internet users have "polled" or sampled and decided to visit and stay. As a result, web sites' popularity appears to be self-reinforcing and determined by a sort of historical process in which references from previous users, friends, and acquaintances, drive sites growth[10]. Second, suppose an Internet user visiting a particular web site. It is plausible that while navigating within the site, he will be tempted to click on related or suggested links that drive to other web sites. That means, which sites an Internet user decides to visit also depends on the number of other sites pointing to it. The more *in-links* a site has, the more users will visit it. Recent work in the area of web navigation patterns has shown that although it is not always the case, pages with high in-degree will also have high-ranking positions [13].

The first stylized fact describes a process that is similar to the individual consumers' reliance on word-of-mouth communication when they decide to buy a product with performance unknown ex-ante (in the sense that the real performance of

---

[9] In the sense that they include these web sites into their *portfolio of frequently visited sites* (see footnote 4).

[10] Evidence to this story is provided by a recent story published by The New York Times (22.03.200). *Marketers Try Infecting the Internet:* Overwhelmingly, Web users are relying on friends and family for new site recommendations, the report said. Fifty-seven percent say word of mouth or viral marketing is their main source of information about new sites. So instead of relying on banner advertisements and expensive marketing campaigns to promote a site or service, companies are looking to their customers as a source of publicity.

the product, and its suitability to purchaser's particular needs, will be proved only after use). Under these circumstances, the potential purchaser will probably try to reduce this uncertainty by asking previous purchasers about how they have evaluated the different products in competition. However, as demonstrated by Arthur and Lane [14], Banerjee and Fundeberg [15], Ellison and Fudenberg [16], reliance on this sort of easily obtained information (through sampling or "pooling") may affect the aggregate outcome by introducing an informational feedback which can cause, in certain cases, market shares to become self-reinforcing. Arthur and Lane [14] use the term *information contagion* for this informationally generated linkage between a product's prevalence and its likelihood of being purchased. We adopt the same view about how information is transmitted among Internet users and how this introduces an information feedback into the process of web sites competing for market share. In our model, the sites that users learn about depend on which sites others users have visited and "stayed", so Internet-users, through word-of-mouth feedbacks, are likely to learn more about popular sites than unpopular ones, sites with few previous visitors. The second stylized fact relates somehow to the *linkages* story that explained the formation of physical cities [6]. The idea is that firms and people are finding benefits to be near other firms because they want to explore potential backward and forwards linkages. Almost the same process takes place in the web where sites find benefits to be "near" sites that have large in and out degrees (surfing-path generated linkages). In our model, web sites are positioned along a transport network, defining relational paths between web sites that make navigation very hierarchical.

3.2 Computational Implementation

The model is computationally implemented using object-oriented programming. Two populations of software agents have been created: a population of Internet users making "purchasing" decisions among several products-web sites, and a population of web sites to which we attribute different performance characteristics. The Agent Based Environment gets functionality from *Mozart,* a distributed software architecture developed by SICS[11].

3.3 Set-Up of the Model

Fig. 2 represents our web model economy, consisting of M Internet consumer agents and N web sites agents (M and N increase linear over time). Each agent's internal parameters are printed inside its eclipse.

A1: Initial conditions. Initially (t=0), Internet consumer agent i, $i \in (1... M_0)$, select randomly lp_0 web sites, among N_0, to create an initial version of its *portfolio of choices* (therefore portfolio, a subset of their bookmarks folder). Web site agent j, $j \in (1... N_0)$, has performance characteristic r_j that determines its performance in practice (that is, its "intrinsic value"). A random uniform distribution describes sites' performance at t=0; I, *performance interval,* illustrates the interval between upper and

---

[11] See Mozart Consortium: The Mozart Programming System (http://www.mozart-oz.org/).

lower performance values. We suppose that these performance characteristics do not change over the course of the locational choice process described by the model.

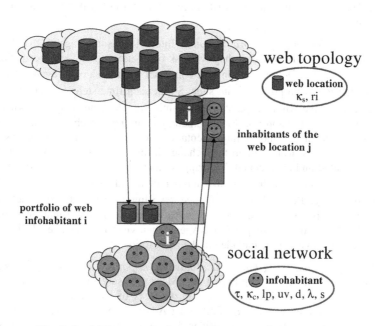

Fig. 2. Graphical representation of a simulated web economy

A2: Agents' activation. Internet consumer agents are activated at each time step t. Agents are activated exactly once during a single period (we suppose uniform activation, at least at this implementation of the model). When an agent is activated, starts a new surfing session (i.e. navigation across different web sites) that ends when time step t expires. Naturally, agent i starts a new surfing session (at time t) from visiting a subset *uv* of the web sites included in the portfolio it has composed during the previous time step (t-1).

A3: Portfolio's composition and update. The surfing behavior of consumer agents is crystallized in their portfolios. In fact, frequently visited sites are selectively organized into a portfolio of choices, which is different from one agent to another. The length of that portfolio, *lp*, remains constant over the model course (at least at this implementation of the model). Agents' portfolio is regularly updated (at each time step t) as follows. From time step t_0 (t=0), individual agents have randomly selected lp_0 sites to create an initial version of their portfolio of favorite sites. As the process evolves, agents learn about new sites via a word-of-mouth-based information gathering mechanism (A4) and through personal exploration of the web (A5). Agents evaluate sites they learn about according to a utility function *U*, and include in their portfolio the sites with the highest perceived utility (i.e., high-ranked sites after a performance check). In addition, we assume agent i to be relatively loyal to its portfolio: a new site will be included in it, only if agent i perceives a high utility for that site over a longer period of time (i.e., we require that consumer agents retain a site and include it in their portfolio if they perceive a higher utility after number λ of positive checks during a period of s iterations; formally we call λ the number of times agent i calculates that a particular site j gives a higher utility before including it in his portfolio).

A4: Learning through word-of-mouth. Internet consumer agents that have been activated, decide first whether they will ask other users to collect information about "interesting sites". Only a fraction α of consumer agents ask other agents (friends and acquaintances) to propose favorite sites. So, at each time step t, agents α, randomly selected from the whole population, randomly sample τ other agents, where τ is a stopping rule (a decision rule for terminating sampling, which is supposed the same for all agents, in this model implementation). Of course, consumer agents interact with other agents near to them to exchange information about web sites they have already visited and appreciated. We suppose a *small world* structure[12] describing the dynamics of this interaction; κ the number of initial neighbors in the local social network and β the probability of edge rewiring in this network. Each sampled individual proposes to the agent who poses the question, one (number 1) web site, randomly selected from his portfolio. Agents then visit these sites, evaluate them and select the sites that will be included in their portfolio.

A5: Exploration along hierarchical navigation paths. Consumer agents surf from one web site to another along hyperlinks. More precisely, at each time step t, agent i visits a number of d sites following the *out-links* of the sites it has visited earlier during the iteration (uv_i plus τ_i). Following Adamic [18], the *underlying network* of links connecting web sites is considered as a *small world* graph, where vertexes define web sites, and edges define links among them[13]. Agents then visit these sites, evaluate them and select the sites that will be included in their portfolio.

A6: Use's evaluation method. We assume that the utility U_{ij} agent i perceives from visiting site j is $rj + e$, where e represents agent-specific idiosyncratic shocks, which could capture either variations in sites' download time (for example, how fast, today, one can access this or that site), or variations in agent's willingness to explore the site.

---

[12] It is largely accepted that social networks are described by a *small world* structure, that is: even when two persons are not friends or do not have common friends, there is a sort chain of acquaintances that connect these two persons. Watts [17] define small world networks according to two basic properties: i) The average shortest path from any two users is small and, ii) the clustering coefficient (that is a measure of the extend with which users band together) is large, compared to the clustering coefficient of random graphs. He proposes three different network models that appear to embody the defining characteristics of the small world structure. In our model, we use Watts' β-model in order to generate a graph representing a social network transmitting word-of-mouth information. The algorithm starts with a highly ordered graph, a perfect 1-lattice, in which each vertex has precisely κ neighbors, and randomly rewires the edges of the lattice with probability β. In the resulting graph, which illustrates the characteristics of small world graphs, vertices have an average number of neighbors equal to κ with small variance.

[13] We again use Watts' β-model to generate a graph representing the network defining navigation paths (β and k take different values in the social and underlying network).

We suppose that *e* are individually independent distributions (i.d.d.) over time and across agents and sites. For simplicity we assume that *e* has a normal distribution with mean *0* and standard deviation σ_{ob}.

3.4 Aggregate Dynamics: Distribution of Web Sites' Sizes

In this sub-section we describe typical realizations of this model. Results are still exploratory and presenting initial observations, rather than describing definitive conclusions and sensing trends.

3.4.1 Evolution in Time of Web Sites' Sizes. From Fig. 3 it can be seen that our model reproduces a power law distribution that appears as a straight line in log-log coordinates (parameter assumptions: α=0.2, τ=1, d=2, lp=15).

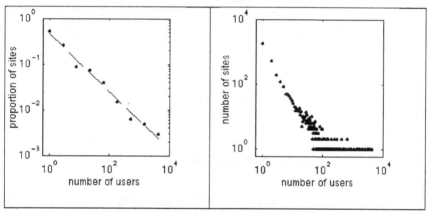

Fig. 3. Distribution of web sites by size, iCities project results (vertical axis: proportion of sites/number of sites, horizontal axis: number of users)

The above figure is a simple run of a model of a web economy initially consisting of 10,000 Internet users and 5,000 web sites. Web sites size distribution at the iteration number 50,000 (t=50,000) is described by a power law with exponent ρ=0.63. Interestingly, numerical results are pretty close to these provided by Xerox Internet Ecologies Project with AOL data.

Table 2. Distribution of user volume among sites: iCities and Xerox Internet Ecologies Project results

% sites	% users volume	
	all sites/Model results	all sites/Xerox results
0.1	13.98	32.36
1	63.54	55.63
5	84.31	74.81
10	90.92	82.26
50	98.44	94.92

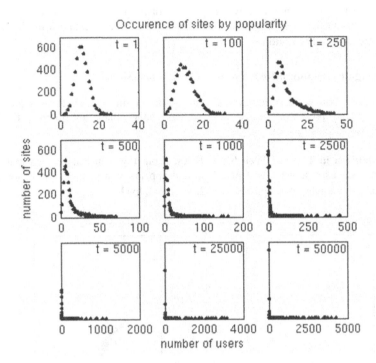

Fig. 4. Histogram "number of sites/number of users": evolution in time

We started the run (t=1) with a non-even distribution of Internet consumer agents across the 5,000 web locations (Fig. 4). As agents are being activated and new consumers and sites entering the game (M_{final}=19,880, N_{final}=9,909), the pick of the histogram gets closer and closer to 1 (t=2500). Already at time t=2,500, a group of sites appears to gain large proportions of unique visits. Hereafter, most of the sites progressively lose their appeal while few sites continue to gain more and more visitors. As a result, the shape of the curve changes and progressively takes a L-like form. This is an evidence of the transition from a normal distribution with a small mean to a power law distribution. Regarding the exponent of the power law distribution, it stabilizes close to 0.63 after time step t=25,000. Notice also another property inherent in the model dynamics. We have established that a few locations would become big by exploring word-of-mouth information diffusion and by navigational hierarchies, but, according to our experiments, neither of these effects (case a=0 or d=0) would alone produce a power law distribution result.

3.4.2 Unpredictable Evolution Paths, Variable Growth Rates, and Relative Performance Awards. Our results give also some indications about eventual patterns of self-organization that should be further investigated to get definitive conclusions. First, we should notice that the "game" is very uncertain at the early stages of the model course (up to t=2,500). Of course, (early) success begets success, but there is always the possibility for sites that had a slow start to accelerate, during later stages, their rate of growth and finally rank with the more popular web sites. The same applies for new sites, entering the competition at later stages. Necessary condition for this is that they are *strongly connected* with already popular sites. In addition, small differences in initial conditions seem to have large effect on the final outcome. Second, web locations with the largest sizes seem to belong to small groups of co-evolving locations (Fig. 5). This may not be strange given the small world topology of the *underlying network* but it is interesting to observe that the web space organizes itself into a structure composed of groups of sites of similar size with a characteristic distance between them.

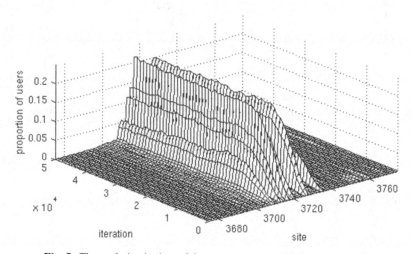

Fig. 5. The evolution in time of the stronger group with the most popular sites

Third, a very interesting result comes from observing growth rates of different web locations. For locations that succeeded to rank into the upper positions, size seems to fluctuate considerably at the early stages of the process but it progressively stabilizes. On the contrary, sites with very limited success, or no success, remain with highly fluctuating growth rates over the whole model course. Is that also a sign of self-organization? Fig. 6 illustrates the differences in growth rates between the winner location and the site ranked into the 125th size position.

Finally, no strong correlation seems to exist between web sites' ranking and the performance characteristics. Figure 7 confirms that in many cases, sites with comparatively low performance have been attracting more users than sites with high performance values.

Notice that the word-of-mouth mechanism displays all the increasing returns properties of informational feedbacks: not only does it privilege sites that became quickly established and early well known, but it also acts as a powerful mechanism of exclusion for others sites with a relatively good performance.

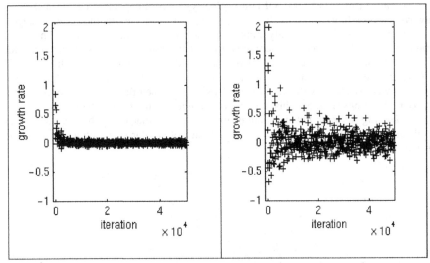

Fig. 6. Differences in evolution of growth rates for sites ranked into 1st and 125th positions

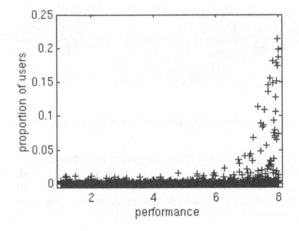

Fig. 7. Size versus performance ranks

3.4.3 Robustness of the Results and Issues under Further Investigation. The results we presented in this paper are highly exploratory and require further investigation in two directions. First, we need to better understand the behavior of the power law distribution, especially the dependence of its exponent ρ on basic model assumptions. Second, we need to experiment with other underlying network topologies, closer to the Internet reality. Broder et al. [19] have recently revealed a more detailed and subtle picture of the web architecture, much richer from a small world-like connectivity: "in a sense the web is much like a complicated organism, in which the local structure at a microscopic scale looks very regular like a biological cell, but the global structure exhibits interesting morphological structure (body and limbs) that are not obviously evident in the local structure (i.e. bow-tie graph)".

References

1. Sairamesh, J., Nikolaou, C., Kavassalis, P., Haridi, S.: Building an Information City over the Internet: Design Principles and Architecture. Digital Communities Conference (2001)
2. Isida, T., Isbister, K. (eds): Digital Cities: Technologies Experiences and Future Perspectives. Lecture Notes in Computer Science, Vol. 1765, Springer-Verlag, Berlin Heidelberg New York (2000)
3. Henderson, J. (1998) Urban development: Theory, Facts and Illusion. Oxford UP.
4. Gillet, S.: The Self-Governing Internet. Coordination by Design. MIT ITC Working Paper
5. Adamic, L., Huberman, B. The nature of Markets in the World Wide Web. QJEC 1 (2000) 5-12
6. Fujita, M., Krugman, P., Venables. A.: The Spatial Economy. Cities, Regions and International Trade. MIT Press (1999)
7. Kleniewski, N.: Cities, Change and Conflict. Wadsworth Publishing Company (1997)
8. Krugman, P.: The Self-Organizing Economy. Blackwell Publishers (1996)
9. Arthur, B.: Increasing Returns and Path Dependence in the Economy. University of Michigan Press (1994)
10. Arthur, B.: Industry Location Patterns and the Importance of History. In: Arthur, B.: Increasing Returns and Path Dependence in the Economy. University of Michigan Press (1994) 49-67
11. Bailey, J.: Intermediation and Electronic Markets: Aggregation and Pricing in Internet Commerce. Ph.D. Thesis. MIT (1998)
12. Simon, H.: On a class of Skew Distribution Functions. Biometrika 42 (1955) 425-440
13. Brin, S., Page, L.: The anatomy of a large scale hypertextual web search engine. 7th WWW Conference (1998)
14. Arthur, B., Lane, D.: Information Contagion. Increasing Returns and Path Dependence in the Economy. In: Arthur, B.: Increasing Returns and Path Dependence in the Economy. University of Michigan Press (1994) 69-97
15. Banerjee, A., Fundenberg, D.: Word of Mouth Learning. Working Paper. Available at http://fudenberg.fas.harvard.edu/mouth.htm.
16. Ellison, G., Fundenberg, D. Word of Mouth Communication and Social Learning. QJE 110 (1995) 612-643
17. Watts, D.: Small Worlds. The Dynamics of Networks Between Order and Randomness. Princeton University Press (1999)
18. Adamic, L.: The small world web. 3rd European Conference On Digital Libraries (1999)
19. Broder, A., Kumar, R., Maghoul, F., Raghavan, P., Rajagopalan, S., Stata, R., Tomkins, A., Wiener, J.: Graph Structure in the Web. 9th WWW Conference (2000)

Communication of Social Agents and the Digital City – A Semiotic Perspective

Victor V. Kryssanov[1], Masayuki Okabe[1], Koh Kakusho[2], and Michihiko Minoh[2]

[1] Japan Science and Technology Corporation, Japan
[2] Center for Information and Multimedia Studies, Kyoto University,
Kyoto 606-8501, Japan
{kryssanov, okabe, kakusho, minoh}@mm.media.kyoto-u.ac.jp

Abstract. This paper investigates the concept of digital city. First, a functional analysis of a digital city is made in the light of the modern study of urbanism; similarities between the virtual and urban constructions are pointed out. Next, a semiotic perspective on the subject matter is elaborated, and a terminological basis is introduced to treat a digital city as a self-organizing meaning-producing system intended to support social or spatial navigation. An explicit definition of a digital city is formulated. Finally, the proposed approach is discussed, conclusions are given, and future work is outlined.

1 Introduction

A digital city may be very generally defined as a collection of digital products and information resources made of a large distributed database of heterogeneous documents of various digital genres – (hyper)texts, photographs, maps, animated images, and the like – deployed to provide services aimed at facilitating social and/or spatial navigation in a virtual (e.g. "information" or "communication") or physical (e.g. geographical) space. Paramount to any digital city mission is the ability to deliver information of interest in a timely manner to its users. To do this, digital cities exploit a computer network and a client-server protocol, allowing the user to browse across digital documents through appropriately ordered hyperlinks and retrieve information as needed. An effective digital city supports access to all its repositories of relevant knowledge and data in both the raw and quality-filtered forms, and there can be several search engines installed to carry out the retrieval process. Naturally, networking and information retrieval are considered key issues in the development of digital cities.

As part of the information delivery, a digital city seeks to enable uncomplicated and correct interpretation of the results of a user's query. Examples of this include but are not limited to: providing the user with the related context as an aid for understanding the results (or even the query itself, in the case of exploratory search), illustrating the results with a suitable metaphor or analogy, and utilizing feedback from the user (or some data about the user) to adjust the strategy for retrieving or displaying the information to make it more accessible and meaningful to the user (the so-called "adaptive

M. Tanabe, P. van den Besselaar, T. Ishida (Eds.): Digital Cities, LNCS 2362, pp. 56-70, 2002.
© Springer-Verlag Berlin Heidelberg 2002

navigation support"). Another important issue that is thus immediately falling under the purview of digital city developers is human-computer interface.

Reflecting the present understanding of the concept of digital city, which is far from unified and is subject to discussion (and yet confusion), the literature abounds in technical descriptions of implemented and projected digital cities [18][1]. The authors typically approach the task of the development with a narrow focus, defining a digital city through its functions or even contents with vague terms, such as "useful information," "communication," "social agent," "community network," and the like, and with *ad hoc* "common sense" design decisions, which may have unpredictable (especially, on a long-term scale) consequences, and which are often of arbitrary relevance to the users' needs. Evidence of the latter can be found already in the very attempt to characterize digital products intended for different purposes (e.g. social *vs.* geographical navigation) and different types of users by utilizing the loose metaphor of city without clarifying which, if any, aspects or features of the city original concept – the material grounding, functionality, dynamics, structure, or other – are to be adopted. Besides, it is admitted that the inter-disciplinary theoretical study of digital city remains in its infancy and is currently of little help to the practical developers.

The presented work aims to establish a basis for scientific investigation of digital cities, and to explore fundamental properties of a digital city as an information structure. In this paper, a definition of a digital city as an organization of interacting social agents is introduced, based on a semiotic interpretation of a system-theoretic model of communication. The definition is to explicate the concept of digital city and to elaborate perspectives on the research and development for the future.

The rest of the paper is in four parts. The next section analyzes the concept of digital city. Section 3 develops a semiotic view on the subject matter. This is followed by a section that strives to define a digital city in a manner sufficiently precise for both the academic and practical needs. The final section then discusses the study theoretical findings, formulates some conclusions, and gives information on forthcoming research.

2   Concept of Digital City

2.1 Metaphor of City

It is evident that "digital city" is a metaphor. Metaphors (from Greek *metaphora* – transfer) serve to create new meanings by transferring the semantics of one concept into the semantics of another concept. Metaphors are habitually used to interpret an unknown "world" (perception, experience, etc.) – the target – in terms of a familiar world – the source. Metaphorical explanation often helps us understand highly abstract and complex phenomena by relating them to phenomena we know well (or, at least, better). In so doing, a metaphor preserves (part of) structure of the original con-

---

[1] Throughout the paper, we will use this publication as a representative collection of studies of digital cities.

cept, but substitutes its functional contents, anticipating the corresponding change in its properties and meaning.

A metaphor can be expressed with worlds, gesture, in a graphical manner, or through behavior – essentially, metaphors are (combinations of) signs. To successfully apply a metaphor, one should understand not only the systemic organization of the source, but the rôle of the source's larger context that has to be realized and presented in the context intended for the target. (Proper) metaphors are not merely somehow convenient selections of signs. Rather, they are selections of consistent logical systems or theories, with which one can generate new meaningful signs from signs already existed [37]. It seems rational to assume that the logic of a digital city could root in the logic of real cities, if this metaphor is to be properly used. Another (perhaps, stronger) assumption can be made that digital cities as "virtual structures" have much of the properties inherent in the social communities.

Juval Portugali, in his survey of the study of urbanism, described a present-day city as a conglomerate of people together with their artifacts – buildings, roads, communications, etc. – that is "actually not a city but a text written by millions of unknown writers, unaware that they are writers, read by millions of readers, each reading his or her own personal and subjective story in this ever-changing chaotic text, thus changing and recreating and further complicating it" [30, 29]. A city is *complex*. It consists of numerous components, which interact, and which are created by (and from) other components, thereby continuously re-producing the fabric of the city. A city is *self-organizing*. It, like all self-organizing systems, exchanges the resources – matter, energy, and people – and information with its environment and is, in this sense, *open*. At the same time, a city is *closed* (to a degree) in the sense that its structure is determined internally (again, to a degree), and the environment does not control how the city organizes itself. In complex system theory, complete closure means that every component of a system is produced solely by other components of the same system without influence from the outside – a requirement hardly reachable in social or even biological organizations. However, once a city starts to distinguish itself from the environment by creating a *boundary*, it can achieve a sufficient degree of organizational closure to be seen (though, controversially [25]) as an *autopoietic system* that is a form of self-organization [24].

Due to its composite make-up and the complexity of internal interactions, a city is generally indescribable in terms of cause and effect or in terms of probabilities [7]. This makes it extremely difficult to study the city basic properties. Recently, however, some conceptual and mathematical approaches (such as dissipative structures, synergetics, and cellular automata), borrowed from the natural sciences, have successfully been applied to the study of cities with the focus on not to control or predict behaviors of city components, but to deliberately participate in and sensibly "shape" the city development by acting at the global, social and organizational level [30].

Turning now to the case of digital cities, one can quickly prove the openness and the complexity of the virtual organizations. Intuitively, digital cities should be open, since they constantly exchange information with their environments, and they are indeed complex, each comprising a number of dynamic information resources. Not so straightforward is the question of organizational closure: it is unclear what a digital city produces and how it reproduces. A still more difficult question is, how can a digital city separate itself from the environment and what is the boundary? By answering these, we would clarify whether and to what extent the logic of cities and social systems in general is applicable to an information web-structure called "digital city."

2.2 Navigation with Digital City

Even at the level of parts, self-organization does not really mean freedom but a controlled collective behavior towards achieving a common (for the entire system) goal in an environment [16]. There is a controlling mechanism "hidden" and distributed over all the system parts that determines a strategy for the system, which is usually implemented as more or less inclusive constraints imposed on each part's behavior. While the principal goal of any ("living") self-organizing system must imply its long-term survival in a variable environment, i.e. the maintenance of the system invariant structure – its *identity*, the tactical (or transient) goals usually determine the system parts' behavior in every local situation and at every particular time. To "survive" for a digital city would mean to uphold the stability of its structure with the designated functionality supporting (social, geographical, spatial, etc.) *navigation* despite environmental disturbances.

Perhaps most generally, navigation in an environment[2] was defined in [34] as a four-stage iterative process that includes: 1) *perception* of the environment, 2) reconciliation of the perception and cognition (i.e. *understanding*), 3) deciding whether the current goal has been reached (i.e. *decision-making*), and 4) choosing and performing the next action (i.e. *adjustment* of the behavior). Among these stages, the last two have a noticeably subjective character and are solely on the navigator's side, whereas the other two depend on "objectively" available – sensed – information about the environment. It is perception that first represents "raw" sensory data and provides for further interpretation by putting the resultant representations into a context of the scene perceived (e.g. by simply combining the representations). When information obtained through the senses is not enough for establishing or re-establishing meanings of the environment necessary for successful decision-making, the navigator may ask for help a guide – someone, who could presumably know more about the environment. A digital city may be thought of as such a guide: in the navigation process, it works to enhance and complement the navigator's sensing capabilities. In other words, a digital city is to "produce" information about the navigation space.

Perceptual Control Theory [31] proposes an explanation of the control mechanism for complex self-organizing systems. The theory tells us that a perceiving system normally seeks to bring the perceived situation to its goal or preferred state by utilizing (negative) feedback from the environment: if the situation deviates from the goal, the system acts and adapts, possibly changing its own state and the state of the environ-

---

[2] It should be noted that for the digital city, the environment as surroundings may or may not coincide with the environment as navigation space. We will not, however, distinguish these two environments for the purpose of this study: the latter is often part of the former, and in both cases, the environment is "that, which is not the digital city."

ment, and the new situation is again sensed and estimated in respect to the goal. The loop repeats and keeps the system in a stable goal-directed state, environmental perturbations and compensating actions notwithstanding. Although a digital city can, in principle, sense its environment directly (e.g. through cameras and transducers, as in the "Helsinki Arena 2000" project [22]), there is no other way for it to determine the context and, hence, semantics necessary for making the sensed information *meaningful* for the navigation process, but (ultimately) by drawing on expertise of its users and utilizing feedback from them. The users together with their knowledge can and in fact should be considered as indispensable and *constitutive* parts of the digital city.

Each user's knowledge is supposed to be a subjective reconstruction of the locally and selectively perceived environment (for justification, see [20, 38]). No user possesses perfect knowledge, but being connected by means of the digital city, the users can gain access to "collective knowledge" – once sensed or created information about the environment that, owing to the spatio-temporal dynamics uniquely allocating each user (and yet the natural cognitive limitations), is far more complete and encompassing than knowledge of a solitary user.

Perception is, obviously, effective only when it provides the navigation process with comprehensible and meaningful – useful – information. This requirement defines the strategy for a digital city. To ascertain the usefulness of a particular perception, the digital city puts it into the context of a situation associated with a user's query and then attempts to evaluate the user's reaction and/or feedback. There can be different and even conflicting interpretations of the same situation made by different users that would, in the long run, destroy the digital city by denouncing its very rationale. In order for a digital city to "survive," its functionality is kept up by enabling context-sensitive (i.e. dependent on the user's prior experience and personal understanding of the situation) interpretation of its contents. The latter sets conditions for the tactics. Thus, the global organizational stability of a digital city (that actually determines its functional stability that is supporting navigation) is naturally maintained at the expense of the stability of its parts (i.e. at the expense of the uniformity of the representation and understanding of the environment – see, for instance, the adaptive interface concept for the Kyoto Digital City described in [17]), just like as it happens in physical cities [30].

It is now understood that a digital city can become self-organizing, if it separates itself from the environment by developing an eventually autonomous structure allowing for generating meanings – forming a "sense" – of the environment for the needs of navigation. In addition to plain separations in matter (there is not such a thing as information, but a digital city is a representation of things; on the other hand, "the environment contains no information; the environment is as it is" [10]) and time (the timescales of a digital city and its environment usually differ), a self-organizing digital city should develop a meaning boundary: it should maintain and reproduce its own functionally invariant meaning-making structure not just by storing some observations, but by recursively producing pertinent observations using other observations, while acting independently (perhaps, to a degree) of environmental disturbances.

3 Approach

3.1 Semiotics

An issue of great (by its consequences) significance that is sometimes overlooked by theorists and, fairly often, by practical developers dealing with human-computer interface is the fact that information transmitted by means of computers tends to loose its meaning. Digital signals, such as arrays of bits forming raster graphics, do not bear semantics and have to be interpreted subjectively. There is no context-independent or "absolute" meaning, but the meaning of a signal emerges through the process of interaction between a local perception of the signal and a global (in some way) vision of the corresponding situation [1, 8].

Contrary to the objectivism dominating AI research, human navigation in an environment builds on information conceived (not just perceived!) by the navigator [34]. For instance, observing a map is useless for the purpose of navigation unless the map can be related with the navigator's current location and goal that, as a rule, requires additional "information processing," such as (re)interpretation of sensed information about the surroundings and the map itself. People, through their activities and practice, subjectively and locally but always internally create meanings of the environment. These meanings are then "externalized" to be disseminated and proliferated, while their validity (in respect to the environment) is continuously and again subjectively examined in an attempt to identify currently effective and supportive meanings. Semiotics studies these in essence meaning-making processes, construing elements of the environment as signs that need to be interpreted to obtain meanings for their contextual use.

In Peirce's formulation [28], semiotics studies the process of interaction of three subjects: the sign itself – the *representamen* or signifier, the object – that which is signified by the sign; and the *interpretant* – the meaning that follows semantically from the process of interpretation of the sign. It is postulated that no sign is directly connected to an object: signs have meanings only when they are embodied into a system of *interpretance* that is just a (larger) system of signs – a sign system, which constrains and relates its constituents, thereby creating a context. A representamen is necessarily a sign of an object for a certain sign system but not for any sign system: depending on the context, the same sign may have different meanings while signifying different objects, or different signs may have the same meaning while signifying the same object, and so on. Designated *semiosis processes* determine the meaning(s) of signs in all the specific situations.

The science of semiotics has a long history of development and application, presently offering a set of generic concepts and procedures to a variety of disciplines, such as art theory, film theory, linguistics, theoretical biology, complex system theory, anthropology, and philosophy of mind, among others (see [6] for a nice introduction into the study). Often thought of as "the mathematics of humanities" [2], semiotics has developed analytical apparatus for qualitative characterization of various representation and re-representation processes involving signs. This has later been applied on a more formal basis in natural sciences, putting forward a common language for treating information-processing aspects of inter-disciplinary problems [9]. In computer science, semiotics has traditionally been focused on analyzing the reciprocal influence of the computation and interpretation processes, and classifying representations by type of relation to their objects [2, 11]. From a semiotic point of view, many (if not all) information processes in a digital city – from "purely" technical, such as data storage, to experiential and cognitive, such as understanding of data – are semiosis processes [36]. Semiotics appears particularly apt for explicating the structure of the mechanism "producing" *meanings out of perceptions.*

3.2 Structure for Producing Meaning

Semiotics teaches us that people perceive an environment through signs, which may be interpreted and which serve to mediate meanings of the environment. Although human perception is relatively uniform and consistent, the meaning assigned to a single sign can vary significantly, resting on the subjective dynamics of perception and cognition, as well as on a larger context (e.g. orientational, functional, or operational) of the situation encountered. A semiosis process is the process of determining the meaning of some distinctions in an environment that entails representation and re-representation of these distinctions over several levels of interpretation, each of which is governed by and adopts certain *norms* – developmental rules and relational constraints for the signs. The norms reflect different aspects of human behavior that can be classified into five major groups [35]: perceptual – to respond to peculiarities of sensing; cognitive – to deal with cultural knowledge and beliefs; evaluative – to express personal preferences, values, and goals; behavioral – to delineate behavioral patterns; and denotative – to specify the choice of signs for (further) signifying.

From a system-theoretic viewpoint, the complexity and richness of many natural organizational processes, such as adaptation and self-organization, derives from the ability to arrange smaller units into larger ones, which are in turn arranged into larger ones, which are arranged into still larger ones, and so forth [33]. Semiosis is a natural organizational process [21]: it organizes signs in a partial hierarchy by ordering them so that representamina of objects (that can be other signs) of level N-1 for processes and structures of level N+1 are placed on level N. The lowest-level signs, e.g. (manifestations of) physical objects, behavioral dispositions, emotions, and the like, are perceived or realized through their distinctions and get a representation at an "intermediary" level of norms, reflecting interpretive laws of a higher, experiential and environmentally (physiologically, socially, technically, economically, etc.) induced level, which accommodates interpretants and gives meanings to the representamina. This simple three-level structure corresponds to and is set up by a single semiosis process, whereas various semiosis processes defined on the same realm will create a complex partially ordered structure, where one sign gets multiple meanings, depending on both the signified contents of the lower levels and the contextual constraints from the interpretive levels (see Fig. 1).

Navigation within a digital city activates a number of semiosis processes (e.g. by different users) and results in the creation of a multi-level sign system with a potentially infinite hierarchy of interpretive levels, where signs on level N are dynamically composed of signs on level N-1 so that only those of all the possible combinations of that lower-level signs persist, which are allowed by boundary conditions effective at level N+1. Signs on level N-1 serve as constitutive units for level N signs, which are constitutive for level N+1 signs, which can be constitutive for yet-higher-level signs. Besides, signs on higher levels are constraining for signs on their adjacent lower levels. The levels have different dynamics, such that the probability of changing the relationships among signs within a level decreases for higher levels [21].

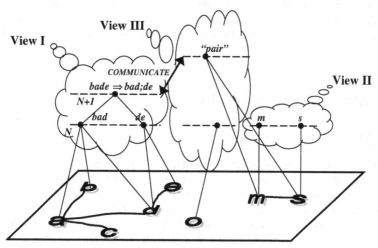

Fig. 1. A simplistic example of the composite partial hierarchy for producing meaning: in View I, entities "*b, a, d*" and "*d, e*" are represented at level *N* as *connected* for level *N+1*, and a new (in respect to *N*) meaning may emerge (e.g. be inferred) for *N+1*: "*b* and *e* are connected." There are some other systems of interpretance in the structure, and the one that recognizes, for instance, *pairs* of connected entities – as in View III. By referring to (i.e. communicating with) III, View I may apparently learn (e.g. *syntactically* – see [38]) to also recognize pairs of entities. It may then reconsider "*bade*" as a pair "*bad;de*" (that will become of interest to III). Thus, the meanings in the system may change as I and III communicate.

A user of a digital city typically deals with a fragment of the global system of signs, which is loosely shared by all the users in the environment (that may be seen as the lowest semiotic level) (Fig. 1). The fragment is, however, distinctively ordered in an interpretive hierarchy peculiar to the user's experience and the norms he or she adopts. Hierarchies created by different users may be different in terms of the order as well as the coverage, and they may run on different time-scales (see [20] for general argumentation). Combined into one structure (e.g. by means of a community network [12]), the fragments may form a global but partial and often implicit "hierarchy". This global hierarchy constitutes the functionally invariant structure of a self-organizing digital city.

It allows for producing "meanings" for the system internal needs (adaptation), out of (represented) perceptions that are based on the currently prevailing experience of the digital city users (received through, for instance, feedback – see Section 2.2). The hierarchy has an essentially ordering dynamics that affects the interpretive levels rather than the signs within a level [27].

Unlike the case of individual navigation, where perceived and conceived signs may need not be articulated explicitly, the development and operation of a digital city neatly builds on communicative use of a multi-level sign system representing the environment and the digital city itself. This sign system can be externalized – derived from the digital city structure – as a language defined in a very general way and not confined to handling verbal constructions. The digital city "describes" (and interacts with) its environment with this language, which has a syntax reflecting the organization of the environment, semantics defining meanings of the environment, and pragmatics characterizing the effect of the language use. (See, for instance, [12] presenting the Campiello System that works to construct and utilize such a language.)

4 Self-Organizing Digital City

4.1 Communication

Users of a digital city, although acting individually, are not isolated from the surroundings: their behavior is determined not only by their aims, but considerably by the material processes taking place in the environment, by the actions of others (both users and non-users), by the existing time- and functionality-constraints, by the actions of groups, by the current state of the digital city, etc.. The users interact with the digital city (yet being parts of it), their environments, and simply with each other. The users are, nonetheless, autonomous, in the sense that they possess a representation of the environment adequate to sustain their purposeful behavior for some time. Also the digital city is autonomous, as it is recursively (through its users) closed with respect to meaning. In this situation, the operation of a digital city heavily depends on the social context of the semiosis associated with the navigation process – it depends on how the users and the digital city receive and interpret information in the course of navigation, i.e. how they communicate.

From a behaviorist point of view, an individual engaged in navigation develops an internal representation, using those distinctions of the environment that turn up successful solutions [5]. Signs of such representations arrive as "tools for indication purposes" [32]. These signs (i.e. the distinctions they stand for) serve to orient the navigator, independently of their "actual" meanings and roles in the environment. The navigator is not really interested in "getting to the truth," but in knowing what happens or what are possible consequences – *expectations*, when a sign is encountered. In this aspect, signs are signifiers emerging from successful interaction between an individual and an environment. They are "pointers" not just to an object standing in a referential relation with the sign, but also to the outcomes desired (or, at least, anticipated) by the user. Signs can be considered "anticipations of successful interactions of referral" [32], which emphasizes their origin and predictable influence on behavior.

One can show that the behaviorist view of the process of forming the meanings of signs is just an elaboration of the classical view that defines information as "a difference that makes a difference" to the interpreter [4]. This view, however, makes it difficult to explain communication as mere exchange of signs. Indeed, in the case of navigation within a digital city, not objective reality but subjective experience is the basis of signs (also see discussion in [19]). The navigator cannot frequently succeed in developing an interpretation of a sign received through communication by simply referring the sign to the observed part of the environment. The navigator's personal experience has first to be "synchronized" to a certain extent with the experience underlying the creation of the sign. This, however, appears impossible or inefficient (e.g. because of time-limitations) in most cases of the use of a digital city.

A solution to the above problem comes with an advanced explanation of communication that includes aspects of information (sign) exchange as well as behavioral coordination between *autopoietic systems*. An autopoietic system is a dynamic system maintaining its organization through its own operation: each state of such a system depends on its current structure and a previous state only [24]. The structure of an autopoietic system determines the possible (i.e. non-destructive) behaviors that are triggered by the interactions between system and environment. If the system changes its state, enforcing changes of the structure without breaking autopoiesis, the system is *structurally coupled* with the environment. If the environment is structurally dynamical, then both the system and the environment may mutually trigger their structural changes, sustaining the system's *self-adaptation*. When there is more than one autopoietic system in the environment, the adaptation processes of some of the present systems may become coupled, acting recursively through their own states. All the possible changes of states of such systems, which do not destroy their coupling, create a *consensual domain* for the systems. Behaviors in a consensual domain are mutually oriented. Communication, in this view, is the (observed) behavioral coordination resulting from the interactions that occur in a consensual domain (see [8] for details).

(Human) users of a digital city are (higher order) autopoietic systems [24]. Besides, the environment of a digital city is supposed to be structurally dynamical or even self-organizing (to a degree), as in the case of social systems [14, 23, 38]. Therefore, a digital city should be autopoietic (at least, to a degree), i.e. to be a system *internally* producing meanings for its own (adaptation) needs, to endure communication.

4.2 Definition of Digital City

Based on the system-theoretic and semiotic analysis made in the previous sections, we can now define a digital city as follows:

A digital city is an autopoietic organization of social agents communicating by way of computers, such that every social agent is a realization of a semiosis process engendered by navigation taken place in a common (for all agents) environment.

It is important to notice that the above definition builds on the understanding of communication as the (observed) coordination activity in a consensual domain, and it does not "humanize" the social agency. People, computers, and systems can be social agents as long as they interact and produce meanings in the navigation process. Following [34], the term "navigation" is understood here in a broad sense.

It can be seen that the proposed definition is general enough to encompass all the realizations of digital cities reported in the literature, which have a common identity, constituting a distinct class of digital products. On the other hand, it is sufficiently precise in giving not only the functional (i.e. *what* goes on) but operational (i.e. *how* it goes on) characterization of a digital city. By the definition, an agent does not have to be physically embedded within the navigation space but does have to be engaged in the navigation process. The latter allows us to clearly distinguish a digital city among other web-based digital products, yet leaving plenty of freedom for dynamically including and excluding resources and agents appearing in it. One should not, nevertheless, be confused by the process-orientation of the definition: not every navigation (e.g. on the World Wide Web – see [14]) is the source of the emergence of a (self-organizing) digital city, but only that, which is supported by (and supports) the functionally invariant structure for navigation in the specified space.

5   Discussion and Conclusions

Within descriptions of digital cities, there is often little attention to the precise definition of basic concepts, with which a digital city is characterized. This imprecision results in weakly motivated developments, which easily loose their identities when compared with other digital products, such as map repositories or Web-portals (e.g., , the Turin and AOL digital cities [18]). Moreover, although it is assumed by default that a digital city is deployed for a group of users rather than for a single user, most of the reported projects habitually focus on and address specific aspects related to the personal adaptation (e.g. of the interface), while the issue of the appropriateness of a digital city to a particular society remains opaque. Even less is known about possible mutual influences of a digital city and the society, and about the life cycle of a digital city. All this could be a serious reason to question the very rationale of digital cities.

In this paper, an attempt was made to find a theoretical basis for the development of digital cities. Starting from an assertion that "digital city" is a metaphor called to denote a complex digital product with properties structurally similar to the ones of physical cities, the concept of digital city was gradually refined throughout the study. We started to analyze it functionally, then continued with a semiotic analysis, and finally analyzed it from a system theoretic perspective. The definitive function of a digital city is the (information) support of the process of navigation in an environment. Navigation utilizes meanings of the environment resulting from perception and interpretation. Interpretation is intrinsic of semiosis. Different meanings are developed by semiosis processes, which create and order signs of the environment into partial hierarchies. Semiotic sign-hierarchies emerged during navigation can internally generate new semiosis processes and, therefore, new meanings owing to communication. If this generation is maintained regardless environmental variations, the organization of semiosis processes becomes autopoietic, and it constitutes a digital city.

The authors are quite aware of the difficulties and controversy attributed to any attempt to define a "not obviously living" system as autopoietic. By arguing that a digital city should be autopoietic, we follow the German sociologist and philosopher Niklas Luhmann [23], who was first to explicate the autopoiesis of social systems. The concept of digital city is, in our opinion, to organically expand the communication-driven autopoiesis of social systems to the new "digital" dimension. It should be stressed that neither semiotic meaning-making nor self-organization alone is an entirely new and unexplored issue in the fields of Human-Computer Interaction and Computer Supported Cooperative Work (see, for instance, [1] and, especially, [26]). Somewhat different to the previous works, we see the advantage of the application of semiotics and complex system theory not only in their suitability for theoretical exploration of digital products, but in their appropriateness for a rigorous computational treatment and technological validation of the theoretical findings, as it became apparent with the recent advent of algebraic semiotics and category theory [11], as well as evolutionary computation [8].

The view of digital city developed through the study is not only fully compatible with the contemporary vision of urban communities as self-organizing systems (a city as "a text written by millions of unknown writers..." [29, 30]), but it specializes and details the mechanism of self-organization by advocating that digital cities are autopoietic. By extending the recently popular idea that not just biological, but also psychic and social systems can be autopoietic [23, 24, 14], autopoiesis can be considered as a general form of system development that draws on self-referential closure [9, 15]. It was argued in the paper that in the case of digital cities, the concept of life, which is exploited in biology and (in a sense) sociology and urbanism, is to be replaced with the concept of semiosis as a kind of autopoietic organization. Along with systems theory that is used in the study of urbanism [30], semiotics forms the basis for investigation of (self-organizing) digital cities.

Semiosis of a digital city arranges a structure required for the reproduction of meanings by the digital city for its own "internal" needs. The meaning-(re)producing autopoiesis gives more room for a system to "survive" by letting it be autopoietic to a degree: a digital city can be less (and trivially) autopoietic if it mainly produces meanings out of perceptions, and it can be more autopoietic if it produces meanings out of meanings. For the former, consciousness of the users is the source of meaning reproduction that is typically fairly dependent on the environment, i.e. on what is not the digital city. For the latter, meanings are reproduced in the course of communication that powers the autopoiesis without paying much attention to the environment. "Meanings out of perceptions" assumes a hetero-referential closure of the digital city: the system produces meanings for other (possibly "external") meanings (e.g. it learns to send an image for clarifying a text). "Meanings out of meanings" implies a self-referential closure: the digital city produces meanings for communication (e.g. it learns to send an image for adjusting its own interface). Resembling social systems [23], self-reference for a digital city is the ability to distinguish between hetero-reference and self-reference.

The proposed definition of digital city departs from the criticized studies (also see [38] for a more general critique), which tend to focus on the micro-scale phenomena of the interaction between a user and a (part of a) digital city, but ignore (or artificially "fix") the global social dynamics of the digital city. All the users, through their social agents that are realizations of semiosis processes, are constitutive parts of the digital city, and its dynamics is determined by behaviors of the users. It is obvious that the concept of digital city becomes incongruous if the users are not included into the definition in the case of hetero-referential closure: the system would then be anything –

from a database to a game –, depending on the purpose of the user, i.e. on what is the motivation or "driving force" causing the system of interpretance for the semiosis processes representing the user in the interaction with the digital city. Besides, the concept is just absurd if devoid of the users in the case of self-referential closure: how to call a digital product, which acts for its own purposes, leaving an external user unaware of them, and which is generally unpredictable in its behavior? Contrasting these two extreme points, the global and inclusive treatment advocated in this paper is not only comprehensive, but it allows for applying the rich apparatus of social studies to the study of digital cities to examine the macro-phenomena. At the same time, the proposed approach well recognizes the micro-scale dynamics: any user, whether an individual or a group, can uniquely be defined through characteristic semiosis processes. This gives us a happy opportunity to apply various theories of human-computer interaction as well as semiotics to the research and development. Combining the micro- and macro-level visions, the meaning-making self-organization implies the emergence of some ontology (following the terminology coined by the knowledge-sharing research community [13]) of the navigation space, which is understood as the functionally invariant structure of a digital city. This ontology, however, has a structural dynamics and changes throughout the life cycle of a digital city. New technological perspectives might be discovered when examining this evolution (e.g. how networking and information retrieval mechanisms should react when the digital city undergoes a change from hetero- to self-referential closure), allowing for "deliberately participating" in the digital city development (compare with the study of urbanism, [30]) that would lead us to the creation of a "participative virtual city," e.g. as discussed in [3].

The presented work offers one new contribution: the clarification of the concept of digital city. This contribution is based upon the extensive analysis supported by the literature. Another contribution of the paper would thus be providing the reader with an introduction (though, by no means complete) to the semiotic and system-theoretic aspects of the study of social system.

We do not expect our approach be perfect. The presented study seeks to explain a particular view of digital cities that would be found somehow inappropriate. We believe, however, that this is better than discussing the subject in such an elusive way, that no one can tell if it is inappropriate. This work also is to stimulate critical discussions of the concept of digital city.

Building on the conceptual and terminological basis developed through the study, our future research plans include: 1) elaboration of a semiotic theory of communication for a digital city, 2) its verification by both analysis of practical examples and computational experiments, 3) exploration of possible implications of the study of digital cities for the study of urbanism.

Acknowledgement. The presented work is part of the Universal Design of Digital City project in the Core Research for Evolutional Science and Technology (CREST) program funded by the Japan Science and Technology Corporation (JST).

References

1. Andersen, P.B.: A theory of computer semiotics. Semiotic approaches to construction and assessment of computer systems. Cambridge University Press, Cambridge (1990)
2. Andersen, P.B.: What semiotics can and cannot do for HCI. Paper presented at the CHI'2000 Workshop on Semiotic Approaches to User Interface Design. To appear in Knowledge Based Systems (2000)
3. Aurigi, A.: Digital City or Urban Simulator? In: Ishida, T. and Isbister, K. (eds): Digital Cities: Experiences, Technologies and Future Perspectives. Lecture Notes in Computer Science, Vol. 1765. Springer-Verlag (2000) 33-44
4. Bateson, G.: Steps to an Ecology of Mind. Ballantine Books, New York (1972)
5. Bickhard, M.H.: The emergence of representation in autonomous agents. In: Prem, E. (ed.): Epistemological Issues of Embodied AI. Cybernetics and Systems. 28(6) (1997)
6. Chandler, D.: Semiotics for Beginners. WWW document. Posted at URL http://www.aber.ac.uk/media/Documents/S4B/ (1994)
7. Dendrinos, D.S. and Sonis, M.: Chaos and Socio-Spatial Dynamics. Springer-Verlag, New York (1990)
8. Di Paolo, E.A.: An investigation into the evolution of communication. Adaptive Behavior. 6(2) (1998) 285-324
9. Emmeche, C.: Closure, Function, Emergence, Semiosis and Life: The Same Idea? Reflections on the Concrete and the Abstract in Theoretical Biology. In: Chandler, J.L.R., van de Vijver, G. (eds): Closure: Emergent Organizations and Their Dynamics. Annals of the New York Academy of Sciences, Vol. 901. The New York Academy of Sciences, New York (2000) 187-197
10. von Foerster, H.: Observing Systems. Intersystems Publications, Seaside CA (1981)
11. Goguen, J.A.: An introduction to algebraic semiotics, with applications to user interface design. In: C. Nehaniv (ed.): Computation for Metaphor, Analogy and Agents. Lecture Notes in Artificial Intelligence, Vol. 1562. Springer-Verlag (1999) 242-291
12. Grasso, A., Snowdon, D. and Koch, M.: Extending the Services and the Accessibility of Community Networks. In: Ishida, T. and Isbister, K. (eds): Digital Cities: Experiences, Technologies and Future Perspectives. Lecture Notes in Computer Science, Vol. 1765. Springer-Verlag (2000) 401-415
13. Guarino, N.: Formal Ontology, Conceptual Analysis and Knowledge Representation. Int. J. Human and Computer Studies. 43(5/6) (1995) 625-640
14. Heylighen, F.: The Global Superorganism: an evolutionary-cybernetic model of the emerging network society. Posted at URL http://pespmc1.vub.ac.be/Papers/Superorganism.pdf (2000)
15. Heylighen, F.: The Growth of Structural and Functional Complexity during Evolution. In: Heylighen, F., Bollen, J., Riegler, A. (eds.): The Evolution of Complexity. Kluwer Academic Publishers, Dordrecht (1999) 17-44
16. Holland, J.H.: Hidden Order: How adaptation builds complexity. Addison-Wesley (1996)
17. Isbister, K.: A Warm Cyber-Welcome: Using an Agent-Led Group Tour to Introduce Visitors to Kyoto. In: Ishida, T. and Isbister, K. (eds): Digital Cities: Experiences, Technologies and Future Perspectives. Lecture Notes in Computer Science, Vol. 1765. Springer-Verlag (2000) 391-400
18. Ishida, T. and Isbister, K. (eds): Digital Cities: Experiences, Technologies and Future Perspectives. Lecture Notes in Computer Science, Vol. 1765. Springer-Verlag (2000)
19. Latour, B.: On interobjectivity. Mind, Culture, and Activity. 3(4) (1996) 228-245
20. Law, J.: Organizing Modernities. Blackwell, Cambridge (1993)

21. Lemke, J.L.: Opening Up Closure: Semiotics Across Scales. In: Chandler, J.L.R., van de Vijver, G. (eds): Closure: Emergent Organizations and Their Dynamics. Annals of the New York Academy of Sciences, Vol. 901. The New York Academy of Sciences, New York (2000) 100-111

22. Linturi, R., Koivunen, M.-R. and Sulkanen, J.: Helsinki Arena 2000 – Augmenting a Real City to a Virtual One. In: Ishida, T. and Isbister, K. (eds): Digital Cities: Experiences, Technologies and Future Perspectives. Lecture Notes in Computer Science, Vol. 1765. Springer-Verlag (2000) 83-96

23. Luhmann, N.: Social systems. Stanford University Press, Palo Alto (1995)

24. Maturana, H. and Varela, F.J.: Autopoiesis and Cognition: The Realization of the Living. D. Reidel Publishing Company, Dordrecht (1980)

25. Mingers, J.: Self-Producing Systems: Implications and Applications of Autopoiesis. Plenum Publishing, New York (1994)

26. Nadin, M.: Anticipation – A Spooky Computation. Lecture given at the 3rd Int. Conference on Computing Anticipatory Systems. Liege, Belgium. Posted at URL http://www.code.uni-wuppertal.de/de/computational_design/who/nadin/lectures/anticipa.html (1999)

27. Pattee, H.H.: The Physical Basis and Origin of Hierarchical Control. In: Howard H. Pattee (ed.): Hierarchy Theory. George Braziller, New York (1973) 71-108

28. Peirce, C.S.: The essential Pierce: Selected philosophical writings, Vol. 2. Indiana University Press, Bloomington (1998)

29. Portugali, J.: Notions concerning world urbanization. In: Amos, F.J.C., Bourne, L.S., Portugali, J. (eds): Contemporary perspectives on urbanization. Progress in Planning. 46(3) (1996) 145-162

30. Portugali, J.: Self-Organizing Cities. Futures. 29(4-5) (1997) 353-380

31. Powers, W.T.: Behavior: the Control of Perception. Aldine, Chicago (1973)

32. Prem, E.: Semiosis in embodied autonomous systems. In: Proceedings of the IEEE International Symposium on Intelligent Control. IEEE, Piscataway NJ (1998) 724-729

33. Salthe, S.: Development and Evolution. MIT Press, Cambridge (1993)

34. Spence, R.: A framework for navigation. Int. J. Human-Computer Studies. 51(5) (1999) 919-945

35. Stamper, R. and Liu, K.: Organizational Dynamics, Social Norms and Information Systems. In: Proceedings of the Twenty Seventh Hawaii Int. Conf. on System Sciences (1994) IV645-654

36. Stamper, R.: Signs, Information, Norms and Systems. In: Holmqvist, B., Andersen, P.B., Klein, H., Posner, R. (eds): Signs of Work. De Gruyter, Berlin (1996) 349-399

37. Turner, M. and Fauconnier, G.: Conceptual Integration and Formal Expression. Metaphor and Symbolic Activity. 10(3) (1995) 183-204

38. Viskovatoff, A.: Foundations of Niklas Luhmann's Theory of Social Systems. Philosophy of the Social Sciences. 29(4) (1999) 481-516

Digital Cities and Digital Citizens

Doug Schuler

The Evergreen State College
2700 Evergreen Parkway NW
Olympia, WA 98505-0002
The Public Sphere Project
Computer Professionals for Social Responsibility
P.O. Box 717
Palo Alto, CA 94302
douglas@scn.org

Cities are providing the physical environment for an increasing number of the world's citizens. They are also becoming the locus for a variety of "virtual", networked digitally-based economic, political, and cultural activities. Digital cities represent a new manifestation of this phenomenon. Digital cities, like their physical analogies, geographical or "real" cities, are only so much infrastructure unless animated with human social presence. This paper focuses on this social presence, particularly the type of social presence typified by the idea of "citizen," for it is primarily through the work of this social entity that social problems get addressed and social "progress" is furthered. Several socio-technical innovations such as community networks are explored as are possible roles for the computer professional.

1 The Digital City

The world is becoming increasingly urbanized (or de-ruralized) and digitized. More people both absolutely and in relative terms live in cities than ever before; more than half of the world's population now, for the first time, live in cities. At the same time, digital communications are shrinking the globe, connecting people and institutions with terabytes of information every day. Thus the idea of a "digital city" naturally becomes significant.

A digital city has at least two plausible meanings: (1) a city that is being transformed or re-oriented through digital technology and (2) a digital representation or reflection of some aspects of an actual or imagined city. In the first case, that of the city becoming more digitally-oriented, the physical and non-physical attributes of the city itself are changing [1]. It is true that the physical nature of the city is undergoing change: miles of fiber optic cable snake under the city's streets and up into its dwellings and workplaces; vast server farms transfer massive amounts of information from computer to computer while voraciously consuming electricity; and spidery antennas service millions of cellular telephonic conversations and exchange information with satellites circling the earth. The more profound changes, however, are in the non-physical realm. The fields of media, telecommunications, finance, among others, are increasingly dominant in the new world and they rely on digital information and digital communication and they are generally city-centric.

M. Tanabe, P. van den Besselaar, T. Ishida (Eds.): Digital Cities, LNCS 2362, pp. 71–85, 2002.

In this essay we will look at the second meaning of "digital city." We will concentrate on digital representations and manifestations of cities. Instead, however, of focusing on the presentation of the city's superstructure (its buildings, streets, and topography) or on the services that can be found there (bus schedules, maps, and restaurant reviews) this essay will discuss the possible and actual roles of *people* in these virtual venues, particularly in their role of citizens, citizens of *virtual* cities as well as *actual* cities. Here the two seemingly distinct types of digital cities overlap and blur – what happens in one realm affects the other; the technology, for example, conceived in the non-virtual digital city helps create a finite number of digital (virtual) cities from the infinite number of possible digital cities, the online interactions and conversations of digital citizens in turn will shape the tone and usage of the emerging digital (geographical) city. This essay sets out to explore civic-oriented options for the new digital cities, electronic spaces that are connected in a real sense to actual cities. It is possible that we can create opportunity spaces that make it easier for the creativity and the concerns of people from all over the world to be made more prominent and vital.

The Internet is new, the web even newer, and the virtual migration of large numbers of non-technical and non-academic people into cyberspace newer still. What we are seeing in the new medium at this time may prove to be quite fleeting; many of the digital venues currently popular may ultimately be only transitional. The Internet's ubiquity and the openness of its protocols combined with the fluidity of digital representation of information are currently promoting experimentation in many areas. These conditions may encourage widespread socio-technical innovation in the civic arena. On the other hand, it is, of course, possible, that the period of development prior to standardization – both in technical and social terms – for the new medium is largely over and the various forms we're seeing now (search engines, electronic brochures, periodicals online, streaming audio, individual web pages, weblogging, etc.) may be the basic forms that we will live with for a long time to come.

As socio-technological innovation has progressed thus far, it appears that any organization, process, community, or interest, is, at least for the time being, fit grist for the new electronic mill. The idea of a city, of course, has not escaped this imperative. Hence "digital cities" of various forms, and for various reasons, have been established on the Internet. Thus far, these fall into a handful of categories which I label as commercial, governmental, community network, and representational. These categories are intended to illustrate the broad characteristics and most digital cities are probably hybrids that manifest features of more than one type. The Digital City (http://www.dds.nl) in Amsterdam, for example [2], started life as a "community network" and is now apparently in the process of becoming commercial. Also, particularly in the area of representational types there is currently a lot of effort (including much academic research [3] so this particular form may be more dynamic and likely to change over time.

The commercial digital city, as its name suggests, concentrates on commercial information and has the ultimate purpose of making money for its owners. These systems function largely as an information bank or "yellow pages" containing restaurant reviews, retail store hours, tourist destinations and other information of interest to consumers. Although there are a variety of small business ventures dedicated to representing a single city or town (http://www.glasgow-ky.com/ or http://www.weippe.com), many of the more prominent ventures employ a "chain store" approach. The basic model is intended to be replicable so that economies of scale can work in favor of profitability. These systems include Digitalcity.com, Citysearch and, until it was recently sold to citysearch, Microsoft's Sidewalk. Needless to say, local digital cities developed along these lines are not "locally owned and operated." The "chain store" model, interestingly enough has not proved to be particularly competitive. It is not clear that these "chain" digital cities have driven other efforts out of existence.

Governments, also, have substantial claims on cities and information about cities, and are making a great deal of relevant services available online. These generally contain static information about government functions, but some governments are beginning to develop new ways for citizens to obtain licenses, pay fees, file for permits, etc. A few are exploring new participatory venues for gathering citizen input. Many city government sites have links to non-governmental, though "establishment" sites, such as chambers of commerce or tourist bureaus. The two somewhat contradictory impulses, that of government as publisher of information and that of government as listener and facilitator of public conversations, are both in evidence, although the latter is quite rare. Also, as has been pointed out elsewhere [4], when governments focus more on electronic forms of information they may be inadvertently widening the "digital divide"; people without access to those capabilities (the "information-poor") are likely to become even more isolated.

The third form of digital city is the "community network." Community networks are descendants of Free-Nets originally pioneered and championed by Tom Grundner at Case Western Reserve University in Cleveland. The Cleveland Free-Net, the world's first Free-Net, was soon emulated by an estimated 100-200 other Free-Nets in providing the first community- and civic-oriented public access to the internet [4]. Community networks (like their predecessors) gathered a large number of information and communication resources related to their community and organized them in a consistent way for relatively easy "one-stop shopping." The early Free-Nets also promoted community-oriented discussion forums. Community networks, at least in the US, are generally organized as non-profit organizations. More will be said about this particular form later in this essay but, for now, it will suffice to say that community networks are still in existence in the developed world and are viewed by many as an important civic and community resource that should be increasingly supported in the developing world. Community networks are, in general, financially struggling, surviving on user donations and some government and foundation support. Thus far the search for financial "sustainability" has not yet yielded the reliable funding model that community network proponents are hoping to find.

The fourth type of digital city is "representational" in which some physical aspects of the geographical city are emulated in ways that preserve or carry over information more directly. The early Free-Nets through their use of the building metaphor ("schoolhouse" for educational information, "townhall" for government, etc.) suggested this as did Amsterdam's Digital City with its numerous Pleins (or *squares* in English – environment, death, sports, books, tourism, social activism, government and administration, and others). These metaphors were employed for grouping information, however, not for linking the virtual space directly to actual physical aspects of the city they were representing. Toru Ishida in his Digital City Kyoto work [5] has developed "2 1/2-D" fly-through models of Kyoto while Risto Linturi has done similar work based on the city of Helsinki [6]. While technically proficient and compelling on many levels the diversity of possible citizen uses of the systems that take advantage of this fidelity to the physicality of the city has not been thoroughly explored either conceptually or empirically via software prototypes. One use of representational digital cities would be in helping people make civic decisions related to existing and proposed built structure (building a new museum or shopping mall, or tearing down a highway, for example). This use could focus on the consideration of various options through open-ended community deliberation aided by the digital representations. This idea could be used with static representations but could readily be extended to include dynamic simulations and interactions in the digital space. This is similar to the UrbanSim system Paul Waddell and his colleagues [7] have developed (under the GNU Open Public License) to facilitate urban transportation planning. This, of course, reminds us of the opportunities and limitations of the idea of *connections* between the (virtual) physicality of the city representations and the geographical city it represents. Communication, a critical capability within a city's systems, is generally not visible on a physical level. One such method of communication on a physical level in a geographical city is via billboards and some version of billboards could be adapted for digital city use.

A hybrid of all of these types is likely to evolve as work proceeds in all of these areas. Whether this new hybrid will be as collaborative, multicultural, and multipurposeful as geographic cities are, is unknown. Perhaps the new digital city will simply be the union of all the digital services and web sites that correspond to a specific city. This open-ended view, however, doesn't seem to preserve the integrity of a "city." Instead it seems more like a random collection of web pages and networked applications with little except their shared   referent   in common. Questions of authenticity and ownership also come into the picture. There is only one physical "Seattle" yet there can be several "virtual Seattles" coexisting in the potentially infinite dimensions of cyberspace. Each one, however, must be associated in some way with the real one. Cyberspace can be dynamic, interactive, malleable, collective and collaborative, making the digital media much more easily manipulated than the bricks, mortar, and steel that go into the construction of actual cities. Thus a digital city, in theory, can be as life-affirming as the "real thing". But will this occur "naturally"?

2 Digital Citizens in the Digital City

The concept of a digital city is of recent vintage. Consequently it has an ambiguous and, possibly, temporary meaning. A digital city, nevertheless, that has any right to the name must have certain characteristics. These characteristics must reflect those found in the "real" city, the non-virtual one. A "real" city is host to a wide range of people and activities – public and private, commercial and non-profit, individual and collective – and, therefore, must be a combination of at least the first three of the four forms discussed above. A digital city can't be, any more than a "real" city, devoted to a single purpose or be under the guardianship of a single, all-powerful ruler, either individual or corporate. That there must be a role for "digital citizens" is probably the defining characteristic of a genuine digital city. If the citizen can not "enter" the city and then, once there, go from place to place freely, engaging with other citizens to influence policy and take part in governance, possibly, even establishing a residence or business there, then it is difficult to conceive it as a city, digital or otherwise, any more than a photograph of a house can be considered a house, or a map of a country to be a country.

2.1 New Opportunities

Although many observers have shown that digital networking has helped consolidate and extend the reach and influence of the institutions who presently wield power [8,9] few dispute the idea that the Internet and digital networking in general provide a number of provocative opportunities for those presently without power or voice, opportunities which may have a quite finite window. This section discusses some of the opportunities that digital cities may provide and some of the services and capabilities that digital citizens could use.

As discussed above, digital cities need to help promote digital citizenship. This is not recommended solely because it is the "right thing" to do. It is recommended because society relies on the creative collective intelligence of its citizens to develop appropriate ideas, machinations, and institutions for meeting individual and social needs and for addressing civic problems. Robert Putnam points out [10] that in the early twentieth century social entrepreneurs in America devised a great number of innovative institutions and organizations to help alleviate social problems then. Putnam believes that a similar period of crisis is now before us and renewed social entrepreneurism is required. Digital cities can be established to consciously promote social entrepreneurism. Although explicit policy and technological infrastructure is important, the most important precondition to this objective is the conscious acceptance of this objective. Accepting this objective means necessarily embracing an open-ended experimental phase where multiple and competing ideas are encouraged in the evolving digital world.

2.2 New Responsibilities

Who and why and how "responsibility" is assigned is, of course, an eternal question. It can't be answered here, nor, probably, will it ever be answered with definitude. We can, however, note that new circumstances lead to increased responsibilities at the same time they lead to increased opportunities. Why? Part of the answer comes, ironically, from the fact that we have more information available to us. It's impossible to help rectify a problem situation if you don't know it exists. Also, many would argue that *knowledge* of another person's plight is incentive enough to move us to action. But beyond just learning that a problem exists, the type of knowledge that we are now learning informs us greatly about the world's situation and the roles of various individuals, communities, organizations, interest groups, and nations.

For one thing, there is a growing recognition of the interconnectedness of life on earth. Part of this, of course, is the result of the growing influence of ecology and environmentalism which, after an extremely brief historical period, is now truly a worldwide phenomenon [8,11,12]. Now, thanks to humankind's swelling population and our ability (and seeming dedication) to seriously degrade our shared ecosystem and fight with one another, we are faced with enormous global problems.

Our social systems, too, have globalized: trade is globalized and globalizing, consumption in one area of the world (say, of beef in the US) can change the environment elsewhere (in, say, Costa Rica); financial systems, music and other cultural products circulate faster and faster, while tourism and migration for jobs or to escape war are reaching new unprecedented levels [13]. For these reasons and others, the links between "us" and "them" are entirely palpable although often indiscernible.

The unpleasant truth, at least for those who live in the U.S. or in other developed countries, is that in some cases, *their* problems are caused or exacerbated by *our* practices. The U.S., as is widely known has 5% of the world's population yet owns 32% of the world's cars. The average American uses 168 times more energy than a Bangladeshi. The fact that many resources used "came with the territory" which was seized or purchased does little to counter the sad truth that the accelerated patterns of consumption are non-sustainable, cannot be emulated by other countries, and may help usher in catastrophes in the not-too-distant future. Homer-Dixon, for example, has presented clear evidence for the case that conflicts over renewable resources often result in wars and other major struggles.) Besides, as Thomas Jefferson made clear, "Commerce between master and slave is despotism." Under desperate situations people may be forced to sell things they'd be unwilling to sell under more comfortable situations including, increasingly, their own body for purposes of prostitution in Thailand and many other countries [15]. In other cases, resources are sold by those with little right to them to those who are little concerned with the niceties of legitimacy. And, the "free market" imperative, in spite of litanies and homilies by its high (and low) priests is not necessarily a moral one: In nearly all the cases of major famines, for example, the people who starved to death did so because of a shortage of *money*, not food. The food existed, the money necessary to purchase food, did not. It is also cold comfort that the people in other nations may aspire to a similarly unsustainable level of consumption and that individual Americans are not necessarily greedy and mean-spirited (many environmentally-friendly innovations and ideas, in fact, come from the U.S.). Predominant systemic forces in the world (epitomized by American capitalism) are contributing in many cases to the social and environmental ills confronting the planet. The fact that these forces affect not only *others* but also *ourselves* as well as all future generations seems to suggest a need for increased responsibility, no matter which particular version of responsibility a person might adopt.

2.3 New Challenges

By making it easier and less expensive to find and share information, new ICT systems are creating new opportunities for community and civic engagement. That these opportunities, however, may be alarmingly short-lived is suggested by other historic trends. The "media monopolies" that Ben Bagdikian has written about [16], although focused on pre-Internet communication and information systems, are rapidly integrating Internet-based systems into their electronic empires. Time-Warner now controls a vast amount of Internet content and traffic while commercial web sites, forbidden on the Internet less than a decade ago, now account for over 90% of all web content. Fighting at a public policy and education level for the conceptual and actual "space" on the Internet and other network systems for engaged and responsible digital cities is an important task.

At the same time, the apparently infinitely vast repository of information now available can lead us to assume that all the information civil society would need is or will be available. The increasing glut of commercially sponsored and oriented information unfortunately serves to diminish the relative amount of non-commercial information. This makes non-commercial information harder to find, while simultaneously helping to "brand" the new medium as a commercial one, without civic purpose. We know that knowledge creation through the gathering, describing, editing, and presenting of information requires time and effort and, of course, money. The late media critic Herbert Schiller in an insightful (but depressing) indictment of American information policy and practices [17] relates how ideological forces have helped purge an enormous amount of information from the public domain. Long-term rigorous collection and maintenance of, say, health related data is very costly; for that reason, it's not a cost-effective or profitable endeavor for a commercial concern. National governments or coalitions of national governments are therefore the only entities who are capable organizationally and financially of managing such an enterprise – but digital cities – and networks of digital cities – can promote the creation, archiving, and distribution of such information.

Information and communication are usually means to an end as opposed to ends in themselves.   (Although supporting policy and institutionalization of public information and communication systems such as libraries, schools, open meetings and freedom of information, freedom of expression, etc., etc., are indispensable in a free society.)   A danger, then, at least theoretically, exists that people will focus on information rather than on action based on information. If the discussion is entirely "virtual" or, indeed, if no genuine discussion actually occurs the impact will be minimal.

Digital cities need not be merely reflective of activities and attributes in geographical cities, insofar as they are "spaces" in their own right they can develop attributes independent of their own geographical referent.   These attributes, for example, include virtual "lights" in virtual "buildings" to indicate presence of people in, say, a chat room associated with that building. On a deeper level, it will probably involve the governance of the digital city itself. This potential independence from their referent (the geographical city) has some problematical implications from the point of view of promoting citizenship and a democratic culture; namely that the enterprise would ultimately divorce itself entirely from the realm in which it was supposed to be intimately involved becoming, in effect, a digital city "game".

When the digital city strives to become as multifaceted as a geographical city, particularly in terms of conversational venues and opportunities for genuine engagement and involvement, several issues arise. Digital cities could unwittingly be widening the "digital divide," for example, if economic or other barriers keep people from citizenship in the digital city. Digital cities can, in general, manifest any of the characteristics, for good or ill, of geographical cities. Thus balancing "globalism" and "localism" is an issue that faces citizens in geographical and digital cities alike, as do the issues of who, why, what, and how the civic work is accomplished.

In the next section, the "community network" model, as exemplified by the Seattle community Network (SCN), is examined as a platform which is likely to be suitable for cultivating new types of digital citizenship. In the section following that, a number of other socio-technical ideas for realizing that goal (including non-commercial search engines, deliberation systems and open CSCW protocols) are discussed.

3   Socio-Technical Systems That Promote Citizenship

How can digital cities and related socio-technical innovations help in a transformation of our democracy? Certainly new algorithms, new architectures, faster processors, and more recently, more financial transactions on the web can not be expected *on their own* to help address deficiencies of democracy. With few exceptions these advances are not sufficiently linked to the realities of civic and community life to be of widespread benefit.

3.1 Community Networks

Community networks [4] offer a plausible technological and philosophical platform for this work. Developed and maintained by civic and community activists all over the world, community networks are intended to be a new type of public institution similar in spirit to the traditional public library, but built upon more recent modes of communication. These new modes are generally digital and, unlike the public library's focus on *consuming*, extend the idea of access to include *producing*. Moreover, like public libraries, community networks are non-commercial. Well before Hotmail offered free e-mail and Geocities offered free web page hosting, community networks were providing these services with little or no cost as a public service to anybody who requested them.

The Seattle Community Network (SCN) may be considered typical insofar as any community network can be labeled. SCN was launched in 1992 as a project of the Seattle chapter of Computer Professionals for Social Responsibility. SCN is an all-volunteer effort to develop and maintain a public network system in the U. S. that focuses on, but is not limited to, the Pacific Northwest region in Washington State. SCN's "Statement of Principles" (below) reflects the ideals its founded hope to promote.   SCN has thirteen categories ("Activism," "Arts," "Civil," "Earth," "Education," "Health," "Marketplace," "Neighborhoods," "News," "People," "Recreation," "Sci-Tech," and "Spiritual") on its web site, each of which is maintained by a volunteer editor. SCN currently hosts a wide variety of community information including the Sustainable Seattle Indicators project, the Seattle Crisis Resource Directory by the Peace Heathens, the Vintage Telephone Equipment Museum, the Uganda Community Management Program and the web site for Seattle's coalition against the war in Afghanistan.

Seattle Community Network was not conceived as a profit-making enterprise, a source of entertainment, or as a digital billboard for commercial messages. The original developers of the Seattle Community Network hoped to build a new arena for social discourse, an arena in which all citizens – not just those drawing salaries from big corporations or the government – can be active players in the continuing unfolding of the future. Providing a space for connecting people without power with those that may have too much is SCN's implicit goal.

SCN Principles

The Seattle Community Network (SCN) is a free public-access computer network for exchanging and accessing information. Beyond that, however, it is a service conceived for community empowerment. Our principles are a series of commitments to help guide the ongoing development and management of the system for both the organizers and participating individuals and organizations.

Commitment to Access

- Access to the SCN will be free to all
- We will provide access to all groups of people particularly those without ready access to information technology.
- We will provide access to people with diverse needs. This may include special-purpose interfaces.
- We will make the SCN accessible from public places.

Commitment to Service

- The SCN will offer reliable and responsive service
- We will provide information that is timely and useful to the community.
- We will provide access to databases and other services.

Commitment to Democracy

- The SCN will promote participation in government and public dialogue
- The community will be actively involved in the ongoing development of the SCN.
- We will place high value in freedom of speech and expression and in the free exchange of ideas.
- We will make every effort to ensure privacy of the system users.
- We will support democratic use of electronic technology.

Commitment to the World Community

- In addition to serving the local community, we will become part of the regional, national and international community
- We will build a system that can serve as a model for other communities.

Commitment to the Future

- We will continue to evolve and improve the SCN
- We will explore the use of innovative applications such as electronic town halls for community governance, or electronic encyclopedias for enhanced access to information.
- We will work with information providers and with groups involved in similar projects using other media.
- We will solicit feedback on the technology as it is used, and make it as accessible and humane as possible.
- We will build a system that can serve as a model for other communities.

Fig. 1

3.2 Other Ideas

While a community network represents a plausible way in which community and civic use of ICT can be institutionalized as a coherent entity, the community network as a model doesn't appear to be *the* public access model for ICT as, say, the public library is said to provide *the* public access model for access to the printed word. Therefore the following future services might not ultimately be hosted on today's community networks. Hopefully, however, they'll ultimately find expression in some form in tomorrow's digital cities.

There is large body of relevant work in the realm of computer-supported cooperative work or CSCW. This work, though historically associated with research labs, has been incorporated into commercial product such as Lotus Notes which is now used in thousands of offices around the world. In general, CSCW supports cooperation in three ways: process-based, structured-information-based or common-space-based. In the first case the computer helps to ensure that a number of procedural steps are correctly followed, in, say, the processing of insurance claims. In the second case, people cooperate through the use of shared structured information (work orders or schedules, for example). In the third case, software helps to promote a "shared space" (for example, through video conferencing or desktop sharing) in which people can communicate. Mixtures of the three types are, of course, possible.

Historically neither the research labs nor the commercial "groupware" purveyors have focused their attention to the "real world" outside of networked white collar workers. This is largely due to historical (and economic) circumstances (which still largely persist) in which only a privileged few had access to the Internet. Also "cooperative work" particularly the sort that computers could assist was implicitly perceived as white collar work either academic (writing for journals, for example) or commercial (processing a purchase order, for example). While we've seen in recent years, a vast increase of "regular people" populating cyberspace as well as the amount of people engaged in civil society and community *work* there has not been a corresponding amount of CSCW research in those areas [18].

The development and deployment of public CSCW systems is one recommendation that comes easily to mind. These systems should make it easier for citizens to schedule meetings and work on projects of shared interest. A student of mine, Jakob Kaivo, suggested that the development of a public protocol for exchanging the full range of collaborative work information would provide a useful foundation for a great variety of tools and systems. (See http://dmoz.org/Computers/Software/Groupware/Open_Source/ for links to a variety of open source groupware tools and projects.) Another idea, unexplored to a large degree, is that of deliberative systems, since deliberation may be the most important process underlying civic and community work. Robert's Rules of Order [19], for example, which is in everyday use in thousands of assemblies both large and small throughout the world, appears to be a reasonable model to use as a starting point. Promoting effective deliberation on the web, at least in theory, vastly increases opportunities for developing advocacy networks which connect people who are physically removed from each other. On the other hand, connecting (and further empowering) people who are already "wired" to some degree, can lead to situations with "winners" (those with access to ICT) and "losers" (with no or poor access). People in rural areas, for example, are often poor, isolated and unconnected. Clearly, public policy and education that promotes access to these spaces must keep apace with any development in public CSCW.

The development of a public classification system (or systems) could also be expected to provide a foundation and impetus for various projects. Currently most web users rely on commercial search engines which employ their own proprietary schemes for storing and retrieving information. Search engines are known to have many drawbacks including the fact the people can pay to have their site placed higher in the list of sites than the search engine itself would have placed it according to its own criteria [20]. The existence of a public scheme, perhaps on the order of the

Dewey Decimal System (itself not public, but readily licensable), would enable people to provide classification information in their own pages (via, say, a meta tag), build local digital libraries, and, even, create search engines that were not subject to the same deficiencies that commercial search engines are. Search engine purveyors generally want to keep their ranking algorithms secret to prevent clever web page developers from artificially elevating the "importance" ranking of their pages (and hence, position, among the links retrieved) thus raising, at least, the specter of abuse with public schemes [21].

Working with community organizations and *non*-technical people over a sustained period of time is the best way to design and implement systems that meet the needs of a democratic society. We need to ask whether all people – including those at the economic and other margins of society – are getting the information they need. Do the existing communication channels work for them? How could these systems be improved? Do they promote economic development, neighborhood awareness or community collaborative work? CSCW tools, for example, perhaps customized in some way, may prove to be very useful for marginalized communities [22]. But they've rarely, if ever, field-tested under those circumstances. The assumption, usually implicit, is that these tools are supposed to ultimately find their way to users with fewer resources. But CSCW professionals know that the context is of critical importance to the success or failure of a CSCW application [23] and contexts vary considerably. There is little reason to assume that low-income or other marginalized communities will play any role in a participatory design process of a CSCW application for their community without a concerted outreach effort.

4 Computer Scientists, Digital Citizens, and Digital Cities

Computer professionals are usually specialists; it is their job to understand, maintain, and advance the world's digital infrastructure. What role should computer professionals play in the consideration of our broadest affairs when their focus is so specific and arguably narrow? They are likely, certainly, to be cast in the role of what Gramsci calls an "organic intellectual" [24] whose agenda has been determined by others. Does this mean that computer professionals can't or shouldn't participate in broad civic issues and initiatives? Not at all. I believe that their understanding of these critical technologies compels them to accept greater responsibility and their engagement with the world – not as "organic intellectuals" but as engaged citizens with important specialized knowledge to contribute.

How might this transformation take place? It will be necessary to take a hard look at the activities of computer professionals and how they conceptualize their work. Is their discipline construed narrowly as a purely technical, *instrumental* discipline or is it a practice that, although intimately connected with digital technology, is an *embedded* practice that necessarily relates to and interacts with the rest of society. Part of this entails bringing the "real world", including the vast majority of the world's population who have never used a computer, into a more central position in their consideration. Another part of this is entails more strongly engaging with the rest of the research and scholarly community, especially the social sciences, but also, the humanities community. Professional organizations such as the Association for Computing Machinery (ACM) or Computer Professionals for Social Responsibility

(CPSR) can certainly help promote this transformation of a disembodied practice into an embedded one; funding agencies like the National Science Foundation (NSF) and non-governmental foundations such as the Markle Foundation, the Rockefeller Foundation and others can also help. Computer professionals by themselves can also reprioritize their professional and personal lives to some degree. They can choose to work on collaborative community teams, on policy or social work, or on developing new democratic technology.

Computer professionals can assume a stronger role working with community networks or with other digital city projects. For one thing, community networks provide an ongoing and ready-made test-bed for "real-world" applications. I propose that Computer Science department (or Information and Library Science or Public Policy or other academic departments) become long-term "partners" in community networking and other digital city projects. At The Evergreen State College where I teach, Randy Groves and I worked with 50 undergraduate students who built web applications for 12 community groups over a nine-month period (http://www.scn.org/edu/tesc-ds/2001-2002/). In this way, students would have the opportunity to experience first-hand technology development projects that were designed for actual users. Students (and faculty) would play a role in the shaping of public applications and would come to appreciate the importance as well as the challenges of supporting a democratic culture with technology. For their part, the community network practitioners would – ideally – become exposed to innovative ideas, skilled partners, and invigorating enthusiasm.

Only through involvement at several levels at once can computer professionals realize their historical possibilities. Working with community activists, researchers, independent media producers, policy makers, and librarians are all good places to start. Other intriguing possibilities include working with activists in the Free Software Movement to develop CSCW technology that could be used by people in low income communities who can't afford the advanced CSCW technology employed in today's businesses. The operative expression in all of the cases above is "working with;" the design process itself should be democratic and participatory [25]. Technologists and researchers should also forge partnerships with local government and the citizenry. The city of Seattle's groundbreaking "Indicators of a Health Technology City" [26] project is a good example of this. This project has worked with Seattle region citizens to develop a set of "indicators" that, when measured over time, will reveal important trends about the uses and effects of communication technology in the region. These indicators include several types of indicators (access; literacy; business and economic development; community building; civic participation; human relationships to information technology; and partnerships and resource mobilization) and are intended to explore negative as well as positive implications about technology. As a matter of fact, one of the guidelines in the developmental phase was to think about these from a citizen point-of-view that overlaps but is not completely coincidental with points-of-view of government or business. Clearly a project such as this helps to build a civic culture by helping to surface the issues and concerns that people have in relation to computer and communication use in an era of rapid change. Projects like this can serve as both motivator and evaluative yardstick for computer professionals who are interested in long-term development of democratic technology.

If computer professionals are exclusively organic intellectuals destined for academia or industry who see themselves as practitioners of a purely *technical* discipline, their ability to be a proactive and progressive force in society will be insignificant. It must be mentioned, however, that there are countless examples of computer professionals who are actively working to create new institutions, bridge the "digital divide," educate the public, and build new technologies specifically for marginalized communities. The evidence of this involvement is overwhelming and largely unprecedented. Witness the outpouring of papers for the "Shaping the Network Society" Symposium, May 2000 [27] and the resulting "Seattle Statement" [28] calling for a "new public sphere." In spite of these hopeful signs, I would sound the caution, that this type of work is still the exception and moving it more into the mainstream is an important but daunting task.

5 Actions for the Future

Global forces – economic, political and technological – are extending their influence on people and institutions everywhere. As a result, people may feel like they're isolated and alone or part of an undifferentiated crowd. In either case, people – especially those with fewer economic resources – often feel that they have little control over their future. The consequences of this sense of powerlessness, real or perceived, transcend the individual; society as a whole suffers for it is deprived of social intelligence and energy which could be used to strengthen the polity and address social and environmental problems. History has shown that it has been *people* – not government or business – who first raised last century's most pressing issues – the environment, women's issues, sexual freedom, and others [29]. It is likely that tomorrow's social entrepreneurs will use the socio-technical systems that we build today.

Digital cities can help promote social meliorism while simultaneously cooperating with, and fighting against, policies and practices of business and government, and by building bridges between the powerful and the powerless. If civil society is successful in this work, the tensions between cultures, critical environmental stresses, capitalistic demands for more markets, resources, labor, etc. can – we hope – be lessened. If, as Immanuel Wallerstein believes [30], humankind is at a historic threshold, the information and communication resources and services offered by tomorrow's next digital cities might help humankind enter this next phase in our development with less turmoil. Digital cities can play a positive role in rebuilding community by strengthening its core values. Whether these aims are realized will depend on citizens from all walks of life. Truly democratic systems can only be developed through broad participation. This endeavor must not be a charitable good-works project of elites, or a rebellion of the underclasses. It should be open to citizens of all races, economic classes, ethnic origins, religions, genders, ages, and sexual preferences. It must be global in nature, because a confluence of perspectives, experiences, and skills is needed in order to succeed.

Why should people care about digital cities outside of their own region? The answer is that the cities and people of the world are bound to each other; the world is shrinking, and globalism – with positive and negative connotations – is becoming the defining characteristic of our era. We all share the planet; national citizens are also planetary citizens. No society can rely solely on large institutions – either commercial or government – to provide all of its information and communication needs. People are developing digital cities that reflect their own cultural values. That is how it should be. On the other hand, all of us are human, and we are more similar to each other than we are different. Clearly virtual networks are needed to connect digital cities and digital citizens. Robert Putnam [10] explains the importance of "bridging" social capital (which provides effective connections across communities) in addition to "bonding" social capital (which connects people within communities).

The rapid computerization of the world and the immense attention it's receiving represents an unprecedented opportunity for computer professionals. Computer professionals can seize this historic opportunity and engage in interdisciplinary and collaborative work involving other researchers as well as practitioners in education, development, social services, social activism, and the government to help build (and, in some cases, rebuild) a civic culture. Additionally, computer professionals and other digital city developers must also be aware of the numerous barriers –conceptual, structural, economic – to this work. For one thing there is a disquieting lack of critical analysis of the immense economic and other forces that are shaping our world. These forces tend to crowd out efforts that don't fit within the dominant ideological framework. Some authors [31] for example, have suggested that tragedies such as the World Trade Center attacks may become increasingly more prevalent as conditions in the "global south" become increasingly desperate. Yet ideas such as these, however critical to our understanding of the complex interrelatedness of our world and our work, are often pushed aside and banished from public consideration. For that reason and many others, working to develop information and communications technology and systems that foster deep democracy will face many obstacles.

This article was finished two weeks after the tragic attack on New York City and Washington, DC several days after president George Bush's announcement regarding America's military and other responses. The global dream of collective intelligence and harmony and peace is, once again, severely called into question. Far from being its death knell, recent events have demonstrated the indispensability of a shared vision for our survival. Digital cities, insofar as they help develop a truly inclusive "public sphere" [32] through engaged information and communication technology, could be a part of that vision.

Some of this article, particularly paragraphs related to the role of the computer scientist, was published before in Communications of the ACM, January, 2001; *Computer Professionals and the Next Culture of Democracy.*

This work was supported in part by the National Science Foundation, 0002547.

References

[1] Graham, S. and Marvin. S.: Telecommunications and the City. Routledge, London (1996)
[2] Lovink, G. and Riemens, P.: A Polder Model in Cyberspace: The Contemporary Amsterdam Public Digital Culture, In Shaping the Network Society. MIT Press, Cambridge, MA:. (2002)
[3] Ishida, T. and Isbister, K. (Eds.): Digital Cities, Technologies, Experiences, and Future Perspectives. Lecture Notes in Computer Science, Vol. 1765. (2000)
[4] Schuler, D.: New Community Networks: Wired for Change. Reading, MA: Addison-Wesley. http:/www.scn.org/ncn. (1996)

[5]   Ishida, T. Digital City Kyoto: Social Information Infrastructure for Everyday Life. Communications of the ACM (CACM) (to appear)

[6]   Helsinki Arena 2000 - Augmenting a Real City to a Virtual One, Risto Linturi, Marja-Riitta Koivunen, and Jari Sulkanen, LNCS 1765, p. 83 ff. (2000)

[7]   Waddell, P.: UrbanSim: Modeling Urban Development for Land Use, Transportation, and Environmental Planning. http://www.urbansim.org/papers/UrbanSim-JAPA.pdf. Revised version forthcoming in the Journal of the American Planning Association. (2001)

[8]   Castells, M.: The Rise of the Network Society. Blackwell, Oxford (1996)

[9]   Sassen, S.: Electronic Space and Power, from Globalization and its Discontents, Saskia Sassen. The New Press, New York (1998)

[10] Putnam, R.: Bowling Alone. Simon and Schuster, New York (2000)

[11] Keck, M. and Sikkink, K.: Activists Beyond Borders: Advocacy Networks in International Politics. Cornell University Press, Ithaca, NY (1998).

[12] Runyan, C.: Action on the Frontlines. World Watch (November / December 1999)

[13] Sassen, S.: Guests and Aliens. The New Press, New York (1999)

[14] Homer-Dixon, T., Boutwell, J., and Rathjens, G.: Environmental change and violent conflict. Scientific American. (1993, Feb.)

[15] Goldstone, P.: Making the World Safe for Tourists. Yale University Press, New Haven (2001)

[16] Bagdikian, B. : The Media Monopoly. Beacon Press, Boston, MA (1992)

[17] Schiller, H.: Information Inequality: The Deepening Social Crisis in America. Routledge, London (1996)

[18] Schuler, D.:   Computer   Professionals   and   the   Next   Culture   of   Democracy. Communications of the ACM (January, 2001)

[19] Robert, H.: Robert's Rules of Order, Revised. William Morrow and Co., New York (1971)

[20] Kopytoff, V.: Searching for profits: Amid tech slump, more portals sell search engine results to highest bidder. San Francisco Chronicle (June 18, 2001)

[21] Introna, L. and Nissenbaum, H. "Shaping the Web: Why the Politics of Search Engines Matters." The Information Society, 16(3) (2000)

[22] Schuler, D.: Computer Support for Community Work: Designing and Building Systems for the "Real World." Tutorial. CSCW '98 ACM Conference on Computer Supported Community Work. ACM. Seattle. http://www.scn.org/commnet/cscw-tutorial-1998.html (1998)

[23] Grudin, J.:   Why CSCW Applications Fail: Problems in the Design and Evaluation of Organizational Interfaces. Proceedings of CSCW '88. New York: ACM (1988)

[24] Said, E.: Representations of the Intellectual. Vintage, New York (1996).

[25] Schuler, D. and Namioka, A. (Eds.) Participatory Design: Principles and Practices. Erlbaum, Hillsdale, NJ (1993).

[26] City of Seattle: Information Technology Indicators for a Healthy Community. Seattle: Department of Information Technology. http://www.ci.seattle.us/tech/indicators.htm (2000)

[27] Day, P., Holbrooks, Z., Namioka, A. and Schuler, D. Proceedings of DIAC-00, "Shaping the Network Society" Palo Alto. Computer Professionals for Social Responsibility. (2000) http://www.scn.org/cpsr/diac-00/ (2000)

[28] Seattle Statement. http://www.scn.org/cpsr/diac-00/seattle-statement.html (2000)

[29] Castells, M. The Power of Identity. Blackwell Publishers, Malden, MA (1997)

[30] Wallerstein, I. The End of the World as We Know it. University of Minnesota Press, Minneapolis (1999)

[31] Sassen, S.: Voices from the Global South. Guardian (London), (September 12, 2001)

[32] Habermas, J.: The Structural Transformation of the Public Sphere: An Inquiry into a Category of Bourgeois Society. Polity, Cambridge (1989)

Designing Democratic Community Networks: Involving Communities through Civil Participation

Peter Day

School of Information Management, Faculty of Information Technology, University of
Brighton, Watts Building, Moulsecoomb, Brighton and Hove, BN2 4GJ, UK
p.day@bton.ac.uk and p.day@btinternet.com

Abstract. Outlining issues of significance from investigations of a range of
community ICT initiatives in the UK and Scandinavia, this paper presents a
normative framework of democratic design criteria of relevance to community
networks. Community networking or community informatics as it is
increasingly called, provides the platform for a more participatory and
democratic vision of the network society. However, before the opportunities
presented by this vision can be embraced, the challenges of embedding such
initiatives in community practice to stimulate community ownership and
identity must first be addressed. Additionally, the enthusiasm of emergent
community informatics practitioners should be informed by the experiences of
early community ICT initiative pioneers. The issues presented in this paper
provide salutary lessons for community networkers, researchers and policy-
makers alike.

1 Introduction

Around the world, civil society and local communities are utilizing ICTs to underpin
the creation of a more participatory and democratic vision of the network society. A
growing interest in the social and technical form and function of these community
ICT initiatives has led to the emergence of a movement of practitioners and
researchers engaged in community networking and community informatics. Grounded
in and drawing from a diversity of socio-economic cultures, this movement concerns
itself primarily with the social shaping of ICTs as tools that underpin and support
existing social networks in geographic communities and assist in developing new
ones [1].

The notion that the digital city metaphor can be used as a platform for such activities
is conceptually of great academic interest and certainly worthy of investigation.
However, it is contested here that any consideration of the future of community
networks, whether as digital cities or some other form of socio-technical
manifestation, should seek to understand and learn from the experiences of
community ICT initiatives both past and present.

Based on the empirical evidence of a social sciences Ph.D. study of Danish, Swedish
and UK community ICT initiatives [2] this paper identifies several areas of concern

M. Tanabe, P. van den Besselaar, T. Ishida (Eds.): Digital Cities, LNCS 2362, pp. 86-100, 2002.
© Springer-Verlag Berlin Heidelberg 2002

relating to the design,[1] implementation and development of such initiatives during the last two decades. A normative framework of democratic design criteria for community ICT initiatives, drawing from a range of social and computer science traditions,[2] is then presented to stimulate consideration of these concerns.

However, because community networking/informatics is located in the real-world activities of social practice and policy, theoretical contributions such as these must embrace the opportunities and challenges found in inter-disciplinary and cross-sectoral[3] communications and inter-action, if they are to be of any practical value.

2   What Is Meant by Community?

This paper seeks to contribute to the development of such interdisciplinary/cross-sectoral knowledge by considering the design of community ICT initiatives[4] from a social science rather than a computer science perspective. However, in order to share knowledge and build on our existing understanding of community networking, it is imperative to acknowledge the difficulty of developing a mutually acceptable understanding of the term 'community'. A complex task in itself.

We know that communities comprise both active community groups and individual citizens but in terms of essential characteristics such as socio-economic environments, their cultures, social norms and values, needs and behavior no one community is alike. There are commonalities but there are also differences and consequently communities cannot be modeled and homogenized. Rather than seeking to develop a hard and fast definition of community therefore this paper recommends a more flexible approach. Drawing on Butcher's three interrelated senses of community [8] not only provides a starting point for discussion but enables practitioners, researchers and policy-makers to identify the characteristics, resources and needs of their own communities and design community initiatives accordingly.

2.1   Three Distinct Yet Interrelated Senses of Community

The first sense of community identified by Butcher is *Descriptive Community*, which draws on the word's etymological origins of having 'something in common'. This

---

[1] Within the context of this paper, the notion of design is applied to community ICT initiatives as social organizations and networks as opposed to technological systems and technical artifacts.

[2] Human-centered systems [3] and participatory design [4], [5], [6]; democratic technology [7]; community policy [8] and practice [9]; and the emerging field of community informatics [10], [11]

[3] Cross-sectoral refers to interaction between public, private and not-for-profit sectors of society.

[4] Uses of ICTs by geographic communities vary in their form and function – from online community newsletters, community radio and TV to community telecottages and telecentres to community information networks and digital cities. As such community informatics as an area of practice and study is socially and technologically complex. The use of 'community ICT initiative' is intended here as an 'catch all' phrase that accommodates this diversity.

'something in common' can refer to a neighborhood, village, town, etc. but can also refer to other social determinants such as ethnicity, religion, sexual orientation, etc. In this way, two forms of community - geographical communities and communities of interest - are identified.

At this stage it should be noted that communities based on location or interests are not necessarily mutually exclusive. Indeed geographic communities often comprise different cultures and it is not uncommon for groups and individuals to share knowledge and draw from each other's experiences, creating new forms of common interests as a consequence. Of course, the opposite can also be true and conflict can and does arise in and between communities.

For communities to be sustainable, especially where diversity of culture and social values exists, Butcher's second insight - *Community as Value* – is of import. In this context the existence of community is based on certain shared values, identified as the principles of solidarity, participation and coherence. Solidarity sustains community members at an emotional level, inspiring affection and loyalty towards the group through mutuality and co-operation in relationships. Participation benefits individuals through the recognition of their contribution to collective life and the aspirations of the group. Coherence connects the individual to the community and leads to an appreciation and comprehension of self and situation that give meaning to and awareness of themselves and their social world. [8]

Although community values are open to interpretation and can be contested, Butcher asserts that such principles provide the *value* base of community initiatives and policies. However, it should not be assumed that the communal is always subsumptive of the individual. A need for balance between community and self and community and group is required, providing adequate amounts of privacy, autonomy and localism. Shared public spaces, community associations and activities providing people with the chance to engage with one another should be tempered with spaces that shield from unwanted interaction by offering privacy and respect for a diverse range of cultural principles. Such considerations might also be applied to the design, implementation and development of community networks.

Community values then, are the social product of individual people living in and identifying with a specific 'something', often but not always a geographical space. The collective community, in the context of this paper, comprises individual community members that have developed an inherent interest in each other. In order to co-exist in the same geographical space and share social experiences, community members need to respect and celebrate the diversity of human interests. This diversity distinguishes the individual from the collective but at the same time contributes to that collective. This is the paradox of community.

Butcher's third insight into community - the *Active Community* – leads from this sense of community identity. It is from the sensation of belonging to the local community that people become actively involved in everyday community life. The *Active Community* refers to collective action by community members embracing one or more communal values. Such activities are purposively undertaken through the vehicle of groups, networks and organizations. Community and voluntary sector organizations such as these form the bedrock of civil society and although often under resourced and over stretched have a significant role to play in community building.

The *Active Community* is based on the participation of community members, groups and organizations in shaping community life. However, a shared value base between community and policy makers is crucial to the formulation of policies that build, develop and sustain active communities. A method for promoting such policies is community practice, described by Glenn as comprising three elements: [9]

1. *Community services approach* – identified as the development of community-oriented organizations and services. In a community networking context, examples of this might include: the provision of online information services, public access centers, low cost ICT provision schemes, and education and training programs.
2. *Community development* – identified as the promotion of community self-help and empowerment. Within this context this would require a continuation of the community services approach but with a view to building the capacity of communities. Stimulating dialogue, collaboration and mutual support within and between social networks are key goals here.
3. *Community action* – identified as campaigning for community interests and community policies. Elements 1 and 2 are continued but with less input from community policy and professionals. The aim here is sustainable community through democratic communicative action.

2.2   Community Practice and Community ICT Initiatives

As a social phenomenon then the concept of community can be loosely described as an active group of people having something in common, who from a shared value-base work to improve the quality of life for the collective and individual alike. Transposing this notion to a community networking context both Schuler [10] and Gurstein [11] subordinate ICT systems and artifacts to the needs of people living in geographic communities. Indeed, by studying geographic communities, their constituent communities of interest and their community ICT practices, [2] it is possible to establish what Community Network or Digital City initiatives can and/or do to maintain and deepen knowledge about design issues in local communities. By developing such an understanding at the local level, it is possible to develop Community Networks and/or Digital Cities that are meaningful and relevant to their citizens. Community practice therefore is of significance to the design, implementation and development of community ICT initiatives. [13], [14], [15], [16], [17], [18]

3 Lessons from Previous Community ICT Experiences

Before introducing a normative framework intended to assist the process of stimulating participative community ICT practice, it is important to consider the experiences and lessons of community ICT practice pioneers. This section identifies issues relating to earlier community ICT policy and practice and is drawn from the empirical evidence of a PhD research project. [2] The headings presented here are intended to provide the basis for the start of such consideration and are not therefore exclusive.

3.1   Community Involvement

Today, much of the development of local digital network initiatives is driven by local authority-led partnerships yet despite this, some authorities/partnerships appear not to recognize the potential of ICTs to stimulate and promote community life. Failure to engage with the not-for-profit sector in equitable and meaningful partnerships often results in restricted public access and limited local content. Consequently, opportunities for the acquisition of skills and the distribution of benefits are limited to selective, or self-selecting, elements of a community or locale. In addition to failing to engage with the not-for-profit sector, especially community and voluntary groups, partnerships often fail to include interactive communication facilities for citizens and community groups in community service type initiatives. The lack of opportunities for community groups to publish local information electronically themselves, is another area of concern.

The importance of a sense of community ownership of, or identity with, an initiative, is often underestimated or overlooked by sponsoring agencies and partnerships. The initiative at Vejle, during the Danish 'Social Experiments with IT' program in the 1980s, is a classic example of this. Despite being driven by a community development agenda at partnership level, the Vejle Datariet initiative failed mainly as a result of its failure to engage with the local community and community groups at grass roots level. [2], [13] The Wiltshire Telecottage Network (WTN) was another example of partnership 'experts' knowing what was best for the community rather than engaging with them. [2], [13] Community involvement cannot be manufactured. It is born of community participation and is understood by community practitioners to be the cornerstone of community practice. [9] For initiatives to succeed they must be embedded in the practice of local communities.

3.2   Community Practice

Glen's community practice framework is helpful in developing an understanding of the community role and function of community ICT initiatives but it also enables some identification of differences between social intention and social practice. Indeed, all the initiatives in the investigation, [2], [13] displayed to varying degrees, some evidence of attempting all three community practice approaches but it should be noted that the community services approach dominated.

However, there is some evidence of balance emerging in the social practice of community ICT initiatives. A number of initiatives have started to incorporate outreach work and the promotion of active community participation in their service and activity portfolio. The contention here is that in order for community ICT initiatives to flourish, a greater degree of balance in community practice is necessary, enabling initiatives to promote social inclusion through self-directed action rather than focusing on the important but more socially passive activity of training.[5] To this

---

[5] Government funded ICT initiatives have a tendency to focus on training individuals rather than complementing this with exploration and promotion of collective uses of ICTs in the community.

end, initiatives such as the Sussex Community Internet Project (SCIP) and the Manchester Community Information Network (MCIN) are embracing outreach and development programs to work with community and voluntary sector groups within diverse community settings. [2]

An important point to note at this juncture is that many of the initiatives investigated are viewed by policy as social experiments, e.g. Datariet, Vejle. As social phenomena community ICT initiatives are fraught with political complexities and difficulties, which can only begin to be addressed by a more formal linking of community practice and information society policies at national and local government levels. If social exclusion in the information society is to be addressed, then public access to ICTs must be recognized as a complex social issue that requires the identification and meeting of community need.

It is simply not enough to expect the location of ICTs in public places to meet community need. Despite its importance, this is the main weakness of the currently dominant community services approach to policy development. Large amounts of resources and energy are currently invested in physical public access with little consideration given to the broader social context. In the UK, for example, local authorities and public agencies are confronted with the intricacies of partnership, the technicalities of network definition, and the bureaucracy of large funding bids. It appears to be easier to contrive policy programs that locate public access points in public libraries and local schools in an attempt to address social exclusion, than identifying the social needs of local communities and designing programs flexible enough to address them.

3.3   Social Inclusion

Attempts by community ICT initiatives to utilize ICTs in addressing social exclusion pre-date the fashionable policy use of the term. Some initiatives in Europe, such as the Grimethorpe Electronic Village Hall (GEVH) - established by unemployed miners in a community ravaged by the UK program of pit closures in the 1980s - constitute bottom-up community responses to social exclusion. [2], [13] Most initiatives result from partnership activities, usually driven by local government. However, unless clear community ICT policies exist, attempts to address social exclusion in the network society by bridging the 'digital divide' become dissipated. To understand the reasons for this, two central priorities dominating local government information society strategies must be identified:

1)   Improved efficiency and savings through the provision of electronic services, and
2)   Stimulating local economic competitiveness through ICTs.

Whilst some local authorities have understood that such objectives need not over-ride other social goals, others have yet to do so, underlining the importance of the awareness raising and advocacy work of the community informatics movement.

3.4   Technology

Although the research of this project was not technology centered, two technology-related issues emerged that warranted attention. Firstly, the increasing use of broadband infrastructure, e.g. local area Intranets, often led by local authorities, frequently bypasses community and voluntary sector organizations, despite the importance of such bodies in building community and addressing social exclusion. Even today, much community ICT initiatives do not form part of, or are marginalized from, locally developed information and communication infrastructures.

Secondly, technological platforms become rapidly outdated. What was state-of-the-art technology in the early 1990s[6] had by the mid-1990s become outdated, creating difficulties in providing the services and activities required by their local communities. In one initiative in Manchester, formerly promoted by the City Council as part of its 'Community ICT Flagship', the PCs were so old that they simply could not perform the functions required of them and their networking consisted of cables running down through holes in the ceiling. Imagine a room of such networked PCs being used to provide the latest ICT training and the challenges facing many community ICT initiatives become clearer. Such a state of affairs led to disillusionment among staff and users alike. In order to address local needs and retain community relevance in a rapidly changing environment, urgent consideration must be given to the development of technology policies at local and national policy level.

In a number of UK initiatives, the cycle has been completed. As a result of the government's 'ICT Learning Centres' program [14] they again possess a cutting-edge technological infrastructure and a renewed sense of enthusiasm for the task ahead, even the initiative in Manchester cited above. However, they have been in this position before and if they are to contribute to addressing social exclusion, through community access to ICTs, their present circumstances must be sustained.

3.5   Funding

The initiatives studied in this research [2], [13] point to dependency on a wide range of funding sources. Funding regimes range from low cost basic models to the substantial European, national government and Lottery grants attracted by initiatives in major metropolitan areas. The most important issues relating to funding are reliability and permanence of these contributions.   Attempts to address social exclusion at community level should receive core public funding. However, it is important to emphasize that this should not be at the expense of other forms of public services, such as libraries. Indeed, it is felt that public libraries have a significant role to play in community ICT initiatives. Neither does it mean that *all* the funding required by community initiatives need come from the public purse, or that it should always take the form of money. Funding in kind, for example, in the form of free premises can make a significant contribution toward financial sustainability. Public funding does however, commit policy to an obligation of permanent support. It should

---

[6] When many of the initiatives studied first started.

also be noted that *supporting* community ICT initiatives does not mean *controlling* them.

All the initiatives investigated [2], [13] utilized a mix of funding to perform their role in the community, and managers were often involved in proposal writing. Large funding schemes, such as those provided by the EU and national governments, require a disproportionate amount of investment in terms of time and human resources, and have a tendency to favor those experienced and knowledgeable in the proposal writing culture. Other funding agencies have a tendency to focus on their core business, e.g. employment training, and show little concern for the needs of local communities.

The short-term nature and unfair distribution of funding for community initiatives are examples of negative aspects of social policy mechanisms. They can be extremely demoralizing for community members and practitioners and appear to contradict policy's stated aim of addressing social exclusion in the information society. It is true, that examples exist of great achievements on the back of these funding mechanisms, but it is as equally true, that many hopes have also been dashed and communities damaged as a consequence. This was certainly the case when the preliminary findings of the research were presented to a meeting of community ICT practitioners held in Bristol in 1997. The latest round of National Lottery grants had just been announced. Some practitioners, the successful applicants, were happily discussing future plans, whilst others, the unsuccessful applicants, were fearful for the future sustainability of their initiatives.

The issue here is one of appropriateness of funding mechanisms. At all the initiatives studied there was a perception that community development was subordinate to financial targets and performance indicators. If community ICT initiatives are crucial to social inclusion, and this is a view now adopted at UK government level, e.g. the 'ICT Learning Centre' program, [14] then this should not be the case.

3.6   Organizations and Partnerships

The organization and management of partnerships is an increasingly fundamental component of community ICT initiatives. Despite this, little consideration appears to be given to the range of skills required by those involved in such enterprises. It is clear that partners could provide a more organizationally supportive role. Initiatives overseen by management boards comprising of people with jobs and responsibilities elsewhere, are heavily dependent on staff, volunteers and initiative managers. These roles can be extremely demanding and often receive a low level of recompense, accounting for a high level of staff turnover. The Manchester EVHs and the Danish initiatives at Vejle and the Åben Datastue for Kvinder in Odense - a computer workshop initiative for unemployed women - suffered particularly from this, although it was common in all initiatives. [2]

The role of initiative manager especially, can be extremely demanding and requires wide ranging skills in marketing, promotion, partnership building, fund management, building management, proposal writing, information service provision, administration and public relations, to name but a few. Such skills span from strategic planning to highly specific operational work, and would be highly sought after in the private sector.

Although many partners have the resources and expertise to assist initiatives with such tasks, either in the form of training or basic practical help, few appear to concern themselves with such matters. Another reason for the demise of WTN was the lack of adequate support from the founding partners. [2], [13] Partners often see themselves as Board members that ratify decisions and provide occasional financial support, leaving initiative staff to *do* things. A more appropriate approach might be to view their role and responsibility within a community partnership as a 'working group that does things'. That is to say, actively engaging with the community to identify and address community needs, as opposed to sitting in remote rooms *talking* about them. The adoption of such a community mentoring approach by the public and private sectors would go a long way to achieving initiative sustainability.

3.7   Sustainability

If community ICT initiatives are to succeed in addressing social exclusion in the information society, then sustainability is essential. However, sustainability of initiatives is often achieved as a result of the heroic efforts of initiative workers, who regularly sacrifice their personal lives and give far more than their job descriptions require. The support needed to nurture initiatives in their early years and encourage the strength and capacity they need to achieve sustainability, is an urgent issue for policy-makers. It should not be left to the sacrifice and dedication of initiative workers.

Community ICT initiatives are essentially long-term endeavors. Short-termism, in terms of policy development and funding mechanisms work to the detriment of such initiatives. The 'project culture' and 'social experiment' approaches are inconsistent with sustainable attempts to address social exclusion. In addition to this, achieving a sense of community identity with an ICT initiative requires the active participation and involvement of local communities in all stages of its life cycle. A sense of community ownership is crucial if an initiative is to be sustainable.

Drawing on the relationship between community practice and the design of community ICT initiatives, the next section presents a framework of democratic design criteria for community networks. The framework informs community ICT policy and practice by providing a tool-kit for the consideration and resolution of the kind of problems outlined in this section.

4   Democratic Design Criteria for Community ICT Initiatives – A Normative Framework

The framework is structured in five sections. The first three are based on Sclove's organizing principles of institutional setting and association in a democratic society: democratic community, democratic politics and democratic work [7] and are deemed as essential to establishing democratic community ICT initiatives. The fourth relates to criteria aimed at securing the democratic sustainability of initiatives whilst the fifth introduces criteria intended to perpetuate democratic participation. In order to achieve democratic design, implementation and development processes in community ICT initiatives, the five stages should be viewed as complimentary, however, attempting to develop any of the sections is a positive step in the right direction.

4.1   Toward Democratic Community

A.   Seek initiatives embracing one or more community value (solidarity, participation and coherence).

B.   Promote community development through the empowerment of citizens to define and meet their own needs.

C.   Relate goals and outcomes to the needs of communities and their citizens.

Criterion A states that democratic community ICT initiatives should be based on one or more community value. Solidarity inspires affection and loyalty through mutuality and co-operation in relationships, sustaining community members at an emotional level. Participation benefits individuals through the recognition of their contribution to collective life and self-development. Coherence connects the individual to the community, and leads to an appreciation and comprehension of self and situation that give meaning to and awareness of themselves and their social world. [8] Related to these community values is the advancement of community development through the use of ICTs as empowering tools. Criterion B calls for community ICT initiatives to promote community development by empowering citizens to democratically define and meet community needs. The development of community ICTs promoting the autonomy of local communities whilst facilitating collaboration and co-operation through community action is crucial to community conviviality. To fulfill criterion B, methods of needs analysis that are inclusive and participatory should be harnessed to identify the scope and diversity of a community's social needs to which community ICTs can be applied (Criterion C).

D.   Develop activities and services that meet community need, identified through sustained and meaningful dialogue of citizens and service providers.

E.   Give priority to the needs and interests of a community's socially excluded citizens.

The implementation of initiative activities and services must be effective in meeting community need, if initiatives are to remain sustainable. Criterion D requires sustained and meaningful dialogue between 'experts' (social and technical) and the local community through the forging of democratic partnerships, to ensure that initiatives continue to meet community needs. To ensure social inclusivity (Criterion E), priority must be given to the needs and interests of the disadvantaged and marginalized members of a community.

4.2   Toward Democratic Politics

F.   Avoid policies that establish authoritarian or elitist social relations.

G.   Ensure initiative independence to encourage participatory community action to achieve community goals.

The important issue with respect to Criterion F is that ICTs should be harnessed to underpin democratic community. To achieve this it is crucial to select technologies that do not establish authoritarian or elitist social relations, either within partnerships or the community itself. For example, community initiatives, with the best of social intentions, when run by a small number of self-appointed leaders, run the risk of developing an atmosphere of elitism and being unrepresentative of community wishes. Although many initiatives are started in this way, there comes a time when their governance must be placed in the hands of the broader community, if they are to remain democratic. It is also essential that community ICT initiatives retain some degree of independence from funding agencies or partnership organizations. There may be occasions when the views of the community come into conflict with those of such bodies and some form of community action is required. Criterion G states that initiatives must be independent and free from the influence of vested interests if they are to be used by an empowered community acting to identify and achieve community goals.

H.   Contribute to a public space for shared communications that facilitate inter/intra community conviviality.

I.   Recognize and celebrate diversity of opinion, beliefs, values and cultures and avoid policies that promote intolerance and disrespect.

Underpinning all community ICT initiatives should be a public space [1] dedicated to open communications (Criterion H). Such a public space supports inter and intra community communications. If community-driven ICTs are to underpin social activities within local communities, by providing an extra forum of communication, then electronic public spaces should be afforded the same importance that sociologists give to 'actual' public spaces or 'third places' such as parks, community centers, civic squares, cafes and pubs. The utilization of ICTs to provide a public space for shared communications at both inter and intra community levels, supports participatory democracy and encourages the valorization of diversity.

Modern society is both pluralist and multicultural. Whilst this diversity enriches the human experience, it also produces complex social problems. The many communities, groups, associations, etc. that comprise society often coexist quite peacefully, however conflict also often exists within and between communities. Criterion I holds that community ICTs should both respect and protect society's diversity. They should not be used to promote views hurtful or damaging to the cultural heritage of others; for example, racist or sexist materials should not be stored or disseminated on community systems. The resolution of problems of conflict can only be achieved through democratic determination within or between communities.

4.3   Toward Democratic Work

J.   Promote self-actualization through activities and services that stimulate lifelong learning and active citizenship in the community.

K.   Invest in social capital by promoting common community interests and concerns.

L.   Seek to stimulate both social and formal economies of local communities.

In this context democratic work applies to activities engaged in as part of the social economy, but policies could be developed here that relate to telework and other forms of community-based revenue generation. Criterion J relates to awareness raising, training and education activities and services at community ICT initiatives, and states that they should enable self-actualization and enable community capacity building. The development and application of skills through activities in the social economy enable citizens, through engagement, to contribute to community life in new ways. Consequently, facilitating self-actualization and capacity building activities in community initiatives is a way for policy and practice to invest in the social capital of a community. It can be done by supporting common interests and concerns, as a recognition of the importance of a community's social wealth[7] (Criterion K). By adopting more holistic approaches to the social development of communities, a range of mutual community economic development activities can also be supported and/or identified (criterion L).

4.4   Securing Democratic Sustainability

M.   Enable meaningful engagement with groups and organizations active within local communities through the development of tripartite partnerships.

N.   Promote social innovation by harnessing the indigenous knowledge and creativity of communities with the resources and expertise of public, private and third sectors.

O.   Develop a sense of community identity and ownership.

Some form of cross-sectoral partnership often shapes the structure, function and organization of community ICT initiatives. This is because the highly competitive and profit motivated nature of modern capitalist society makes it difficult, if not impossible, for community-driven grassroots initiatives to survive without support of this nature. Therefore, partnerships are an increasingly important component of civil life. Criterion M necessitates the establishment of tripartite partnerships to secure initiative sustainability. By harnessing the existent knowledge and creativity of communities with the resources and expertise found in the public, private and third sectors, social innovation can be promoted (Criterion N). Criteria M and N make significant contributions to the development of a sense of community ownership and identity. This community identity and sense of ownership are essential if community ICT initiatives are to be sustainable (Criterion O).

---

[7] The wealth of knowledge, skills and expertise possessed by citizens and groups of a community.

4.5   Enabling Active Community Participation

P.   Promote universal participation.

Q.   Seek 'local' technological flexibility and 'global' technological pluralism.

Central to promoting democratic participation is the recognition that whilst policy must enable active community groups to participate in the three organizing principles of a democratic society, this in itself does not represent an inclusive approach to participation. Community groups, whilst important to active communities, do not constitute complete communities. The facilitation of universal participation, where every citizen that wishes to, has the right to participate in these principles in some way (Criterion P) goes some way to achieving this. Clearly, it is impractical to enable full citizen participation in every stage of the design, implementation and development of community ICT initiatives. However, a range of participatory community methods exist that can be utilized where appropriate, e.g. consensus conferences, citizen panels and scenario workshops. It is important that the community socio-technical order remains flexible and democratic. If it becomes too rigid, social relationships become more inflexible and subsequent structural alterations prove difficult. Whilst flexibility is important at the local level, it is also significant globally. Valorizing diversity by ensuring local flexibility in all communities, ensures the preservation of cultural pluralism and affords communities and individuals the ability to communicate with and learn from other cultures (Criterion Q) in the network society.

5   Conclusion

This paper contributes to the inter-disciplinary activities of the 'Second Kyoto Meeting on Digital Cities' by presenting insights into a social science research project that investigated thirteen different UK and Scandinavian community ICT initiatives. The issues identified as of significance to community networking, based on investigations of community ICT practice, [2] reveal interesting insights into the challenges faced by community ICT practitioners, and forms the basis for the development of a normative framework of democratic design criteria for community ICT initiatives. Although the framework represents community ICT initiatives as social artifacts to be shaped by community need, it would be wrong to interpret this as suggesting that technological infrastructure, platforms and artifacts are unimportant. Although this paper argues that technical issues should be subordinate to the needs of community in community networking/informatics, they are still of significance and require a fuller understanding within the context of community.

The democratic design criteria presented here need to be supported by similar design criteria from the technological perspective. This is the challenge facing the community systems and software developers of the community informatics movement. The development of technical democratic design criteria is an area where important research can be conducted in the future. Synergy between the social and technical components of community ICT research, practice and policy is crucial to building socially inclusive pathways to the information society and the synthesis of social and technical democratic design criteria for community ICT initiatives is presented here as a prerequisite to achieving them.

One final point needs to be emphasized at this juncture. The framework is *not* intended as a blueprint to be imposed, by policy, on local communities. Its value lies in its applicability across the diversity of community ICT practices. The *Taylorist* notion of 'best practice' is rejected here as being contrary to the diversity of social practice found in communities. Through the promotion of social cohesion, diversity of communities, and consequently of community ICT initiatives, is seen as a strength within, and between, communities, especially as the community informatics movement gathers momentum worldwide. [1], [12] In order to facilitate this diversity, the design criteria are deliberately left open. It enables enough flexibility for communities to identify design criteria that reflect indigenous culture, communication and information needs, and that promote the needs of the socially excluded.

The framework also enables initiatives to evaluate their activities by facilitating an ongoing analysis of initiative role and function. In this way, the framework provides communities with a tool to ensure that practice does not become rigidified in ritual and custom, but remains flexible enough to respond to the changing needs of community citizens and their environments.

References

1. Day, P., Schuler, D. (Eds.): Shaping the Network Society: The Future of the Public Sphere in Cyberspace. Proceedings of the DIAC 2000 International Symposium in Seattle, Washington, May 21-23,2000a. CPSR, Seattle
2. Day, P.: The Networked Community: Policies for a Participative Information Society. [Unpublished Ph.D. thesis] (2001)
3. Gill, K.S.: The Foundations of Human-Centred Systems. In: Gill, K.S. (ed.): Human Machine Symbiosis: The Foundations of Human-Centred Systems Design. Springer-Verlag, London (1996) 1-68
4. Ehn, P.: Work Oriented Design of Computer Artefacts, Arbetslivscentrum, Stockholm (1988)
5. Emery, M.: Participative Design for Participative Democracy. Centre for Continuing Education, The Australian National University, Canberra (1993)
6. Schuler, D., Namioka, A.: (eds.) Participatory Design – Principles and Practices. LEA, Hillsdale, New Jersey (1993)
7. Sclove, R.E.: Democracy and Technology. Guilford Press, London (1995)
8. Butcher, H.: Introduction: Some Examples and Definitions, In: Butcher, H., Glen, A., Henderson, P., Smith, J. (eds.): Community and Public Policy. Pluto Press, London (1993) 3-21
9. Glen, A.: Methods and Themes in Community Practice. In: Butcher, H., Glen, A., Henderson, P., Smith, J. (eds.): Community and Public Policy. Pluto Press, London (1993) 22-40
10. Schuler, D.: New Community Networks: Wired for Change. Addison-Wesley, Harlow, UK (1996) http://www.scn.org/civic/ncn/
11. Gurstein, M. (ed.): Community Informatics: Using Technology to Enable Community Processes. Idea Group Publishing, Hershey, PA (1999)
12. Day, P., Schuler, D.: Shaping the Network Society - Are Citizens Actors--or Just Part of the Audience? *The CPSR Newsletter*. 18 (3). Summer. (2000) http://www.cpsr.org/publications/newsletters/issues/2000/Summer2000/

13. Day, P., Harris, K.: Down-to-Earth Vision: Community Based IT Initiatives and Social Inclusion. [The Commit Report]. IBM/CDF, London (1997)
14. Policy Action Team (PAT) 15: Closing the Digital Divide: information and communication technologies in deprived areas - A Report by Policy Action Team 15. Department of Trade and Industry, London (2000) http://www.pat15.org.uk/consult.htm
15. Department of the Environment, Transport and the Regions: Preparing Community Strategies – Government Guidance to Local Authorities. DETR, London (2000) http://www.local-regions.detr.gov.uk/pcs/guidance/
16. Community Development Foundation (CDF): The New Community Strategies: How to Involve Local People. CDF, London (2000) http://www.cdf.org.uk
17. Social Exclusion Unit (SEU): National Strategy for Neighbourhood Renewal: Policy Action Team Audit. Cabinet Office, London (2001)
18. Shearman, C.: Local Connections: Making the Net Work for Neighbourhood Renewal. Communities Online, London (1999) http://www.communities.org.uk/

TeleCities – Digital Cities Network

Ingrid Götzl

Chief Executive Office – EDP and Information Management
1082 Vienna, Rathausstrasse 1
ged@mdi.magwien.gv.at
http://www.wien.at/

Abstract. The TeleCities telematics network consists of more than 120 European cities with key business partners participating as associated members. Telecities, which is currently under the presidency of the City of Vienna, acts as a Europe wide network for urban policy issues relevant to the information society. Many of the member cities whose administration is based on a long and successful EDP tradition have come to call themselves "Digital Cities". They all increasingly rely on the new information and communication technologies (ICT) as well. The following article provides a comprehensive outline of TeleCities, along with its strategic goals and projects; the City of Vienna is used as an example of a "Digital City" which places great significance on the implementation of eGovernment.

Keywords: network, Digital City, eGovernment

1 TeleCities

TeleCities is an open network of more than 120 European cities of all shapes and sizes: capitals, metropolitan cities, cities of regional significance, as well as small towns; its main aim is to promote development in these cities with the help of ICT; it has set itself the goal of advancing the information society to promote economic and social development and to provide maximum quality services on the part of the administration. All of these strategies are guided by the principle of "Cooperation and Social Inclusion".

TeleCities was initiated in 1993 as a "sister network" of Eurocities, an association of approximately 100 European cities with more than 250,000 inhabitants each in over 22 countries. It is now an independent network governed by a TeleCities president and a steering committee; both are elected democratically according to TeleCities' own statutes. Financially, it is largely independent of Eurocities.

TeleCities encourages participation of key players in the information society based on cross-border cooperation and knowledge transfer. Within the TeleCities network itself *cities* as such are considered pilot projects for research and project development. TeleCities serves as a forum for knowledge exchange between members seeking information on other cities' expertise and experience in order to implement their own innovative plans without running into the risks otherwise entailed. TeleCities is ac

M. Tanabe, P. van den Besselaar, T. Ishida (Eds.): Digital Cities, LNCS 2362, pp. 101-109, 2002.
© Springer-Verlag Berlin Heidelberg 2002

tively involved in establishing public-private partnerships to promote participation of the European business sector.

TeleCities is based on four pillars:

- Knowledge Transfer: within the information society, exchange of experiences, project results and "lessons learned" among the cities concerned is to facilitate local and global processes of learning.

- Policy and Dialogue: TeleCities acts as a platform of dialogue for cities and EU institutions, particularly with regard to information and communication technologies. This is to place increased emphasis on the position of cities vis-à-vis EU institutions in the above context.

- Dissemination Activities: knowledge, experience and Best Practices are spread through international TeleCities conferences, regular working groups, exhibitions, publications, TeleCities' own website, training courses as well as a virtual discussion forum.

- Support and Assistance: TeleCities is also highly appreciated among its members for its efforts in preparing new projects, searching for partners for EU proposals, providing information on programmes, initiatives and EU funding.

TeleCities activities are carried out at several levels:

- Policy Papers: this is one of TeleCities' more recent activities which has helped to establish its official position on ICT issues of political interest. It relies on participation of representatives from city administrations as well as on the expertise drawn from within cities themselves. It has given considerable political weight to TeleCities as a city network, and as speaker on behalf of millions of people in Europe. TeleCities is cooperating with Eurocities to create widespread understanding within pertinent EU institutions for ICT issues of relevance to city administrations, and to engage in constructive dialogue on such issues. Policy papers on eLearning and eDemocracy are currently being prepared.
- Working Groups: TeleCities Working Groups were established as open discussion forums. Participants physically meet four times a year during TeleCities conferences to discuss topical issues of vital significance to city administrations. Each working group is coordinated by a city chosen for its experience with and practical knowledge of a particular subject matter. There are four working groups currently in progress on: eEducation, Organisational Changes in the City of Tomorrow, Smart Government, and TeleDemocracy. Three additional working groups are active within the PACE project (see below).
- EU projects: TeleCities has become a favorite partner for such EU projects as enable it to pursue its primary objectives, which are: "to raise awareness, exchange of best practices among all relevant actors and of state-of-the-art urban IS technologies by means of events and information dissemination." TeleCities is a partner of "DEBUT - Data Exploitation and Best Utilization Trail", the aim of which is to encourage public private partnerships between private partners and public administrations. It also participates in "EDEN – Electronic Democracy European Network", a project developed in support of Natural Language

Processing (NLP) Tools and subsequent citizen participation in urban policy plans. TeleCities is also actively involved in the LEONARDO project "Exchange of Skills", the eContent projects "eCT – Electronic Call for Tenders" and "ODA – Open Digital Administration", as well as the IST eCommerce project PACE (see below). The latter might serve as an example to illustrate TeleCities' commitment to project activities. "PACE – Public Administration and Electronic Commerce in Europe", one of TeleCities' main projects, is supported by IST, a funding programme established by the European Commission. The purpose of this programme is to encourage implementation and utilisation of new technologies in public or more specifically in city administrations. PACE wants to support cities in developing new ways of utilizing eCommerce as a means of interacting with citizens, suppliers and other administrations. It has triggered a sustainable process of studies, knowledge distribution, training, awareness raising activities and working groups, etc., within public administrations, to open the doors to the European eCommerce market. To increase the chances for successful development and implementation of eCommerce, TeleCities deals with various important socio-economic issues. Among those are the effects of technological trends and of market developments, legal and ethical considerations, worldwide Best Practices and the impact of eCommerce on the employment situation.

2 Digital Cities and eGovernment

During the Vienna's term at the presidency of TeleCities, the following strategic issues will be dealt with:

- Advancing eGovernment for increased citizen orientation, promoting the Inclusive Digital Society by placing special emphasis on ICT activities for all citizens concerned.
- Strenghtening TeleCities as a speaker on behalf of European cities representing their ICT objectives and requirements within relevant EU institutions.
- Intensifying cooperation among EU cities, paying particular attention to the fact that cities with highly advanced information and communication technologies will support those seeking increased development of their ICT activities.

The above choice of issues is a clear indication that cities need to be strengthened in their role as primary promoters of well-being and wealth. Special efforts need to be undertaken to support information and communication technologies and the essential role they have come to play in urban policies in recent years.

For many decades, city administrations in Europe have been relying on information technologies to meet their many obligations in practically all spheres of competence. In the early days, applications were largely pragmatic and operational and only loosely connected. Since then, a sophisticated infrastructure has been developed, with a system-wide network of computers covering the entire administration.

To meet the need for increased efficiency, city administrations must undergo a series of change processes. They have had to adapt to fundamental changes in their scope of activities in recent years, in the course of which information and communication technologies have been recognized as strategic tools of urban development capable of influencing the make up of public administrations. Digital cities as we have come to know them are already beginning to feel the impact of new public management, business process reengineering, "administrations as service corporations", and their practical implications, among others citizen-oriented front-desk services. The term digital cities as interpreted by TeleCities refers to cities that rely on a high degree of, albeit traditional, EDP in most of their institutions.

As requirements are changing, as organizational structures are adapting to these changes, and as EDP is gradually turning into ICT, many digital cities are beginning to draft ideas for new administrative processes. The Association for Informatics and the Association for Information Technology, in their joint memorandum, have defined electronic government [1], as "implementing processes of public will formation, of decision-making, and providing of services in politics, government and administration based on intensive utilization of information technology." The City of Vienna has adopted these views to a large extent, for the development of electronic government processes.

The Society for Informatics

For DiMaio et al. [2], eGovernment is the "transformation of public-sector internal and external relationships through Net-enabled operations, information and communication technology to optimise government service delivery, constituency participation and internal government processes." GartnerGroup detects a close link and partial overlap of eGovernment and the Digital Society: "A digital (or information) society is a society or community that is well advanced in the adoption and integration of digital technology into daily life at home, work and play, and has advanced in the adoption of the connected (or "new") economy. Many governments see the development of a digital society as an essential aspect of continuing economic development."

The following infrastructure and regulatory measures are considered criteria for digital cities:

- Enhancing language and computer training at preschool age, introducing compulsory computer courses for teachers; subsidizing PC acquisitions for students and teachers.

- Introducing infrastructure measures, setting up all-round network infrastructures.

- Supporting ICT applications in the business sector.

- Providing legal security by emphasizing security, privacy, etc.

Taking into account GartnerGroup's definition of digital societies, we can therefore conclude that "a digital city is a city whose administration is well advanced in the adoption and integration of new information and communication technologies into everyday practice, and which already includes principles of New Economy in its administrative processes."

3 Digital City Vienna

The Strategy Plan for Vienna 2000 [3] states that "cities and urban regions worldwide are gaining importance. They play an active role in shaping economies and societies as well as in spreading global responsibility for sustainable and environmentally oriented developments. This has led to the establishment of new, universally accepted criteria for international, and above all European city networks. The guiding principle for all of them is to create sustainable living environments."

For this purpose Vienna, by its own definition *a city of vision,* has drawn up a catalogue of guidelines for future development:

- Creating sustainable development.
- Participating in the European Association of Cities and Regions.
- Creating a competitive business center for a strong region.
- Pursuing future-oriented labor market policies.
- Creating a center of knowledge and culture.
- Achieving social balance.
- Promoting coexistence of different cultures, religions and life styles.
- Promoting equal chances for everyone.
- Becoming a pioneer in "Gender Mainstreaming".
- Achieving a high quality of life.
- Spreading environmental awareness.

3.1 ICT Strategies Developed by the City of Vienna

ICT strategies are developed for the sole purpose of putting into practice overall urban strategies; this principle also holds true for Vienna where strategies have been developed to pursue the following objectives:

- Citizen services
Administrative activities are drawn up in accordance with citizen or rather customer needs; the efficiency of measures is measured by how they are actually experienced.
- Promoting the city as a business location
Due to regional circumstances special attention must be given to the needs of small and medium sized enterprises.
- Economy of operation
The efficiency of administrative processes and activities as a whole must be raised.

Vienna has approximately 1.7 million inhabitants. The City of Vienna employs more than 70,000 in the fields of education, health care, public administration, social services, environmental matters, housing, urban planning, water management, waste water management, and others.

The figures quoted below are to illustrate the significance of information and communication technologies for the City: for more than 35 years, the city administration has been relying on EDP in all of its spheres of competence; approximately 25,000 employees have access to 22,000 personal computers, all equipped with e-mail functions; 15,000 employees have direct Internet and Intranet access; roughly 1,100 members of staff are employed in ICT, approximately ATS 900 million annually are spent by the City on ICT services (not including staff costs).

ICT applications are rated in accordance with the following priorities:

1. Benefits for citizens
2. Economy of operation
3. Process optimization
4. Innovation

In principle, all ICT expenditures are meant to improve the performance rendered by the commissioning party. Customer satisfaction is an important measure for the quality of services rendered the costs and quality of which must be comparable to similar services available on the market. Yet one of the decisive criteria for eGovernment services in particular is how the final customers of the City Administration, i.e. the citizens and the business community of Vienna, accept them.

Members of staff and municipal departments engaged in ICT are considered key factors in the successful implementation of information and communication technologies in Vienna.

Information and communication technologies departments have taken the role of internal service providers and general IT entrepreneur, to support the City of Vienna in becoming a citizen-oriented and efficient service corporation. ICT departments are mainly concerned with those areas that are crucial to the city's business routine. This includes technical consulting, ICT-relevant project management, handling of central and sensitive applications, software support, etc.

New developments in the technology sector are to provide continuous quality improvement of ICT services in order to give maximum support to crucial processes and procedures, and to open up new opportunities for maximum performance. Like other businesses with a long EDP tradition, the City of Vienna will benefit from the fact that the globalization sustained by the Internet and its many options is forcing manufacturers of software tools – especially development tools – and hardware to make their products progressively more compatible with others. In other words, the Internet potentially may create universally accepted solutions. Market developments have made it possible to solve, or at least bypass, many of the problems caused by technical incompatibilities. The use of these technologies will also facilitate the integration of legacy systems.

3.2 eGovernment in Vienna

"eVienna" was initiated by the City Administration as an eGovernment umbrella project to respond to the growing significance of information and communication technology applications.

The services provided by the City should come across as simple, accessible, up-to-date and competent; citizens are to get a sense of being taken care of but also of being well informed and included in relevant processes. Members of the business community are to actually feel the advantages of being located in Vienna, a place where all technicalities are dealt with quickly and smoothly by their business partner "the City of Vienna".

"eVienna" is based on a concept where supply is regulated by the needs of the citizens: it is a concept for all circumstances and problems of life. ICT makes it possible to apply for services of different public or private suppliers at the same time, as the case may be or as the situation requires (moving home, starting up a business, etc.). These services are then offered as a package without the customer being aware of the interfaces between the different suppliers involved in handling their case and without the customer having to get in touch with individual service suppliers.

"eVienna" was created with four objectives in mind:

a) Information and Services
With ICT it will be possible for citizens to communicate with authorities interactively whenever the need arises.

b) Transparency
ICT offers new ways of strengthening people's confidence in business and the City Administration by making relevant administrative processes increasingly more transparent: by accessing the Internet, citizens and members of the business community can find out how their "case" is progressing. The public administration is no longer a "Black Box" to them – as customers they assume responsibility for part of the quality control of their "case in progress".

c) Co-Decision
With the help of information and communication technologies citizens are to be made part of decision-making and planning processes carried out by political committees and by the City Administration. To achieve this, information will be made available electronically via the Internet. In addition, customers will be given the opportunity to participate in Internet discussions.

d) Participation
ICT is to provide support as certain tasks traditionally performed by the public administration are delegated to the citizens of Vienna. Apart from the core areas of public administration which will, of course, continue to be the sole responsibility of these authorities, there are a number of tasks currently in public hands which could easily be carried out by private individuals or private communities. The City Administration is offering Internet support as a communication tool and information source to help restructure these responsibilities. As responsibilities are redistributed between the City and its citizens, society as a whole is given more scope for commitment, and the City's budget can be used more efficiently.

The Internet is an important means of communication between the City Administration and its customers. It provides a useful addition to the many traditional ways of interacting with institutions, e.g. personal contact, written or telephone communication.

Below is a list of the means of access currently available, bearing in mind that this is a multi-channel approach:

- Appearing in person
- By telephone
- By letter
- By fax
- By e-mail
- Via SMS
- Via WWW and WAP

As citizens are to be supplied with all the required services and information at their chosen points of access, the administration needs to be restructured to include both a front office (actual contact with customers) and a back office approach (handling of the "case"). Restructuring activities are currently in progress.

A call center about to be installed will handle the different access channels, i.e. telephone, e-mail, SMS and fax. "One Stop Shops" are to take care of "personal contacts". Internet access is available via (www.wien.at), Vienna's own homepage, which provides all the details on required information and services.

Internet technology will be used to support the handling of information and services at the call center and the One Stop Shop. It will also help to establish the link to the EDP solutions prepared at the back office which are basically the same for all front office applications.

3.3 Other ICT Projects

Bearing in mind the infrastructure and regulatory measures set out in the Gartner-Group criteria for digital cities the following projects may also be of interest:

- Vienna education network: all the schools and out-of-school educational facilities run by the City will be interlinked and provided with Internet access. Schools will be equipped with personal computers and printers. Content preparation and distribution will be handled by an association established for that purpose.

- City network: "City network" was commissioned in 1996. It was established as a Virtual Private Network and equipped with the necessary bandwidth to provide a general network infrastructure for EDP and telephone communication; it is now in full operation as a backbone for the City Administration as well as for the Vienna Hospital Association.

- WELCOM: the project "WELCOM – Wiener Electronic Commerce" was initiated by the City in early 1999 as an Electronic Commerce (eC) – umbrella project incorporating all relevant activities, measures and projects. The aim was to integrate the entire spectrum of eC facilities into the City Administration and thus to make Vienna "fit for eC", i.e. to offer interfaces for electronic handling of transactions between the City of Vienna and the Vienna business community. Small and medium-sized enterprises in particular were to receive the full potential of eCommerce. Procedures were chosen based on their capacity to facilitate cooperation between the business community and the administration and to create the necessary eCommerce infrastructure.

- Legal security: the City of Vienna is participating in a nationwide working group of federal and regional governments which was established to install a legal framework for eGovernment. The basic legal provisions for digital signatures already entered into force on January 1, 2000 in accordance with the relevant federal act. The working group is also engaged in preparing proposals on amendments of relevant legal acts.

References

[1] Electronic Government als Schlüssel zur Modernisierung von Staat und Verwaltung. Ein Memorandum des Fachausschusses Verwaltungsinformatik der Gesellschaft für Informatik e.V. und des Fachbereichs 1 der Informationstechnischen Gesellschaft im VDE, Gesellschaft für Informatik e.V. (GI), Bonn; Informationstechnische Gesellschaft (ITG) im VDE, Frankfurt, September 2000 (- "Electronic Government – the key to modernizing government and administration, memorandum published by the technical committee for administrative informatics of the German Association for Informatics, in cooperation with the technical committee 1 of the Association for Information Technology")
[2] A. Di Maio, C. Baum, F. Caldwell, E. Fraga, B. Keller, G. Kreizman, Where E-Government Ends and Digital Society Begins, Research Note, QA-14-0716, © Gartner, Inc., 31.7.2001
[3] Strategieplan Wien (Vienna Strategy Plan), City of Vienna (Ed.), © City of Vienna, 2000
[4] E. Binder, Th. Skerlan-Schuhböck, eVienna, working paper, © City of Vienna, 2001

TeleCities Network, www.teleCities.org , © Eurocities, 2001
    PACE, www.pace-eu.net , 2000

The Camfield Estates-MIT Creating Community Connections Project: Strategies for Active Participation in a Low- to Moderate-Income Community

Randal D. Pinkett

MIT Media Laboratory
20 Ames St., Room E15-120B, Cambridge MA 02139 USA
rpinkett@media.mit.edu

Abstract. This paper shares the early results of a study that is investigating strategies to bridge the "digital divide" [15, 16, 17, 18] — the gap between those who benefit from new technology and those who do not — by examining the role of community technology for the purpose of community building and economic development in a low- to moderate-income housing development. Since January 2000, the Camfield Estates-MIT Creating Community Connections Project, a partnership between the Camfield Tenants Association and Massachusetts Institute of Technology, has taken place at Camfield Estates, a 102-unit, low-to moderate-income housing development in Roxbury, Massachusetts, and its surrounding environs. With support from the W.K. Kellogg Foundation, Hewlett-Packard, RCN Telecom Services, Microsoft, and others, every family at Camfield has been offered a state-of-the-art desktop computer, software, high-speed Internet connection via cable-modem, and eight weeks of comprehensive courses – free of charge. Camfield residents are also supported by the Creating Community Connections (C3) System, a web-based, community building system designed at the MIT Media Laboratory, to establish and strengthen relationships between community residents, local businesses, and neighborhood institutions (e.g., libraries, schools, etc.) and organizations. Of the 102 units at Camfield, approximately 80 are presently occupied, while approximately 60 units have elected to participate in the project in some capacity, from among two rounds of sign-ups in September 2000 and January 2001. This paper is a case study of the Camfield Estates-MIT project to-date, including the history and background of the project, the theoretical frameworks guiding the initiative, the project methodology that has been employed to foster resident engagement and integrate community technology and community building, early results, and a set of recommendations and lessons learned for other initiatives.

1 Introduction

The digital divide [15, 16, 17], the gap between those who benefit from new technologies and those who do not, has received considerable attention in the new millennium as organizations from the public, private, and nonprofit sectors have partnered with communities to address this critical issue [25]. In urban and rural neighborhoods across the country there are examples of successful initiatives to

M. Tanabe, P. van den Besselaar, T. Ishida (Eds.): Digital Cities, LNCS 2362, pp. 110-124, 2002.
© Springer-Verlag Berlin Heidelberg 2002

provide economical access and promote meaningful use of technology, as a means toward achieving tangible and sustainable outcomes in areas such as education, employment, and health care [2, 3, 4, 5, 6, 10, 11, 24, 27, 31].

Historically, one of the major challenges associated with community collaborations is the "inside-outside tension" resulting from the delineation between internal and external actors, which is perhaps best characterized as the distinction between "us" and "them" [30]. This tension manifests itself in a variety of ways. From the "inside" perspective, neighborhood residents and governing boards seeking to leverage the resources and expertise of researchers, funders, and technical assistance providers, must do so in a way that advances, and does not compromise their own goals and objectives. From the "outside" perspective, non-residents seeking to support and learn from community members and organizations, must do so in a way that fosters ownership and empowerment, as opposed to dependence. As corporations, foundations, government bodies, universities, partner with non-profit organizations and expand the scope of their work to include high technology in low-income and underserved communities, the inside-outside tension will undoubtedly arise as it has in the past. However, the need for a greater awareness of, and sensitivity to these issues is only heightened by the challenges associated with the ongoing use of technology, such as installing new systems and maintaining and upgrading existing systems. Without careful attention to this dilemma, community-based organizations could easily be saddled with a prohibitively higher total cost of ownership than experienced before.

The ideal scenario for communities to truly work together as partners with the public, private, philanthropic, academic, and non-profit sectors, is one where the needs of both parties are met and the community's capacity is strengthened as a result of the partnership. These goals are most likely to be met (and the inside-outside tension is most likely to be resolved) in projects that engage community residents as active participants in the process, ensuring that they have a strong voice in determining outcomes for *their* community, while still leveraging the contributions from these entities. As Kingsley, McNeely, and Gibson [8] explain:

"Community participation" is not enough. The community must play the central role in devising and implementing strategies for its own improvement. This does not mean that outside facilitators cannot help show them the way, or that they cannot accept outside help or accomplish goals by partnering with outside agencies, but neighborhood residents must feel that they "own" the improvement process.

The Camfield Estates-MIT Creating Community Connections Project, a partnership between the Camfield Tenants Association (CTA) and the Massachusetts Institute of Technology (MIT), has endeavored to exemplify this notion.

Started in January 2000, the Camfield Estates-MIT project has the goal of establishing Camfield Estates as a model for other housing developments across the globe as to how individuals, families, and a community can make use of information and communications technology to support their interests and needs. This multi-sector collaboration [25] has joined to create an infrastructure at Camfield Estates that combines the three primary models for *community technology* [14, 1] – a *community network* whereas state-of-the-art desktop computers, software, and high-speed Internet connectivity have been offered to every family, a *community technology center (CTC)* located on the premises in the community center, and *community content* delivered through web-based, community building system, the Creating Community Connections (C3) System, designed at the MIT Media Laboratory – along with a *community building* agenda [8, 12, 30]. Note that there is a parallel, and related initiative being conducted at Camfield to build empowerment and self-sufficiency amongst residents that is beyond the scope of this paper. This paper is a case study of the Camfield Estates-MIT project to-date, including the history and background of the project, the theoretical frameworks guiding the initiative, the project methodology that has been employed to foster resident engagement and integrate community technology and community building, early results, as well as a set of recommendations and lessons learned for other initiatives.

2 History of the Camfield Estates-MIT Project

Camfield Estates, under the leadership of the non-profit, Camfield Tenants Association (CTA), Inc., is one of the leading housing developments in the greater Boston area. Camfield is a participant in the US Department of Housing and Urban Development's (HUD) demonstration-disposition or "demo-dispo" program. Demo-dispo was implemented by HUD in 1993, as a strategy to deal with its growing inventory of foreclosed multifamily housing, much of which was in poor physical and financial condition (MHFA, 2001). Through this national demonstration program, approved only in the City of Boston, the Massachusetts Housing Finance Agency (MHFA) was designated to oversee the renovation and sale of HUD properties to resident-owned organizations. Camfield residents, through the efforts of CTA, identified needs of not only affordable housing, vis-à-vis demo-dispo, but also closely related areas such as building community to address existing social, economic, and technological disparities.

Under the leadership of CTA, the 136 apartments of Camfield Gardens were demolished in 1997 and residents were relocated throughout the greater Boston area. Reconstruction of the property was completed in 2000 as residents returned to Camfield Estates - 102-units of newly built town houses. The renovated property also includes the Camfield community center which houses meeting space, management offices, and the Neighborhood Technology Center (NTC) – a CTC and HUD Neighborhood Networks site, managed by Williams Consulting Services, and supported by MHFA. Finally, on June 22, 2001, HUD disposed (transferred ownership) of the property to CTA, making Camfield the first of several participants in the demo-dispo program to successfully complete the process.

The Camfield Estates-MIT Creating Community Connections project was initiated in January 2000, by graduate students and faculty from the MIT Media Laboratory, MIT Department of Urban Studies and Planning, MIT Center for Reflective Community Practice, and MIT Laboratory for Computer Science. These researchers shared an interest in the role of technology for the purpose of building community, empowerment, and self-sufficiency in a low-income community. Camfield was identified as an excellent site to examine these issues and conduct a longitudinal study for numerous reasons, including the strong leadership exemplified by CTA, the cable-modem Internet capabilities in each unit, and the presence of NTC, along with its associated course offering and ongoing technical support. However, what made Camfield particularly attractive were the prospects to sustain the initiative as a result of their leading role in the demo-dispo program and impending ownership of the property.

The W.K. Kellogg Foundation provided primary support for the project in the form of a monetary grant, followed by in-kind donations from Hewlett-Packard Company (computers), RCN Telecom Services (cable-modem Internet service), Microsoft Corporation (software), and ArsDigita Corporation (software and technical support), with additional support from MHFA, Williams Consulting Services, Lucent Technologies, HUD, US Department of Commerce, the Institute for African-American eCulture (iAAEC), YouthBuild of Boston, and the William Monroe Trotter Institute at the University of Massachusetts at Boston.

Exploratory meetings between CTA, MIT, Kellogg, and Williams Consulting took place during the winter 2000, culminating in final approval of the project by CTA. Under CTA's leadership, in spring 2000 a nine-person committee was established to oversee the project's implementation, which consisted of three Camfield residents, two representatives of CTA, two members of Williams Consulting staff, and two researchers at MIT. The project officially began in June 2000.

3 Background & Theory: Sociocultural Constructionism and an Asset-Based Approach to Community Technology and Community Building

One of the project's goals is to explore the synergy between *community technology* [14, 1] and *community building* [30, 8, 12]. *Community technology* has been referred to as "a process to serve the local geographic community – to respond to the needs of that community and build solutions to its problems" [14], and defined as "using the technology to support and meet the goals of a community" [1]. *Community building* is an approach to community revitalization that is focused on "strengthening the capacity of residents, associations, and organizations to work, individually and collectively, to foster and sustain positive neighborhood change" [30].

To date, three primary models have emerged for community technology – *community networks, community technology centers (CTCs), and community content* – all of which have been deployed at Camfield and combined with a *community building* agenda.

Community networks are community-based electronic network services, provided at little or no cost to users. Every family at Camfield has been offered a state-of-the-art desktop computer, software, and high-speed Internet connectivity via cable-modem. *Community technology centers (CTCs),* or community computing centers, are publicly accessible facilities that provide computer access for people who can't afford a computer, as well as technical instruction and support. As mentioned earlier, the Camfield Estates Neighborhood Technology Center (NTC) has been established in the Camfield community center where comprehensive courses as well as technical support are provided. *Community content* refers to the availability of material that is relevant and interesting to a specific target audience (e.g., low-income residents) to encourage and motivate the use of technology [10]. The Creating Community Connections (C3) System, a web-based, community building system, has been co-designed between MIT students and Camfield residents at the MIT Media Laboratory, using the application service provider (ASP) model – Camfield residents create and maintain the content, while MIT administers and maintains the associated hardware and software.

To promote *community building,* Camfield residents and MIT researchers have been actively involved in "mapping" and "mobilizing" community assets and resources to create connections among residents, local organizations and institutions (e.g., libraries, schools, etc.), and neighborhood businesses.

Since the project's inception, a heavy emphasis has been placed on engaging the residents at Camfield as active agents of change, as well as active producers of community information and content. This orientation is grounded in the theories of *asset-based community development (ABCD)* [9] and *sociocultural constructionism* [22] which, in concert, constitute an asset-based approach to community technology and community building [31]. These theoretical frameworks have proven extremely useful for conceptualizing how this partnership can foster community empowerment, rather than dependency.

Asset-based community development (ABCD), a particular model, or technique, for community building, assumes that social and economic revitalization starts with what is already present in the community – not only the capacities of residents as individuals, but also the existing commercial, associational and institutional foundation [31]. Asset-based community development seeks to leverage the resources within a community by "mapping" these assets and then "mobilizing" them to facilitate productive and meaningful connections. Asset-based community development is an approach to community building that sees community members as active agents of change, rather than passive beneficiaries or clients.

Sociocultural constructionism, here applied to community technology, is a synthesis of the theories of *social constructionism* [28] and *cultural constructionism* [7], both extensions of the theory of *constructionism* [20]. *Constructionism* is a design-based approach to learning, drawing on research showing that people learn best when they are active participants in design activities [20], and that these activities give them a greater sense of control over (and personal involvement in) the learning process [23]. *Sociocultural constructionism* argues that "individual and community development are reciprocally enhanced by independent and shared constructive activity that is resonant with both the social setting that encompasses a community of learners, as well as the cultural identity of the learners themselves" [22]. Sociocultural constructionism yields an approach to community technology that regards community members as the active producers of community information and content, rather than passive consumers or recipients. In practice, the asset-based community development and sociocultural constructionist frameworks help operationalize a methodology for integrating community technology and community building.

4 Camfield Estates-MIT Project Methodology

In June 2000, the project committee outlined a methodology to integrate community technology and community building, consisting of five interrelated, and at times parallel phases (Figure 1)

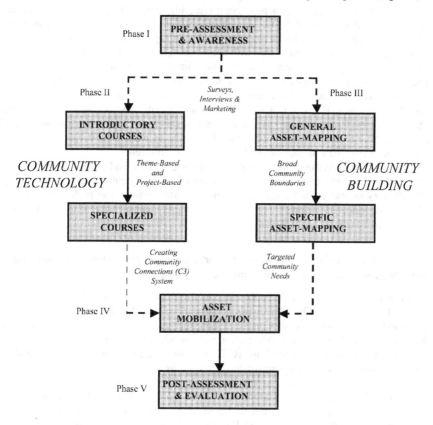

Fig. 1. Project Methodology

Phase I: Pre-assessment and Awareness

During the summer 2000, we developed a pre-assessment survey instrument to collect data in the following areas: *community interests and satisfaction, social networks (strong and weak ties), neighboring, awareness of community resources, community satisfaction, community involvement, empowerment, self-sufficiency, computer experience, hobbies, interests and information needs, assets and income, and demographics.* The survey was designed for two purposes. First, to provide strategic direction for the community building and community technology initiative by identifying the interests and needs of residents. This information would shape the nature of online and offline activities to be planned in the future. Second, to provide baseline and formative data for the research study. This information would be used to perform a comparative analysis of a similar data set to be gathered approximately one-year later.

During this same period, an awareness campaign was conducted to inform residents about the initiative. A series of mailings were distributed describing the project's goals and objectives, and offering a new computer, high-speed Internet connection, and comprehensive courses at NTC, for adults 18-years and older that completed the courses, completed the preliminary interview, and signed an informed consent form granting permission to track the web-traffic at Camfield through a proxy server (aggregate patterns of use only, and not individually attributable). An open forum was also held in the community center for questions and answers. While families were encouraged to attend the training, at least one adult from each household had to fulfill these requirements in order to receive the computer and Internet access. Given the fact that NTC was primarily used by youth at this time [19], it was the decision of the committee to restrict participation to adults only, as we believed it would motivate parents to attend the training for the benefit of their children.

August 2000 marked the deadline to sign-up for the project, and 33 of the 66 occupied units at Camfield elected to participate in Round I. Subsequently, and just prior to the introductory courses, three committee members administered the preliminary survey via one-on-one interviews with each of these participants (lasting between approximately one and four hours).

Phase II: Community Technology – Introductory and Specialized Courses and the Creating Community Connections (C3) System

From September to October 2000, introductory courses were offered at NTC to Round I participants. The project-based curriculum lasted eight weeks (two sessions per week, two hours per session) and covered various aspects of computer and Internet use. In November 2000, specialized courses were offered on how to use the Creating Community Connections (C3) System, available through the Camfield Estates website (http://www.camfieldestates.net), as shown in Figure 2. Whereas the introductory curriculum was designed solely by Williams Consulting Services, with input from MIT, the C3 curriculum was co-designed by both parties. C3 is a web-based, community building system designed to establish and strengthen relationships between community residents, local businesses, and neighborhood institutions (e.g., libraries, schools, etc.) and organizations. Designed at the MIT Media Laboratory using the ArsDigita Community System, and based on the principles of sociocultural constructionism and asset-based community development, C3 facilitates community communication and information exchange, as well as asset-mapping and asset mobilization.

In November 2000, 31 families received computers, software, and subsequent high-speed Internet access, having fulfilled the aforementioned requirements. In January 2001, a second awareness campaign was conducted and aimed at the 47 families still eligible for the project (the number of occupied units had increased from 66 to 80), including another round of mailings and meetings. After the second deadline passed, only 8 families elected to participate in project, the majority of whom were Spanish-speaking, as we were late distributing the flyers in their native-language during Round I.

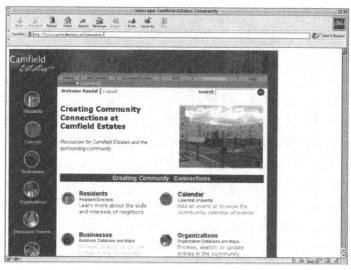

Fig. 2. The Creating Community Connections (C3) System

Phase III: Community Building–General and Specific Asset-Mapping

Per the asset-based community development approach, a resident-led general asset-mapping took place during the summer 2000, with technical assistance from researchers at MIT. It consisted of mapping all the organizations, institutions (e.g., libraries, schools, etc.), and businesses within an approximately 1.5-mile radius of Camfield, as shown in Figure 3. This broad attempt to identify community resources was done to obtain local information of potential benefit to residents that would eventually be made available through C3, and as a preparatory step for more specific asset-mapping to be conducted after analyzing the results of the pre-assessment. Not surprisingly, the mere process of gathering this information served to heighten residents' awareness of assets in their own neighborhood. For example, the first-pass general asset-map was conducted within a few square blocks of the property. Residents soon discovered there were very few organizations and institutions in this catchment area, and only a small cluster of businesses. The decision was then made to expand the radius of the asset-map to 1.5 miles, which captured approximately 757 businesses, 178 organizations, 67 churches, and 29 schools.

Specific asset-mapping began in November 2000, and consisted of mapping the formal and informal skills of residents, as well as a more detailed mapping of a targeted sample of the organizations, institutions, and businesses previously identified during general asset-mapping. The former activity took place during the final two weeks of the introductory and specialized courses. Using C3, residents entered their formal and informal skills and interests, by selecting from an inventory of more than 150 items. Given this information, residents could now use C3 to identify neighbors who could perform plumbing, babysitting, web design, etc., or, neighbors who were interested in learning these skills. Again, residents were often pleasantly surprised to learn about the talents and abilities of their neighbors. The latter activity is presently underway, and is being informed by the results of the pre-assessment. For example, Table 1 lists the issues deemed important according to residents.

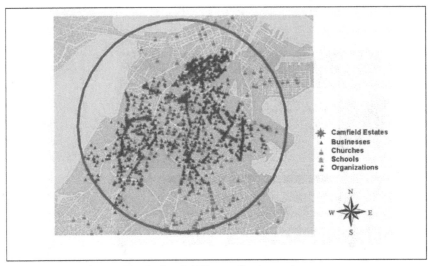

Fig. 3. Camfield Estates Catchment Area

Table 1. Issues Deemed Important by Residents

Issue	Rank	*Issue*	Rank
Safety/environment	1	Child care	6
Employment	2	Parenting	7
Housing	2	Community activism	8
Education	4	Political involvement	9
Health care	5		

During general asset-mapping, only basic information was obtained for community organizations, institutions, and businesses (e.g., name, address, contact information, products/services for businesses, programs/services for organizations and institutions, etc.). During specific asset-mapping, to begin addressing issues such as child care and health care we can obtain more detailed data (e.g., hours of operation, eligibility, fees, etc.) on this focused subset of the community resources deemed important to residents, who can then publish this information online using C3. We can also involve the resident social services coordinator in connecting residents to these programs/services.

Phase IV: Online and Offline Asset-Mobilization

Asset-mobilization involves devising strategies to create community connections between residents, organizations, institutions, and businesses, which previously did not exist, toward achieving specific outcomes. Asset-mobilization will be heavily informed by the pre-assessment, and will likely involve outreach and the formation of new community partnerships. For example, Table 2 identifies items residents would like to see made available on the Camfield website.

Table 2. Items Desired for Website by Residents

Item	Rank	Item	Rank
Employment opportunities	1	Volunteer opportunities	10
Camfield resident's information	2	Organization information	11
Education	3	Weather	12
Local news	4	Sports	13
Safety	5	Regional and national news	14
Government information	6	Classifieds (want ads)	14
Health care	7	Electronic commerce	14
Community calendar of activities and events	7	Online forums and discussion groups	17
Business information	9	Arts and entertainment	18

Several of these items are now available through the C3 system, such as the resident profiles module. However, based on these results we will continue to add new modules including a job posting board, and education- and safety-related features, by partnering with relevant community entities.

We anticipate residents connecting with other residents (e.g., leveraging neighbors skills, interests, etc.), local organizations and institutions (e.g., utilizing services, programs, etc.), and neighborhood businesses (e.g., identifying products, services, etc.). Some examples include parents exchanging their child-rearing practices via e-mail, NTC classmates relying on one another to solve technical problems in a chat room, residents identifying volunteer opportunities from a discussion forum, or adults obtaining a new job from employment postings available online.

We also anticipate residents producing information and content on the Internet that reflects their interests and needs, and explicates knowledge indigenous to the community. This will be done by creating personal websites, configuring e-mail lists, posting messages to the discussion forums, and contributing activities to the community calendar of events. Some examples include a group of single mothers creating an e-mail list to discuss their experiences, a senior creating a website containing her favorite recipes, the tenants association publishing their newsletter electronically, and the social service coordinator advertising activities on the community calendar of events.

CTA and MIT will continue to work closely with residents and the broader community to leverage the established infrastructure and demonstrate the possibilities resulting from an asset-based approach to community technology and community building.

Phase V: Post-assessment and Evaluation

In summer 2001, a post-assessment and evaluation will be conducted. At that time, a comparative analysis will be performed against the pre-assessment interviews and other sources of data (proxy server logs, C3 server logs, direct observation) to quantify and qualify our progress to-date.

5 Recommendations

The following five recommendations are offered for other community technology and community building initiatives. They are not presented as strict rules to follow, but rather lessons learned as a result of our experience with the Camfield Estates-MIT project thus far.

- *Demonstrate relevance clearly.* At times, it has required nothing short of going door-to-door to demonstrate the relevance of technology, as evidenced by the grassroots mobilization required to solicit Round II participants. We have endeavored to demonstrate relevance in two particular ways. First, by providing a curriculum that is project-based and combines a variety of learning objectives, rather than focusing on narrow skill development such as how to use a mouse or a keyboard. For example, to teach participants how to use a browser and the printer, they are instructed to use a search engine to locate information on a topic of interest to them, print out each of their results, and summarize which search terms and associated results they found to be useful. Second, by emphasizing outcomes instead of access. For example, an elderly woman at Camfield was one of the project's staunchest opponents. Upon initial contact, she flatly refused being involved. Rather than focusing on the computer and Internet service (access) as a selling point, one of the instructors introduced her to the information she could obtain online and the people with whom she could communicate to improve her quality-of-life (outcomes). A few weeks later, she commented, "This computer is better than all of my medication combined!" Other initiatives have expressed similar observations [4].

- *Link curriculum to outcomes.* One of the areas we improved upon between the Round I courses and the Round II courses, was linking the curriculum to our desired outcomes. The Round I curriculum was more generic when compared to the Round II curriculum, which achieved greater depth with respect to how technology could support community building. We dedicated more time to learning the C3 modules, and exploring how these modules could improve communication at the development. Furthermore, once the results of the pre-assessment were compiled, we were able to follow-up the project-based curriculum, and couple it with a theme-based curriculum. These thematic workshops (e.g., using online educational resources) were designed around the areas deemed important by residents, as articulated during the preliminary interviews.

- *Establish multi-sector collaborations to build capacity and promote sustainability.* CTA has established relationships with universities, government agencies, corporations, foundations, nonprofit organizations, and neighboring tenants associations. HUD and MHFA have played a critical role with respect to the demo-dispo program, which will ensure NTC remains operational. Support from Kellogg, Hewlett-Packard, Microsoft, and others, has been instrumental in establishing a state-of-the-art technological infrastructure. MIT's strength in areas such as research, education and technology positioned the institute to provide useful technical assistance, evaluation, software development, and more. Similarly, each of the remaining entities, which span the public, private, and nonprofit sectors, has contributed something different, yet valuable to sustaining this initiative.   However, it is CTA's demonstrated commitment to internal capacity-building, which is strengthened by their ability to cultivate and leverage these relationships, that ultimately bodes well for these efforts to be sustained.

- *Engage residents as active participants in the process.* Although the Camfield Estates-MIT project was initially proposed by MIT to CTA, MIT researchers did not approach this initiative as if we had all the answers. Instead, we have worked hard to create an atmosphere of trust and mutual respect with CTA and the broader community at Camfield. The process has not been easy, rather, it has required relationship building, commitment, patience, and empathic listening on both sides. From the beginning, CTA and MIT recognized that these foundational elements were fundamental to the project's success.   Collectively, we acknowledged that for residents to feel a sense of ownership and empowerment, they must be actively involved in the process.

6 Conclusion

The digital divide is a modern day reflection of historical social divides that have plagued our society for years.   Over the past decade, the community technology movement has gathered momentum toward closing the gap with programs targeted at areas such as education, health care, employment, economic development, and more. Meanwhile, the community building movement has wrestled with directly related issues such as the war on poverty, and instituted programs aimed at identical outcomes, for more than a century.

The intersection between these domains holds tremendous possibilities, as both efforts seek to empower individuals and families, and improve their overall community. Ironically, approaches that combine these areas have received very little attention in theory and in practice.   In fact, community technology efforts are often completely decoupled from community building initiatives.

From among the three models of community engagement with technology – community computing centers, community networks, and community content [1] – there are a limited number of projects that have engaged community residents as active participants in using technology to define processes for neighborhood revitalization.   Conversely, from among the multitude of models for community engagement with revitalization – such as community organizing, community development, community building, and comprehensive community initiatives (CCIs) [32] – we are only beginning to witness the benefits that are afforded by incorporating new technologies into these approaches in a way that truly leverages their potential.

The best practices of community technology see community members as the active producers of community content.   Similarly, the best practices of community building see community members as active agents of change.   As community technology and community building initiatives move toward greater synergy, there is a great deal to be learned regarding how community technology and community building can be mutually supportive, rather than mutually exclusive.

In this regard, our goal to establish Camfield as a model for other communities manifests itself in two ways. First, as a methodology that can be replicated in other communities seeking to strengthen relationships between residents, organizations, and businesses in their neighborhood. Second, as an example that demonstrates the limitless possibilities when community members are engaged as active, rather than passive participants in the process. We are only beginning to witness the wonderful stories that will emerge from the Camfield Estates-MIT Creating Community Connections project. Years from now we expect to see new areas within cyberspace that belong not only to residents at Camfield Estates, but other low- to moderate-income communities across the globe.

References

[1]   Beamish, A. (1999). Approaches to Community Computing: Bringing Technology to Low-Income Groups. *High Technology in Low-Income Communities: Prospects for the Positive Use of Information Technology* (pp. 349-368) D. Schön, B. Sanyal, & W. J. Mitchell (Eds.). Cambridge, MA: MIT Press.

[2]   Benton Foundation. (1998). *Losing Ground Bit by Bit: Low-Income Communities in the Information Age.* Washington, DC: Benton Foundation.
       (http://www.benton.org/Library/Low-Income/home.html)

[3]   Bishop, A P., Tidline, T. J., Shoemaker, S., & Salela, P. (1999). *Public Libraries and Networked Information Services in Low-Income Communities.* Urbana-Champaign, IL: Graduate School of Library and Information Science, University of Illinois at Urbana-Champaign.

[4]   Cohill, A. M. & Kavanaugh, A. L. (1997). *Community Networks: Lessons from Blacksburg, Virginia.* Blacksburg, VA: Artech House Telecommunications Library.

[5]   Chapman, G. & Rhodes L. (1997). Nurturing Neighborhood Nets. *Technology Review,* October.

[6]   Chow, C., Ellis, J., Mark, J., & Wise, B. (1998). *Impact of CTCNet Affiliates: Findings from a National Survey of Users of Community Technology Centers.* Newton, MA: Education Development Center, Inc. (http://www.ctcnetorg/impact98.html)

[7]   Hooper, P. (1998). They Have Their Own Thoughts: Children's Learning of Computational Ideas from a Cultural Constructionist Perspective. Unpublished Ph.D. Dissertation. Cambridge, MA: MIT Media Laboratory.

[8]   Kingsley, G. T., McNeely, J. B., Gibson, J. O. (1999). *Community Building Coming of Age.* The Urban Institute. (http://www.urban.org/comminity/combuild.htm)

[9]   Kretzmann, J. P., & McKnight, J. L. (1993). Building Communities from the Inside Out: A Path Toward Finding and Mobilizing a Community's Assets. Chicago, IL: ACTA Publications.

[10]   Lazarus, W. & Mora, F. (2000). *On-line Content for Low-Income and Underserved Americans: The Digital Divide's New Frontier.* Santa Monica, CA: The Children's Partnership. (http://www.childrenspartnership.org)

[11]   Mark, J., Cornebise, J., & Wahl, E. (1997). *Community Technology Centers: Impact on Individual Participants and their Communities.* Newton, MA: Educational Development Center, Inc. (http://www.ctcnetorg/eval.html)

[12]   Mattessich, Paul, Monsey, Barbara. (1997). Community Building: What Makes It Work: A Review of Factors Influencing Successful Community Building. Saint Paul, MN: Amherst H. Wilder Foundation.

[13] Melchior, A., Thorstensen, B., & Shurkin, M. (1998). *The Uses of Technology in Youth-Serving Organizations: An Initial Scan of the Field.* Waltham, MA: The Center for Human Resources, Bandeis University.

[14] Morino, M. (1994). *Assessment and Evolution of Community Networking.* Paper presented at Ties That Bind, at Apple Computer, Cupertino, CA.

[15] National Telecommunication and Information Administration (1995). *Falling Through the Net Full Report.* (http://www.ntia.doc.gov/ntiahome/fallingthru.html)

[16] National Telecommunication and Information Administration (1997). *Falling Through the Net II: New Data on the Digital Divide.* Full Report.
(http://www.ntia.doc.gov/ntiahome/net2/falling.html)

[17] National Telecommunication and Information Administration (1999). *Falling Through the Net III: Defining the Digital Divide.* Full Report.
(http://www.ntia.doc.gov/ntiahome/ digitaldivide/)

[18] National Telecommunication and Information Administration (2000). *Falling Through the Net:Toward Digital Inclusion.* Full Report.
(http://www.ntia.doc.gov/ntiahome/fttn00/contents00.html)

[19] O'Bryant, R. (2001). Establishing Neighborhood Technology Centers in Low-Income Communities: A Crossroads for Social Science and Computer Information Technology. Forthcoming in *Projections: The MIT Student Journal of Planning–Making Places through Information Technology* (2) 2.

[20] Papert, S., A. (1993). Instructionism vs. Constructionism. In Papert, S. *The Children's Machine.* New York, NY: Basic Books.

[21] Pinkett, R. D. (2002). The Camfield Estates-MIT Creating Community Connections Project: High-Technology in a Low- to Moderate-Income Community. Forthcoming in *Managing IT/Community Partnerships in the 21st Century.* Lazar, J. (Ed.). Hershey, PA: Idea Publishing Group.

[22] Pinkett, R. D. (2000). Bridging the Digital Divide: Sociocultural Constructionism and an Asset-Based Approach to Community Technology and Community Building. Paper presented at the 81st Annual Meeting of the American Educational Research Association (AERA), New Orleans, LA, April 24-28.
(http://www.media.mit.edu/~rpinkett/papers/aera2000.pdf)

[23] Resnick, M., Bruckman, A. & Martin, F. (1996). Pianos Not Stereos: Creating Computational Construction Kits. *Interactions*, (3) 6, September/October.
(http://el.www.media.mit.edu/el/Papers/mres/chi-98/digital-manip.html)

[24] Resnick, M, Rusk, N. & Cooke, S. (1998). The Computer Clubhouse: Technological Fluency in the Inner City. *High Technology in Low-Income Communities: Prospects for the Positive Use of Information Technology* (pp. 263-286) Schön, D., Sanyal B., & Mitchell, W. J. (Eds.). Cambridge, MA: MIT Press.

[25] Robinson, R. (2000). *The Role of Information Technology in Economic Development of the Inner City.* In Proceedings of the 2000 Inner City Business Leadership Conference, Boston, MA, November.

[26] Massachusetts Housing Finance Agency (2001). MHFA's Demonstration Disposition (DemoDispo) Program History. (http://www.mhfa.com/dev/dp_ddhistory.htm)

[27] Schön, Donald A., Sanyal, Bish, & Mitchell, William J. (Eds.). (1999). High Technology and Low-Income Communities: Prospects for he Positive Use Of Advanced Information Technology. Cambridge, MA: MIT Press.

[28] Shaw, Alan C. (1995). Social Constructionism and the Inner City: Designing Environments for Social Development and Urban Renewal. Unpublished Ph.D. Dissertation. Cambridge, MA: MIT Media Laboratory.

[29] Shaw, A. & Shaw M. (1998). Social Empowerment Through Community Networks. *High Technology in Low-Income Communities: Prospects for the Positive Use of Information Technology* (pp. 316-335) D. Schön, B. Sanyal, & W. J. Mitchell (Eds.). Cambridge, MA: MIT Press.

[30] The Aspen Institute. (1997). *Voices from the Field: Learning from the Early Work of Comprehensive Community Initiatives*. Washington, DC: The Aspen Institute. (http://www.aspenroundtable.org/voices/index.htm)

[31] Turner, N. E., & Pinkett, R. D. (2000). *An Asset-Based Approach to Community Technology and Community Building*. Proceedings of Shaping the Network Society: The Future of the Public Sphere in Cyberspace, Directions and Implications of Advanced Computing Symposium 2000 (DIAC-2000), Seattle, WA, May 20-23. (http://www.media.mit.edu/~rpinkett/papers/diac2000.pdf)

[32] Hess, D. R. (1999). *Community Organizing, Building and Developing: Their Relationship to Comprehensive Community Initiatives*. Working paper series for COMM-ORG: The On-Line Conference on Community Organizing and Development, June. (http://comm-org.utoledo.edu/papers99/hess.html)

Community Websites as a Local Communication Network: "Directory Westfield", an Experience Report

Karrie J. Hanson and Gerald M. Karam

AT&T Labs-Research, Florham Park, NJ USA
karrie@research.att.com

1. Introduction

A small crisis occurred in the town of *Westfield, New Jersey* (NJ) in 1999 when *NJ Transit* (the local commuter railway), citing safety problems, changed their policy of allowing organizations to drape signs for town events and celebrations along the Raritan Valley railway trestles that form a gateway to the downtown area. Newspaper articles, window postings, even mailings to the homes are far more onerous and expensive, and much less effective than a couple of huge banners proclaiming "Jazz Week", or the Community Players latest show over the two major arteries into town. Even in the age of seemingly ubiquitous information, the loss of a sign across a railroad trestle was cause for uproar. The crisis reflected the recognition by townspeople that communications form the core of the community, and they had just lost an important node in their local social network.

We are approaching the day when every local community will be up on the web, yet we are still far from making those sites even approach the dynamic interactive social and commercial node that exists at the corner of Main and Elm in town on a Saturday morning or have the impact of the sign across the bridge trestle. We define a "community site" as not only an information source, but also a site that supports the dynamic and unedited contributions of many people, and includes the discussions and transactions that constitute the normal business of a community. In this sense, we are far from the goal.

To understand the type and design of Internet and telephony tools that would be needed for a local community site, we created an ad hoc service in the town of Westfield, NJ, starting in July 1996. The site was titled *Directory Westfield* (DW). Our notion was to design a site in a generic fashion – which might apply to any town or community - but tailor it to fit Westfield's needs. The objective of the DW project was to create a set services that would evolve into a collaborative "intranet website" that would foster the existing connections and activities already occurring via the existing person-to-person "networks" in the town.

Many other communities have built useful and interactive sites. An often-cited example is Blacksburg, Virginia, which has several sites including one sponsored by the local government, http://www.blacksburg.gov, and the classics "Blacksburg Electronic Village", http://www.bev.org and Seattle Community Network, http://www.scn.org. Community sites for local town and neighborhoods are so prevalent that it is unusual to find a town without a site (NJ has over 400), and many communities have a number of sites covering different aspects of the town. But a

M. Tanabe, P. van den Besselaar, T. Ishida (Eds.): Digital Cities, LNCS 2362, pp. 125–138, 2002.

personal survey of over 200 local sites confirms that the management of content continues to be a challenge. Outdated content is prevalent. To manage the "information maintenance problem", many town sites have posted only a very low level of information (for example lists of services with no way to contact them). Community sites tend to follow one of two models. The most common approach is (A) "webmaster approach", where all the content and updates are funneled through a "webmaster" (a single person or small group of people) who convert the information to html and loads the pages to the server. This approach is workable for a small site but rapidly overwhelms the webmaster. "Webmaster controlled" sites have few uncontrolled community contributions other than discussion boards and possibly event calendars. They have the advantage of being cohesive, with a common "look and feel" and coherent navigation. Also, contributions from web novices is possible, because the webmaster does the actual technical work. Another approach is (B) the "page hosting" or "hackers paradise" model (for example, the Seattle Community Network), where participants may upload entire web pages to a common community server. The community site is essentially a page of links to independently produced content. This approach lacks a common look and feel, and frequently has navigational disconnects to the common site. Although it is a terrific solution if the community is technically advanced, the lack of the ability to publish is currently a "show stopper" for the majority of participants in a local community at this time. Tools to support community networks are beginning to appear that will offer a third approach. Simple self-publishing sites, such as http://www.sidewalk.com , http://clicktown.com offer systematic approaches to manage and categorize "mini-sites" within a geographic community. These sites can be attractive collections of announcements or advertisements, but the advertising model of support is waning, and the economic viability of this approach is as yet unproven. (A list of site references is included in the appendix.) We began an experiment "self publishing type" community site five years ago in Westfield NJ that is the subject of this paper.

In this paper, we review the DW project and describe the evolving software. We summarize the relationships with the business and community contributors to the web site. We evaluate the reaction to the project from three groups involved: the public, the business owners, and the business partners. And finally, we discuss the software innovations that we believe would be helpful in achieving a highly interactive, communications-oriented and manageable community experience on the web.

2. The Site

We began building a directory-based town website about January 1996. The target town was Westfield, NJ, a community of about 28,000 people in central New Jersey. Westfield is located within a comfortable commuting distance to New York City as well as to the technology and pharmaceutical companies in northern New Jersey. It is an "upscale" town, with a base of turn-of-the-century housing, an excellent public school system and a long tradition of civic volunteering.

We chose a directory structure for the site because it is a well-understood and comfortable format for users, and easily extensible as nearly every part of a directory listing could be turned into a "clickable" choice. A flexible, and technologically advanced directory could be evolve to become an exciting portal or town square for a real community and it had the potential to become a revenue generator for the sponsor or owner of the site.

2.1 Site Tour

The home pages from the original and current "Directory Westfield" (DW) are shown in Figure 1. The original page consisted only of a simple navigation path to the DW listings, and offered a "Westfield-only" version of a white pages directory. The page eventually evolved to a "community portal", as shown below.

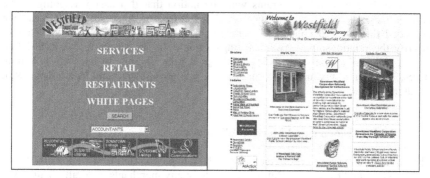

Fig. 1. The original (left) and current home page for "Directory Westfield."

A typical DW listing is shown in Figure 2. The data consisted of an image, the store name, a small image of the store logo, the store hours, the address, the phone number, the fax number, an email address, and a text field used for the store description. We discovered that this was not enough information for many merchants; so each listing is allowed to have up to three additional links for images of menus, other photos or text pages.

Fig. 2. The DW Listing Page

The data for each merchant is stored in a database and the pages are dynamically created upon a web query. By using this approach, we were able to allow the user to make a limited set of queries to the database to view collections of listings organized in different ways that take advantage of the relational properties of the information. For example, we offered queries such as "show me the other stores on the same block" (NEIGHBORHOODS), or "show me other stores related to this one" (PSST!). For example, clicking on NEIGHBORHOODS from the children's bookstore retrieves a page of links to the directory listings for all of the stores on the same street as the currently displayed listing.

The PSST!, button is aimed at revealing relationships between the listings that the user would find helpful. For example, the movies and entertainment listings were related to the cafes and restaurants with the notion that if a user was going to the movies, they may also want to have a cup of coffee or dinner in town. Later we expanded this idea to consumer segments (people with children, seniors, etc.) to identify the relationships between listings. For example, selecting the PSST! link from a children's shoe store listing produces a page of links to children's clothing stores, children's matinee performances at the symphony, and restaurants with children's menus.

2.2 Initial Provisioning and Merchant Responses

The initial directory was restricted only to the downtown merchants (about 100), and was provisioned "by hand". Before approaching any merchants, a "draft" listing was prepared for them by taking a photo of their storefront and inserting the name and address into the template. The Chamber of Commerce, the Downtown Mainstreet Organization[1] and the Westfield Police Department were also notified of the project. Each of the first 20 merchants was approached individually. We described the project and showed them a paper mock-up of their directory listing, with open spaces for the information needed. We also described the project as an unbranded trial of *AT&T Labs-Research* (Research), and we made the commitment to keep the directory online for one year. The listings were offered for free. If members wished to change the data on their website, they contacted us by email or phone.

The project was positioned to the local merchants as a marketing opportunity, as well as an inexpensive way to become familiar with a new technology. The reaction from the local merchants was ultimately very positive, but they did not make their decisions quickly. Most opted to join the directory and decided in about a week. Reactions varied from complete lack of knowledge of the Internet ("can you explain this internet thing again?") to suspicion of the Internet (about half felt irritated by the whole idea of the internet- "why do I need this?") to gratefulness and relief (about 30 to 40% welcomed the project because they felt they should be doing something with the internet but didn't know how to start). Typically the merchant requested time think about it, then called the police, the Main Street Organization or the Chamber of Commerce in town to see if they knew about the project, then finally requested a listing. At the end of the two-month initial sign up period, about 90% of the stores we approached decided to participate. The major driver for most merchants, was

---

[1] The "Main Street" program is a national organization affiliated with "National Trust for Historic Preservation" located in Washington D.C. Their website: http://www.mainstreet.org

knowledge that their neighboring stores were participating. Several merchants agreed to be part of the directory, not because they expected it to impact their business, but because they perceived that it would be "good for the town".

At the time of the launch, there were about five nationally branded stores in Westfield including The Gap and Woolworths. Because no one on-premises in these stores was able to be a decision-maker for this offer, the arrangements had to be handled at corporate headquarters -- a drawn-out interaction. Although interested in the offer, the national firms felt that they needed a company-wide Internet policy. At that time, none of the national stores had Internet sites of their own. The local network that enticed the local stores had no impact on the corporate headquarters' decision. However, once national stores started to participate in the directory, the local stores because more eager to join.

2.3 Debut

The initial site went live as http://www.quintillion.com/westfield on July 23, 1996. The site was featured in several newspapers and a New York City local news team covered the story for the local ABC news affiliate. The site is currently hosted at http://westfieldnj.ataclick.com.

3. Site Design

There are at least four perspectives on the DW project, and each of these roles had different needs and expectations for their portion of the site. The four roles we consider here are *public*, *member*, *sponsor* and *webmaster*. Each of these roles had access to a different set of information on the website.

The public site is open to anyone but targeted to the town residents. We envisioned an "insiders" portal – a site rich with relevant information that would make living in the town easier and more interesting. Later we realized that another perspective on the public view of the page was that of people living *outside* of the town – either former residents or people looking to move to the town, shop in the town or apply for a job in the town. Their need was for information that was organized in a different way, with more explanations and guidance.

The member role is the retail or service merchant, a businessperson or a member of a non-profit group. The member site is restricted to those with the user name and password obtained at provisioning. Members needed a simple and quick method of posting their information (or someone to do it for them), and feedback on whether people were looking at their site. As we worked with this group over several years, a number of ideas for of web services that would "plug in" to their listing emerged. Most of these, such as "audio message" were concepts that members felt would enable them to improve their businesses or work. We developed and trialed a few of these ideas and describe the results later in the paper. Other "plug-in" services were related to messaging, transactions, and image handling or information management.

The sponsor role is a local representative of the town who supplies an affiliation to the project and may also supply or provide editorial review of the content, as well as staff. This role is distinct from that of "owner" - defined as the owner and operator of the service. Three different groups occupied the "sponsor" role over the course of this project. At the start of the project, Research acted as owner and sponsor, but we realized that we needed a local partner, both to be a local contact for the members, and a supplier of interesting top-pages content. We also felt that the results of the partnership would help us understand how to build a credible business case for a local directory. During the course of this project, we worked with both a local paper, *The Westfield Leader* and a local downtown development group called *Downtown Westfield Corporation* (DWC) in the role of sponsor.

3.1 The Public Site

The public site structure has a top page (shown in Figure 1), about 20 *subject* pages to support the primary content and the directory (about 20 category pages and the directory, which fluctuated between 200 and 350 listings. The original directory structure was based on a local downtown directory that was published by the Main Street organization. The listings were organized into two tiers of categories. The top-level categories (Shops and Stores, Services, and Restaurants) led to a collection of sub-categories, and each sub-category page shows a collection of listings. This top set of categories later expanded to "Entertainment", "Services", "Shops and Stores" and "Food and Drink". The user browses through these sets of categories and sub-categories to find a listing.

Although the key feature of the DW site is the collection of owner-maintained listings, we found that the listings alone were not sufficient to sustain a reasonable level of public interest in the site. This led us to develop the home page and top levels of the site as a community portal, which would serve to draw people into the site. Thus, we had to expand our role of "owner" from simply fixing technical problems with the site, to becoming a "local correspondent" for reporting the events and some news. The home page evolved to feature current events, a town calendar, pointers to listings in the directory and a collection of important links for the town. We converged on a mix of calendar and community event information as well as more detailed information about the downtown and schools. Later we offered a threaded bulletin board service for town discussion groups.

Drawing attention to the listings. Treating all directory listings in the same way, from the point of view of navigation, led to a problem. This approach treated merchants who actively updated their site equally with merchants who never touched their site, and did not encourage updating. Readers were not pointed to the most recent content, and merchants were not rewarded for their efforts to keep the site current. We addressed this issue by altering the software to selectively promote recently modified listings ("bubble up") and by adding a feature called "Click of the Week" to promote active site owners with additional marketing on the top page.

Bigger than a listing, not quite a website. The core of the DW design is the listing page, shown in Figure 2. Since these pages are effectively all advertisements for the owners, the first impression for a reader would establish the branding of the page. Therefore, the directory template was designed to be as transparent as possible, so that the owner's content and message would dominate the page. Since photographs can convey a strong and emotional impression to the viewer, we chose a single photograph of the storefront as the dominant feature of listing page. This choice proved to be a workable solution as the image conveys, for better or for worse[2], a snap shot of the actual image the merchant conveys to their customers, including their signage and branding.

We found that sports teams, or scout troops, or non-profit groups were also interested in using the directory to bring their messages into a community space. Since we had based our design on storefronts, the option of only one template was somewhat limiting for these groups.

3.2 The Member Role

About two years after the launch, we released the *Member Update* version of the site that allowed members of the directory to easily provision and update their listing. The member site is a collection of forms that allow the user to add, edit and delete text and image data. It was designed for the novice Internet user. Text data was typed in and images could be uploaded from the client PC. Figure 3 shows an excerpt from the user interface of this site.

Fig. 3. The "Merchant Update" site

Early in the project we realized that we were asking shop owners to place ads or communicate with their customers (from their point of view) in a medium that most of them could not see. At that time, most had no Internet connection at all, and those that did were connected at home and not at the store location. Nevertheless, there was intense interest in the web and the possibilities for their businesses. There was a need for listing owners to be able to use the communications devices they had on hand, a telephone and in some cases, a fax machine, to update and interact with their website.

---

[2] A couple of merchants actually changed their signs and straightened up the front of the store after we posted the directory. Apparently the peeling paint became visible when viewed from this perspective.

The *Audio Daily* service was devised as method to update a listing without using a PC. The Audio Daily is a link to an audio file that appears on a directory listing. When clicked, the public hears an audio message on their computer that had been recorded by the storeowner using a conventional telephone. The members provisions the actual text of the link through the merchant update website, and once activated, the audio file is updated using a telephone. The user experience was designed to be simple and intuitive – similar to that of an answering machine. The service is implemented with a toll-free phone number, user ID, and a personal identification number (PIN). To record a new message, members call, and authenticate with a user ID and PIN, and then are prompted to record, listen to, or delete their message. This service is used most by restaurants to record the daily specials for the evening meals.

3.3 The Sponsor Role

One problem we faced early on was the issue of getting relevant, interesting and timely content for the site to attract viewers on a daily or weekly basis. The content issue drives an important aspect of the project: a sponsor was needed who was local, credible, able to provide a source of interesting content, and have a vision for creating a community site.   From this perspective, the possibilities in Westfield included the two town papers, the town government, the Chamber of Commerce, and the Westfield Mainstreet program, a downtown improvement association.   At the time, most of these organizations were new to email; none of them had a website, so we needed to bolster the web capabilities of the partner. We felt that a local paper would be the partner with the most local content, an existing relationship with the local merchants, and a potential business case for a local website.

Newspaper Relationship:
Westfield has two small weekly town newspapers, The Westfield Leader or Leader and the Westfield Record. The Westfield Leader is a family-owned local paper that has been in business in Westfield for 112 years and has paid circulation to about 8000 homes (in 2001). We approached the owner of the Leader in October 1996 to begin talks on establishing a joint web presence in Westfield. At that time, the newspaper had no web presence but one owner believed that the Internet was a critical piece of their long-term strategy. After several talks we initiated a business relationship with the following agreements:
- Research would co-develop a website for the newspaper and host the site for 1 year. Both the DW and Leader site would link to each other. We would jointly promote the site.
- The Leader would provide local news content up for the front page of the directory site.
- Leader could sell enhanced DW listings – i.e. sites with additional pages, menus, etc., and retain all the revenue from the sales.

Based on this agreement, Research developed a series of web templates and designs for the Leader, and the new Leader news site was launched January 1, 1997. This site then provided a news feed to DW. The relationship lasted the full year of the agreement and did have some modest successes, but was not extended for 1998.

From the point of view of both parties, the relationship ultimately did not meet the original goals. In fact, as the relationship played out, the interests of the two parties became not aligned, but divergent. The main issues were as follows:

- The Leader really didn't have the staff, expertise, or time to post daily content to the web site. New updates of content were frequently weeks after the last installment. The news up on the site was usually dated and sketchy. The additional news on the site ultimately did not produce a significant increase in hits to the site. The staff was resistant to the project because they felt that the website would cut into their subscription base.

- The two web sites were in competition with each other. Both were seeking to become the dominant or premier site or portal (in terms of hits), for Westfield, and neither had the complete solution for the audience.

- The Leader's business case relied upon selling Directory listings, but since they were not custom sites, but simple template-based listings, they didn't feel they could charge very much. They tried to bundle advertising in the newspaper with a web presence but the estimated profits did not warrant the work involved. This reflected the fact that the merchant community was not ready for the Internet. Most merchants saw no real advantage to having a web presence, and did not have the capability or time to get involved.

- We had different visions for the project. The Leader vision for merchants was to create a small "marketplace" of custom sites (for which they would charge a nominal fee and bundle with newspaper advertising.) The Research vision was a complete directory of the downtown "sponsored" by the Leader with the merchants updating the site themselves.

Both groups realized that the market was not yet ready for this approach, and the relationship ended amicably, with both sites linking to the other on the front pages.

DWC Relationship:

Without the newspaper relationship, we needed a local affiliation and a source for content. In January 1998, we approached the newly formed Downtown Westfield Corporation (DWC) as a possible sponsor for the local directory/portal site. In return, the top pages of the site would be restructured to reflect the image of the DWC and prominently displayed information they wished to make public. The executive director was enthusiastic and the Board of Directors agreed. Initially, all the content management was done by the Research with some editorial review by DWC. In 1999, the DWC assumed responsibility for the content management and employs a part-time (about 10 hours/week) local "webmaster" to work with the merchants and update the top pages in the site. The site is positioned as a service to the local merchants (as part of the dues they pay to the DWC) and to the community.

This relationship has gone very smoothly and has benefits for both parties. The DWC needs were for local and regional marketing of their programs and events, establishing a point source for their information, establishing a brand image for themselves, and providing an interface for tourists and visitors for shopping or visiting the town. As they got more comfortable with the site, they began to use it in a more interactive way. For example, to build support for a downtown-parking garage, they established a "parking" forum in the threaded bulletin board on the site and the executive director directly answered many of the questions. This issue gripped the community and most of the town council and the mayor responded to questions on the bulletin board.   As town leaders were clearly involved in the discussion processes on the web, the site gained credibility.

Recently the DWC has taken a greater interest in contributing content and "look and feel" branding to the site, as well as continuing to provide Research with useful feedback regarding the Internet needs of local businesses and government. This information contributes to our work on Internet services and service infrastructure.

3.4 The Webmaster Role

The Webmaster view of the site had separate authentication and allowed access and editing of any listing. There is also a limited set of tools available, including tools to count the number of merchants, maintain email lists for merchants, and view the server logs.

4. Responses to the Project

4.1 Public

Log data and user surveys shows that the DW readership has steadily risen in the five years of the project, as shown in Figure 4. We can track the result of promotions and events such as elections (election results were posted on the site) in the daily servers logs of the site, but the general upswing in audience is likely due to the increase in Internet access in Westfield, consistent with national trends. Since the early phase of this project, the pages in the site that show consistent reader interest are the top index page (including the calendar information), the movie theater and restaurant listings. In the last year, certain retail sites have generated more interest. The top ten listings in the server logs are the theater, the DWC, four restaurants, and three clothing stores.

The DW audience hourly distribution is shown in Figure 5. This example shows an average over one month in 1999, but this pattern has not changed in the course of the experiment. During the week, there is a bimodal distribution of daily viewing, with over 60% of the pages viewed between 9AM and 5PM. An analysis of the domain names of the requests during the day revealed that the majority were from local employers in the area. Apparently readers are viewing the site from their place of work. Interviews with residents confirm that they use the site to stay in touch with their local community during breaks at work. They also appreciate the high-speed Internet connections in the workplace. The pattern of having a significant readership at work is important for the merchants to understand, as readers would like to interact with their local merchants online (and pick up the merchandise later).

An online survey, performed early in the project with about 150 self-selected web users, showed a great deal of interest in the *potential* of the site. The features most cited as attractive were the "availability of current information", "movie listings", "coupons", "the fact that it was truly local", and the "community calendar". This is corroborated by an analysis of the pages served.

There were also many issues for the public users. Feedback from our site and surveys indicated that, besides trouble with modem speeds, our readers had the following issues: "out-of-date information", "couldn't buy anything", "not interactive enough", "desire for an interactive Westfield government site", and "desire for only one Westfield community site, instead of many". More recently these comments have shifted to requests for more features, such as video of events and inside the stores, and transaction services.

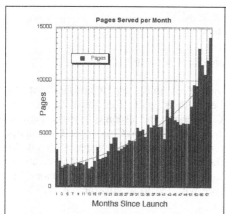

Fig. 4. Pages served per month since the launch of "Directory Westfield"

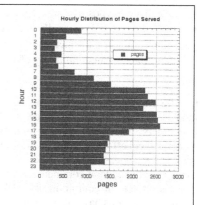

Fig. 5. Average distribution of pages served during a day.

4.2 Members

We had up to about 300 merchants on the site. Most were local Westfield merchants, although a few from outside the Westfield area found the site and listed themselves. At the end of one year, most merchants were enthusiastic about the site. However, updating the site was a major issue. Interviews with merchants revealed that the primary problem was a lack of an Internet connection and computer *in the store*. Although they liked the idea of having complete control over the site, they simply didn't have the means to update. Until the merchants or store workers can do the updating as a part of the business day, this will continue to be an obstacle. This initial behavior has been charged with markedly however and new merchants are updating their sites independently.

Nationally branded firms were interested in the site, and willing to update, but few actually did. We speculate that updating a local website was too great a stretch from the local store managers normal responsibilities. That early resistance is also yielding.

We also noted other issues for merchants updating their sites, including difficulties getting images in digital format for the site, and our lack of tools to provide feedback from the readers to the merchants. Without email or transaction tools to be in contact with their customers, merchants did not know if people were really using their site.

In contrast to the merchants, the non-profits groups, churches, teams, and clubs have responded very positively to the updating features and are much more willing and interested in using the site as an interactive meeting place.

4.3 Partners

A partial list of the goals and objectives of the Downtown Westfield Corporation for the site include:

- establishing a positive public image for the DWC
- market the DWC regionally and nationally
- attract and assist businesses in town
- unify the current community of web providers in Westfield

This year, the DWC has taken a more active role in the appearance and content of the site and this has brought the site closer to their goals of establishing a positive image and providing a rich source of DWC material. The response from the merchant community has been overwhelmingly positive, The DWC is poised to sharply increase their efforts to market the site in their literature and newspaper advertising. We have not measured the effect of the site on attracting new people and businesses to town, but anecdotal comments have indicated that it has been positive factor. Also, there is interest in combining the DWC site with the local government site, but no substantive actions have been taken.

5. Discussion

Can a community site on the Internet foster a real network as large as a town?

A team trying to build a community site continuously faces a dilemma of balance – if they define the community too narrowly, there is not enough interest or traffic to justify the work involved.   If they define the community too broadly, the content is shallow or not particularly interesting to anyone. In general, community sites seek to be a "one click" source of information for a community – and indeed, directories of information form the basis for many sites. The portal concept arises from the desire to become a valuable site for the largest possible number of people in the community in order to draw traffic to the site and justify the investment of time and money in the site.   But the specific interests and points of view of the contributors drive involvement in community projects.   As the portal sites become richer in any particular set of subjects, it will create tension from other groups with different points of view. For this reason, the goal of a single site for a community is a challenge to achieve. A thriving community is likely to have a number of large websites, each striving to become a portal. They will likely have a great deal of information in common. Coalitions of similar groups to sponsor sites will evolve as the demands of content generation and site management become apparent, and eventually the number of portal sites in a community will stabilize as competing needs become balanced. Stated or unstated, the goals of the competing sites are likely to be different.

The sponsor of a community website will determine, if not all the content, certainly the point of view and focus of energy.

The content in the site will then expand into new areas in the need to increase traffic to the site. The major interest groups that emerged from this study were the downtown (merchants, restaurants, theaters, as represented by the DWC), the schools, the non-profit groups, the local political parties and the municipal government. The interest group that had the strongest appeal to our readers, based on the server logs, was the downtown – especially the restaurants and theaters. However, the group most likely to publish new material, i.e. update their site, was the non-profit group, including the schools. The DW site encouraged involvement from all of these groups, but emphasized the downtown community. This captured a shared interest in the town, but relied upon the participation of merchants who were mostly reluctant or unable to write directly to the site. As we incorporated more content and involvement from non-profit groups, conflict emerged from time to time over the presentation of the public face of the town. This tension arises from conflicts between the community contributors over the goals for the site.

Consider the interaction with a local group called "BRAKES". The group was active in trying to make the streets safer by encouraging motorists to slow down and trying to get people to walk and bicycle more. After several tragic accidents in town, content for this group was added to the DW top page to publicize their efforts to increase safety. Although the DWC was sympathetic to the causes, they were most alarmed by the inflamed debates on the top pages of the site, and moved some of the content to more obscure areas of the site. While the debates represented best efforts at enabling the community to engage in spirited discussions of great importance to the town, they also had the effect of presenting the community as fractional, divided and dangerously unsafe when a major goal of the sponsor was to draw new people and businesses to the town.

Can Technology Help? Achieving a dynamic, interactive and popular community site that is an asset to the local community is mostly a social, not technical challenge. However, when the social issues are understood, technologies can reinforce social structures that are effective in communities.

Healthy community sites need to have many people, with different perspectives contributing content with different perspectives to a site. In Directory Westfield, the only current sources of unedited content are the merchant content, and the discussion forums. Ideally, other types of un-reviewed content would be welcome by the public. Examples might include public service announcements, election results, emergency notices from the police or mayor or superintendent of schools, or general interest columns from people or organizations (such as the Historical Society). Since we understand that a sponsor will want to exert some editorial control over that content, the technology needs to support the sponsor by allowing them to select the authors and control the placement of content. This approach could be realized by carefully understanding the different roles in the site. We described the roles of public, member, sponsor and webmaster in some detail, but other roles need to be developed for a thriving site. For example, "community leader", "feature writer", or "classified ad writer" are roles we have contemplated for the site. As more members of the community become authors as well as readers, the site will become more interesting and have more impact in the community. From a technology perspective, web software that supports a role concept, including how authentication of contributors in this roles, and the placement of their content, would help the sponsor exercise technical support of this compromise of social relationships.

Another problem was the lack of feedback from the public to the members. New messaging technologies can also help make the site more interactive and provide needed information to both the readers of the site and the merchants. Tools such as email mailing lists, threaded message boards, "instant messaging" and forums need to move into the domain of the member role so that they can be customized and adapted for specific retail, government and business purposes.

In addition to finding a balance between the site goals and achieving a reasonable audience, the stability of a community site is ultimately related to how well the technology reduces the human intervention needed to manage the content. This is a constant challenge to web site designers, but it is particularly tough in a community where funding resources are limited, but demand for service is not.

Acknowledgements. Many people contributed immensely to this project, including Martha Desmond, Beth Robinson, Mark Plotnick, Yi Gong Lu and John Perry who built the service; Nancy Gannett Vickers and Carrie Mumford, who maintained the content on the site and provided the interface to the Westfield Community; Horace Corbin, of the Westfield Leader, and Michael LaPlace and Sherry Cronin, of the DWC, and Spencer Seidel, Ben Cohen, and Andy Cytron who helped maintain the service. We gratefully acknowledge the many discussions with and support of Steve Crandall.

6. Appendix: Community Network References and Resources

1. References, Papers and Conferences on Digital Communities:
   http://www.bev.net/project/digital_library
2. Association for Community Networking:
   http://www.afcn.net
3. Discussion of the Celebration, Florida Community Experience:
   http://www.firstmonday.dk/issues/issue4_11/cisler/index.html
4. Community Express, Bell Canada sponsored sites for Repentigny, Quebec and London, Ontario:
   http://www.telepres.com/case_stu_bell.shtml
5. Seattle Community Network:
   http://www.scn.org
6. Software infrastructure for communities:
   http://www.realcommunities.com
7. Franchise town sites:
   http://www.clicktown.com
8. Douglas Engelbart's Bootstrap organization:
   http://www.bootstrap.com
9. City search:
   http://www.citysearch.com

Ennis Information Age Town: Virtuality Rooted in Reality

Helen McQuillan

Research Dept. eircom Ennis Information Age Town , Ennis, Co. Clare, Ireland
hmcquillan@ennis.ie
http://www.ennis.ie

Abstract. This paper describes the progress of Ennis, Ireland's Information Age Town, in its bid to become 'The Largest Community Technology Project in the World'. An overview of the project outlines the goals, organization, participation and evaluation of the Information Age Town project - confirming the town's 'digital' status. Four key initiatives are examined in detail: the creation of the town's ICT infrastructure; investment in education and training; the development of public sector projects aimed at increasing civic participation and the evolution of the Ennis website as the community's premier communication medium. In conclusion, the paper highlights the potential of a virtual community to enhance social cohesion within a community which has an existing, strong physical community and a collective pride in its history, culture and technology.

1 Introduction

Ennis, a medieval market town in Mid-West Ireland, hosted its thirtieth Fleadh Nua[1] festival in May 2001. The town's cobbled streets and traditional style pubs played host to its annual festival, which celebrates traditional Irish music, song and dance – cultural expressions handed down from generation to generation; musician to musician. Live webcasts blended traditional entertainment with modern technology, matching the number of visitors in the town with virtual visitors – linking the Clare diaspora with Ennis residents and revelers; seamlessly connecting real events with the virtual. For Ennis residents, this interconnectivity is commonplace. With a household PC ownership rate of 83% and active internet usage by 77% of its population, Ennis boasts the most active and ICT fluent citizens in Europe; a community comfortable with their identity as 'Information Age' citizens.

2 Ennis Information Age Town: An Overview

In October 1996, Telecom Éireann (now Eircom), the Irish telecommunications provider, announced a flagship project to accelerate Ireland's progress towards the

---

[1] Fleadh is Irish for cultural feast. Seemain activities at http://fleadhnua.ennis.ie/index.htm and http://www.fleadhnua.com

M. Tanabe, P. van den Besselaar, T. Ishida (Eds.): Digital Cities, LNCS 2362, pp. 139-151, 2002.
© Springer-Verlag Berlin Heidelberg 2002

Information Society.[2] The aim of the Information Age Town initiative, with an accompanying investment of 19 million, was to develop a unique integrated ICT infrastructure within an urban district, to assess its social, educational and economic impact. A highly publicised, nation-wide competition attracted entries from 50 Irish towns, all anxious to provide evidence of their capacity and commitment to exploit the potential of ICT across business, education, community and public sectors – to assess what would happen when their town became 'wired'.

A public/private partnership, spearheaded by a Task Force comprising 11 men and 5 women active in business, community, education and public service championed a successful bid for Ennis, resulting in the town (population 18,000) becoming Ireland's Information Age Town in September 1997. The development of a strategic plan for the project over a six-month period quelled the expectation that Ennis would develop instantly into a digital town.   A process began to build an organizational framework that would be representative of the Ennis community and have the technical skills to develop a robust network infrastructure and manage the project.

While the definition [1] and goals [2] of digital cities are diverse, typically they provide a communication link between citizens and the public sector, using a city metaphor. Their objectives can be interpreted in different ways but are influenced by their management and organizational structure, cultural context, users' motivation and participation, technologies employed and their development process and evolution. [3] [4] [5]. As an ICT development model, the Ennis project was undoubtedly technology driven, initiated by a telecommunications operator. However, over three years the model has evolved towards social pull because of the mobilization of interest groups within the community who have been able to adapt the technology to their own needs and integrate it into their daily lives, endorsing the project through high level participation. [6] The scale of support and participation across all sectors in Ennis is reflected in the project's positive public perception - 90% of people in Ennis consider the Information Age Town project to be a good idea and 83% of the population consider that Ennis has an advantage over other towns. [7]

Since 1998, Ennis Information Age Town has had clear goals - to provide the tools of the Information Age to the largest number of citizens, to teach them how to use them and to encourage people to become electronic contributors, rather than consumers. To achieve these goals, the project team, supported by voluntary Task Force members, advisory groups and community advocates, are implementing ICT programs in partnership with five constituent groups; Residents, Business, Community, Education and Public Sector. These five key programs aimed at increasing awareness, facilitating access, developing skills, building capacity, trialing new technologies and promoting effective use of ICT have ensured that the Ennis Information Age Town project is a catalyst for widespread ICT adoption and the acceleration of electronic communication, community and commerce.

3 Confirming Ennis' Digital Status

As an Information Age Town, the development of an integrated ICT networking infrastructure, allied with the opportunity to trial emerging technologies has provided

---

[2] The Irish Information Society policy is outlined in a number of publications at www.isc.ie

the opportunity for residents and businesses to engage with new technologies.   Since 1998, the Ennis project has provided a test-bed for:

A fiber-optic ring, the first in any Irish town, connecting all areas of the town with 24 fiber-optic conduits.

- High speed internet via ADSL (asymmetric digital subscriber line), an experimental AODI (always on dynamic ISDN) connection and a 3,000 capacity ISDN exchange. High speed connectivity has allowed multimedia industry to thrive in Ennis and has become the standard for public and school internet access – allowing the potential of the internet for publication, communication and transfer of knowledge to be fully appreciated.

- Public internet access via internet kiosks. Stand alone internet kiosks were tested for 18 months in Ennis in hotels, shopping centers and tourist offices. These proved to be problematic from a technical and management perspective and have been replaced by PCs with free public internet access in staffed community network centers and in the county library – which provided 24,000 hours of free internet access in 2000.

- Smart cards. Ennis hosted a 12 month electronic purse trial to evaluate a smart card alternative to cash – an experiment centered on the concept of a cashless society. This experiment provided invaluable research into the uses and limitations of smart card technologies. While very successful in unattended sites – public car parks and public phones, for retail businesses, the transactions were too slow and the technology too cumbersome. The long established, conventional financial systems remain.

- WAP trials, pioneering e-commerce transactions via WAP. Using a smart card and WAP phone, bank customers were able to transact on-line, secure transfer of cash. Although this trial had a short life, the surrounding publicity has impacted on mobile phone use in Ennis – 82% of the population owns a mobile phone, 10% higher than the national figure. [8]

- Mobile services through ODIN[3], an EU funded project which is developing just-in-time, geo-spatial mobile applications and services. Ennis is experimenting with mobile tourism and public services with both high-end and naive ICT users.

- Digitizing cultural objects and archives through COINE (Cultural Objects in Networked Environments), a fifth framework, European IST project. This will allow cultural organizations, ranging from large scale museums to small scale traditional music festivals to digitize their collections, facilitating wider access to these precious cultural resources and collective heritage.

For the media, technology trials glamorize the town's information age status and serve to label the town alternatively as 'Smart, Intelligent, Digital, Wired, Virtual or Electronic', defining the town as 'futuristic or cutting edge'. For the project sustainability, however, more 'mundane' and popular software applications and ICT support systems provide familiarity, security and relevance for project participants,

---

[3] www.odinproject.org

encouraging active participation across all sectors. The main program supports are outlined below:

- 4,600 households (83%) received subsidized, internet-enabled computers, supported by free PC familiarization training. Managed by a residents coordinator, the program aims to maximize access to computers at home, encourage internet usage and ICT skills acquisition. Three years on, in households that have an internet connection (76%), the average time spent 'surfing' per month is 15 hours – 3 times the national figure. Formal ICT skills have been acquired by 41% of Ennis residents, ranging from basic IT and Internet skills to web design and programming. Informal training also has an important role in skills acquisition, provided by family, friends and neighbors.

- 550 businesses (90%) in Ennis are affiliated with the Ennis project and have developed an ICT plan, facilitated by a Business Liaison team. The business program aims to heighten awareness of the benefits of using ICT to consolidate and develop business opportunities and remove barriers to ICT adoption and e-commerce innovation. ICT consultancy, subsidies for hardware and software, web hosting service and training aim to stimulate e-business in Ennis. Businesses also get the opportunity to participate in technology pilots and trials and can serve as exemplars for other businesses by being promoted as Business Champions. Case studies of these businesses highlight their e-business goals, technologies employed and the effectiveness of the chosen solutions in terms of economics and human resources.[4]

- 100 community and voluntary organizations are active in the Community Program. The problems of inclusion for the voluntary sector in the information age are well documented [9,10,11]. From the outset, the Ennis project sought to address this. A strong partnership has been built with development organizations, culture and heritage associations, sports clubs and groups that provide community care. Managed by a community -coordinator, the program provides hardware, software, assistive technologies, high speed internet access and dedicated technical support to constituent organizations. Four community network centers and ten community training centers also avail of these supports and are active in tackling social inclusion and promoting e-citizenship. Training courses from basic IT and ECDL to web design are tailored to the needs of the different groups. Web-building templates offer clubs and societies the opportunity to publish their information electronically, and several of the more ambitious organizations are utilizing and evaluating electronic publishing tools[5] developed by MIT Media Lab.

- Young people in Ennis are often described as the 'Jewels in the Information Age Crown' and the education program is central to the project's success. Twelve first and second level schools are equipped with networked computer laboratories with ISDN and ADSL connection, maintaining the 5,000 student e-mail accounts created over the past three years. Ennis is widely recognized as a center of

---

[4] A description of Ennis business champions is published at www.ennis.ie
[5] An excellent example is an electronic newsletter produced by senior citizens in Ennis http://sunset.ennis.ie

educational ICT integration and innovation.[6] With a ratio of one internet-enabled PC to every nine students, and access to multimedia projectors, digital cameras, scanners and video conferencing equipment, the youth of Ennis enjoys the best ICT facilities in Ireland.

From the outset, social inclusion has been a key goal of the project. The challenge has been the provision of appropriate supports for people to capitalize on the town's investment in a technology infrastructure. Ongoing evaluation of the project aims to document the project's success in achieving these goals as well as recording people's experience of using technology.[7]

4 Key Initiatives: Four Building Blocks

Many factors contribute to the development of a community technology project. Below, four elements are highlighted that are recognised as key building blocks for the Ennis project. Individually they are all essential components for a town or city to be titled 'digital'. Collectively, however, they facilitate technical, social and educational synergy, allowing the tools of the information society to benefit the largest amount of citizens, enabling community in its widest sense.

4.1 Creating an ICT Infrastructure: Facilitating Access and Integration

In 1997-1998, the telecommunication infrastructure of Ennis was enhanced significantly. Ennis was the first Irish town to develop a digital self-healing broadband ring connecting all areas of the town, with a capacity to handle three million calls simultaneously. Ennis also boasts Ireland's only ADSL (Asymmetric Digital Subscriber Line) exchange which allows business, education, community and public service sectors to exploit the potential of always-on, high speed internet. A consultancy and technical support service is also provided by the project, advising on all aspects of ICT installation, connectivity, networking and management. This advisory, demonstration, and trouble shooting service has been crucial in eliminating many of the technical fears and frustrations associated with ICT, and has been used by 33% of households who have had a problem with their computer.

The residents PC program was the biggest step towards the town's ICT integration. The most eagerly anticipated aspect of the project was the offer of subsidized computers and one year's internet subscription to all (5,600) households within the Ennis Urban District. During the summer of 1998 50 Pentium-II multimedia PCs were installed daily in Ennis. Participating households (4,600) contributed 330, which was reinvested in the project. A waiver scheme was offered where appropriate. Six

---

[6] SIP (Schools Integration Project) details ICT activities within Ennis primary schools.
http://www.sip.ie/sip058/index1.html

[7] A research report on Ennis Information Age Town is available on the Ennis website http://www.ennis.ie/evaluation_report.pdf. Results from a major residential survey released in Autumn 2001 are also published here.

hundred households that had never had a telephone also availed of free telephone connection and all homes in Ennis were enabled with enhanced telephony services.

The community and voluntary sector is widely recognized as a sector with most to gain from ICT, yet one which encounters the greatest barriers to ICT adoption. Lack of financial resources, limited access to training and technical support, literacy problems, perceived lack of relevance of computers and internet to organizational goals and limited awareness of best ICT practice within the community sector are all exclusionary factors. Conscious of these barriers a community infrastructure has been developed in Ennis which provides ICT resources and supports directly to the organizations that provide education, training, support and services for diverse community groups, and particularly for disadvantaged members of society. A superior ICT infrastructure - hardware, specialist software, assistive technologies, multimedia equipment and web publishing tools, allied with advice, technical expertise and training, are supporting the development of a lifelong learning environment within the Ennis community.

Additional ICT facilities are also available in community and business network centers, which provide free internet access to residents, businesses and visitors. The network centers, in strategic locations – library, community centers, business centers and chamber of commerce, ensure that people without personal computers can participate and benefit from the Information Age Town project.

Ennis schools' advanced ICT infrastructure is unique in an Irish context and serves as a model nationally and internationally.[8] Although a Government schools' ICT initiative[9] provided one computer with internet access for each school in Ireland, the national ICT education infrastructure remains underdeveloped. Ennis schools have state of the art computer facilities, which facilitate best practice in ICT integration, multimedia authoring, transnational projects, website development and electronic publishing.[10] The schools' resources are also widely used outside of school hours, by parents and the wider community.

---

[8] The Ennis Education programme served as a model for Pennsylvania Digital School District initiative http://www.padigitalschooldistricts.com

[9] IT 2000 http://www.irlgov.ie/educ/it2000/it2000.htm

[10] Examples of Best Practice are available at http://bestpracticeawards.ennis.ie/educat.htm

4.2 Developing Skills :   Providing a Progressive Training Route

Capacity building, through progressive ICT training provision, is a key objective of the Ennis Information Age Town project. Investment in ICT training concentrates on five main elements, whose collective aim is to facilitate and promote life-long learning, for social, education and economic benefit for the Ennis community.

Basic IT and internet training provide a foundation for further ICT skills development. 2,400 people availed of free PC familiarization training, offered to people who received Information Age computers. Numerous training courses and workshops over the past three years have been organized in a diverse range of learning environments in an attempt to introduce hundreds of people to basic IT concepts and content in a context that is relevant to their lives and their interests.   As well as proving a basis for further training, the emphasis on basic training in Ennis is on enhancing people's ICT skills for social interaction, to exploit the internet as an effective communication and information medium.

Since 1998, the training environment in Ennis has been enhanced significantly. Twelve training centers now offer wide-ranging certified ICT courses commercially. Ten community training centers, serving disadvantaged clients, deliver high quality ICT training to their service users, both in the centers and electronically. Ennis has the highest rate of ECDL (European Computer Driving License) participation in Ireland, with ten accredited test centers offering taught and computer based ECDL training. Six schools offer computer courses to students, teachers, parents and community organizations, using funds raised to supplement and upgrade their ICT facilities.   Purpose built training suites, with video conferencing and multimedia facilities are also heavily utilized in the Clare Education Center and the project headquarters, the Information Age Center.

Since 2000, Ennis has also supported e-learning.   With e-learn@ennis[11], residents and businesses are offered a selection of 300 online courses with professional certification including MOUS, MCP, MCSE, MCDBA as well as a range of business courses. A combination of flexible delivery and tutor training offers the possibility

---

[11] http://elearn.ennis.ie

for the majority of people to choose a training method which suits their individual learning style and budget.

Collaborative learning has been introduced in schools – cross phase and cross community. Conferencing software, FirstClass™, facilitates collaborative projects between pupils in schools, teachers groups and between third level colleges and second level schools. An ambitious plan, involving all thirteen schools, designed around sharing resources, showcasing pupils' work and communicating between school, home and the community has been developed, but is still awaiting funding from the Department of Education and Science.

As important as the support for high-level skills is the creation of a community culture which fosters a collaborative learning environment. This is a notable characteristic of the Ennis project.[12]   Family, school friends, work colleagues and volunteers willingly pass on their newly acquired tips, skills and knowledge – a learning and teaching method often more effective than formal learning in an institutional setting.

4.3 Public Sector Projects: Preparing for E-citizenship

Public service providers in Ennis aim to be at the forefront of e-democracy by providing dynamic, relevant and up-to-date information on all types of services available to the population of Ennis and County Clare.

Clare County Library[13] is an exemplar of good ICT practice and has been proactive in the project since the beginning. The library's IT department has been developing and adapting its ICT strategy since 1996. The library is the primary public information source for the county and is increasingly providing that information electronically. Its WISE (Web and Internet Service for Ennis) project provides a complete information retrieval system which manages bibliographic records as well as maps, press cuttings, video, recorded music, photographs and journal articles. De Valera library, Ennis was

---

[12] Research published in September 2001 confirms the high volume of informal training.
[13] http://www.clarelibrary.ie

the first public library in Ireland to develop an online catalogue, and has developed an extensive website, which regularly publishes local historic records and documents, facilitating electronic access to rare manuscripts – normally the preserve of academics. Its projects make diverse information sources available on-line, which can be accessed by people locally, as well as globally via the internet. Since March 2000, the library has provided high-speed internet access through 15 PCs to its members and visitors. The busiest community network center in Ennis, there is heavy demand for the 3,000 hours of free internet access provided by Ennis library each month.

Clare County Council and Ennis Urban District Council have a clear objective of best ICT practice for local government. In partnership with Ennis Information Age Town, they are developing an ambitious local authorities' website project – EOLAS[14] (Ennis Online Local Authority Services).   The launch of EOLAS is scheduled for Autumn 2001, giving members of the public electronic access to local authority databases, housing lists, planning applications, tenders and contracts. The EOLAS project has enormous potential for e-democracy through dynamic, up to date information delivery and interaction. Its phased development will allow ongoing evaluation and change where necessary, to respond to individual and community information needs and to deliver tailored services and information. Local authority staff are active in ICT training and public representatives in Ennis aim to champion local e-government in Ireland, using Ennis as a model. Over the next few years, the EOLAS project aims to be at the forefront of mobile e-government and e-democracy, the ultimate challenge to Information Society promises and rhetoric. Whether the local authorities can deliver what they promise remains to be seen, but they are in a uniquely fortunate situation of having a captive, ICT fluent audience for its services.

4.4 The Ennis Website; the Evolution of a New Communication Medium

The Ennis website www.ennis.ie is the public face of the Ennis Information Age Town project. The site aims to be a virtual 'window to the world' for Ennis citizens as well as reflecting the broad ranging activities, interests and culture that are central to the Ennis community – facilitating the sharing of news and information between its physical and virtual community. The role and goal of a community website is dependant on the definition of community, adopted by a group or organization that claims to represent 'the' community. The balance between the freedom to experiment in a virtual environment and the responsibility of reflecting reality affects our definition and representation of community. For Ennis Information Age Town, which claims to be the largest community technology project in the world, Ennis community has a broad scope, encompassing local and global, immigrant and emigrant, physical and virtual.

The graphic representation of the Ennis website illustrates the main features of the site. A web team of three – designer, content editor and manager – ensures that the site is content-rich and interactive and that its four services are fully functional: Web hosting, Ennis Mail, e-learning and directories. Dynamic content is contributed through a daily local and national news service, business news, live local radio

---

[14] EOLAS is Irish for knowledge.

Ennis Information Age Town's Website http://www.ennis.ie

streaming[15] and regular contributions from the public to the community news section.The major sources of information on the site include Information Age Town updates, business, community and tourism sections, and a research page. Photographic content is provided via a webcam, focused on activities in the town centre, photo essays of recent community events and galleries which display local artists' work. A bulletin board, teen-zine and sports e-zine provide space for contribution and interaction, articulating the interests of the website's users.

The website is considered to be in its embryonic stage although it has had three iterations – evolving according to user needs and interests, trying to balance the needs of its members and establish itself as a sustainable community resource. Representing a physical community virtually is not an easy task and the Ennis project has learnt many valuable lessons. A website is resource intensive – its sustainability is dependant on good design, frequent iterations, dynamic content, regular contributions from all sectors of the community, feedback from new and regular visitors and responsiveness to local and global information needs and interests.

The most crucial element, however, and the most difficult, is to develop a sense of community ownership. Over its three year development the Ennis website has gathered a huge amount of data, hosted and published personal, business, school and community websites, documented events in the locality, presented daily news and attempted to present a snapshot of present day 'life' in the town. While these have contributed to a steady increase in site traffic (10 % rise per month) and a large volume of communication via e-mail with the web team, local visitors and commentators represented only 20 percent of visitors. A recent initiative, however, has changed that dynamic. The development of an online photographic gallery 'Through the Years'[16], depicting historic images and video clips of the town's 'faces and places' has generated huge interest in the community. Photographs from public and private collections have been generously donated, with donors anxious to contribute to the town's, and its people's, collective history and memory. This collection is one of the community's greatest electronic resources, depicting the shaping of the town's tradition and culture – a resource that bridges all the social divides; age, gender, class and ethnicity – rooting historic reality in virtuality.

5 Conclusion

The challenge in Ennis has been the development of appropriate supports and resources for people to capitalize on the town's unique technology infrastructure, and become contributors to the town's new, and potentially most democratic and empowering, communications medium. This cannot be achieved without public support for the project, active participation by all sectors of the community, sustainable partnerships and finance.

In terms of training, engagement with the project, skills development, capacity building and internet usage, the Ennis project has been very successful. Examples of

---

[15] CLARE FM http://www.clarefm.ie
[16] http://gallery.ennis.ie

Best Practice[17] in all five programs qualify this success. Whether social cohesion is enhanced through the Ennis Information Age Town project is harder to measure and is dependant on a multiplicity of factors, many of which the project is attempting to address, in partnership with a wide variety of actors and agencies.

Despite high levels of participation, discrepancies persist in computer ownership between social classes, computer confidence and skills in different age groups and computer and internet usage between genders. Thus, the Ennis project challenges the simplistic Information Society assumption that access to ICT will ensure equality.

It is also recognized that the pace of participation and progress has been uneven. Some organizations instantly became ICT champions – publishing their own HTML websites within weeks of initial training. Others have struggled with the technology but have slowly accepted the challenge, working at their own pace to familiarize themselves with applications, determined to make the technology work for them, as a quote from a community organization illustrates:

"In our experiences with Information Technology we have had our preconceptions about computers shattered, have been frustrated by them, have struggled with them but ultimately we have learnt a lot about them and enthusiasm for them has crept in. We are now determined to put them to work for us and get as much out of them as we can."

We have learnt that there are many incentives as well as barriers to meaningful use of PCs and internet – motivation, time, financial resources, access to training, technical support, literacy skills, relevance and awareness of best ICT practice.

As an experimental project, Ennis hopes to highlight the project's learning process; the successes and failures, expectations and disappointments; factors that inhibit or encourage a community with a strong physical network to develop confidence in their virtual citizenship.

Whether the internet becomes the community's premier communication medium remains to be seen. Evidence in Ennis, however, affirms the potential of a virtual community to enhance social cohesion within a community which has an existing, strong physical community and a collective pride in its history, culture and technology.

References

1.   B. van Bastelaer *Digital Cities and Transferability of Results,* Proceedings of the 4th EDC Conference on Digital Cities, Salzburg October1998.
2.   T. Ishida, *Understanding Digital Cities,* Digital Cities, LNCS 1765, Springer-Verlag, 2000.
3.   P. van den Besselaar, I. Melis and D. Beckers D*igital Cities, Organisation, Content and Use,* Digital Cities, LNCS 1765, Springer-Verlag, 2000.
4.   A. Aurigi *Digital City or Urban Simulator?* Digital Cities, LNCS 1765, Springer – Verlag, 2000.

---

[17] See http://bestpracticeawards.ennis.ie for examples of best practice in 4 sectors.

5.   E. Mino *Experiences of European Digital Cities,* Digital Cities LNCS, Springer – Verlag, 2000
6.   2001OECD, *Information and Communication Technologies and Rural Development* OECD 2001
7.   Behaviour and Attitudes *Ennis Information Age Town –Residents Survey* 2001.
8.   OTDR, *The Internet in Ireland – Communications Transmission and Delivery Issues,* OTDR 01/47, 2001
9.   S. O'Donnell, B.Trench and K.Ennals, *Weak Connections: Final Report of the Research Project – The Voluntary Sector in the Information Age,* Dublin City University, 1998.
10. INSINC *The Net Result: Social Inclusion in the Information Society.* IBM, 1997
11. P.Gaskin, K.Harris and J.Patterson *Information Technology in the Community and Voluntary Sector: A Selected Bibliography* CDF, 1993

Feasibility Study of Digital Community through Virtual Enterprise Network

Kikuko Harada[1] and Hiroshi Hoshino[2]

[1]KRP, 17 ChudojiMinami-machi Shimogyo-ku Kyoto JAPAN, 600-8813
Tel: +81-75-315-9103, Fax: +81-75-315-9134
harada@krp.co.jp
[2]ASTEM RI, 17 ChudojiMinami-machi Shimogyo-ku Kyoto JAPAN, 600-8813
Tel: +81-75-315-6724, Fax: +81-75-315-2899
hoshino@astem.or.jp

Abstract. A Digital Community emerges from a virtually created network community and is expected to change according to the needs of real human community. An ideal digital community is built on harmonized relations between virtual and real communities, and should be a common place for which its participants feel both ownership and liability.

Japan Network of Virtual Companies (JNVC) is a simulated business training program. JNVC provides its members with an enterprise community in which educational institutions of all levels can participate, under the precondition that people from businesses in the local region are involved in the virtual company's operations.

This paper outlines the result of a feasibility experiment on how interaction between real and virtual communities is affected by the virtual enterprise network. How does this contribute to a strengthening of the local community network? We argue how a digital community like JNVC can make participants aware of the resources they have, how it may promote their ownership and liabilities toward their local community, and whether it has an impact on the development of the social infrastructure in the local community.

1 Introduction

A digital community is usually formed voluntarily for the purpose of information sharing on a certain common theme. It provides infrastructure for communication and social interaction without the restriction of regional boundaries. Social interaction is said to be one of the main goals in network communities [1]. However, an incentive is required to motivate members to take their roles in the community. When there is a strong incentive in a community, people actively interact, gradually create rules, and play their roles under mutual agreement of its members [2]. Incentives can be practical benefits or something that promotes people's skills, talents, or knowledge. It can be said that community member's real lives are enriched through the networking community. In this sense, we can say that an active digital community is a place formed by mutual beneficial interaction between the real world and the virtual world.

M. Tanabe, P. van den Besselaar, T. Ishida (Eds.): Digital Cities, LNCS 2362, pp. 152-163, 2002.
© Springer-Verlag Berlin Heidelberg 2002

In this paper, we introduce a test case project called Japan Network of Virtual Companies (JNVC) as one future community model that has the above mentioned mutual beneficial interaction between the virtual and real world.

The JNVC project was launched in September 1999, and has been in it operation for two years. This project began with the purpose of raising entrepreneurship among the youth and having business people in the community get involved in education. JNVC is formed under a partnership with educational institutes and industries in the community. It is a combined unity of real and virtual worlds. JNVC members create VCs and experience business operation by interacting with other members. Members are expected to acquire real skills and knowledge through simulated business operation. At the same time, this network community aims to offer an opportunity to make members aware of the resources they have in the region, promote their ownership or liabilities toward their community, and eventually people who participate in JNVC will hopefully be leaders in the creation of new businesses that contribute to the local economy.

This paper argues how real and virtual communities can affect each other and the way local networks are formed by partnerships such as those JNVC offers.

2   Japan Network of Virtual Companies (JNVC)

The Japan Network of Virtual Companies (JNVC) is a community for virtual companies. Participants are students of all levels, teachers, business people, and students' parents; or in other words anyone who is engaged with the operations of a VC. JNVC is one of the national networks of virtual businesses that are linked together under a global educational scheme [3]. These national networks cover 38 countries with about 4000 virtual business enterprises and provide a simulated economy and market to its participants. The first four VCs were set up in September 1999 in Japan, 25 VCs in the following year, and the number will expand to over 80 in November 2001.

2.1   Aim of the Project

Virtual Company (VC) is a simulated enterprise that is set up and run by its students with support from an educator (facilitator) and a real company (business partner). JNVC offers an opportunity for community members to experience e-commerce and international business.

The concept of VC aims to promote students' entrepreneurial sprits and develop their employability due to IT skills and business knowledge gained during the program. Students are also expected to develop personal qualities and attitudes such as leadership, decision-making, problem solving and communication skills in a team working environment. These attributes are essential requirements of employability as a whole.

Secondly, this program aims to have students become more aware of the way in which people can make a living and of the resources they have in their local region. This may extend their career options. Through operating a VC within the JNVC community, students obtain an opportunity to work with people from regional companies. In this way, students communicate closely with the real world, and are exposed to adult society. Such interaction helps students become aware of the possible roles and responsibilities that they can expect to have when they become adult members of society.

And, more importantly, in this program, adults in the local area get involved in the education of the youth, and the whole community can play a role; including schools, parents, industry, and the government. Within JNVC, people in the local community assist to create a safe virtual environment where students can try out various things, make mistakes and learn from failure, and when necessary, get support from others; including classmates, teachers, or people in the community. The virtual environment provides a foundation for stepping into the real world, by using real skills.

This educational method of VC can be one of the tools that people at various levels of the community have to get involved in a joint project working on better solutions for making a community more attractive – especially from a business point of view.

2.2   Virtual Company

VCs conduct business with other VCs in a simulated market economy on a local, national or international level. This program educates students (members) in every aspect of business operation. As employees of a VC, students take their roles in various departments like administration, financial, sales/purchases, personnel, and undertake market research, advertise, buy and sell goods etc.; they work out pay rates, assess employees' work performance, and pay them virtual salary. Although there is no actual transfer of goods or money, all the usual business transactions take place: orders are sent, invoices issued, financial records maintained, and a business plan and marketing strategy developed and monitored.

Acting as one of employees of a VC, the students (members) play a role of the consumer as well. Employees receive salary from a VC and spend it in the JNVC simulated market. This network offers an opportunity for students to experience both B to B and B to C businesses.

A VC requires students to learn business and IT skills that are necessary as members of the work force. By accomplishing one's roles and responsibilities in its operation, he or she learns the importance of self-learning. International trading with VCs in other countries enhances understanding of international business and culture. Participation in a VC gives student's real business insights and awareness of business sensitivities. They develop skills in decision making, problem solving, and in working with clients towards a positive outcome. They learn to work effectively in a team and prioritize their work; they learn about accountability and daily work routines.

2.3   Business Partner

A business partner is a real organization or company that gives support and guidance to the operation of a VC and its educator (facilitator). When it comes to choose a line of business, most of the schools are willing to introduce firms that deal with special resources or traditional art in a local area. These business partners are usually small or medium size enterprises located in its schools region and have good reputation in producing services or products, in business management, and in employee training. The business partner is essential to a VC for learning and applying economic and business operation processes in as real a world as possible. They provide education and support of many functions to a VC. These business operation areas can include product development, marketing, public relations and personnel assessment, just to name a few. Business partners play key roles of connecting a virtual network community and a real community.

Business partners should also gain benefits from working with a VC. A VC promotes the business partners' social recognition and its product or service on a national or international basis. It can be a potential training opportunity for new employees of business partners. They can present company information and provide guidance to the operation of a VC, etc. Students can also undertake useful market research of a new product within or outside of JNVC.

2.4 Central Office

The Japanese Central Office for JNVC was established in 1999 within the Center for Entrepreneurship Education (CEE) [4] with the mentorship of ANPF [5] (The Australian Network of Practice Firms). The Central Office has an information and coordination role for the VC Network and it assists schools when setting up a VC. It offers the following support services:

- Consultation for VC curriculum development or class management.
- Training and workshops on different aspects of a VC.
- Supporting schools with set up and operation of a VC.
- Monitoring a VC operation.
- Supporting domestic and international trade activities.
- Providing virtual operation of taxation, public services and insurance.
- Providing companies available for trade.
- Acting as a simulated Japanese Central Bank and offering common banking functions such as account administration, on-line banking, and e-trade service for on-line shopping.
- Planning and supporting special projects or events in order to enhance interactions among members in the community.

CEE is an offshoot of the "Kyoto Committee for the Cultivation of Entrepreneurial Spirit and Development of its Environment". This Committee was established in January 1999, for the purpose of discussing methods of implementing community support systems necessary for developing entrepreneurial spirit and employability of students who have to confront a rapidly changing information society. The Center is expected to function as a bridge between the worlds of government, industry, and academia in order to realize necessary supporting systems in the community.

2.5   E-trade Banking System

The first four VCs were set up in September 1999, and they founded JNVC. In the following year, e-trade banking system was developed and installed in the network. JNVC Central Office has also started to offer its service for 25 new VCs in Japan.

The e-trade banking system was developed in order to facilitate manual transaction procedures required in traditional trading, and to ensure that students experience e-commerce in a more realistic way. Students are expected to learn the concept of electronic money, the potential of e-commerce, and the risks of on-line shopping. This system also enabled students without any background in bookkeeping or accounting to trade and communicate with students in other schools.

3   Experiment of Case Study: JNVC 2000

In January 2001, the Japanese Government issued "The Education Reform Plan for the 21st Century" [6] based on the recommendation of "The Final Report of the National Commission on Education Reform". This plan introduces the overall picture of the future efforts needed for educational reform. One of the major objectives is to revitalize the school board by improving parental participation and to establish new types of schools that fit the needs of the different communities. Schools are also asked to encourage youth to participate in community activities and learn through their own experience. A key theme of the reform is to involve schools, families, and communities in the education system.

In line with the educational reform in past years, practical work experience has been encouraged at the elementary and secondary school levels. The purpose of this is to nurture students' occupational consciousness and their understanding of the importance of career development. Many schools have started to implement internship or have professionals visiting their class activities. Due to lack of organized planning and prior training, however, work experience like this tends to remain a one-time event, without achieving much of its purposes. Schools fail to develop a lasting partnership with people who have assisted.

Under such circumstances, four educational institutions participated in JNVC in 2001 and tested this educational program as one of the solutions to revitalize schools and communities. By building a bridge between education and industry, they aimed to develop students' employability and establish stronger partnerships with businesses in the area.

Next, we will outline and describe the results of the feasibility experiment that was started by JNVC in 2000.

3.1 Participants

The following four educational institutes participated in JNVC and created 25 VCs in the year 2000:
1. Goko High School: three VCs
   One teacher for one class, 25 3rd year students in the Mechanics program, and three people from area businesses.

2. Ooe High School: two VCs
   Four teachers for one class, 28 3rd year students in the Information Processing program, and four people from area businesses.
3. Saikyo Commercial High School: twenty VCs
   Six teachers for two classes, 75 3rd year students in the Information Processing program, and about 25 people from area businesses.
4. Otemon Gakuin University: one VC
   One head teacher, one assistant teacher, six 2nd year students Majoring in Business Management, and five people from area businesses.

In total, 184 people (134 students, 13 facilitators (teachers) and 37 people from business partners) were concerned in forming the JNVC community. Students at three high schools set up and operated these VCs under the support of business partners. A group of Otemon Gakuin University took a different approach. They had business representatives' lecture on specific themes and created a company on their own.

3.2   Project Schedule

For most of the schools, VC Program was a one-year project and schools underwent the following stages:

1st stage: Prior preparation
Teachers who took the role of facilitators in the VC program were required to attend the teachers' workshop, to conduct a feasibility study, to develop their own curriculum, and to find a business partner for their VC. VCs were instructed to sell the same products or services as their business partner. By adding a complementary item or a new feature to a product or service offered by their business partner, VCs were allowed to introduce their own invented products or services as well. Through this cooperative work, schools were expected to establish a stronger partnership with businesses in the area.

2nd stage: Introduction (1st term, April to June)
At first, teachers introduced the VC program and how they would run it. Class schedules, objectives, assignments, and how students were to be assessed were announced to the students. Additionally, each school planned its own curriculum.

3rd stage: Operation of the VC (2nd and 3rd terms, September to January)
All schools set up a VC and started to trade within JNVC. The following is a rough schedule of the operation of the VCs of the four schools from September to January (5 months)
  - Decide on the VC's capital, number of employees, their roles, salaries and any bonuses.
  - Discuss each task and write a job description and schedule.
  - Decide which products or services are sold in the JNVC community.

- Create promotional tools, first leaflets and then a web page with an on-line shopping service.
- Start promotional activities by sending e-mails or leaflets.
- Start trading in JNVC: Members buy products both as a consumer and a company.
- Make a financial statement and a presentation at a board meeting with the business partner.
- Discuss what has been learned, and discuss their own career path.

3.3 Collaboration with Businesses and Its Outcomes

Each school found its own business partner in their local region, and arranged a cooperation-scheme according to its own curriculum.   Students of the four educational institutes set up 25 VCs in 2000. In the process of running a VC, they decided on the details of company structure, on the goods to sell, and on how to run and manage their companies. A rough business plan was prepared, and promotional tools both in Japanese and English were developed.   Then, they started to communicate with other participants. When ready to sell or buy products, they registered with the Central Office bank, and sent an announcement of the opening of their business via e-mail, attaching promotional leaflets if available.

Below are the structures and outcomes of the collaborations the four institutions adopted in 2000.

Goko High School: Business partners: Mitsutoyo and Kureryohai Cooperative Association.

With the support of the business partners, three VCs were created with seven to nine employees, and each sold business partners' products such as digital body fat meters, wheat germ oil, and rice. Representatives of supporting companies gave lectures and advised on certain topics such as the vision and the organization of their company, on promotion and sales strategies, or on bookkeeping, etc. In addition, they responded to e-mail inquiries from students and evaluated the outcomes of students' efforts. Finally, they attended the opening and closing ceremonies of the three VCs and commented on students' presentations and achievements.

Compared to the other two high schools, Goko students did not have prior knowledge of accounting, usage of spreadsheet software, e-mail, or web page development. The students and the teacher had no business knowledge whatsoever. However, this encouraged the teacher to get active support from the business partners.

Ooe High School
Business partners: Gunze Miyazu Factory, and Ooe Town Chamber of Commerce and Industry (OTCCI).

There were no formal lectures by business partners.   Their representatives participated in the classes and responded to students' questions.   They discussed certain topics, gave suggestions to solve problems, consulted on product development, and evaluated web page design. They also joined the presentations of the midterm and final reports of the two VCs and they gave advice on how to improve them.

Ooe High School created two VCs with 14 employees each.   One VC called 'Tanaka Hadagi' dealt with Gunze underwear. The other VC called 'Sol*C' sold the same goods characterized demon that OTCCI was selling. 'Sol*C' also invented a few new demon's goods. A mobile phone strap and a scent bag shown in fig.1 have become real products with the help of the OTCCI and are sold to the public. This was one of the good examples of a VC actually creating real business.

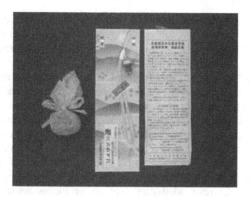

Fig. 1. Real products Ooe High School sells.

Saikyo Commercial High School
Business partners: 23 shops from the Association for the Promotion of Kyoto Sanjokai Shopping Street, Osaka Gas, and Kyocera.

In the first term of the year, Saikyo students established 20 SOHO style businesses with three to four employees for each business. Each SOHO team interviewed the owners of 23 shops in Sanjokai shopping street and created their web pages. The owners of the shops evaluated the web pages and gave the students feedback. These web pages are introduced in the web site of Saikyo High School.

In the second term, these 20 SOHO teams introduced their newly invented goods and services. Representatives from Osaka Gas and Kyocera gave lectures, but were not involved very much in creating the VCs. This weak interaction between the business partners and the students affected the way the VCs operated. Their products ended up being too virtual, discouraging other participants from buying their products. This illustrates that the more business people are involved in learning, the better students gain practical ideas. Support of the real society is important in order to save the project from ending up as an imaginary art class.

Otemon Gakuin University
At Otemon Gakuin University, one VC consisting of six students was established. Business partners were ED-CONTRIVE, TAMI Research Lab for Information Education, NEC, Osaka Gas, and Langate.

In the spring semester, professionals in special areas and entrepreneurs of IT ventures gave lectures, and had discussion-sessions with the students. Student's acquired basic concepts of enterprise from the series of lectures were required to write their own business plans and submit them to a competition. In the fall semester, six students who were interested in running a simulated business formed a team and joined JNVC. This team consisted of Japanese and Chinese students and it created a virtual software company without the support of business partners.

4 Evaluation

We conducted a survey in the middle of January during the final term of the year. Here we present the responses to the questions and some of the comments. It was a Yes-or-No questionnaire.

The numbers in Table 1 show that more than 90% of students were interested in the VC program and in working as a group. More than 75% of them answered that they actually acquired the skills to work as a team and to take responsibility. Computer skills and creativity followed next with about 60%. All the participants - students, teachers, and business partners - set a high valuation on the opportunity for students to learn from business people rather than teachers. Business partners see the VC Program as an ideal program for students to learn practical business skills.

The major issue coming from this survey was that this educational concept of VC is a very new way of teaching and learning, and both the teachers and the students were puzzled at the beginning. It took some time till they could act flexibly and make the best use of the support from business partners. While 94% of the students regard teamwork and student oriented self-learning like the VC method beneficial, only 56% of teachers (See Table2) responded they had no problems acting a facilitator and

Table 1. Students' self assessment and evaluation of the VC program

	Questions	Yes	No	Valid Answers
1	It was easy to understand the structure of the class	72 64%	41 36%	113
2	I understand the aims and objectives of the program.	93 82%	21	114
3	I understand my role and responsibility in the group, and tried to complete my work.	76 67%	38 33%	114
4	I participated in class activities with interest.	108 96%	5 4%	113
5	I was interested in group work	103 90%	11 10%	114
6	It is beneficial for me to learn from business people rather than teachers.	98 94%	6 6%	104
7	Simulated business program like VC is helpful to help me think about my career options.	65 62%	40 38%	105
8	Team working and student oriented self-learning methods like the VC program are beneficial for me.	94 91%	9 9%	103
9	Choose skills you learned in this program (You can choose more than one skill).			
	Working as a team	79	76%	104
	Responsibility	78	75%	104
	Computer skills	67	64%	104
	Creativity	61	59%	104
	Communication	54	52%	104
	Problem solving	49	47%	104
	Making decisions	46	44%	104
	Judging	43	41%	104
	Expressing self and presenting	40	38%	104
	Posing problems	34	33%	104
	Establishing a challenging spirit	31	30%	104
	Leadership	12	12%	104
	Language ability	8	8%	104

Table 2. Teachers' self assessment and evaluation of the VC program

	Questions	Yes	No	Valid Answers
1	I could introduce the VC without difficulties.	2 20%	8 80%	10
2	There was no problem to act as a facilitator and develop self-learning skills in my students.	5 56%	4 44%	9
3	Students were clear about the rationale of the class and were interested in the group work.	7 78%	2 22%	9
4	Students expressed their opinions and tried to understand and accomplish their roles or responsibility in the group work.	7 78%	2 22%	9
5	It is beneficial for students to learn from business people rather than teachers.	9 100%	0 0%	9
6	Simulated business programs like VC are helpful for students to think about their career options.	6 60%	4 40%	10
7	I discussed well with other teachers on the rationale and aims of the VC, understand them fully, and taught the class.	5 50%	5 50%	10
8	I exchanged opinions with business partners about aims, problems and things to improve, so that they felt it easy to support us so we could make the best of the program.	3 30%	7 70%	10
9	It is beneficial for teachers to have business people in the class.	8 80%	2 20%	10
10	Not only students but teachers also learned from the VC program.	7 78%	2 22%	9

Table 3. Business Partners' evaluation of VC program

	Questions	Yes	No	Valid Answers
20	Students understood the aims and objectives of this class, expressed their opinions and asked questions.	5 71%	1 14%	6
21	It is beneficial for students to learn from business people rather than teachers.	7 100%	0	7
22	It is beneficial for teachers and schools to have business people in the class.	7 100%	0	7
23	Simulated business operation programs like this are useful for students to experience activity-based learning and to develop their own career options.	6 100%	0	6
24	I myself learned from participating in this program.	7 100%	0	7

managing the class in such way. We can see that teachers need time to change their teaching style, which is currently based on conventional lectures and one-way communication. They need to acquire teaching skills that enable them to act as facilitators, which in turn will enhance students' self-learning skills.

For teachers, having their co-workers understand the aim of the program and getting support from people both in the same school and in the outside community is also a big hurdle to overcome. The extra workload, such as negotiating with business partners, involved in conducting a VC seems to discourage teachers from participating in programs like this. Teachers who were positively involved in the program and went out into the community for support valued this program most and played a key role in the development of the JNVC community. The same thing can be said of the students. The students who had a positive attitude found their roles and tasks in their team, and accomplished them. However, students with passive attitudes, ended up finding nothing to do and did not acquire as much knowledge or skills as the others. This relationship between motivation and outcome certainly simulates a real work place.

The low scores on questions 8 and 16 were due to the fact that all the high school students were in their 3rd year and already had decided on their future profession or academic study.   This indicates that if we aim to develop students' career consciousness, we should implement this type of education in earlier stages in the education system.

We can see that all the people who participated in this program regarded this type of education as beneficial for students. However, until it has been generally accepted, there are some major issues to overcome, and the hardest task will be to change the mindset of people in the educational institutions. This type of education demands an entrepreneurial spirit and management skills.   Business partners indicated that teachers should take some business training or try to develop a network outside of the school. In order to solve this problem, there is a need for training for teachers to learn new teaching methods and skills, in order to be able to cooperate with people outside of the school.

5 Conclusions

Participants that become a member of the network community of JNVC, create a virtual copy of the real world. They set up and operate an enterprise in the protected environment of the virtual community, and interact with people in the real community in the region. JNVC links communities of education and industry, and, at the same time, connects virtual and real communities.

While operating the simulated businesses, all people involved in JNVC take certain roles and accomplish their tasks and responsibilities. In the safe environment of the virtual community, they are encouraged to try out their original ideas and creativity, to make as many mistakes as possible, and to learn from their experiences. They acquire practical skills and knowledge and develop personal qualities including entrepreneurship. All the crucial aspects of employability in the real world can be exercised in this virtual community.

Such simulated experience in JNVC not only connects members in the network to a real society, but also it sometimes helps a virtual world produce a real output. Mobile phone straps or scent bags of 'Sol*C' are a good example of this. Teachers involved with 'Sol*C' worked it out with a business partner (OTCCI) and produced the goods to be put on the market. Now these goods are sold together with other Ooe souvenirs. This year, one of the newly set up VCs from Ooe High Schools is discussing the possibility of developing their product ideas into real merchandise, in cooperation with their business partner, Gunze.   One of the students' ideas has become an experimental product and they are having regular meetings with their business partner.

In the process of running a VC with the support of the local industry, Ooe students had an opportunity to become aware of the resources available in their town.   By developing promotional tools for their local products and by inventing new merchandise themselves, students felt ownership of and responsibility for their local community. They realized that there are things they can do as a member of society, and that they can contribute to their community. At the same time, people from businesses realized what capabilities young people have, and they realized that they can contribute to the education of youth. The same things can be said about other groups involved in JNVC.

When these collaborations are formed well, in good partnership with virtual and real communities, they surely affect the development of the social infrastructure of the local communities.

Taking suggestions from this experiment during the year 2000, the e-trade banking system has been improved. The number of VCs is expected to expand to over 80 in November 2001. Students from elementary and junior high schools and their parents have joined in JNVC as consumers. About 1500 people are currently members of the JNVC network. More cooperation between the educational system and industry is happening on the community level.

The concept of this VC program will be much appreciated by the 'Period for Integrated Study' [9] which has almost the same objectives, and which will come into effect in Japan in April 2002 under National curriculum standards reform. We would like to continue exploring the potential of JNVC and study how the partnership between education and industry can positively affect the development of the social infrastructure within the local community.

Acknowledgements. This work has been supported by CREST of the Japan Science and Technology Corporation.

References

1. T. Ishida, "Understanding Digital Cities", *Digital Cities: Technologies, Experiences, and Future Perspectives, Lecture* Notes in Computer Science, Springer-Verlag, 2000
2. S. Miyagawa, I. Kaneko "The Mutual Development of Role, Rule, and Tool Through the VCOM Project", *Digital Cities: Technologies, Experiences, and Future Perspectives, Lecture* Notes in Computer Science, Springer-Verlag, 2000
3. Europen: http://www.europen.de/english/
4. Center for Entrepreneurship Education: http://entre.kysa.co.jp/e_index.html
5. Australian Network of Practice Firms: http://www.europen.de/english/
6. "Educational Reform Plan for 21st Century", Ministry of Education Culture, Sport Science and Technology: http://www.mext.go.jp/english/topics/21plan/010301.htm
7. Sanjokai Shopping Street: http://kbic.ardour.co.jp/~sanjo/index-j.html
8. Virtual site of Sanjokai Shoppin Street:
   http://www.edu.city.kyoto.jp/hp/saikyo/sanjo/tempo.html
9. "National standards of curriculum reform": Ministry of Education Culture, Sport Science and Technology: http://www.mext.go.jp/english/news/1998/07/980712.htm

Knowledge-Based Economic Services Supported by Digital Experiments

Dieter Rehfeld and Ileana Hamburg

Institut Arbeit und Technik (IAT), Wissenschaftszentrum Nordrhein-Westfalen
Gelsenkirchen, Germany
rehfeld@iatge.de / hamburg@iatge.de
http://iat-info.iatge.de

Abstract. Successful knowledge-based strategies for organizations require to build digital experiments which combine the power of networked information technologies like the Internet and the Web with the creativity and competencies of their own staff. This paper presents such an experiment which refers to the services of German economic development agencies. The presented work is carried out within a German project supported by the Federal Ministry of Education and Research (bmb+f). The development of required economic, social and technical competencies of the agencies staff by using Web-based qualification processes and virtual learning communities has a key role within the digital experiment.

1 Introduction

Discussing knowledge based economies has resulted in an increasing awareness of knowledge as a key factor for economic growth and performance. Technical advances in digital communications support new applications based on structuring of a variety of information and knowledge. Results of research studies (VDI Nachrichten 06.04.01) and of international conferences, e.g. 11th Annual Conference "Strategic Uses of Information Technology", Seattle 2000, show that in Germany there are many technical developments also in networked technologies, but referring to applications, Germany is still a "digital country in development".

In order to improve this situation, there are some initiatives of the German government, e.g. "Bund online 2005", and some national programs on this topic. In this paper, we start with a brief presentation of the use of knowledge management and of networked technologies like the Internet for the development of digital experiments, among others within economic development agencies (part 2). Then, we discuss the role of communities and of regions as nodes in a global network (part 3). In the rest of the paper we describe the objectives of the on-going project "Wirtschaftsförderung als wissensbasierte Dienstleistung" (Economic development as a knowledge based service activity) coordinated by the IAT in Gelsenkirchen, Germany, and supported by the Federal Ministry of Education and Research (bmb+f) (part 4).

The idea of this project is to improve the performance of economic development agencies, which play the role of a spider in nodding global networks, by taking into consideration two main aspects: the building of a vision of the future of the city or the

M. Tanabe, P. van den Besselaar, T. Ishida (Eds.): Digital Cities, LNCS 2362, pp. 164-176, 2002.
© Springer-Verlag Berlin Heidelberg 2002

region in a globally open economy, and the building of competencies to realize this vision. These aspects should be supported by the use of networked information technologies, by knowledge aiming at an intensification of internal as well as external communication, and by building virtual communities of life and learning.

Figure 1 gives an overview about the key issues of the project. The starting point concerns the question of a shared vision. In this first phase of the project research and face-to-face-communication is basic, and digital communication can support it. The core of the project concerns the digital infrastructure, as a tool to make knowledge sharing and effective project management work in a way that we call *learning organization*. Of course there is a need of improved competencies, related strategies and organizational structures. Web-based learning and a learning environment aim at improving the competencies. The aim is to strengthen networking and communication on the local as well as an the global level.

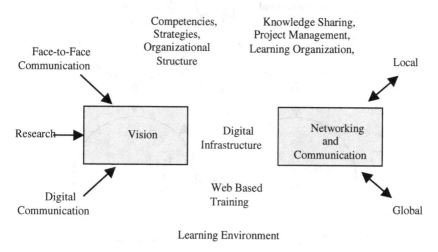

Fig. 1. Digital experiments to improve knowledge based economic development – the project

2 Knowledge Management and the Use of Networked Information Technologies

The concept of knowledge management is not new in information systems practice and research, but nowadays business environment, which is characterized by dynamics, a high level of uncertainty, and inability to predict the future, requires changes in the traditional view of knowledge management.

As figure 2 shows, knowledge means not only what a person knows but also what the organization knows – gathered from internal and external sources for years or even decades (Rosenberg, 2001).

Knowledge can be explicit or implicit (tacit). The explicit knowledge can easily be structured, codified and saved in printed or on-line documents, in databases and in knowledge bases, etc., and can be used for practices and training. It is more difficult to record implicit, tacit knowledge (e.g. heuristics which are often embedded in peoples' experiences of life and work), to document it, and to teach it to others. A combination of factors that are hard to describe or to teach give an inner quality to the implicit knowledge which, in many cases, is more valuable than the existing explicit knowledge. These different types of knowledge require different approaches to knowledge management, and each of them represents unique challenges and opportunities.

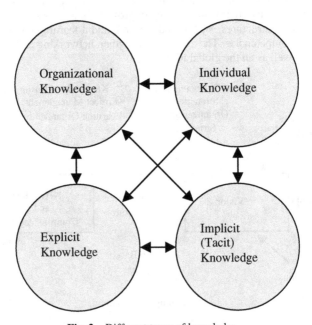

Fig. 2.   Different types of knowledge

In order to perform business activities successfully, all organizations, particularly economic development agencies, have to use a mix of tacit and explicit knowledge of individuals and organizations. So they need adaptable and flexible knowledge-based services based on networked information technologies that support the management of this mix of knowledge, and combine those with competencies and creativity of their staff.

The Internet is one of the most promising networked technologies because it allows two-way communications, e.g., audience as well as the possibility of feedback. It is built around open standards, which means interoperability and the advantage of a large market, and the possibility to integrate one product or process with another.

Intranet and Web technologies facilitate the building of closed, organizational virtual networks like the Intranets or private ones like the extranets (e.g., for the communication with customers).

Learning over the Internet (Web-based training) enables instant updating, storage/retrieval, distribution and sharing of instructions. Therefore, it is one of the "most promising" forms of learning, which can be applied in all kinds of training programs, like in vocational training. Distributed software tools based on Internet and the Web should be developed which facilitate the delivery of right information to the right person at the right time, the acquisition and storing of explicit and implicit knowledge in organizational knowledge bases, and the distribution of it.

Institutionalization of "best practices" by embedding those in information systems might facilitate efficient handling of routine, "linear" and predictable situations in stable as well as in changing environments of an organization. But when these changes are discontinuous, then continuous renewal is required of the best practices stored in organizational knowledge bases.

In literature there are different opinions about the consequences of the use of the networked technologies. Some authors as Rushkoff (as quoted by Graham and Marvin) predict that the diffusion of interactive technologies, such as Web and e-mails "will be used to enhance the individual and to break down the walls between individuals". Opposite to these "utopists", the "distopians" (Postman, 1992) stress that the use of new media will cause a growing social polarization, and that the wealth of information does not necessarily mean that people have more knowledge. The directions of changes due to the Internet and to other new technologies are still uncertain, they have to be discovered yet. But based on the abilities of these technologies, new kinds of social places and services in virtual reality (cyberspace) by can be developed, like the virtual cities and virtual communities, where people can meet, work, exchange experience, acquire new knowledge, and learn without ever seeing each other in the physical world (Ishida, 1998).

One of the main questions to be answered when using the Internet, the Web and virtual spaces remains "how to build digital experiments which bring virtual and real spaces together?"

3   Building Digital Experiments to Link Virtual and Real Spaces

Digitalization is one of the economic driving forces compressing time and space (Sassen, 1999). Nevertheless, the Internet is a social space, too. And because of this, it is helpful to ask for communities that make the Internet a working room where people can collaborate in creation and use of knowledge.

With the advent of computer-mediated communication (CMC) and virtual reality it has become difficult to determine exactly what is meant by the word community. People associate the environment where they work, live and cooperate with other people with the notion of community. This environment is not static: it changes almost every day, it is alive. A community can be understood as "a social group of any size whose members reside in a specific locality, share government, and have a common cultural and historical heritage ...... a social group sharing common characteristics and interests..." (Rheingold, 1994).

Knowledge management fosters the growth of knowledge communities, learning communities or communities of practice. Eric Vogt and Diane Hessan from Communispace Corp. give the following definition:

"A learning community is a trusting group of professionals united by a common concern or purpose, dedicated to support each other in increasing their knowledge, creating new insights, and enhancing performance is a particular domain" (Rosenberg, 2001).

Communities can be built around content or disciplines; they can be also project, process or product specific. Although people within a community have similar interests, and are focused on closely related goals, they may not have the same level of experience or expertise, and they may have different needs for digital experiments supporting knowledge management.

In case of a virtual community, based on CMC and the Internet, the limitations of the geographic and temporal dimensions does not exist. The exchange of information, and the communication within virtual communities are independent of place and time. This leads to an increasing potential of the community members, and to better information sources, both quantitative and qualitative.

Rheingold (1994) says that "Virtual communities are social aggregations that emerge from the Net when enough people carry out those public discussions long enough, with sufficient human feeling, to form webs of personal relationships in cyberspace. This is the conceptual space where words, human relationships, data, wealth and power are manifested by people using Internet technology". It has the potential to change humans, communities, and democracies. Therefore, it is important to understand the nature of Internet-based communication, of the cyberspace, and of virtual communities in every context: politically, economically, socially, cognitively. The use of the Internet adds dimensions to the communities that otherwise would not be present (Pallof, 1999).

The building of learning communities within cyberspaces, which connect tutors, experts and participants in a common course, is of eminent importance, also for economic agencies. This aspect is the essence of Web-based training (see part 4), which we use in our project. There is a great deal of research on the value of communities in support of learning. At many institutes (e.g. at the Institute for Research on Learning in Palo Alto, California) researchers work to reinforce the social nature of learning. People learn best when they can interact with other people as full members in communities of shared interest. Covey (1989) affirms that the collaboration involved in learning in communities creates a sense of synergy, an atmosphere of excitement and passion for learning, for working together, supporting the process of knowledge acquisition. In the traditional model of training, the tutor imparts knowledge to participants, who are expected to absorb it. In the learning processes in virtual communities, the relationships and interactions among people are the main channels for generating knowledge.

Some authors underline characteristics of virtual communities and virtual spaces: "we have to keep in mind, that each community is dependent on a net of responsibility. Without any commitment a community would disintegrate, real as well as virtual ones. To keep a community alive, we need shared visions and joint projects" (Weinstein, 2000). Castells (1997) points out that „Space is the material support of time-sharing social practices." From this point of view, electronic networks are social spaces, too. The space of flows is not placeless, although its structural logic has these characteristics. The electronic networks links up specific places. These places have well-defined characteristics that can be viewed as a profile. Some places are playing the role of coordination for the interaction of all players in the network. Other places are the nodes in the network.. „Location in the node links up the locality with the whole network" (Castells, 1997), or in other words, nodes are linking the local and the global. These aspects referring to nets and nodes constitute a good starting point to discuss the fundamental shift in political and social, as well as in economic terms.

"Telematics and globalization have emerged as fundamental forces in the reorganization of economic space. This reorganization ranges from the spatial virtualization of a growing number of economic activities to the reconfiguration of the geography of the built environment for economy activity. Whether in electronic space or in the geography of the built environment, this reorganization involves institutional and structural changes." (Sassen, 1999)

In her analysis, Sassen is concentrating on global cities and global value chains. But our analysis shows that global change is a more fragmented process in functional as well as in sectoral terms (Rehfeld, 2001). There are different economic flows becoming more and more global and each of these flows has specific geographical dimensions, specific hubs and nodes, specific kinds of networks.

From the local or regional point of view, the key question is how to drag the anchor and to avoid to become subordinated to the flows of a global network. That is the question cities and regions have to answer. The opening of global flows, maybe communication flows or maybe economic flows like products and services, needs a strong local basis. In terms of communication, this needs a high density of internal communication, and in terms of economy it refers to an innovative "milieu" (Camagni 1991). To bring these spaces together is the main topic of our project.

Of course, the future of economy is a network economy. Nevertheless, economic activities remain social activities, and social activities need direct social communication: Trust in order to reduce insecurity, the generation and diffusion of implicit knowledge, especially when intercultural communication takes place, common learning and other social activities are limited in its virtualizing capacity. So there exists a chance for local and regional networking, especially in a world that becomes more and more global.

4   The Project

4.1   Starting Points

In order to use the Internet and CMC for effective digital experiments like virtual cities and virtual communities, it is important to build a "vision" of the space to be transformed, in a globally acting network, and to choose the suitable techniques to collect the data and to process the needed knowledge in order to develop the experiment based on this vision.

In our project we don't look at the hubs, but at the nodes. The regions of our project are not global cities, they are more normal regions that can be found all over the world. Gelsenkirchen is an old industrial city in the core of the Ruhr Area. It is a city in ongoing restructuring and with an unemployment rate up to 18 percent. The Rheinisch-Bergische Kreis is a small and medium companies based location with a high degree in sectoral differentiation.

This is not the place to discuss a vision for these two locations. A vision like this can only be articulated by the people living inside a region. But to make a vision work two aspects are important:

First aspect is to focus the activities on shared projects, innovation projects aiming at sustainability, symbolic architecture perhaps in the built environment. It is important that visions like this include images and symbols which people can see and feel. It is not only a by-side aspect that the articulation of visions because this strengthens internal communication.

Second aspect is to give a profile to a location, a city or a region. A location is not really interesting when it claims to be better, bigger or faster – nearly all locations all over the world try to be attractive in this way. But the crucial point is to become different. In the course of globalization all regions run danger to become identical and that means to become banal. Therefore, the challenge is to improve the difference, because the difference has good chances to be recognized from outside.

In Gelsenkirchen we have started a process to bring out a vision by spring 2001. 40 years ago, Gelsenkirchen had been a booming city. Based on mining, steel generating and steel processing Gelsenkirchen has been known as „city of thousand fires." Today, mines have run empty, steel processing has been relocated, and steel processing has become fragmented in very different companies and markets. Gelsenkirchen runs danger to become a very simple place like a lot of other old industrial places all over the world. Nevertheless, there is some innovative potential left and some new companies had been founded. But the industrial basis is very fragmented, yet. Facing this situation, the key issue of the project aims at connecting local nodes to build a stable basis for global networking. The first step is to improve local networking, aiming at common projects like mentioned above. This is a starting point, and in the long run the hope is to bring a new identity into life.

Doing this, we have to organize communication on different levels (Fig. 1). In this first stage communication means first of all face-to-face-communication. The organizational core is a steering group, consisting of representatives of 15 companies and some members of the local industrial development agency. The companies belong to very different industrial sectors. Old ones, like water management, mechanical engineering, plant construction, and basic chemicals. New ones, like information and communication technologies, solar energy, and electronics. The common interest is to revitalize Gelsenkirchen. This group is in charge of the key decisions, like agenda setting and the selection of priorities. Because this group represents only a small part of the industrial basis of the city, another 50 companies are included through expert interviews. In these interviews we are discussing the company's vision and strategies, and its local integration, and we try to activate their local engagement. Commitment by local authorities is a further level of the project. Therefore the results of the project are presented and discussed with local authorities from time to time.

Finally, face-to-face-communication takes places in the context of workshops. These workshops are organized in order to give additional actors the chance to join the process, and to create a commitment to specific projects. In this context, support by digital communication is helpful. The problem is that we need professional, strategically oriented small workshops, to bring about concrete results, but that we also need new ideas to overcome the old discussions and to bring about synergies. Therefore, from time to time, we are opening the discussion by presenting ideas and results on the Internet, and we are organizing an open space (chat room) to bring in new ideas, and more.

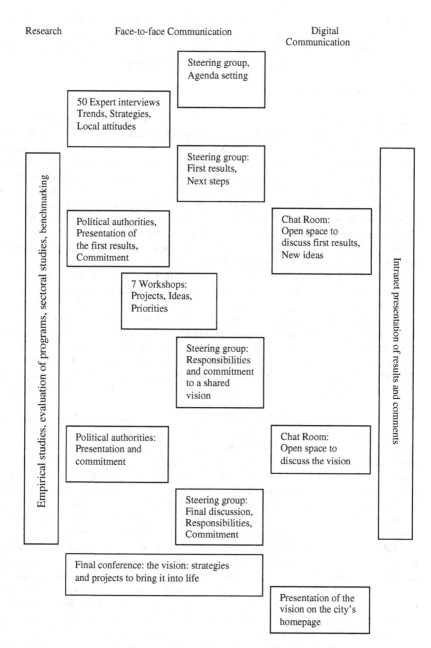

Fig. 3. In search of a shared vision

Our hope is, when the process of local networking has a solid social basis, and when we have an idea of a common vision, communication can be organized digitally. To support this, the members of the local industrial development agencies need further competencies, and an advanced technological basis.

4.2 Objectives of the Project

A lot of competencies are needed to implement visions like mentioned above, which are usually not available in economic development agencies. Up to the 1990s, local development agencies were concentrated on the acquisition of internal investments. But in the course of the last decades, competition for investments has become very strong on a global level. Therefore, the focus of the activities of economic development agencies has shifted to improve the local basis of innovation and economic strength. This is reflected in research by he use of terms like "network-economy", "cluster-development", "learning region", "reflexive urban development", and "knowledge based local infrastructure". Whatever the term refers to in detail, the common focus is to strengthen and improve the local potentials and competencies by networking, learning, and knowledge sharing.

Facing these new tasks, a lot of new competencies are needed, for instance strategic development, location marketing, human resource management, innovation and technology management, internal and external networking, knowledge management, conflict management, or controlling (Bratl & Trippl, 2001). Usually, all these competencies are available in a location, but they don't have a common focus. The function of a local development agency is not to build up all these competencies in house, but to make use of local competencies to improve the local industrial basis. Insofar, a local node in a global network is a potential, not a reality, yet (Appadurai, 1999). To make this potential work, the use of new telecommunication technology can be very helpful.

As pointed out, most of the knowledge that the economic development agencies need to manage their tasks is fragmented, and it is distributed over different economic agents. New strategic solutions for theoretical and practical concepts to improve the economic agencies services are needed by using digital support for these services including Internet-based procedures for an efficient management and for the use of implicit and explicit knowledge of individuals and organization and support for CMC.

The development and testing of such a concept, which includes also Web-based learning modules for the agencies' staff in order to acquire the needed competence for an efficient use of the digital experiment is the main objective of our project.

Interdisciplinary work is planned within the project, by constituting a project steering group. For the implementation and testing of the concept, two pilot agencies have been chosen: the municipal agency of the city Gelsenkirchen, and the regional agency Bergisch-Gladbach. The work within the project will be structured by questions about organizational aspects, management of knowledge resources, development of competencies, and the support of a digital infrastructure. This should strengthen "high quality" communication and information exchange both within the economic agencies as well as with their clients and cooperating partners. It should be supported by Web-based learning processes and the building of learning communities.

4.3 Digital Infrastructure Supporting Knowledge-Based Services

Tom Kelley, the Vice President of World-wide Training, Cisco Systems, Inc. says that "On the Internet, content may be king, but Infrastructure is God". In our project, the digital infrastructure supporting knowledge-based services will be based on Web and on the existing intranets of the agencies, in order to be easily integrated with existing computer facilities, and to assure low development costs. The functionality of the intranets will be extended with procedures for CMC, as well as for knowledge management, e.g., collecting, structuring, distribution, evaluation, using knowledge. Figure 4 shows such procedures for knowledge management and training.

As an example, collaborative services which support an asynchronous co-operation and communication by using discussion forums or News groups or a synchronous one by chat facilities are planned to be developed.

The procedures of communication and knowledge management will be accessible by using a Web portal with easy to use search engines. It is important to use the Web portal as a "gate" to the knowledge world, because often this constitutes the first contact with the clients and other partners. Additionally, the Web-sites which use multimedia and other technologies are a user-friendly media of communication.

Procedures for knowledge management and communication which we would like to develop in our project are important for the two economic agencies not only for their activities as consultant. In order to remain competitive within their area of business, the agencies have to be able to react quickly to world-wide processes of knowledge transfer, and to be able to create new individual and organizational knowledge.

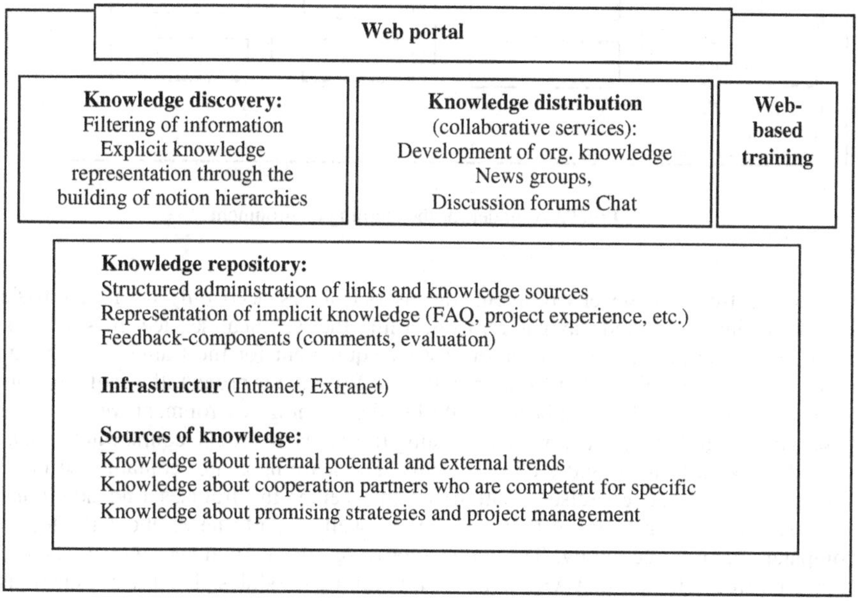

Web portal		
Knowledge discovery: Filtering of information Explicit knowledge representation through the building of notion hierarchies	**Knowledge distribution** (collaborative services): Development of org. knowledge News groups, Discussion forums Chat	**Web-based training**
Knowledge repository: Structured administration of links and knowledge sources Representation of implicit knowledge (FAQ, project experience, etc.) Feedback-components (comments, evaluation) **Infrastructur** (Intranet, Extranet) **Sources of knowledge:** Knowledge about internal potential and external trends Knowledge about cooperation partners who are competent for specific Knowledge about promising strategies and project management		

Fig. 4. Procedures accessible by using a Web portal

In our project we would like to facilitate that those processes of transfer and creating new individual and organizational knowledge take place directly at the shop floor.

4.4 The Learning Environment

The learning processes in the project are supported by a Web-based digital learning environment where self-directed learning is combined with collaborative learning, and sound "generic" know-how is linked with tightly fitting solutions for the economic agencies. As a basis for the environment we use the software developed within the German project FrauTelNet (Engert, 1999). The learning environment is accessible also by using the Web portal (Fig. 5).

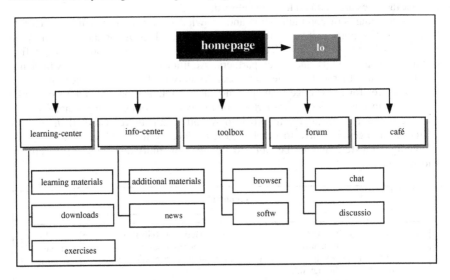

Fig. 5. A model for the learning environment

On the front-end of the environment, the users/learners need only to master basic Internet technologies and navigators. Concerning the technical service, it is a major objective of the project to keep the necessary equipment for the trainees at a minimum, in order to avoid technical discrimination. Within our project, the requirements are Internet access and a Web browser. Within the learning environment we are going to provide the following categories of learning resources and tools: courseware, email, chat, discussion forums, and feedback-forms. The learning-center contains the basic course materials and exercises. Within the info-center the trainees find additional information referring to the offered courses as well as daily news about the topics computer, Internet, economy. The toolbox provides the participants with tools like browsers, free software that will be needed within the modules. The forum functions as communication platform for trainees and tutors. So does the café, which is only used for "social" communication, not directly related to the content of the course.

The chat within the learning environment should be used to ask short questions about the courses and to assign working exercises. We offer a chat-room for every module and a meeting point. In general, the chat is open to the trainees at any time, but during prefixed hours it is accompanied by a tutor to structure the discussion process and to encourage trainees to participate.

The synchronous communication supported by chat rooms allows a fast and efficient exchange of comments on a topic. However, a disadvantage lies in the impossibility to follow different discussions at the same time, and the loss of remarks, which are forgotten along the discussion process.

For longer comments, the different discussion forums can be used. In addition to the advantage of being a structured discussion, the forum allows a certain flexibility concerning the working hours of the trainees. Within our previous projects, we experienced that a discussion forum with is open to all does not work very well. Many participants rather send an email or chat, than contribute to the discussion forum, which is readable for all trainees. Therefore, a strong tutor is needed to encourage the trainees to participate.

Within the training we would like to include sessions (not only on-line classrooms) where trainees and tutors meet face-to-face, unless this is completely unfeasible. These sessions are important to lower barriers, as IT-based learning is unfamiliar to most learners. In our project, the workshops play a significant role also in providing hands-on experience with the required technologies, especially the techniques needed to work with the Web-based learning environment. Furthermore, we would like to stress that it is very important to provide sufficient technical support throughout the course, i.e., to have a person in the team which is permanently accessible, also by telephone, to help with technical questions.

The development of a learning community and of a knowledge community is facilitated by the design of the learning environment described above, and by the delivery methods for the learning material. With respect to the first, the learning environment rests on a dialectic between knowledge which has been fixed in the textbook, supplementary materials provided beforehand, and the generation of knowledge in a guided, but open process of communication of equal partners. It can be done in chats and discussion forums offered by the environment and in the creation of original work by the trainees, e.g. in Web-based small projects during the training.

At the beginning of the training, the virtual learning community has to be stimulated by promoting small teams around the trainee's projects and the tasks. To stimulate the work, and the (electronic) communication, a very active role of the tutors is needed – a role which differs quite fundamentally from the traditional role. Needed are facilitators and moderators, and not traditional lecturers.

5 Conclusions

In this paper we present the first steps of a project about the development of knowledge-based digital experiments for German economic agencies. Because the two agencies have their own economic profile the project team works intensively with the corresponding staff in this early project phase in order to find the right vision for each of them. The experiments should be integrated into the business and cultural environment of the agencies and should contribute to create suitable competences for the staff.

References

1. Appadurai, A., 1999: *Globalization and the research imagination*. In: International Journal of Social Science.
2. Bratl, H. and Trippl, M., 2001: Innovation System Management Austria. Wien.
3. Camagni, R., 1991: Local „milieu", uncertainty and innovation networks: towards a dynamic theory of economic space. In: Camagni, R. (ed.): Innovation networks: spatial perspectives. London/New York.
4. Castells, M., 1997: The Rise of the Network Society. (The Information Age. Economy, Society and Culture vol 1). Malden, Mass.
5. Covey, S., 1989: The Seven Habits of Highly Effective People: Powerful Lessons in Personal Change, Fireside, New York.
6. Engert, St., Hamburg, I., Terstriep, J. 1999:, Kompetenznetzwerke zur Kontext-steuerung von Wissensteilung: Ein Beispiel. In: P. Brödner and I. Hamburg (ed.), Strategische Wissensnetze: Wie Unternehmen die Ressource Wissen nutzen. Gelsenkirchen.
7. Graham and Marvin, 1996: Telecommunication and the city. Electronic space, urban places, Routlege, New York, US.
8. Ishida, T., Isbister, K., 2000: Digital Cities: Technologies, Experiences and Future Perspective, Springer, Berlin/Heidelberg/New York.
9. Murdock, G., 1993: Communication and the constitution of modernity. In: Media, Culture and Society 15.
10. Pallof, R. and Pratt, K., 1999: Building Learning Communities in Cyberspace, San Francisco.
11. Postman, N. 1992, Technopolis: The Surrender of Culture to Technology, Vintage, New York.
12. Rehfeld, D., 2001: Global strategies compared: Firms, markets and regions. In: European Planning Studies vol. 9.
13. Rosenberg, M., 2001: E-LEARNING - Strategies for Delivering Knowledge in the Digital Age, McGraw-Hill, New York.
14. Reingold, H., 1994: Virtuelle Gemeinschaft, 1. Auflage, Addison-Wesley.
15. Sassen, S., 1999: Urban Economies and Fading Distances.
    http://www.megacities.nl/lecture_sassen.html
16. Weinstein, M., 2000: Die Himmelstür zum Cyberspace. Von Dante zum Internet. Zürich.

Community Network Development: A Dialectical View

Murali Venkatesh[1] and Donghee Shin[2]

[1] Ph.D., Associate Professor & Director
School of Information Studies
Community & Information Technology Institute (CITI)
4-279 Center for Science & Technology
Syracuse University
Syracuse, New York 13244-4100
(315) 443-4477 mvenkate@syr.edu

[2] Doctoral Student
School of Information Studies
4-227 Center for Science & Technology
Syracuse University
Syracuse, New York 13244-4100
(315) 443-5618 dhsin@syr.edu

Abstract. Drawing on an ongoing longitudinal research study, we discuss problems in the development of Urban-net, a next generation community network in a city in central New York. The project was funded under a state program to diffuse broadband technologies in economically depressed areas of the state. The network is technologically complex and entails high costs for subscribers. The political economy of the development process has biased the subscriber base toward the resource rich and away from the resource poor, and toward uses like intra-organizational connectivity and Internet access and away from community-oriented uses as originally envisaged. These trends raise troubling questions about network ontology and function, and about the relation between the network and its physical host community.

1 Introduction

In 1995, as part of a settlement of a regulatory case before the NY State Public Service Commission, the incumbent local exchange carrier in the state (hereafter the carrier) committed $50 million to develop and deploy broadband telecommunications services in economically depressed communities across the state. The program that came into being as a consequence established a competitive request for proposals process to solicit proposals from eligible consortia of public institutions (such as city and county government agencies, K-12 schools and higher educational institutions, healthcare organizations like hospitals), social sector non-profits, and small business entities. Subscribers had to be located in or provide services to approved low-income zip code areas to be eligible for subsidies. State government agencies could not

M. Tanabe, P. van den Besselaar, T. Ishida (Eds.): Digital Cities, LNCS 2362, pp. 177-190, 2002.

participate in the program, nor could individual residents. Two rounds of grants were awarded before the program concluded in 2000. In all, 22 projects were funded – fourteen urban/suburban, six rural, with two qualifying as urban/suburban/rural combination projects [14].

Subscribers were eligible for reduced monthly service charges and some financial support toward computer and networking equipment at the user premise (customer premise equipment or CPE). Eighty per cent of every grant went back to the carrier for infrastructure and services development and deployment. The remainder could be applied toward CPE or training at the subscriber site. Grant funds could not be used to hire technical consultants or administrative staff, or to support applications development.

The goal of the program was to bring "advanced telecommunications services to economically disadvantaged areas of New York State that would not be available in the near future on account of limitations in the advanced telecommunications infrastructure and related equipment marketplace" [14]. In other words, these areas would not have access to advanced services if it were left to market forces. Less formally but no less important as a goal, the program sought to encourage public institutions, non-profits and small business entities to come together to meet local needs and solve local problems. Program selection committee members pointed to the strengthening of existing institutional ties and forging of new ones in grantee communities as a program goal. They viewed a program-funded network as a *community network* – an enabler of local and cross-sectoral connectivity where, for example, the city's public schools could connect not just to other schools but to non-profits and the city zoo as well to serve a broad cross-section of residents.

Explaining the decision to use a competitive request for proposals process, a selection committee member said: "We were not interested in putting technology in place. (Proposers) had to make a strong case that the investment would make a difference to the community in economic and social terms". To be eligible for program subsidies, subscribers had to connect to a shared backbone. One respondent emphasized this point: "Recall that…organizations had to connect to a common backbone: this reinforced the notion of community and information sharing". This way, subscribers could connect to the world at large through the Internet but would also be connected to other subscribers locally, in the host community. In the latter sense, a program-funded network was intended to serve as an inter-organizational infrastructure. To qualify for an award, proposals had to show sustainable, broad-based support for the project within the local community.

Program selection committee respondents' construal of "community", "community networking" and "community network" was "aspirational" [21], and envisioned a desired end-state. Analyzing the process by which a community network develops allows us to show how developmental trajectories get deflected from desired goals and why conservative trajectories may persist despite stakeholders' best intentions and transformational aspirations. A process orientation views technological choices as socially constructed, that is, as outcroppings of a social process with conflicting human and institutional interests, the representation of these interests and their relative influence over outcomes. As with technologies in general, a community network is shaped by social, political and economic choices. These are part of the network's history and are "embedded in the social structure which supports its development and use" [19: p.103].

In this paper, we trace the development of Urban-net[1], a next generation community network. We refer to it as a *community network* in the sense that its geophysical context is defined by certain economically depressed areas in a medium-sized city in central New York. The term "next generation" is defined below. The major findings can be quickly summarized. First, Urban-net's technological complexity and high subscription costs have biased subscription toward the resource rich and away from the resource poor. The picture is quite consistent with Castells' argument that high technology mobilizes a dualizing logic, dividing the resource rich from the resource poor [12]. Second, we also found a balkanizing logic, with subscribers using (or intending to use) Urban-net services for inter-organizational connectivity (where, for example, branch campuses are linked to headquarters over the network) or Internet access, not local inter-connectivity. Ironically, the needs analysis effort at the project's outset had revealed a high degree of interest in local and cross-sectoral connectivity via the Urban-net.

The Urban-net currently has 12 subscribers, with a total of 204 endpoints (connections) among them. The list includes public institutions like city and county government agencies, K-12 public schools, a university and hospitals. Small non-profits and small business units are notably absent from the list. These entities often provide key services in low-income neighborhoods. Eight such entities, as part of a separate coalition outside the program and the Urban-net, have negotiated subsidized digital subscriber line (DSL) service with a competitive carrier for Internet access and internal connectivity. The coalition is linked electronically to the Urban-net.

2 Advanced Technology Community Networks

As a broadband network infrastructure, the Urban-net is significantly more complex compared to dial-up community networks (powered by the telephone modem) of the first generation [30]. We refer to the Urban-net as a *next generation community network* (NGCN). Our characterization is limited to the project described here and should not be taken to represent community networks in general.

The Urban-net has the following features, which constitute our definition of NGCN.

➢ *High technological complexity*: The Urban-net is a technologically complex, broadband, open, multi-service and multi-layered community intranet with high-speed Internet access. It can support data transfer at high to very high rates (1.5

---

[1] Urban-net is a pseudonym adopted to protect the identity of the people involved in the project.

Mbps to 1 Gbps range). Gigabit Ethernet and Asynchronous Transfer Mode (ATM) cell relay service are the services available to subscribers. As a broadband environment, the network can support delivery of high-touch services (high-bandwidth services with rich media content, like video-conferencing) while also supporting conventional uses (information exchange and email). The Urban-net is not merely a logically carved-out and locally focused segment of the Internet [30] but inverts the paradigm: it is a hardwired, broadband, intranet (access restricted to eligible organizations) that also connects subscribers to the Internet.

➢ *Costly and complex applications development*: Developing applications for the Urban-net is resource-intensive and technically complex. For example, the county library system would like to digitize its holdings and place them online through a portal accessible over the Urban-net and the Internet. The design and development of such a multi-media application with adequate security and service quality assurance calls for complex skill sets and significant resources.

➢ *Complex services contracting*: Contracting for Urban-net services can be complex for subscribers. As their needs evolve, subscribers will be faced with in-source vs. buy decisions on a broad range of network services, potentially from multiple service providers in a competitive marketplace. While this will benefit subscribers, it will also complicate contracting.

➢ *High subscription costs*: Subsidized subscription charges range from approximately $300 a month for Gigabit Ethernet to 15 times that for high-end ATM service. Subscribers have to pay extra for Internet access, and an additional charge for network management and related services. In 1998, relatively cheaper DSL was eligible for program subsidies. Many non-profits were interested in DSL for its affordability. However, it subsequently became a tariffed service and became ineligible. The Urban-net technology committee suggested variations on the tariffed DSL service that might be eligible for program subsidies, but the carrier was not open to exploring these options.

3   Community Network Development as Dialectic

The dialectical view is focused on analyzing the process by which a social system develops along certain lines, how this trajectory is maintained or reproduced, and how its character changes over time [5]. Marx used the method in his critique of capitalism, but its general perspective is not Marxist. Benson enumerates four principles of dialectical analysis – social construction/production, contradiction, totality and praxis [5]. He defines these principles for use in organizations. We extend their use to the developmental analysis of the Urban-net – which developed within the socio-political context of the city and had explicit and progressive social goals included in its morphology.

We consider each of these principles below.

Social construction/production: Technological artifacts develop within a particular social context through a social process. Their form and function bear the imprint of social forces – political, economic, cultural – at work in the developmental context. The process of social shaping may be analyzed at the micro-scale and the macro-scale. Micro-scale analysis is concerned with human agency: How do the actions of human agents (designers, users) shape design choices? Macro-scale analysis is concerned with the broader social structure: How do societal relations, and the values and needs that shape those relations, influence the actions of human agents? [7] [13] [23] A micro-scale analysis of the Urban-net's development is beyond the scope of this paper. We do, however, touch on the implications of human agency for systemic change. We present below a macro-scale perspective on the developmental process.

The tension between dominant economic interests and the Urban-net's social goals surfaced contradictions and raised fundamental questions about network ontology and function: *Whose network is it anyway*, and *What is it for?*

The dialectical view acknowledges the interaction of political and economic interests in influencing change in social systems. These same forces are acknowledged shapers of telecommunications systems as well: "the driving forces shaping the application and development of telecommunications are the political, economic, social and cultural dynamics of capitalism itself" [17]. Not surprisingly, Urban-net's development was powerfully influenced by the interests of large public institutions. These institutions saw the Urban-net as a means to cut their telecommunications costs by replacing existing services with subsidized services. The public institutions represented large accounts the carrier did not want to lose to a competing provider. The project's social goals receded in importance as the process unfolded, and the economic interests of the large players and their political clout with the carrier emerged as decisive shaping forces. This is not to say that the public institutions, or the carrier, exercised power consciously to manipulate project goals. They were seen by the project steering committee as vital "to get the network up and running" by being early adopters, and their influence stemmed from their putative role as guarantors of the project going forward. As early adopters, their interests were considered crucial to the community having an advanced technology network at all.

The more the use of a network "depends on social organization and mobilization of significant resources, the more it will tend to be controlled by those who are already organized and well-off" [9]. A recent report by an independent consultant, which reviewed all 22 projects funded under the program, reached a similar conclusion: "those institutions already involved in technology and advanced technology such as BOCES (a county-level technology resource organization for K-12 schools), community colleges and hospitals were predisposed to or ready to take full advantage of the program" [14: p. 29]. Continuance of the program subsidies to address the needs of non-profits was proposed recently before the Public Service Commission:

"Because of the funding constraints which they experience…community service organizations in low income areas are often unable to incorporate…advanced technologies into their operations…By focusing the available rate reductions on this sector of service providers in low income communities ...(the continuance of the program) will help bring these customers more directly into the digital economy and...bridge the digital divide". [28: pp. 3-4]

The document continues:

"The non-profit organizations eligible for the reduced rates would include community action agencies, day care centers...community centers, community health care clinics, legal aid offices, and other service providers located within low income communities. By reducing broadband rates for these organizations, real assistance is provided to the organizations which create the social infrastructure on which low income communities depend and, therefore, to the low income families and households which make up that community" [28: p. 3].

Importantly, besides rate reductions (subsidized network access charges), the document seeks assistance to cover technical support resources and support for CPE.

At a critical point during the Urban-net design (technical specification) process, there was an implied threat from program authorities to revoke the grant if not enough subscribers signed on. In response, the project steering committee adopted what we call the "Mall model" of diffusion. The implied justification was: sign on anchor tenants (early adopter public institutions) and then worry about recruiting others. The Mall model was useful in starting up the network. The threat was averted. But the model is unlikely to be successful as a broad diffusion mechanism in the absence of provisions in the project by-laws requiring the resource rich to assist the resource poor to get connected. Currently, there are no such provisions mandating cooperation among eligible institutions. Hence market forces will continue to apply to narrow the subscriber base to those that can afford to pay.

The Mall model was also attractive to the carrier. The carrier operated in a highly competitive market, with competing local exchange carriers vying for the same large accounts. Locking in large accounts early was an outcome attractive to the carrier.

Contradictions: Contradictions, or "ruptures, breaks and inconsistencies in the social fabric" [5 p. 14] – may prefigure change and often result from it. It is critical to analyze contradictions because they are a source of conflict and can limit the developmental possibilities of systems.

The Urban-net developmental effort has abounded in contradictions. As noted earlier, a basic one is that between hard economic realities and the project's progressive social goals. The balkanizing of the network is an offshoot essentially of its economics and is inconsistent with the idea of a program-funded network as a catalyst of cross-sectoral connectivity in the host community.

Contradictions were evident even within subscriber organizations. The "techy" types (information systems and telecommunications staff) represented the interests of public institutions differently from general management representatives from these same sites. The general management reps were interested in innovative uses of the Urban-net, while the techies were driven to cut organizational telecommunications costs through subsidized services. Participation by the techies grew more prominent as the development process intensified, and that by general management reps weakened. The techies grew more prominent for several reasons: they were more attuned to the vocabulary and concepts of the technologies involved, they could authorize and implement systems infrastructure modifications that subscription would entail, and, increasingly, as the process wore on, they represented the financial interests of their institution, which was critical given the high subscription costs. The institution's needs and interests came to the foreground as a result, while those of the *community* (the interstitial needs and interests that collectively made up the common ground) receded.

Totality: A dialectical view requires that "social phenomena should be studied relationally, that is, with attention to their multiple interconnections. Any particular structure is always seen as part of a larger concrete whole rather than as an isolated, abstract phenomenon" [5: p. 4]. In the present research, a key relation is that between Urban-net and its geophysical context. The program required that the network be based in and advance the interests of the poorer sections in the host community, and the project steering committee's aspirations for it were consistent with this focus on locality. Descriptive, non-evaluative definitions of the term start with the notion of locality: a community, in its basic sense, is tied to a particular physical locale [20]. A community network should be "as grounded as possible by primarily gearing toward local users" [3: p. 498].

The project steering committee viewed the Urban-net as a catalyst in the city's social and economic revitalization. But it was seen as little more than high technology by the city's urban planning establishment and, as such, was not part of the city's present social reality or its future. City planners played only a small, non-substantive role in the development process: they generated GIS maps on eligible zip codes at the project's outset. They viewed the project as "too esoteric" and as "not impacting the grassroots". Elected officers and the mass media played no part in the project (one county-level officer participated briefly early on in the process before dropping out; [10] [25] on the need for strong political and mass media participation in community initiatives). This meant the Urban-net was not part of any transforming, inclusive, strategic vision for the city, nor was it viewed in relation to the city's pressing social needs or problems. A master plan for the city has been proposed by the Mayor's office and is expected to reference the Urban-net. However, civic priorities were unavailable to inform, or be informed by, the network in its crucial formative stages, when questions of access equity and network ontology and function could have been debated most profitably (Aurigi notes a similar disconnect between urban planners and digital city projects in Europe [2]).

There are currently no proposals for Urban-net applications targeting the needs of the elderly, the disabled, or the city's many racial and ethnic groups. The poor, whose numbers and spatial concentrations provided the project's physical and moral context, are not covered either. There are no proposals to use the Urban-net to combat urgent social problems such as adolescent pregnancy and infant mortality (in the late 90s, the county's infant mortality rate was among the highest in the nation). Socially responsible and community-oriented applications may yet develop as the network evolves, but will be dependent on the vagaries of external funding. Meanwhile, the community at large may see little benefit from the project.

The disconnect between community needs and the Urban-net raises a fundamental question: Do subscribers have obligations to the host community? Should subscribers be viewed as institutional citizens or merely as consumers? The right of an agency located in or offering services to eligible zip code areas to receive program subsidies came up many times in steering committee discussions on Urban-net development policy. The related notion of subscriber obligations to the host community came up exactly once. A city government agency representative argued: "Since large players are getting such a good deal (from subsidized services), couldn't we require them to provide resources and services to smaller agencies? Large players have to see themselves as resource providers. This is part of their responsibility". This line of reasoning was never pursued. Many "smaller agencies" – non-profits – are part of a community's grassroots social support infrastructure and serve the neediest residents. A system of mandated cooperation [22] where the resource rich assist the resource poor to get connected might have helped equalize access to the benefits of the Urban-net.

Citizenship in a polity confers rights and requires obligations of rights holders. It is central to the ideal of civil society – which is founded on mutuality and reciprocity. Aspirations consistent with these were part of the morphology of the Urban-net. Mandelbaum notes: "the beginning of the search for a craft of community design is the notion of membership. Members are bound to one another by a web of rights and obligations" [24: p. 10]. A community network and its subscribers cannot escape the reciprocity of obligations (if only in the contractual sense), especially when the network is funded with rate-payers' monies. The Urban-net's by-laws do not require obligations of any kind. Subscribers are expected/encouraged, but not required, to "support projects that will benefit the underserved in the community", according to the project leadership responding to the first author's recent biannual survey. In the follow-up interview, respondents talked about their preoccupation with "getting the network off the ground". One of them implied that subscriber obligations would follow:

> "I hadn't thought of that (subscriber obligations). Maybe we could have language to that effect in the by-laws or in the governance somewhere. Currently, each of the large agencies has its own contract with the carrier. But we will have to pull together the board of directors...to begin to think collectively as a community, and think of obligations".

At present, subscribers have no obligations to be citizens, merely to be consumers. This emphasis is consistent with the Mall model of development and was, according to one respondent, occasioned by its imperative to "get the network off the ground". This could only be done by signing up early adopters (public institutions). It is not clear how a generalized expectation or non-specific obligation outside the by-laws, as in "support projects that will benefit the underserved in the community", will be enforced.

In the realm of citizenship, as O'Neill has argued, "it is the discourse of obligations rather than that of rights that is the primary vocabulary of action-centered ethics. When we discuss obligations, our direct concern is with what should be done" [27: p. 105]. Increasingly, the focus is on our obligation as citizens to meet the needs of others in the community [8]. Specialized needs – such as healthcare for the needy – constitute a large part of "our most urgent needs...And a large proportion of the cases in which people are not currently satisfying their own needs are cases in which the social structures in which people find themselves provide them with no feasible opportunity for doing so" [4, p.220]. Community networks can extend the reach of, and access to, the social support infrastructure available in the community for need fulfillment; they can help adapt such structures to the needs of residents with disabilities. As an extension of the support infrastructure, community networks can alter the social structure of choice and make it more convenient for the needy to avail of social services [4].

It is in the enhancement of the quality of day-to-day living, particularly for the less privileged, that technologically advanced networks like the Urban-net must find their true role and justification. Apropos, two types of services are possible. Informational services provide information to and may collect information from residents through electronic forms. High-touch services enable live, synchronous, person-to-person interactive transactions, often video-based, such as telemedicine. Informational services can be (and indeed routinely are) delivered over dial-up technologies; one would not need broadband to deliver such services. High-touch services, on the other hand, are best delivered over broadband. Considering that its costs and complexity have put the Urban-net out of reach of non-profits and their clientele, electronic delivery of services may yet be the only way to spread its benefits in socially responsive ways. How the digital intersects with day-to-day life in the host community is a critical question for a community network. If used well, it can enrich and expand the interface between a community's residents and its social support infrastructures for need fulfillment and, more generally, for what Friedmann and Douglas call "human flourishing" [15]. But whether the digital intersects with community life at all will depend on whether network subscribers see themselves as citizens first.

Praxis: The dialectical view defines a role for human agency in resisting, and in mobilizing resistance to, dominant political economic forces. It resists the determinism of the political economic view and argues that technology choices can be informed through social action. It believes in praxis, or action, by which human agents can challenge and reconstruct the social arrangements that produce biased outcomes. It dereifies "established social patterns and structure...and reveals the mechanisms of transformation" [5: p. 6]. Human artifacts and configurations, technological or social, are socially constructed and thus can be changed through social action.

Broadly, the dialectical view has two implications for human agency in community network development. First, user participation is crucially important. Second, human mediation to help mobilize broad participation by empowering human agents and advocating minority interests is an important corollary.

Given their high aspirations for it, steering committee members were interested in participating in the Urban-net design process. Carrier design staff were open to working with them. In practice, however, the "working together" was frustrating to both parties. Steering committee members were, for the most part, technologically naïve and were unwilling or unable to educate themselves on technology to be competent participants. The design staff were new to collaborative design. They had no personal experience with it. They were open to the idea of collaborative design, but were unsure of their emergent role as participant designers. They were unfamiliar with participative design methods and tools.

Note that grantees could not use program funds to hire technical expertise, and the Urban-net project had no funds from other sources to hire expertise. For effective participation, two kinds of knowledge are usually needed: general technological knowledge, and contextualized understanding of the implications of and opportunities from using technology. Attewell documents the role of knowledge barriers – lack of generalized and contextualized understandings – in the adoption of computing in the U.S. [1] During the Urban-net needs analysis effort, 60% of the respondents said lack of technical knowledge was a "barrier" or "major barrier" to technology planning and acquisition in their organization. Small non-profits continue to be woefully short on technology at this writing, and many lack in-house technical staff. Not surprisingly, participation and representation by such entities in development has ranged from marginal to none.

In community network development, institutions that "mediate" [1] between an innovation and the adopter can play two possible roles: a pragmatic role (facilitating broad participation by helping to lower knowledge barriers) and a political role (empowering the marginalized and advocating minority interests). Given the political economy of NGCNs, the second is as important as the first.

Mediating institutions have to augment generalized knowledge with localized or contextualized knowledge to be effective. They have to be local themselves to be able to work directly and "horizontally" with the needy. The term "horizontal" here refers to hands-on engagement of the user's context in situ. Localized knowledge is "sticky" and resists abstracting out, which means the mediating institution will have to work closely with the user [31]. Outreach programs based in higher educational institutions can be effective as a sustainable mediating mechanism in community network development, and may play both a pragmatic and political role [33]. Outreach efforts must be directed at sustained capacity building in the resource-poor, not at providing a one-way, one-shot "transfer" of shrink-wrapped knowledge. Recipients have to be coached in learning how to learn. The objective should be empowerment and assisted self-determination, not the creation of dependency.

4 Conclusion

The foregoing analysis was not intended to assign blame to the project steering committee or the carrier for the way the Urban-net turned out. The objective was to show the bias inherent in telecommunications [17] and demonstrate how such a bias, which tends to favor the resource rich, may operate less equivocally in the case of advanced technologies. Furthermore, in this case, the bias was in play despite the community-centered aspirations for the Urban-net voiced by stakeholders early on.

Telecommunications design and deployment decisions, in general, are powerfully shaped by market forces. Community networks have the opportunity to follow a different path, to envision new styles of community, a more equitable social order. A dialectical view believes in the possibility of reconstruction and change in social systems. However, fundamental to this conception of social construction of technological outcomes is human agency. As Graham and Marvin have argued, a purely political economic analysis tends to view developmental processes in telecommunications as determined by "abstract and macro-level" power systems [17]. We have tried to avoid this pitfall. While such forces are doubtless important, and have been key in the Urban-net's development, we believe that human agency can yet influence how it *evolves*. Combining the political economic and dialectical views permits analysis of the developmental process at micro and macro-scale levels. Such a combined view is emphatically contra determinism – of the technological or political economic variety.

A community's social structure is made up of social relations that tie its residents to one another and to its institutions. These relations may be described in terms of functions [26]. Needs and values influence and are influenced by the structure of relations [22]. For example, some communities may place a higher value on certain needs than do others. Analysis of the development of community networks at the macro-scale implicates the social structure of the host community. The Urban-net has developed without explicit reference to the community's social structure, with the result that the city's social and economic priorities (needs and values) have had little bearing on its design or use decisions. Community networks have to be explicitly grounded in the social structure of the communities they hope to serve. Efforts at reorienting the Urban-net's trajectory toward the project's social goals must be undertaken in the knowledge that dialectical praxis may affirm some of those relations – and related needs and values – and subvert others in the social order.

Gaps in alignment between the Urban-net's development and the concerns of the social order emphasize the need to locate community networking efforts within the broader context of community development and urban planning. In their 1996 book, Graham and Marvin argued that a 'paradigm crisis' threatened urban studies and planning:

> "...many urban analysts and policy-makers still see cities through analytical lenses which...have less and less to do with the real dynamics of telecommunications- based urban development" [17: p. 48].

They call for education in and improved understanding of telecommunications in urban development. We see the need for the opposite to occur as well: community networking is imperiled if it is not informed by the dynamics of urban development. Community network development cannot be removed from the concerns of the host community. In bridging this distance, community network planners (human agents representing community interests in the network development process) can learn much from the evolution of urban planning to its contemporary emphasis on radical practice:

> "Radical practices emerge from experience with and a critique of existing unequal relations and distributions of power, opportunity and resources. The goal of these practices is to work for structural transformation of these systemic inequalities and, in the process, to empower those who have been systematically disempowered. [29 p. 176]

What then might be the role of the new, radicalized planner in community network evolution? We see three ways into the new praxis:

> Despite their sympathetic view of the project's social goals, the carrier design staff were more attuned to a technical rational view of network development, which seeks to optimize outcomes on conventional design criteria such as network performance and efficiency. The new planner has to ensure that the concerns of the broader social structure are not lost sight of in the shuffle of purely technical rational preoccupations. Design choices can divide and balkanize; they can have the force of implicit policy [18]. The planner has to resist and reorient such trajectories. Technical criteria are critical in design, but so are the larger issues – the ontology, the ends – that design must serve. In her new role, the planner would use means and viewpoints considered vital in current urban planning practice – the ability to question and challenge assumptions (see [29] – and a post-modern sensibility [17], to keep the focus on the *community's* interests and needs.

> The new planner would combine technical and contextualized knowledge with an understanding of 'radical' developmental methods to empower and invite participation from diverse publics. Given the high knowledge demands of NGCN development, the new planner has to fulfill the role of an expert advocate in the network infrastructure design process. However, in terms of ideas for network use, the community should be in charge, with the planner as an ally. Radical methods like applications prototyping can be used to highlight urgent needs in the community and to influence the agenda for network uses around such urgent needs. Working with a mediating institution would be especially beneficial if prototyping is involved, on account of the resources that would be needed. There are other *bottom-up* methods to build a constituency. For example, the new planner can publicize exemplars of innovative uses of technology for pro-social ends to develop grassroots momentum.

> The new planner would be equally willing to adopt *top-down* methods to recenter marginalized interests in the developmental process. She would be an activist willing to take sides and work through politics. She would be effective in converting community-centered aspirations into explicit social policy instruments to secure the interests of the marginalized and further those of the moral economy. As we showed, this conversion has not occurred with the Urban-net

by-laws. It is vitally important that it does occur, and in a timely fashion, to shape the Urban-net's evolution such that it intersects substantively and meaningfully with community life.

Community networking projects cannot only be responsive to a market economy; they have to be informed by obligations of mutuality, reciprocity, and equity. To the extent that a community network purports to have a *community* orientation, market forces need to be balanced with a concern for the *moral economy*, which is exchange "justified in relation to social or moral sanctions, as opposed to the operation of free market forces" [32: p. 203]. The new praxis, we believe, would be needed to press for such a balance in the development of a community network.

References

1. Attewell, P.: Technology Diffusion and Organizational Learning: The Case of Business Computing, Organization Science, Vol. 3, No.1, (1992) 1-19
2. Aurigi, A.: Digital City or Urban Simulator?, Digital Cities, Lecture Notes in Computer Science, 1765, Springer-Verlag, (2000) 33-44
3. Aurigi, A., Graham, S.: Cyberspace and the City: The Virtual City in Europe in G. Bridge & S. Watson (Eds.), A Companion to The City, Oxford, Blackwell, (2000) 489-502
4. Baker, J., Jones, C.: Responsibility for Needs. In G. Brock (Ed.), Necessary Goods: Our Responsibilities To Meet Others' Needs. 219-232 Lanham, MD: Rowman & Littlefield Publishers (1998)
5. Benson, J. K.: Organizations: A Dialectical View. Administrative Science Quarterly, Vol. 22, (1977) 1-21.
6. Benson, J. K.: The Inter-organizational Network as a Political Economy. Administrative Science Quarterly, Vol. 20, (1975), 229-249.
7. Bijker, W.: Of Bicycles, Bakelite, and Bulbs: Toward a Theory of Sociotechnical Change. Cambridge, MA: MIT Press (1995).
8. Brock, G.: Introduction. In G. Brock (Ed.), Necessary Goods: Our Responsibilities to Meet Others' Needs. Lanham, MD: Rowman & Littlefield Publishers (1998) 1-18
9. Calhoun, C.: Community without Propinquity Revisited: Communications Technology and the Transformation of the Urban Public Sphere. Sociological Inquiry, 68 (3) (1998), 373-397.
10. Castells, M.: The Information Age: Economy, Society and Culture. The Rise of Network Society, Vol. I, Blackwell (1996)
11. Castells, M.: High Technology, Economic Restructuring, and the Urban-regional Process in the United States. In M. Castells (Ed.), High technology, space, and society. Beverly Hills, CA: Sage Publications (1985) 1-40
12. Castells, M.: The Informational City is a Dual City: Can it be Reversed? In D.A. Schon, B. Sanyal & W. J. Mitchell (Eds.), High technology and low-income communities: Prospects for the positive use of advanced information technology. Cambridge, MA: MIT Press (1999) 25-41
13. Dobres, M-A., Hoffman, C.R.: Introduction: A Context for the Present and Future of Technology Studies. In M-A. Dobres & C.R. Hoffman (Eds.), The Social Dynamics of Technology: Practice, Politics and World Views. Washington D.C.: Smithsonian Institution Press (1999) 1-19

14. Evaluation Report.: New York State Advanced Telecommunications Project: Diffusion Fund Program. White Plains, NY: Magi Educational Services (2001)
15. Friedmann, J., Douglass, M.: Editors' introduction. In M. Douglass & J. Friedmann (Eds.), Cities for citizens: Planning and the rise of civil society in a global age. Chichester, UK: John Wiley (1998) 1-6
16. Gillespie, A.: Advanced Communications Networks, Territorial Integration, and Local Development, in R. Camagni (Ed.), Innovation Networks. London, UK: Bellhaven (1991) 214-229.
17. Graham, S., Marvin, S.: Telecommunications and The City: Electronic Spaces, Urban Places. London, UK: Routledge (1996)
18. Guthrie, K., Dutton, W.: The Politics of Citizen Access Technology: The Development of Public Information Utilities In Four Cities. Policy Studies Journal. 20 (4), (1992) 574-597
19. Iacono, S., Kling, R.: Computer Systems as Institutions: Social Dimensions of Computing in Organizations. Proceedings of the Ninth International Conference on International Systems, Minneapolis, MN, (1988) 101-110
20. Khatchadourian, H.: Community and Communitarianism. New York, NY: Peter Lang (1999)
21. Kling, R., Courtright, C.: Group Behavior and Learning in Electronic Forums: A Socio-Technical Approach. To appear in: S. Barab, R. Kling and J. Gray (Eds.), Building online communities in the service of learning. Cambridge, UK: Cambridge University Press.
22. Laumann, E.O., Galaskiewicz, J., Marsden, P.V.: Community Structure as Interorganizational Linkages. Annual Review of Sociology, 4, 1978, 455-484.
23. Mackay, M., Gillespie, G.: Extending the Social Shaping of Technology Approach: Ideology and Appropriation. Social Studies of Science, 22, 1992, 685-716.
24. Mandelbaum, S.J.: Open Moral Communities, Cambridge, MA: MIT Press (2000)
25. Mino, E.: Experiences of European Digital Cities, Digital Cities, Lecture Notes in Computer Science, 1765, Springer-Verlag, (2000) 58-72
26. Nelson, L., Ramsey, C.E., Verner, C.: Community Structure and Change. New York, NY: Macmillan (1960).
27. O'Neill, O.: Rights, Obligations, and Needs. In G. Brock (Ed.), Necessary Goods: Our Responsibilities to Meet Others' Needs. Lanham, MD: Rowman & Littlefield Publishers (1998) 95-112
28. Public Utility Law Project and New York State Community Action Association, (July, 2000). Comments filed with the Public Service Commission
29. Sandercock, L.: The Death of Modernist Planning: Radical Praxis for a Postmodern Age. In M. Douglass & J. Friedmann (Eds.), Cities for Citizens: Planning and the Rise of Civil Society in a Global Age. Chichester, UK: John Wiley (1998) 163-184
30. Serra, A.: Next Generation Community Networking: Futures for Digital Cities, Digital Cities, Lecture Notes in Computer Science, 1765, Springer-Verlag (2000) 45-57
31. Stiglitz, J.: Scan globally, reinvent locally: Knowledge Infrastructure and the Localization of Knowledge. In D. Stone (Ed.)., Banking on Knowledge: The Genesis of the Global Development Network. London, UK: Routledge (2000) 24-43
32. Thompson, E.P.: The making of the English working class. New York, NY: Vintage Books (1966).
33. Venkatesh, M., Small, R.V.: Active Learning in Higher Education: A Model and Roadmap. To appear in J. Lazar (Ed.), Managing IT/Community Partnerships in the 21st Century, Idea Group Publishing.

The Complexity of Using Commercial Forces to Counteract the Digital Divide: A Case Study of the TUC of Sweden

Agneta Ranerup

Göteborg University, Department of informatics,
PO Box 620,
SE 405 30 Göteborg, Sweden
agneta@informatik.gu.se

Abstract. This article deals with the tension between commercial aims and activities and more democratic and idealistic ones in projects that are pursued to counteract the 'digital divide'. The article focuses on a project; 'Access Kumla' initiated by the TUC of Sweden. The project is characterized as a very ambitious initiative to counteract the digital divide. Its four aims can be summarized as follows: providing citizens with high quality, low cost computers, creating a Community Network, providing knowledge about IT and improving local democracy with the help of IT. In our project the complex role of commercial activities and forces is emphasized. Firstly, they emphasize the importance of financial autonomy from a short-time as well as a long-time perspective. A further result is the surprisingly high degree of harmony or absence of conflict as regards the various aims and activities in the project. The most noticeable exception concerned the role of the TUC, especially in connection with the commercial activities in the project.

1 Introduction

High access to the Internet as well as widespread knowledge about computers are necessary preconditions in order for Digital Cities, Community Networks, local government websites etc., to be used by large layers of the population. As a contrast, the concept 'the digital divide' denotes the differences in access to information technology (IT) in its broadest sense [13] that often are considered as a serious problem in modern society.

In an article published in January 2001 Ari-Veikko Anttiroiko (professor of local governance) discusses initiatives taken by the European Commission in order to counteract the digital divide: "The eEurope Action Plan [a strategy to address key barriers to the uptake of the Internet that was launched in June 2000] proposes that member states and the Commission commit to achieving three objectives; a cheaper, faster, more secure Internet; investing in people's skills and access; and stimulating the use of Internet" [2, p. 33].

In his article an analysis is made of the various programs and projects financed by the European Commission that are in accordance with these and similar goals. According to Anttiroiko, initiatives like these are seemingly dominated by aims

M. Tanabe, P. van den Besselaar, T. Ishida (Eds.): Digital Cities, LNCS 2362, pp. 191-202, 2002.

to increase access to computers and the Internet as well as knowledge about such technologies. Very often they also include intentions to enhance democracy with the help of IT. However, Anttiroiko argues that in practice commercial intentions and activities dominate these programs and projects. In the light of this critical analysis, it is interesting to notice the tension between mainly pragmatic and commercial aims and activities and, on the other hand, more democratic and idealistic ones. This article explores these tensions within a project aiming to counteract the digital divide, that was financed by the European Commission. Our analysis will be pursued with the help of the Autonomy/Harmony model as suggested by Romm & Taylor [16]. This model was designed to explain the results of projects on the digital divide. The model focuses on the existence of economic autonomy, e.g., in the form of stable funding. Another focus is the presence or absence of conflicts about the aims of a project. Thus, intuitively this model seems to be of relevance to the issues discussed in this article.

Our research is relevant to other activities trying to counteract the digital divide, like Community Networks, Digital Cities, and the like [14, 17]. The main contribution in the following is a discussion of tension between on the one hand pragmatic and commercial aims and activities, and on the other hand, more democratic and idealistic ones. More specifically, our research question can be formulated as follows: what complexities are associated with using commercial forces and activities in projects that are designed to counteract the digital divide?

2 Background

2.1 TUC and Its Activities to Counteract the Digital Divide

The concept the 'digital divide' denotes differences in access to IT, e.g. class differences, and gender differences [13]. According to Swedish statistics from the 1990s, differences exist between workers, civil servants/salaried employees, and academics, regarding the percentage of respective groups that have access to the Internet from home. The ideas behind *Access Kumla* were formulated in 1998. This very year, 26 percent of the blue collar workers, 46 percent of the servants/salaried employees, and 53 percent of the academics were reported to have home-access to Internet [12]. An alternative vision has been formulated in terms of an *inclusive information society* or an *information society for all*, as it was formulated by the European Commission [6]. Similar ideals also appear in research and literature on the digital divide [13]. According to these ideals, there should be no differences between people regarding access to IT in its broadest sense. Another aspect of these ideals is that broad layers of the population should be able to use IT, to enhance their position as citizens, as well as their position as consumers and employees.

Historically, the attitude towards new technology within the TUC of Sweden has been very positive. The TUC sees technological progress as a means to improve the living standard of its members, as well as a means to improve society at large [19].

A motion submitted to the TUC Congress in 1996 discussed the existence of a digital divide, as well as what could be done to counteract this. The motion suggested that a free introductory IT course should be offered to all citizens in Sweden. TUC should also work to accomplish universal access to IT, despite existing differences in economic status etc. between various groups in society. The answer of TUC was given in a positive spirit, and referred to the current activities within the TUC to formulate a program that dealt with these and similar issues [18]. One part of this program was the project *Computerize Sweden*, of which Access Kumla is a part.

The partnership in Computerize Sweden consisted of various organizations, like the TUC of Sweden (2.2 million members), the Association of Tenants (700,000 households), and the two co-operative residence organizations HSB and Riksbyggen (600,000 households) [10]. The unique force of these popular organizations would be used to affect the market, as well as the information society of tomorrow. More specifically, it would be used to safeguard that the costs for high quality IT is kept at a minimum. By using their strength, these organizations can take care of the interests of their members, counterbalancing the market forces [10].

Central as well as local activities were planned, with the aim to give the members of these popular organizations access to good quality information technology in their homes [9]. As mentioned above, the intention was to put pressure on 'the market' (manufacturers, service providers, and network operators) in order to safeguard low cost access, end high quality IT, for the TUC members and their children. The intention was also to create local as well as centrally situated *portals* or *Community Networks*, as a basis for a widened democratic development. The members of the organizations would have unique access to these networks. Here, information would be published under responsibility of persons or organizations. Another function of these networks was to support consumer interests, like safe and secure e-commerce [9].

Another part of the TUC strategy had much stronger focus on the members of the TUC itself and their access to IT. In September 1997, the TUC had launched a project ('Medlemsdatorprojektet') with the aim to provide its members with high quality, low cost computers. This was done by offering a special package, containing among others a multimedia computer, an Internet subscription, and support facilities [12]. According to an evaluation of the first two first years, 55,000 members had bought this package. It is interesting that in average each computer was used by 2.8 users. This meant that in total 154,000 persons were given access to computers and the Internet through this project [12].

2.2 The Project Access Kumla

In the application to the European Commission (DG-V Employment and social Affairs), the purpose of Access Kumla was described as follows: "The overall purpose of the pilot project is to test the main ideas of the larger concept in order for these to later on be applicable in a larger scale. Another purpose is to test different models of how access to computers and networks can be made to include all households in an area and with that contribute to general participation in the Information Society. The aim is to test some models and techniques to increase democracy, participation, influence and information at the local level and to develop activities for an extended integration between work, housing and school. The purpose is also to test new models and technique[s] to increase consumer influence within the Information Society" [3, p. 3].

The most important issue in the project application was that access to IT would become a part of the normal housing standards. The intention was to include – for people living in council houses – as much as possible the costs for networks, hardware, programs, and Internet connection within the rent, acknowledging that some of the costs had to be covered by the residents themselves. The idea was to put pressure on the IT suppliers, to get a favorable offer for high quality computers.

A further feature related to the issue of access is the local server that would be implemented as a part of the project, although the costs for the server would not be covered by the project. The server would host a Community Network with local information and services. Local organizations, like tenants associations, local service institutions, and municipal organizations of various kinds would have considerable influence over the design of its services.

The project application outlined a local partnership, consisting of the local government of Kumla, the local branch of TUC in Kumla, the Kumla Tenants Association, and the local business association. There would also be a partnership at a central level between the TUC of Sweden and other popular organizations such as those described above in connection with the project Computerize Sweden.

The need to provide general knowledge and skills regarding the use of IT to the citizens in Kumla was acknowledged in the application, and it was planned to organize this in co-operation with different organizations of adult education. It was stated that people with a short formal education would be prioritized. The need for education in IT issues among unemployed people, as well as elderly people, was acknowledged.

A fundamental assumption behind the project was the democratic value of universal access to IT. However, relevant experiments to discover various ways of using IT for democratic purposes were also seen as a necessity. The US model of Community Networks [17] was mentioned as a source of inspiration. It was suggested that experiments would take place in municipal politics (for example in the form of a dialogue between citizens and politicians), in the local association life (improved information and local democracy), as well as in connection with public services (improved access to service and information).

3 The Autonomy/Harmony Model

A significant part of the research field of Community Informatics in general, and Community Network projects in particular, focuses on the use of IT by territorial communities [7, 17]. Access Kumla qualifies as one of those projects. The technology is used in order to enhance democracy, as well as to contribute to cultural and economic development in the community. According to Romm & Taylor [16], research on factors that might interfere with the diffusion and use of IT and its consequences for democracy and local development due to such projects, is generally absent. Only a few exceptions can be found. With this a background, a model is suggested containing two dimensions or factors that are seen as determining the success of such projects.

The first suggested dimension is autonomy, which is defined as the degree according to which the projects are resourced, managed, or both, by people within the community in which the projects occur. " 'Low autonomy', refers to a situation where the project is resourced and managed by individuals or organizations outside the community. 'Medium autonomy', describes a situation where the project is resourced by individuals or organizations outside the community (e.g., governmental funding agencies), but managed by members of the community, and 'high autonomy' is where the project is both resourced and managed by individuals or organizations that are a part of the community'' [16, p. 4]. The hypothesis of the model is that a high level of autonomy is associated with higher success. Successful projects are associated with high diffusion and use of the technology, and with other positive effects that are in accordance with the aim of the project.

The second dimension is harmony, which is defined as the degree to which the local community is free of conflicts in relation to the project: ''This dimension is seen as a continuum that ranges between 'low', a situation where the community is torn by conflict and is also in conflict with the leaders of the project; 'medium', where the community is torn by conflict but supports the leaders of the project; and 'high' where the community strongly supports the project and the leaders.'' [16, p. 4]. As might be expected, higher levels of harmony are associated with higher prospects for success in the form of high diffusion and use of the technology, etc..

This model will be used as a basis for our analysis and discussion. However, we use a slightly different interpretation of the concept 'harmony'. We will use the concept to denote not only the absence of conflict between the community and the project leader, but also between the possible different interpretations of the aims of the project by the local community and by the steering committee. In our case, not all activities in the project have includes the whole population in the local community. This extension seems to be relevant, as the steering group was representing the community only to a certain extent. Consequently, the aims of the project - more than the project leader - are an important factor influencing the harmony of the project. In the case of Access Kumla, the project leader was unable to affect the aims of the project.

4 Method

The project Access Kumla has been studied and evaluated with the main focus on the period from its start (August 1999) to its termination (November 2000). However, experiences until March 2001 have been included in the analysis, as well as in the discussion about the larger consequences of the project and its results. During the first phase, we have taken part in two meetings (August 1999, February 2000) during which the activities in the project were presented. The second, more active, phase started in August 2000 and was finished in April 2001. During this period interviews were conducted with various partners within the project, as well as with other people who have been involved directly or more indirectly in the project:

- The local project leader (three interviews in Kumla, as well as four shorter interviews by phone).
- The members of the local partnership in Kumla (three interviews in Kumla and two by phone).
- The local webmaster in Kumla (one interview in Kumla).
- Three representatives from the central and the local level respectively of the TUC of Sweden (three interviews in Kumla and Göteborg, as well as two by phone).

The author has also used documents from the project Access Kumla, as well as from the TUC project Computerize Sweden of which this project is a part. We will now continue with an analysis of our experiences from Access Kumla in the light of the Autonomy/Harmony model. Our main research question focuses on the complexities that are associated with using commercial forces and activities in projects that are designed to counteract the digital divide.

5 Result

The project Access Kumla was carried out in Kumla, a municipality in the south of Sweden with 19,000 inhabitants. The municipality is dominated by high-technology industries like Ericsson, but there are also various other kinds of smaller industries. The project was planned to take place between August 1998 and October 1999. However, due to various circumstances the decision about financial support from the European Commission was delayed. This meant that the actual project period was between August 1999 and November 2000. The financial resources of the project consisted of 367,000 Euro (approximately 300,000 US dollars). Consequently, the project to a large extent depended on financial resources from other sources [3] as described further down.

During the project there has been a local steering group consisting of representatives of the local government in Kumla, the municipal housing company, a non-profit association ('Folkets hus'), the local business association, The Kumla Tenants Association, the local branch of the TUC in Kumla, and a local project leader. The representative from the TUC and the project leader are those that have been most active in the project activities.

5.1 Providing High Quality, Low Cost Access to Computers

As described above, the TUC had previously initiated a project in which its members were offered to buy high quality, low cost computers ('Medlemsdatorprojektet'). In the project Access Kumla a similar offer would be given to a larger audience, i.e. to the whole community of Kumla. During the project Access Kumla, several unsuccessful attempts were made to reach an agreement with potential sponsors, among others telecommunication companies like Telenordia and Telia. According to several of the interviewees the fact that the project was delayed and took place during period of recession that affected telecommunication companies and e-commerce business severely, prevented the negotiations from being successful.

In spite of the difficulties, there has been a strong will in the project to succeed. It is therefore interesting to notice that after the project terminated in November 2000. there have been negotiations between members of the steering group and various external commercial agencies. In March 2001 these negotiations resulted in an agreement in which the local members of the TUC and the local association of senior citizens were offered to buy a high quality, low cost computer. However, the agreed price was somewhat higher than the original intentions. Also, the offer was limited to some groups in the society, mentioned above.

According to the Autonomy/Harmony model [16] financial autonomy affects the success prospects of a Community Network project. In our case the goal of providing citizens with high quality, low cost computers depended on large sums of money from external sources. Also, it is interesting to notice that the project was lead by a very active project leader situated in Kumla. According to the Autonomy/ Harmony Model, Access Kumla in this respect categorizes as a 'medium autonomy' project. This means that the project is associated with medium prospects for success.

However, some of the aims of Access Kumla have been perceived as more important than others. In the case of Access Kumla, providing citizens with high quality, low cost computers has in fact been seen as the most important aim. It was the central issue in application for the project, in the public meetings and press conferences during the upstart of the project, and in the opinion of the citizens in Kumla. As a consequence, the difficulties to reach agreements with commercial agencies have been harmful to the results of the project. Many of the people involved in the project have been aware of the strong dependence on external sponsors. For example, when the project was introduced to the press (June 1999), representatives from the steering group estimated the total costs for the activities to more than three times the actual project budget. A representative from the central level of the TUC mentioned the existence of 'black holes' in the budget of the project [1]. With this as a background, Access Kumla categorizes as a 'low autonomy' project. Generally, projects like thes are associated with low success prospects.

As to the issue of the existence of harmony or conflict from the view of the local community/steering group versus this aim of the project, the situation is much less problematic. There does not seem to be conflicts regarding the aim to provide citizens with equipment. In this respect the project categorizes as a 'high harmony' project.

5.2 Creating a Community Network

A further important feature of the project was that a server hosting a Community Network would be installed and used by civic associations, citizen groups and local companies. A result of the project was that a server financed by a local sponsor Folkets hus was set up in Kumla. However, some features of the Community Network were seen as rather complicated. On several occasions during the autumn of 1999, a broad spectrum of civic associations took an active part in meetings in which the functions of the Community Network were discussed. Also, its design was discussed during informal contacts between these associations and the designer/webmaster. The Community Network would contain general information about local civic associations and local companies, as well as news about their activities. Also, the Community Network would be used by local companies for commercial information as well as for e-commerce.

Within the steering group there was no disagreement or conflict concerning the facilities directed towards the civic associations. The Community Network was in this respect a 'high harmony' issue. As a contrast, the commercial part of the Community Network was seen as more controversial. More particularly, different views existed within the steering group regarding the appropriateness of an arrangement in which commercial activities like e-business are carried out under the influence of TUC and similar organizations. Some appreciated the idea, whereas others feared that this would not be good for business; it was felt that non-members might not appreciate this role of TUC. Also, the local business association perceived the activities of the TUC to create a Community Network as competing with its own attempts to do something similar. As a conclusion, different views existed as regards the Community Network, especially with respect to its commercial features. This means that there was 'low harmony' within the steering group concerning this aspect of the project.

The Community Network in Kumla would function as a pilot, but several other test-sites were planned too. Part of the model was that the commercial agencies and organizations would pay a fee for their presence, and this would finance the local Community Network that was a part of Access Kumla. During the spring of 2001, a new concept has been developed in Kumla. The emphasis was now more on using a Community Network as a means of communications between the members of organizations like the TUC, the Tenants Association and other popular organizations. Similar arrangements have been made on two other places in Sweden. The cost for this new model will be more modest as compared to the model initially suggested for Access Kumla. Consequently, the new concept is to a much smaller degree dependent on commercial sponsors than the previous one. Another interesting feature of the new model is that e-commerce plays a more modest role than in the previous concept. However, according to some of the interviewees, there is still an interest from the commercial side. The main reason is the large numbers of members of the popular organizations that are involved in the Community Networks initiatives. In recent years, commercial companies have tended to use IT in general, and Virtual Communities in particular, as a means of communication with their customers [4]. A Community Network that connects members of popular organizations like the TUC and others might serve as a basis for a Virtual Community. Also from the viewpoint of the TUC, there is still a hope that the arrangements eventually might serve as a platform for safe and secure e-commerce, in which the integrity of the members/customers is preserved.

5.3 Providing Knowledge about IT

An important part of the project was to provide the citizens of Kumla with general knowledge and skills regarding the use of IT. The result of this part of the project was very positive. As a part of the Access Kumla project, the following forms of education about IT and the use of IT have taken place. Firstly, there has been education in the form of introductory study circles arranged by ABF (an educational association in Kumla). The course was offered free of charge, and consisted of in total 21 hours of education with focus on computers, the Internet etc. Approximately 175 people took part in this course. Secondly, a more advanced course consisting of 50 hours of education was offered to eligible groups of citizens in Kumla. This course took place within the program 'Kunskapslyftet' which is a publicly financed program aiming at people with non-academic education. Approximately 200 people took part in this more advanced course. The education could partly be financed within the project, and partly by external sources controlled by members of the steering group.

The latter applies to the education within 'Kunskapslyftet' described above. The steering group also had other recourses relevant within this context, as one of its members was working with the educational association ABF.

According to the Autonomy/Harmony model, the project in this respect qualifies as 'high autonomy' in relation to this aim. This might be seen as an explanation of the positive result. It is interesting to notice that the local community and the steering group alike were very positive towards the educational activities. This does not come as a surprise, as some representatives in the steering group were involved in education. In other words, the project characterizes as 'high harmony' in this respect.

5.4 Improving Local Democracy with the Help of IT

At the beginning of the Access Kumla, a special group was appointed with focus on democracy issues. The group consisted of the representative from the TUC in Kumla, the project leader of Access Kumla, a local democracy activist, as well as some representatives from other municipalities. During the meetings, discussions took place on how IT could be used in local government politics, but this did not result in any concrete measures in Kumla. Also the steering group discussed issues of democracy, in which a representative from the municipality of Kumla took part. According to the interviewees, until March 2001 no concrete activities to improve local democracy using IT resulted form the project. However, some of the interviewees mentioned that the intention to provide the citizens with high quality, low cost computers was perceived as a democratic aim. In other words, in case this aim was attained this would have been considered as a significant democratic achievement.

Also here an important explanation of the result is to be found in our previous discussion about the equipment, and the Community Network. The aim to provide citizens with high quality, low cost computers was seen as the important one, but was severely affected by the 'low autonomy' regarding how it should be financed. Also, we have mentioned 'low autonomy' and 'low harmony' in relation to the commercial features of the Community Network. According to several of the interviewees, these difficulties resulted in postponing some of the activities in the project, including actions to use IT for improving local democracy. Consequently, on the issue of improving democracy, the project categorizes as 'low autonomy' and 'high harmony'.

6 Discussion

Access Kumla had four aims: providing citizens with high quality, low cost computers, creating a Community Network, providing knowledge about IT, and improving local democracy with the help of IT. To realize these aims, the project tried to acquire money from economy oriented EU programs and from commercial sponsors. As explained, the success of the project depended to a large degree on the negotiations about large sums of money to be provided by commercial sponsors. In line with the Autonomy/ Harmony, this was not very successful. The aims of the EU program was social and economic development, and not democracy. However,

Access Kumla with its democratic and idealistic aims was sponsored by this more business oriented EU program. Anttiroiko [2] argues that projects with commercial aims hardly give room for democratic activities. However, in the case we presented here, there was quite some room for combining these diverging commercial and democratic aims.

What more can be learnt from our experiences? A recent study of Danish, Swedish and UK projects on counteracting the digital divide emphasized the importance of reliable and permanent funding [5]. It was suggested that this type of projects should receive core public funding. However, in reality most projects are dependent on a wide range of funding sources [5]. Therefore, it is interesting to notice that projects like for example the Canadian wired suburb 'Netville', studied by Hampton & Wellman [8], as well as Access Kumla, from their very start were heavily dependent on commercial sponsors. In fact, they can be included in the kind of experiments in which local communities are used as test-beds for the information society (hopefully) financed by large (telecommunication) companies [15]. Consequently, problems with sponsors also lead to difficulties in whole project. In fact, in both of the mentioned cases, significant parts of the activities had to be postponed or closed down because of the difficulties with commercial sponsors. Additionally, because of the delays, the projects took place during the recession period that heavily affected the computer industry, the telecommunication companies, and the e-commerce business. As argued by several of the interviewees in the Access Kumla project, the timing of a project might play a decisive role in success or failure. Thus, the opportunities and risks of using commercial sponsors should be emphasized.

It is also interesting to notice that, in terms of the Autonomy/Harmony model [16], financial autonomy is of importance not only from a short-term perspective as described above, but also from a long-term perspective. As an example, idealistic and non-commercial attempts like the Digital City Amsterdam gradually are confronted with increasing difficulties to find external sponsors on a more persistent basis. Instead, funding institutions move away from recurrent subsidies to one-time and project-related disbursements, and therefore limiting the possibilities for creating more permanent, sustainable, and competitive structures [14].

Despite these complexities, it is worthwhile to remember that the TUC of Sweden has had positive experiences with possibilities to enter into agreements with commercial agencies and sponsors. An example is the 'Medlemsdatorprojektet', in which its members were given a special offer to buy computers [12]. In order to receive economic support for the Access Kumla project, the TUC has been judged by the European Commission as being a credible actor. In spite of this, the TUC was unable to attract commercial sponsors.

A further result from the study is the surprisingly 'high harmony' in the educational activities in Access Kumla. This is in line with previous research, which suggests that providing knowledge about computers is the most offered service in projects that are designed to counteract the digital divide [5]. Also, providing high quality, low cost access to computers was seen as uncontroversial in Kumla, like in many other similar projects [5, 15]. The most noticeable exception concerned the role of the TUC with respect to the commercial activities in Community Networks. This phenomenon is of relevance to other attempts to involve organizations like trade unions in Community Networks, Digital Cities, etc.. The problem is that commercial companies might fear that their (potential) customers will perceive the association between themselves and the trade union negatively. More importantly, our experiences show that commercial actors like local business associations might perceive the TUC as a competitor. This means that its potential in this respect is seen as a threat rather than an asset in Community Network projects. It implies that creating a shared vision of a project to counteract the digital divide might suffer from very subtle complexities because of the varying interests among the (commercial) partners.

Lastly, we will comment on the issue of what the TUC hoped to achieve with its activities as discussed. Above we have noticed its interest in providing knowledge about IT as well as access to IT to broad groups. A reason for undertaking this kind of activities may be found in the decline of the *class identities* in modern society. Consequently, trade unions like the TUC needs to approach its old and prospective members in new ways [11]. Providing access to computers combined with the other features of Access Kumla might be a way of doing this. For the TUC it is increasingly important to provide 'value for money' to its membership, and this was explicitly mentioned by the TUC as a reason for the activities.

Access Kumla contained activities with democratic and participatory aims, e.g., the promotion of trade union activities. This has been accomplished with the help of commercial activities. Consequently, the commercial aims and activities have not dominated the project in a way suggested by Anttiroiko [2].

7 Conclusions

Our results indicate that projects with the aim to counteract the digital divide might be heavily dependent on commercial sponsors from a short-term as well as from a long-term perspective. Also, the economic climate at the time when the project takes place might affect heavily the possibilities to attract commercial sponsors. Further research therefore could go deeper into the critical success factors for using commercial forces in projects with the intention to counteract the digital divide.

A further finding is that the majority of the aims associated with this kind of projects are not disputed, and therefore do not result in conflicts. The only exception was the role of the TUC in connection with the commercial activities in the project. As Community Networks increasingly include more commercial Virtual Communities, the role of non-for-profit organizations like TUC in Community Networks has to be rethought. Intuitively, there seems to be a commercial value in its large membership. How to use this, and at the same time avoid confusing roles and conflicting interests with commercial organizations, is a yet unsolved problem.

References

1. Allvin, J.: The project Access: A question of fairness (Access är ett rättviseprojekt, In Swedish) Örebrokuriren, 9th of June, (1999) 9.
2. Anttiroiko, A-V.: Towards the European Information Society. Communications of the ACM, 44, 1, (2000) 31-35.

3. Carlsson, C. G.: Application for Financial Support. 'Access Kumla'. Stockholm, Sweden, TUC (1998).
4. Cothrel, J. & Williams, R. L.: On-line Communities: Helping them Form and Grow. Journal of Knowledge Management, 3, 1, (1999) 54-60.
5. Day, P.: Designing Democratic Community Networks: Participating in an Inter-Disciplinary Approach. In: this volume.
6. European Commission.: eEurope 2002. An Information Society For All. Action plan prepared by the Council and the European Commission for the Feira European Council 19-20 June 2000 (2000).
    (http://europa.eu.int/comm/information society/eeurope/actionplan/index_en.htm)
7. Gurstein, M.: Community Informatics: Enabling Communities with Information and Communications technologies. Hershey USA, Idea Publishing Group (1999).
8. Hampton, K. N. & Wellman, B.: Examining Community in the Digital Neighborhood: Early Results from Canada's Wired Surburb. In: Ishida, T. & Isbister, K. (ed.): Digital Cities. Technologies, Experiences, and Future Perspectives. Berlin, Springer (2000) 194-208.
9. Hansson, C. & Johansson, W.: Computerize Sweden. Raised Housing Standard. Summary of the project. Internal document 27th Nov. 1997. Stockholm, Sweden, TUC (1997).
10. Hansson, C. & Talls, S.: Information Technology (Informationsteknologin, In Swedish). Internal document 10th of September 1997. Stockholm, Sweden, TUC (1997).
11. Kjellberg, A.: Membership of trade unions and power: an international perspective (Facklig anslutning och makt: ett internationellt perspektiv. In Swedish). Arbetarhistoria, 22, 1/2, (1998) 19-22.
12. Larsson, G.: How is the Computer Offered to TUC Members Used? (Hur används LO-datorn 1999. En användarundersökning två år efter starten. In Swedish). Stockholm, LO (1999).
13. Loader, B.: Cyberspace Divide: Equality, Agency and Policy in the Information Society. London and New York, Routledge (1998).
14. Lovink, G. & Riemens, P.: Amsterdams Public Digital Culture 2000. On the Contradictions Among User Profiles. In: Presentation at the Global CN2000 Conference in Barcelona, Nov. 2-4 2000 (2000). (http://www.cnglobal2000.org/)
15. Mc.Quillan, H.: Ennis Information Age Town: Virtuality Rooted in Reality. In: this volume.
16. Romm, C. T. & Taylor, W.: The Role of Local Government in Community Informatics Success Prospects: The Autonomy/Harmony Model. In: Proceedings of the 34th Hawaii International Conference on Systems Science. IEEE (2001).
17. Schuler, D.: New Community Networks: Wired for change. New York, Addison & Wesley (1996).
18. TUC.: Protocol from the 1996 Congress of TUC (Kongressprotokoll LO-kongressen 1996, In Swedish). Stockholm, Sweden, TUC (1996).
19. TUC.: The Technology Policy of the TUC. (Facklig datapolitik. Rapport från LOs dataraåd, In Swedish). Stockholm, TUC/Tidens förlag (1981).

Lessons Learned: Social Interaction in Virtual Environments

Lili Cheng, Shelly Farnham, and Linda Stone

Microsoft Corporation, 1 Microsoft Way, Redmond WA 98052
{lilich,Shellyf,lindas}@microsoft.com

Abstract. With the goal of studying online community, we created two multi-user virtual environment products [1], Microsoft V-Chat [2] in 1996, and the Virtual Worlds Platform [3] in 1998. We analyzed the social interaction that developed in these virtual environments and were particularly interested in better understanding what factors contribute to sustaining online community. Drawing from the design and evolution of physical cities [4] we believed an online community must be able to change over time and evolve the space within a flexible infrastructure. Over the past six years we have learned a number of lessons about the design of community and the effects of design.

1 Introduction: Design Objectives and Background

We believed that the design of the virtual worlds would affect the development of a sustainable community.   Rather than develop one application that supported a particular design approach; we developed tools that supported multiple design solutions and we observed the social interactions that emerged. When we began, we drew heavily from existing work, particularly text-based Multi-user Domains (MUD's) and 3-D multi-player games. Having existed for almost twenty years, MUDs provided a rich set of information about building and maintaining online social environments. MUDs had a number of qualities we expected that would be crucial for building sustainable, dynamic communities [5, 6]. Text-based MUDs supported *multi-user real time* interactions. The people, places, objects, and their interactions were *persistent*, and end users could contribute to the evolution of the *dynamic* environment. We looked at various multi-user games such as DOOM and Quake [7], and virtual social spaces such as Lucasfilm's Habitat [8] and New York University's YORB [9]. We hypothesized that graphics would allow users to be *more expressive*, and would appeal to a *wider audience* than the text-based systems. We believed graphical environments would allow for non-verbal communication and more engaging social interaction and hoped that the virtual environments would be a third place. We were inspired by author Ray Oldenburg, who in his book "The Great Good Place" described the desire for people to have gathering places to nourish "sociability" a third place to visit away from home and work, for personal enjoyment and relaxation [10].   With advances in hardware, software, and networking technology, we hoped that any user would have easy access to a virtual place, full of people they cared about.

M. Tanabe, P. van den Besselaar, T. Ishida (Eds.): Digital Cities, LNCS 2362, pp. 203–218, 2002.
© Springer-Verlag Berlin Heidelberg 2002

1.1 V-Chat & Virtual Worlds Platform: Overview

Over the years, hundreds of communities have built environments using Microsoft V-Chat and the Virtual Worlds Platform software, and thousands of end users have visited these places. These two projects are briefly described below.

Microsoft V-Chat. V-Chat was a graphical chat environment that integrated graphical representations of the user and a 2-D or 3-D graphical background with synchronous text chat (see figure 1). We built V-Chat in 1995 by adding graphical components to the existing Microsoft Network (MSN) [11] v 1.0 text chat client. We incorporated features like MSN user names, profile information. We also incorporated existing MSN tools for managing behavior. Individuals could "ignore" others users (filters out user's text and graphic) and hosts could "ban" or "kick" misbehaving users from the chat room. End users were MSN subscribers. To install V-Chat, users needed to download the V-Chat client/custom graphics, and they needed to re-boot their machine. The entire process took about 20 minutes.

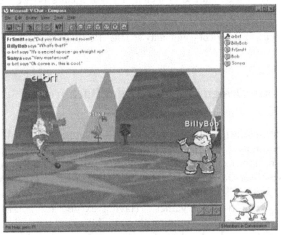

Fig. 1. Image of V-Chat

We built tools for others to create V-Chat spaces. Environments could be text-only, 2-D or 3-D. Design of graphical worlds could be custom or use pre-designed templates. Objects in the 3-D environment could link to content on existing web pages. We also built tools for end users to create custom avatar graphics. World builders could control the artistic design of the space by disabling custom avatars. The MSN product team helped us identify existing MSN chat communities and we worked with these communities to design and build some of the V-Chat spaces. We launched V-Chat in December of 1995 on MSN v1.0, with a variety of general chat spaces and specific community spaces. V-Chat ran for six years, and stopped running in March of 2001.

Virtual Worlds Platform. Based on feedback from V-Chat users and world builders, in 1996 we began to design and develop a new prototype, the Virtual Worlds

Platform. V-Chat world builders wanted the software to support more interesting social interactions than just text chat and they wanted to customize not only the graphical design of the 3-D space, but also the overall user interface. This provided a toolset that lets world builders create custom, web-based virtual environments on the Internet. We released the Virtual Worlds Platform on the Internet in 1998, and provided the platform (including tools and sample code) for free for non-commercial use. In early 1999, we additionally released the source code.

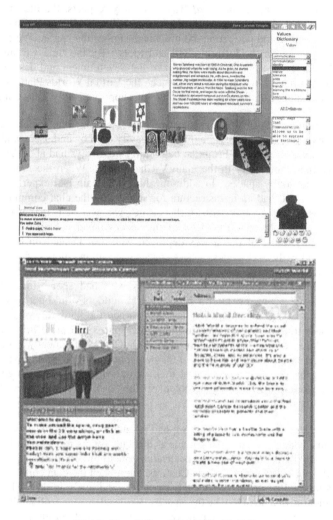

Fig. 2. Zora [12] and HutchWorld, [15]

Two example projects that were built and deployed using the Virtual Worlds Platform are shown above. The Zora project [12,13,14] by Marina U. Bers from the MIT

Media Lab provides social support for sick children via storytelling. The HutchWorld project [15] by the Fred Hutchinson Cancer Research Center [16] and Microsoft Research was designed for cancer patients and their support networks.

1.2 Research Process and Methods

Iterative Design: Learning the Hard Way. In many respects, the life of the online community begins when the space is deployed. When building V-Chat we spent many hours debating and perfecting the graphic design of the space. We also spent a lot of time working on the infrastructure and tools. By the time we launched the space in November of 1995 on MSN, most of the development and design team had moved on to begin working on our next project, the Virtual Worlds Platform. We did not have a dedicated team focused on the ongoing support of the V-Chat community.

From the beginning, some of our spaces were successful, active, social places. The V-Chat Lobby was located on as site that was heavily used by end users, and it always had a critical mass of people. From the beginning, we always had about 20 members of the MSN chat community in the main V-Chat lobby. When the room filled, we created duplicate lobby spaces. In addition, the MSN team had experience running the chat service, and had an infrastructure for supporting the chat communities. We leveraged this support, and with little effort, we watched the V-Chat lobby community evolve. In contrast, many of the spaces never achieved critical mass. Unlike the lobby, most of the spaces deployed were not located on the main chat page, but buried within sub-pages. These spaces were often empty. If a user entered a V-Chat space and it was empty, it was unlikely that the user would ever return. This was extremely disappointing to world builders who had spent time and money building the space. Typically after a failure, world builders would not spend the time and resources to try again. With V-Chat, we learned the hard way, that we should have spent less time perfecting and designing the spaces and more time iterating on the design. A key lesson we learned through the V-Chat deployment was to iterate on the design process early, deploy early in the development cycle, and provide a means for evaluating usage. We also suggest this for our world builders, to give them a better understanding of the design problem so they can better set expectations, and allocate resources.

Evaluating usage. Initially in V-Chat we had no automated way to see which spaces had users and which did not. This made it difficult for us to objectively study the usage of the software, and difficult to determine how to modify designs based on user activity. After our initial release of V-Chat, we automated the data collection process. We then combined a variety of methods to collect and analysis data. To study the social interaction that evolved in the spaces, we used a range of methods. We a) leveraged data collected by other marketing and research groups, b) informally observed world builders and end users in the graphical environments; c) conducted interviews and focus groups, d) conducted online surveys, e) collected and analyzed quantitative usage data, and f) conducted experimental studies. We also completed several longitudinal studies to better understand the change in the online community over time. For example, after releasing V-Chat in 1996, we had two sociologists from UCLA gather and analyze V-Chat usage data across multiple spaces. We studies the evolving V-Chat community over time by repeating the study in 1998, and then again in 1999.

2 Lessons Learned Overview

In 1996 when we launched V-Chat, we could never have predicted the growth of the Internet and online communities. We were able to analysis behavior in V-Chat spaces over the years, and watch the online community evolve over time. The lessons to follow describe not only what helped to aggregate and sustain online community but also provides insight to why environments did not work. The key lessons we learned focused on the individuals, social dynamics, the environment and the user interface.

2.1 The Individual

Unlike in the real world, a digital world builder must design not only the world, but also the people! We found that individuals invest more in their representation and they act more responsibly when they have a persistent identity, a rich representation, and clear understanding of what is being shared and what is private.

Lesson 1: Provide persistent identity to encourage responsible behavior, individual accountability, and to develop lasting relationships. Without persistent user identity (ID), people find it difficult to develop lasting relationships. Providing persistent IDs for users lets them be uniquely identified across sessions. This makes it easier develop lasting impressions of each other. Without persistent identity people feel less accountable for their behavior. This leads to more "bad behavior" such as identity "theft" or spoofing. Persistent user identity allows users to invest in their online reputation, encouraging them to be accountable in their interactions with others.

Design Evolution: The initial V-Chat environment, v1.0, supported persistent identities and a relatively closed community of users. The value of the persistent ID became clear when the second version of V-Chat was released on the Internet to an open group of people without persistent ID's. V-Chat v1.0 provided persistent user IDs by integrating into the Microsoft Network and using MSN IDs; each paying user had a unique MSN user name and password, they appeared V-Chat with their unique MSN name, and it was easy for individuals to identify one another by name. The core group of V-Chat users met over and over in the space, and it was easy for them to identify each other and develop reputations within the space.

The value of the "secure" MSN community and the persistent user identity became clear to the users when it was taken away in V-Chat v2.0. Any user with access to the Internet could access the V-Chat 2.0 rooms and enter with any username. The old users complained that many of the new users were "not behaving responsibly." People were being spoofed, and there was no way to know who was who.

For example, members of the Angel Society club complained of "spoofing." The Angel Society was an end user generated V-Chat club. The club was organized by end user to help new users and helped manage the various V-Chat rooms (note: The Angel Society is described in more detail in Lesson 4 of this paper). Membership in this club was by invitation only, and members had high status within in the V-Chat community. To show membership, the Angels adopted a private angel avatar costume. Spoofers faked membership to the Angel Society club by adopting angel names, e.g., "Angelxxx", and by wearing angel graphics. The members of the Angel Society found these spoofers offensive, and wanted them to be punished. Rather than punish users, we attempted to reduce the ease of spoofing in the space. We prevented users from logging in at the same time with the same name and we put the user's network IP address in the public profile. This made it more difficult for users to pretend they were someone else. In addition, we made the rules of conduct visible during login, and we banned users that did not follow these rules. In sum, we found it necessary to include system features in the environments that let us uniquely identify and ban badly behaving users, to discourage spoofing, and to clearly display the public policy for dealing with bad behavior.

We also found that regular users tended to develop a persistent identity without any technical solutions. For example most regular users had a regular name/names and graphic/ graphics, they had routine habits like showing up in the same place around the same time, and they often knew the habits of their friends. All of the members in our focus groups knew their online friends by user names and avatars, and they tended to meet their online friends in particular places at a particular times of day.

Lesson 2. Support custom profile information, including features that address privacy concerns. Sharing profile information lets users get a sense of who else belongs to the community. Letting users control who and how they share profile information profile information provides a context for starting conversations.

Design Evolution: We expected that the general profile information (name, age, location, sex, etc.) would help initiate conversation and without requiring uses to repeat the same information over and over. However, we many people did not provide even the simplest profile information. When V-Chat was on MSN (a more secure community), more users tended to fill in the optional profile information with "real" information than when V-Chat was released on the Internet. In both cases we found that most people either did not fill in the profile or filled it with false information. For example, a common response to the "Sex:_____" item was "none" or "yes", rather than "male" or "female". The real name item was typically left blank or filled with false information. When V-Chat 2.0 was released on the Internet, in addition to the standard profile dialog, users were prompted to write a description about themselves. If they left their personal description blank, they were described by "This user has nothing to say." The open-ended text description area was filled in by more users and was more interesting to others than the standard profile fields.

In all cases, we found that some of the most common questions in the text chat conversation were questions that could have been answered in the profile. These included questions like, "Where are you from?" "How old are you?" or "ASL?" (age, sex, location). Often people would look at the profile information and then ask "Are you really from {xxx} place?" or "Are you really {xxx} age?" Many users did not provide profile information because it was too much effort, and there wasn't enough perceived value, and that even at a very general level, users wanted to control who had access to the information. Even when this information was filled out, people liked to discuss this common information together in real time. Finally, like in the real world, it was common for V-Chat users to disclose different amounts of information based on personal relationships and level of expertise. V-Chat users disclosed more private information over time. This was not facilitated by any specific privacy related features, but occurred via chatting, exchanging email, instant messaging IDs, photos, phone numbers and face-to-face meetings.

Lesson 3. Encourage users to invest in their self-representation by supporting custom end user graphical representations. We were delighted and surprised by the popularity of the custom avatar graphics, and the impact the graphical avatar had on conversation and status in the community. Users sharing their own drawings and images, and they enjoyed selecting and creating their graphical representations. Most people used the graphic to convey something about their true identity, particularly gender. Graphical avatars were also used to help identify interesting people to talk to and people to avoid.

Design Evolution: We provided a variety of solutions for adding graphics to the user's representation. In V-Chat we provided a standard set of 20 avatar graphics plus the ability for end users to design custom avatar graphics. The graphics included 20 frames, allowing the avatar to animate to different gestures. During the design and development of the avatars, we argued about which style of graphics would be used the most (abstract, photographic, human, animal, etc.). We decided to release V-Chat with a set of 20 avatars. These included a variety of image types—and we watched to see what type of graphics people would actually use. We agreed that users would want to create their own custom graphics, but we argued about how much effort the user would spend. The users needed to download a separate application and create up to twenty separate images for their graphical avatar. In addition, users needed to upload their avatar and specify who could use the image by marking "share, let others use" or "private, for my use only." We wanted to encourage end users to create custom avatar graphics, and given users' reluctance to fill in the simple profile, we thought this process would be too difficult and tedious.

To better understand how people used avatars we a) held an avatar contest, b) informally observed the usage of graphical avatars, and c) had two sociologists from UCLA, Peter Kollock [17] and Marc Smith [18], conduct a study. In the spring of 1996, about 6 months after the release of V-Chat, we held an avatar graphic contest. We were surprised by the number of realistic, human, avatar images. Any adult or child could participate in the contest by submitting an avatar to one of the following categories: male/female/neutral and human/animal/abstract.   A panel of judges determined the best design and winners received t-shirts and buttons, and their names were posted in the avatar contest section of the V-Chat site. Of approximately 75 submissions, over half were realistic (men (33) and women (15)). The rest were equally divided between a variety of objects, and animals. Although no one submitted a photographic avatar, in general, men submitted male figures and women submitted female figures, and most of the abstract, non-human designs were submitted by children.

Fig. 3. General V-Chat avatar designs

Around the same time, Kollock and Smith evaluated the "popularity" of avatar graphics by observing the usage of different types of avatars (general, chatroom specific, end user created) in each different room, and recorded the frequency of use by analysis of V-Chat log files. They repeated this study in 1998. Kollock and Smith's analysis matched our informal observations and the avatar contest data. In V-Chat, each user entered each chatroom as a "default" avatar graphic that was specified by the V-Chat designer. To change the graphic, the user could select a different graphic from the default set of 20, or create a custom graphic. In 1996, almost all users changed their avatar from the default. Of those selected, the most common was a male, then female, and then a variety of animals, objects and other designs. When the study was repeated in 1998, humans remained the most common avatar, but rather than males, young women become the dominant theme for the most popular custom avatars, with many cartoon and science fiction characters present. [19] Like in the avatar contest, photographs of the self were not popular, but users did represent themselves with photos of famous or attractive people. The least used designs were the purely abstract designs.

Kollock and Smith found that custom avatars were one of the most popular features of V-Chat. In the 1996 study, they found that 21% of all avatars used in V-Chat were custom avatars, created by end users. When the study was repeated in 1998, they found that 87% of the avatars in use were custom avatars. This represented a very substantial increase of the number of custom avatars in use [20]. They found that different users invested different amounts of time in the community. The people that used custom avatars visited V-Chat on average for longer amounts of time. In total, 37% of all time spent in an avatar was spent by a user wearing a custom avatar [20].

Like the textual information, the graphical avatar helped users identify those they wanted to interact with and those they wanted to avoid. People would often avoid people with a custom avatar that they found unappealing.   Like text-based profile information, the graphics were a popular topic of conversation. Users often asked an unfamiliar user with a custom avatar "Did you make your custom?" or "Nice custom (avatar)." Unlike the textual profile information, if a person spent time an effort customizing their representation, it was immediately visible in the graphical environment, and ultimately led to creating social status. Creating and exchanging graphical avatars was hugely popular despite the fact that it took considerably more effort to create custom graphics than it took to fill out several text fields.

2.2 The Social Dynamics

Individuals collected to form groups in the V-Chat and Virtual World environments. Supporting the formation of groups and clubs, supporting the development of reputation and status, and providing a mechanism for groups to self-regulate encouraged the development of community in the virtual environment.

Lesson 4. Support the ability for people to form into groups and then self-regulate. When world builders assume responsibility for managing social dynamics it is costly, does not scale well, does not respond to the needs of the community and interferes with community members taking on a more active leadership role. Providing the ability for users to form into groups and self-regulate by moderating the space and managing bad behavior is key for developing a self-sufficient community.

Design Evolution: During deployment of V-Chat, we recognized the need for "setting a tone," managing the space, and scheduling and hosting events, but we did not want to engineer social interactions for the emerging community. MSN provided us with a part-time host for the rooms, but it was unreasonable for her to manage all of the social interactions and be responsible for promoting the development of community in the 20+ V-Chat spaces. We also felt it was not desirable for us to monitor the rooms. Often when a host entered the room, we observed users immediately leaving the room. The host could kick and ban end users and was often viewed as an interfering authority figure, an outsider. In addition, we observed usability problems for new users. New users did not know how to move or interact with others in the graphical environment. Several experienced users wanted to be able to help the new users, and offered to form a club to help others in the V-Chat community.

A helper club would be useful, but we did not want to create status differences by favoring a particular set of users. We consulted with sociologist Peter Kollock to design a system to support the development of user-generated clubs. Kollock suggested that we provide a clearly defined and fair system, such as a mechanism for anyone to create a club. He also suggested that we not give clubs special privileges (such as the ability to kick or ban users from the space) unless absolutely required. We followed his advice and designed a simple system to support the creation of clubs and groups. On the main V-Chat page, we had a club application form. Any users who wanted to form a club needed to submit the user names of 10 people that supported the club. A description of the club, and a specified club owner were also required. Once the club was created, we offered to display a graphic promoting the club in the 3-D V-Chat lobby, Compass. We weren't sure if this simple set of rules would be enough, so we tested it out.

The helper community that emerged called themselves the "Angel Society." The Angel Society was not granted any special privileges, and we did not interfere with the policies and rules they designed for themselves. The Angel Society members created their guidelines and recruited members. Members decided to wear a private custom angel avatar graphic, designed by one of the members. The Angel Society members wore the same custom angel avatar graphic and later developed a naming convention such as "Angel xxx". The Angels self-organized and created a schedule for helping new users. Being a member of the Angel Society became a V-Chat status symbol. In fact, the Angel Society remained with the V-Chat product longer than any of the members of our development team who worked on the project!

People also formed groups by congregation in particular places. Many people wanted to create their own custom spaces to attract their own interest groups, and they wanted to manage, design, and maintain the space themselves. We did not support user-created rooms in V-Chat v1.0, and decided to add this in V-Chat v2.0. To create a room, users simply typed in the room name and a one-line description of the room. In addition, we let users select a room graphic. The owner/creator of the room regulated the space by setting up membership rules and specifying a particular user as a host. Typically key members of the group, hosts could kick and ban users from the room and could assign others with host privileges. To restrict membership in the room, some creators scripted automated bots that would look through user profiles and automatically "kick" users that were not a valid member of their community (filtered by age or other profile field).

The users' ability to create and manage their own rooms made a significant difference in usage of the application. When end users were allowed to dynamically create rooms, the number of rooms created by end users greatly exceeded the number of rooms that were provided by the V-Chat team. In the directory, there were typically about 100 V-Chat environments up and running and of these, about 80% were end user created. Although many of these rooms had only a few participants, many social groups formed around the various user-created rooms.

Lesson 5. Frequent and repeated interactions promote cooperative behavior. Help people coordinate meeting and finding those they care about to increase the likelihood of positive interactions. Frequent and repeated interactions between users encourage users to act responsibly. Users are more likely to cooperate if they feel know they will see others again. Being unable to coordinate meeting friends and find similar people in a virtual environment is a barrier to entry. Often it takes too much effort to find interesting people and social activity. Providing mechanisms to let users find friends, find active groups of people with similar interests, and create user generate interest groups is key for encouraging cooperative behavior.

Design Evolution: In V-Chat V1.0, through survey data [21], we found users wanted to interact with their online and real-world friends. Many frequent users coordinated meeting friends online by using the external tool ICQ [22] for instant messaging and buddy lists. ICQ users reported more frequent and higher quality interactions. In 1996, this was the first we'd heard of instant messaging and buddy lists, and ICQ was the only product that provided this functionality. V-Chat 1.0 users sought out people with similar interests (matchmaking, etc.), but this often took too much time.

To address this issue, we watched when and where different groups of people in V-Chat community congregated. Our general space, named Compass, was the most popular space, and members of different groups, particularly the teen and adult users, would often disturb general chat users and new users (called newbies). We informally supported these groups by describing the room audience in the room name/ description. The teens preferred to socialize with other teens and the adult audience preferred to socialize with other adults. This made V-Chat more pleasant for all of the different audiences to be able to separate into their respective groups.

The adult content users were the most advanced users. They included not only those interested in "adult" behavior, but also those interested in interacting with a mature audience. Some world builders classified their rooms as "adult" to discourage young users from entering (at that time on MSN only users 18 and over could enter rooms marked "adult"). In the adult rooms, the users were generally older and also more advanced. Users tended to have more private conversations (via whispering in text chat) and use more custom avatars. The adult rooms were particularly popular in the late evening. The teen community tended to come online in the late afternoon, after school. This group primarily consisted of teenage boys, and they enjoyed interacting in the 3-D space. They ran around the room, played tag, and zoomed close up to other avatars. They were also very active chatters. The teens group was particularly attracted to a room we called "Lunar Islands," a sci-fi looking landscape. The newbies, mentioned earlier, were often new to text chat, and had little experience using 3-D graphics. The newbies preferred the general space to the newbie room.

In V-Chat 2.0, we integrated a directory service when we added the ability to create custom rooms. The directory let users view all the room names, descriptions, and the number of people currently in the space. In summary, letting users find people they care about increased the likelihood of positive interactions.

Lesson 6. Make social interaction more compelling by supporting the development of reputation and status. We found that the development of reputation and status was an important aspect of a compelling social experience for our V-Chat users. Users developed reputation and status in V-Chat using various mechanisms. The primary items people used to build status were: a) hours online (more advanced skills); b) friends online (having popular friends); c) artistic talent (displayed via avatar creation), and d) exploration of the environment (discovering secret places in the 3-D spaces).

Design Evolution: Most of the items that V-Chat users attached status to were not intentionally designed as a means to build reputation in the community. However, as the status items emerged in the V-Chat community, and as we developed an understanding for their importance in the process of community development, we encouraged the behavior by supporting and emphasizing those features. As mentioned earlier, we found that users enjoyed avatar graphics. In V-Chat, when a user posted a custom avatar, it was stamped with the name of the creator. These avatar graphics were exchanged and worn as status symbols. Several users became famous for creating well-used custom avatars. In fact, the use of custom avatars was so popular that some users began to post custom avatar web sites for others to access and exchange custom graphics.

Another sign of one's status was an awareness of the Easter Eggs-secret items or places to explore and visit. One popular V-Chat room was the Fishbowl. In Fishbowl, there was a small hole in the background collision detection plane. Users could escape out of the hole and go behind the background, to reveal a secret stage set. In another space with a large-scale desk named Desktop, we put a piece of bubble gum under the table and the artist put his own face on the coins that were on the table. In our main lobby, Compass, we hid a triangle high above the center of the room. Inside of the triangle was a bright red room. In our sci-fi landscape, Lunar Islands, we hid words behind the two moons. If you went out to the moons and looked back at the world, the world would seem to disappear. We thought we would surprise the users in our focus group by revealing the secrets of each room. They surprised us by telling us "Oh, we know all of those." Then they surprised us by revealing things that our designers had hidden in the world like initials hidden on the backs of textures, and other secret objects and places. They shared this knowledge with one another and gained status through this exploration of the space.

2.3 The Environment

We found that the design of an environment and its user interface affected the nature of the environment's social interactions. These needs vary depending on the context and nature of the community. For example, small communities have very different needs from large communities due to the need to attract critical mass.

Lesson 7. The communication tools and the design of the environment should support small, dynamical communities and groups. Failure to achieve critical mass is often a problem, so it is essential for the UI to support small communities and that management of the space be planned.

Design Process: Most of our Virtual Worlds Platform builders worried about supporting large numbers (>50) of users. Almost no world builders focused on designing a space to attract and engage small audiences. The majority of the Virtual

Worlds were designed as synchronous communication spaces. This meant that the total size of the user community needed to be large enough to have a critical mass of people online at the same time. In addition, many world builders had no intention of actually posting/managing the online community. Many projects were prototypes or research experiments. For those spaces posted to the public, many never attracted anyone outside the development team. For technical reasons, we were limited to about 25 users simultaneously in one room and a few hundred users in one world. In most cases, these limits of the technology were not a barrier to use. Overall we were disappointed by the small ratio of Virtual Worlds sites that were actually deployed, and the small size of the communities.

We wondered how the usage of our tools compared to the easy-to-use online community building tools like those found on MSN Communities [23], Yahoo Clubs [24], and AOL Groups [25]. To compare, we collected data from five thousand randomly selected online communities that were made using standard web based tools. We found that about half of the online community sites that were created were not used. We defined an unused site as one that attracted no members (aside from the creator) and had no information (no messages, announcements, file or photos). Of the majority of the sites that were active, about 75% were small communities with less than 25 total members. Very few sites (<4%) had more than 100 users [26]. Our analysis also showed that most used tools were bulletin boards and photo sharing, both asynchronous communication tools. Less than 3% of the communities used the synchronous text chat. Clearly the asynchronous communication tools integrated in the online community were more used than the synchronous tools [25]. From the analysis of online communities and experience working with world builders using V-Chat and the Virtual Worlds Platform, we found that most online communities are small (<25 users). For small communities, where users tend to not be online at the same time, the use of asynchronous communication tools is essential for success. Tools for world builders to attract and manage small, dynamic groups would be used much more than tools to support large online communities.

Lesson 7: Graphical environments provide valuable context for non-verbal communication and gesture. Graphical environments allow people to communicate non-verbally. Users can express emotions through gestures, and communicate interest and direction of attention through their orientation and position in the 3-D space. However, the use of graphical features to communicate nonverbally often interferes with verbal, text communication.

Design Evolution: As with the avatar graphics, before releasing V-Chat we discussed the different gestures and the different ways of "talking." We were not sure which gestures would be used (wave, smile, flirt, sad, silly, etc.) and we were unsure how often the different ways of speaking (say, think and emote) would be used. V-Chat users could interact with one another in the 3-D space by typing or explicitly controlling their graphical avatars. In some cases, the gestures were automatically triggered via the content of the text conversation (for example, by typing "hello" the avatar would wave) and in other cases pushing buttons in the user interface would trigger gestures. We found that the most popular gestures were positive gestures: waves (23%), smiles (17%), and flirts (11%). The least used gestures were negative gestures: angry (8%), shrugs (6%), and sad (5%) [19]. Over time, the use of positive gestures continued to be the most common gestures. [20]. Graphical gestures were used less than expected for a couple of reasons. Many began their sessions by exploring the 3- space, but then as they engaged in text chat, they would minimize the size of the 3-D window and not move in the 3-D space while focusing on the conversation. It people seemed to forget to gesture graphically when engaged in conversation, although use of emoticons such as ;-) or ;-(embedded in the conversation was popular.

Casual observation suggests that users were quite aware of non-verbal communication in the spatial context. Phrases such as "someone coming over to me," "someone in my face," "someone walking through me," "come here," and "look at me," were common. We also observed small clusters of two or three people positioning themselves off in the distance in what looked like private conversations. To explicitly study non-verbal communication in the 3-D space, for several weeks in 1999 we collected position and conversation data of users in several of the public V-Chat spaces. [27] We found that many people did use the 3-D space for non-verbal communication. They used their ability to position in the 3-D environment to stand near and look at the person with whom they were talking.

Lesson 10: User interface design for communication is most successful when it proves the user with a continuum of interaction levels, from lightweight awareness to full-focused attention. Many social interactions are informal, spontaneous, and lightweight. 3-D graphics and synchronous communication (text chat) demand the user to pay full attention to the screen. This often requires too much from the end user, and is not necessary when engaging in lightweight or spontaneous interactions.

Design Process: Over the years we have not seen the use of 3-D virtual environments grow, aside from those built for entertainment purposes, primarily shooter games and role-playing games. We found that all V-Chat users always also used text chat, but only a small percentage of text chatters used the graphical chat communities. Despite improvements in networks, home personal computers, graphics and rendering technologies, and public awareness of online community, chat, and the Internet, the graphical environments were only used by a subset of the population. Why?

We believe that people are more concerned with reaching critical mass and being accessible to anyone with any computer than providing a cool, more compelling experience for a subset of the user community. Getting critical mass often means the tools and access to the online community should be simple and easy as possible. Many people don't have a lot of time to waste. Synchronous communication (text chat) can be difficult to follow, and is often does not lead to productive conversation. For example, if ten people want to coordinate a meeting time, coordinating in text chat is extremely difficult and frustrating due to conversation errors and lack of threaded conversation. In addition, often people are not in the same space at the same time. The 3-D graphical worlds add further usability challenges for the user. Just installing software often requires users to wait for the graphics to download and render. Many users don't want to wait for graphics when their primary goal is to communicate. Just remembering to go to check the status on a text based online community, and taking the effort to go to a simple web page can be a barrier to entry. As seen by the usage of buddy lists in combination with applications like V-Chat, users want to know "who's there that I care about" before bothering to interact. In summary, 3-D virtual environments are immersive and compelling, but world builders should make sure the user experience matches the lightweight, spontaneous nature of the community and social interaction.

3 Summary

Our main lessons focused several areas: *Individuals:* Support persistent identity, custom profiles and privacy, and graphical user representation. *Social Dynamics:* Support the ability of groups to form and then self-regulate and the ability of individuals have frequent interactions with others, and to build social status and reputation. *Environment:* The design of the environment should support small, dynamical communities and groups. When there is critical mass, users use the 3-D graphics for non-verbal social interaction and for providing context for communication. *User Interface*: User interface design for communication is most successful when it proves the user with a continuum of interaction levels, from lightweight awareness to full-focused attention and engagement. Our initial belief that adding 3-D graphics would appeal to a wider audience has not proven to be the case. In V-Chat, we found that the 3-D graphics features were used by a *subset* of text chat users rather than by a wider audience than text chat. Despite advances in technology over the past six years, multi-user 3-D environments still have difficulty achieving critical mass, particularly in productivity-focused scenarios. For many communities, the demands on the users' attention and the networking and machine requirements will continue to be a barrier to building critical mass. Nevertheless people are meeting others in regular places and making friendships online. As today's teenage population of users continues to mature, we expect this trend to continue, and we hope the realization of the Third Place will evolve in many unpredictable ways.

References

1. Virtual Worlds Group/Social Computing Group, Microsoft Research, Microsoft Corporation, http://research.microsoft.com/scg/.
2. The Microsoft V-Chat software (1995), produced by Microsoft Corp., Redmond WA.
3. The Virtual Worlds Platform software (1999), produced by Microsoft Corp., Redmond WA, http://vworlds.org/.
4. Bacon, E. (1976) The Design of Cities, New York: Random House.
5. Vellon, M., Marple, K., Mitchell, D., Drucker, S. (1998) *The Architecture of a Distributed Virtual Worlds System.* Unpublished report for Microsoft Research.
6. Reid, E. (1994) *Cultural Formations in Text-Based Virtual Realities.* Masters Thesis. English Department. University of Melbourne.
7. The DOOM and Quake PC computer games (1993, 1997), produced by ID Software, Mesquite TX.

8. Morningstar, C., Farmer, R., (1991) The Lessons of Lucasfilm's Habitat. In Benedikt, M. (Ed) Cyberspace: First Steps, Cambridge MA: MIT Press, pp. 273-302.
9. The Yorb project (1994), produced by O'Sullivan, D., New York University, NY.
10. Oldenberg, R. (1989) The Great Good Place, New York: Paragon House.
11. The Microsoft Network v1.0 software (1995), produced by Microsoft Corp., Redmond WA.
12. The Zora project (1999), produced by Bers, Marina U., MIT Media Lab, Cambridge, MA http://lcs.www.media.mit.edu/ ~marinau/Zora/.
13. Bers, M., Gonzalez-Heydrich,G., DeMaso, D. (2001) Identity Construction Environments: Supporting a Virtual Therapeutic Community of Pediatric Patients undergoing Dialysis. Proceedings of Computer-Human Interaction, ACM Press, pp. 380-387.
14. Bers, M. (1999) Zora: a Graphical Multi-user Environment to Share Stories about the Self . Proceedings of Computer Support for Collaborative Learning, ACM Press, pp. 33-40.
15. Cheng, L., Stone, L., Farnham, S., Clark, A. M., and Zaner-Godsey, M. (2000) Hutchworld: Lessons Learned. A Collaborative Project: Fred Hutchinson Cancer Research Center & Microsoft Research. Proceedings of Virtual Worlds Conference 2000, Paris, France, pp. 12-23.
16. The Fred Hutchinson Cancer Research Center, Seattle WA http://www.fhcrc.org/.
17. Kollock, P., University of California, Los Angeles. http://www.sscnet.ucla.edu/soc/faculty/kollock .
18. Smith, M., Microsoft Research, Redmond WA. http://research.microsoft.com/~masmith/.
19. Kollock, P. and Smith M. (1996) An Ethnography of MSN V-Chat, Unpublished report for Microsoft Corp., Redmond WA.
20. Smith, M. and Kollock P. (1998) What do People do in Virtual Worlds? An Analysis of V-Chat Log File Data, Unpublished report for Microsoft Corp., Redmond WA.
21. Barnett, T. (1996) V-Chat surveys and V-Chat Analysis, Unpublished report for Microsoft Corp., Redmond WA.
22. The ICQ software (1996), produced by Mirabilis Ltd. http://web.icq.com.
23. MSN Communities. http://communities.msn.com/home, 2001.
24. Yahoo Clubs. http://dir.clubs.yahoo.com/clubhouse, 2001.
25. AOL Groups. http://groups.aol.com/, 2001.
26. Farnham, S. (2001) Unpublished report, Microsoft Research.
27. Smith, M., Farnham, S., and Drucker S. (2000) The Social Life of Small Graphical Chat Spaces. *Proceedings of CHI*, ACM Press, pp. 462-469

Worlds Apart: Exclusion-Processes in DDS

Els Rommes[1]

Twente University
Faculty of Philosophy and Social Sciences
P.O. Box 217, 7500 AE Enschede, The Netherlands
e.w.m.rommes@wmw.utwente.nl

Abstract. More and more interfaces are designed for 'everybody', instead of with a specific user-group in mind. In practice, most of them are still used by the 'typical Internet-user', the highly educated, white young male with extensive computer and Internet-experience. Amsterdam-based digital city DDS is no exception to this rule. In this article, the interface of DDS is studied with the help of ten first-time users with a more diverse background. Did they face any barriers in using DDS? And what kind of work did they need to perform to use the interface? This study shows that the most serious problems the first-time users faced were not caused by a lack of skill, but by the different technological frame they had. Thus, a script-analysis with the help of 'outsiders' seems to be an effective way to uncover some exclusion-processes of a digital city.

1 Introduction

In October 1996, a new user-interface was introduced in the well-known, Amsterdam-based Digital City DDS. This interface was the third to be introduced, and it incorporated the latest features of the WWW. The design-team had very idealistic and convincing arguments for the design-choices they made. They wanted to make DDS original, dynamic, innovative, and commercially viable [16]. Perhaps most of all, they wanted to make a design that was user-friendly, so that 'everybody', 'even my granny' as one of the designers stated, could use it. But, as with most digital cities, hardly any 'grannies' use DDS. Although the user-population of DDS has become slightly more diverse, it is still a very biased group, mostly consisting of young, highly educated, white males [5]. Could it be that the interface of DDS poses barriers for users with a more diverse background?

For my analysis of the potential barriers in the interface of DDS, I use the concept of 'script'. Akrich [1: 208] defines the script of technical objects as follows: 'technical objects define a framework of action together with the actors and the space

---

[1] I would like to thank Ellen van Oost, Sally Wyatt, Anne Sofie Laegran, Nelly Oudshoorn, Agnes Bolso and participants from the Lomskole, the EMTEL-network and three anonymous referees for their helpful comments on earlier versions of this article. I also would like to thank the designers, users and first-time users of DDS who gave me their time and the opportunity to interview them.

M. Tanabe, P. van den Besselaar, T. Ishida (Eds.): Digital Cities, LNCS 2362, pp. 219–232, 2002.
© Springer-Verlag Berlin Heidelberg 2002

in which they are supposed to act'[2]. This script is, often unconsciously, made in the design-process by the designers who construct images of the users and use-situations [2: 168]. If the images the designers make do not fit with the use-situation of potential users, the resulting script can work excluding. Orlikowski [14] gives some insight into when such a script works particularly excluding. She shows how designers often have different expectations, assumptions and knowledge about some key aspects of ICT, than users have. She calls these expectations, assumptions and knowledge about ICT the 'technological frame'. Designers and users tend to have a different technological frame "by dint of their membership in particular social groups and the different roles and relationships they have with technology" [14: 179]. As this frame gets inscribed in the technology, it can be expected that the script of a technology will exclude the members of the groups which differ most from the social group to which designers belong. Following this line of reasoning, it would make sense that the script of the Internet in general and of DDS more specifically tends to have an excluding effect on people with a lower education, unemployed people, inexperienced computer-users, women, ethnic minorities and elderly people.

The terms I use, such as 'exclusion' and 'barriers', seem to suggest that users are static entities who are influenced by the script in a particular way. This suggests a technological determinist view on the script of technology. Of course, people in society and technologies constantly change, mutually influencing each other. The level of education may rise or drop amongst different groups in society, images of technology in society evolve, barriers may vanish while new barriers appear and groups of people who were formerly excluded get included while others are excluded again. So the script-analysis I want to perform is an analysis of the 'mechanisms of adjustment' [1: 209] or the failure to adjust between a technology and a potential user. In other words, it is about whom has to perform what kind of work in order to be able to use a certain technology in present society. With 'work' I not only mean the time and effort spent by the users to learn how to use the interface, but also frustrations, self-doubts and even anger users feel during the process. As DDS is meant to be used for pleasure and users are in no way obliged to use it, this work can form an important barrier for their continuation of the use of DDS[3].

I start with describing the method I used. Then I describe the interface I studied and some of the backgrounds of the design-choices. Next, I study the problems first-time users faced as they tried to deal with the interface. I focus on the problems they

---

[2] This definition can be specified for DDS to show that DDS can exclude potential users at several levels. Potential users need to have access to a computer and Internet, they need to have the skills and knowledge to be able to use the interface of DDS and the concept of DDS has to be attractive to them. Similar barriers are distinguished by others [19], [26]. See also research on universal access and usability [12], [20], [22].

[3] Tyre and Orlikowski [24] have shown that most of the work of experimentation and modifications by users is performed during the introductory-phase of a new technology. Thus, it can be expected that the work in this phase poses too big a barrier and some potential users will give up their attempts to learn using DDS. According to Suchman [23: 4], "making sense of a new artifact is an inherently problematic activity." This does not, however, take away the urgency to reduce the amount of work involved in this phase of making sense of an interface.

had with the metaphor and with the learning-process. Finally, I will discuss whether and to whom the script of DDS has posed barriers for using it and I discuss the effectiveness of the method I used in bringing these to light.

2   Methods

What makes a script-analysis complicated is that designers make many of their design-choices unconsciously as they are based on their technological frame. A frame which I, for a large part, share[4]. Asking the designers what kind of assumptions they build into the technology, or even analyzing the script myself, will not bring to light every part of the script that may exclude potential users. And, according to Akrich [1: 211], the 'study of the ordinary user is not very useful because he or she has already taken on board the prescriptions implied in interaction with the machine.' So analyzing the script with users, who have already integrated the script, is not helpful as both the script and the mechanisms of adjustment have become invisible. To 'de-script' DDS, to decipher the technology back to words, I will use the perspective of 'outsiders', which is a well-known technique in both feminist studies and anthropology[5].

Because this is an explorative study, qualitative analysis is used to get more insight into the particular mechanisms of adjustment and the potential reasons for its failure. I have chosen a case-study approach, in which I went back and forth between analyzing the design-process and the information I got from 'outsiders' experiences with the interface. I got my information about the design-process of DDS 3.0 by interviewing key-informants, reading the archives and analyzing the resulting interface. For this article, I have tried to find some of the elements of the technological frames of the designers, which led to the design-choices with which the outsiders I chose seemed to have the biggest problems. Quantitative data provide some insight into which groups of users are included or excluded by a technology at a certain point in time, in other words, for which groups the processes of adjustment require or do not require too much work. Thus, references to quantitative research will be used to give a first impression about the generalisability of the findings in this study.

2.1   Selection of the 'Outsiders'

I wanted to select people who had no previous experience with DDS, because first-time user experiences make particularly visible what kind of technological frames people use as they try to make sense of a new interface [14: 182]. A second criterion I

---

[4] By analyzing the script as a single analyst, I run the risk of getting caught in the same trap against which I warn designers: resolving to the I-methodology [17]. Many designers of ICT use themselves as exemplary for 'the user' they are designing for, forgetting the fact that they differ in many ways (such as technical competence and confidence, income, educational background, age and gender) from their intended users. See also Nielsen [13: 13] on a description of 'why designers are not users': 'It is almost impossible to disregard the information one already knows when trying to assess whether another piece of information would be easy to understand for a novice user.'

[5] And a technique which is also suggested by Latour and Akrich [3: 260] as the 'exotic' position which they describe as being faced with a new or foreign setup.

used is a common criterion in usability testing practices. According to several usability experts, it is good practice to study interfaces with the 'least competent users' [18: 129] and 'not just those who happen to have the same characteristics as the developers themselves' [13: 46]. These kinds of 'first-time' or 'novice' users offer 'excellent indicators of a product's overall usability and ease of learning' (ibid). Certainly, these kinds of users are outsiders in the sense that they are rarely taken into consideration in present design-practices [12: 56], [15], [20: 90]. Moreover, their skills in handling computers and the Internet are very different from those of the designers, as is their confidence in handling these technologies and their expected enthusiasm for it.

Because I was not so interested in observing the very basic struggles of these first-time users with the mouse and Windows, I found nine of my ten first-time users in a free course to learn the basics of computers and the Internet, organized by the municipality of Amsterdam[6]. Thus, most of them were interested in computers and the Internet. The tenth first-time user, 60 year old Truus who had been a lab-assistant, was not interested in following the course as she was not interested in computers. I included her to get some impression about the difference the attitude towards computers and the Internet could make. The first-time users had different levels of experience with computers and the Internet. For five of the participants, the course was their first 'hands-on' experience with computers and the Internet, though most of them had observed a family-member or friend while they used the Internet. I took care to study them half-way through the course, after they had had an introduction to the computer and Windows, but before they were introduced to the Internet, so that their interpretation of DDS would not be influenced by their impression of other parts of the Internet. Two of the participants to this 'course in basic skills' had extensive experience with the Internet: Judith had used the Internet for two months on a daily basis and Jan had spent the last year surfing the Internet for up to eight hours a day. This shows the diversity in opinions about what basic computer-skills precisely are.

Because I am interested in issues of diversity, I took care that the participants in this study had a diverse background. I wanted the first-time users I selected to have a different social-cultural background than the designers, as I expect this to have influence on their technological frame. So when I asked participants of the course to participate in my research, I tried to diversify them on the basis of gender, age and cultural background. This was the third and last criterion I used in selecting my first-time users. Six of my first-time users were female; their ages ranged between 44 and 70 and three originated from another country than the Netherlands. They were also different in their family-situation and their educational and professional background. Only two of them had a job. The professional background of the first-time users was very diverse[7].

---

6 As part of the project 'digitale trapveldjes' (digital playgrounds), a project in which people are given free education and access to computers and the Internet via community centers, in this case community center 'Verzet' (resistance).

7 The following description of the first-time users I interviewed shows the diverse backgrounds. In this article, I will refer to some of them. To protect their identity, I changed their names.
Judith: 44 year old female born in the Netherlands, drama-school in London, translator, presently in between jobs, 2 children (4, 10) who live at home, divorced. Since two months extensive user of Internet.

I held semi-structured interviews with the first-time users in which I focussed on what they thought of computers and the Internet, what they found attractive and unattractive about it and what they would want or expect of a 'digital city', in other words, about their technological frame. Moreover, I observed each of them as they tried to make sense of the interface of DDS, to find out how their frames of reference influenced their use of DDS. I used the 'thinking aloud' method as I asked them to formulate the thoughts they had as they tried to use the interface. During their attempts, I noted which parts of the interface attracted them, which parts they (dis)liked and which parts were (un)clear to them. According to Nielsen [13: 195], with this method "the test users enable us to understand how they view the computer system". As I want to get more insight into the technological frame of the first time users, this method seems to be particularly useful. Because I did not have access to an official testing environment and because I wanted them to feel comfortable, I performed the interface-part of the research in the classroom in which they were given their course.

As with all methodological choices, the choice of these methods has some drawbacks. The presence of a researcher may cause the first-time users to show interest in other parts of the interface than they would have had if they had been exploring the interface by themselves. And, as I asked them to use the interface, it is also less clear when they would have stopped had they been alone. By asking them to use DDS from the start-page, how and if they would 'find' DDS themselves is invisible, or even if they would enter DDS by using the start-page. Finally, the presence of a researcher may have helped them overcome some of their fear to 'just press buttons', as they knew the researcher would act if something went wrong.

Anna: 59 year old female born in Indonesia, secondary school, secretary, no job because of care for retarded son (38), divorced. No experience with computers or Internet.

Truus: 60 year old female born in the Netherlands, basic education, lab assistant, one son (35), widow. No experience with computers or Internet and does not want it. Not a course-participant.

Ine: 62 year old female born in the Netherlands, secondary school, seamstress, cleaner and worker at blood transfusion-service, no job, two children (42, 37), married. No experience with computers or Internet.

Stella: 66 year old female born in the Netherlands, 4 year course in Blawatski-doctrine, writer and course-leader on chakra-psychology, three children (34, 41, 44), single. No experience with computers or Internet.

Eva: 71 year old female born in Surinam, intermediate education, kindergarten teacher, 7 children (41-50) married. No experience with computers or Internet.

Aram: 48 year old man born in the Netherlands, higher education, English teacher, single. Experience with computers, no experience with Internet.

Jan: 54 year old male born in the Netherlands, academy for arts, voluntary work in theatres and radio, no job, single. Since one year extensive use of Internet.

John: 57 year old man born in UK, secondary school, hotel and catering industry worker presently on a disability pension, single. No experience with computers or Internet.

Joop: 70 year old male born in the Netherlands, secondary school, metalworker and house-painter, no job, two children (43, 45), divorced. Some computer-experience, no experience with Internet.

3   The Design-Choices in DDS 3.0

The successful integration of a new artifact in society can be said to mean that it is fitted into the prevailing cultural frames. One way to make this 'fit' easier is to use a metaphor, which links the new artifact to a familiar image [13: 126, 127], [28: 11]. This is what the designers of DDS did in 1993. To make the integration of the then new Internet-technology in society easier, they used the city as a metaphor for the virtual space and community they created. They tried to avoid unfamiliar technical terms by using metaphors related to the city, such as squares, houses and a post-office. They did not want it to relate too much to the physical city Amsterdam (Interview with Stikker, founder of DDS). In other words, they wanted to use the metaphor in a 'not grounded' way.

Because the founding organizations of DDS were Amsterdam-based and the city council of Amsterdam sponsored DDS, the city-metaphor was also used in a 'grounded' way. The 'grounded' use of the city-metaphor on web-sites means that they "relate coherently to the development of specific cities (...) and concentrate on integrating Web content located within the physical space of one city" (Graham and Aurigi as cited in [4: 12]). DDS related in several ways to the city of Amsterdam. The logo of DDS is reminiscent of the coat of arms of Amsterdam, the names of several squares in DDS are based on districts in Amsterdam and DDS represents a lot of information about Amsterdam. Because the original founders of DDS either worked for political-cultural non-profit organizations in Amsterdam or had close ties with them, the information represented in DDS is mostly provided by these kinds of organizations. This shows how the technological frame of the designers influenced their interpretation of the city-metaphor.

For commercial reasons, gradually DDS came to represent less information about Amsterdam. The management of DDS needed the money organizations would bring in, so they were not selective in allowing non-Amsterdam based organizations to represent their information inside DDS. About two thirds of the information inside DDS is not locally based anymore [5: 24][8]. The commercialization of DDS did, however, not lead to considerably more information from shops, banks, restaurants or other companies which can be found in a real life city.

During the design of DDS 3.0, the designers never questioned the use of the metaphor 'city' and the way the original designers had envisioned its use. So although DDS contained not nearly as much information about Amsterdam as when it was founded, the designers of the new interface DDS 3.0 maintained the references to Amsterdam in their design. At the same time they wanted to use 'city' only metaphorically. So they designed a very abstract, two-dimensional graphical interface, in which only the language reminded of a 'real' city. All in all, the use of the metaphor 'city' in DDS 3.0 remained an ambivalent combination of grounded and not grounded.

How did the designers use the metaphor of city? At the home-page, the most visible use of the metaphor is that the potential user who wants to enter DDS has to decide whether to 'pay a visit to the city' (access the interface) as an 'inhabitant' or as

---

[8] Another reason for this was that the designers wanted to attract users from outside Amsterdam. Nowadays, the number of users from Amsterdam dropped from 45 % in 1994 to 23% after the introduction of DDS 3.0 in 1996 [5: 5].

a 'tourist' (see figure I: 'bezoek de stad als bewoner' or 'toerist'). 'Inhabitants' of DDS are users who have filled out an on-line form in DDS with their name, address and phone-number. Inhabitants of DDS get an e-mail account (accessible via the 'post-office'), they can 'build a house' (design a homepage) and they can participate in the 'café's' or other interactive environments of DDS. These kinds of facilities are denied to 'tourists', users who have not subscribed to DDS, because the designers of DDS want to have 'some control about the content in DDS' (interview help-desk participant). Entering the city as a tourist will take the user to the 'central square', an octagon which is connected to several other such 'squares', each with their own theme. In the following figure, the main part of the home-page of DDS 3.0 is shown.

Fig. 1. The home-page of DDS 3.0

The icon on top of the interface is very similar to the coat of arms of the city of Amsterdam. Users suggested an index as a navigational method after the initial introduction of DDS 3.0. The button 'A-Z index' in the menu on the left side of the screen, was made to accommodate them and contains an alphabetical index of the information-providers in DDS. This index and the 'map', which is presented on the next page of the interface, offer ways to navigate through DDS. The 'map' button links to a colorful honeycomb with in each octagon a symbol that represents the theme of the square inside DDS to which it links.

The advertisement-buttons at the bottom of figure I ('sun, 'uunet', an outdated one and 'tron') were introduced for commercial reasons. The designers thought they would cause no problems, as they had asked inhabitants of DDS at a real life meeting what they thought of the introduction of banners in the city. According to the designers, none of the inhabitants had objections against advertisements[9].

Although help-texts were available in DDS, these were not introduced at the opening screen of DDS. These texts were made by help-desk participants, often volunteers. According to one of the designers: "There were not enough texts by far, of

---

[9] None of the seventeen inhabitants of DDS, who I interviewed for my thesis, indicated any problems with this form of commercialization of DDS.

course. And documenting is a profession. And of course here it was given no priority at all." (Interview with Van Eeden) The choice not to give many help-texts and to put them in one central place, was partly made because the designers wanted users to learn how to use DDS by 'playing around'. This was the learning-methodology the founders of DDS had introduced from the start and which they personally found most attractive [17].

By this description of the design-choices, it becomes clear that the designers often used themselves (e.g. in their ambivalence regarding the use of the metaphor, in their choice of the organizations of which they represented information and in the choice for the 'playing around' methodology) or the inhabitants of DDS (in the case of the decision to use advertisements) as exemplary for the user they wanted to attract. In the next paragraph, I will discuss my interpretation of the consequences of these choices for my first-time users.

4   The First-Time Users Understanding of DDS

4.1   The Metaphor

What did my first-time users expect from something called 'a digital city on the Internet'? This question seems hard to answer, especially because more than half of the participants had not heard of DDS before. Nevertheless, the name 'Digital City' evoked a lot of inspiration amongst the first-time users about what they expected or hoped they could find in such a thing. Their expectations were partly formed by their expectations of the Internet: a lot of information and also communicating with people[10]. Partly their expectations were formed by the name 'digital city'. The 'digital'-part of the name presupposes that potential users have some idea about what digital means. Obviously, this is not the case with people without much experience with new technology. Indeed, three female[11] first-time users either remarked that they did not know what it meant or compared it with for example 'electrical cooking instead of on gas' (interview with Anna). The 'city' part of the name evoked more responses from the first-time users. It made them expect and want to find lists with shops for clothes and furniture (preferably with pictures and ways to compare the different shops), pubs, restaurants, information on public transportation, maps and information for people looking for a house. Most importantly, they expected and preferred all this information to be focussed on Amsterdam[12]. Graphically, they ex-

---

[10] Surprisingly, many of my informants were inspired by the teletekst information system on their televisions. During their use of DDS, they kept comparing the way of navigating DDS with their navigation of teletekst, and the way in which information was ordered in DDS with the way it is ordered on teletekst.

[11] The fact that none of the men made a similar remark does not necessarily mean that they did know what digital means. Several feminist authors [11, 25] have suggested that in our present culture it is harder for men than for women to admit that they are ignorant about a specific technology.

[12] In their study of a project to introduce 'ordinary citizens' of Pittsburgh to the Internet, Kraut ed al found a similar preference: "The Internet is global, but local Pittsburgh and neigh-

pected to find pictures of buildings in a fysical city, some even hoped to find pictures of their own neighbourhood. Two participants hoped they would find pictures and information about what Amsterdam used to look like when they were young.

The designers of DDS had based their use of the metaphor on the city they knew, a public domain where citizens can discuss and non-profit political and cultural organizations give their information. This use of the metaphor contrasted with the reading of the metaphor by the first-time users. Whereas the designers understanding of the metaphor city was informed by their work, the technological frame of the first-time users was informed by their daily-life experiences with a 'city'. These daily activities involved shopping, travelling by public transportation or going to a café. For them, 'city' meant Amsterdam, a geographical location where their homes, activities and their memories are situated. Moreover, a remark of sixty year old widow Truus made me realize that 'city' is not a neutral metaphor. She said she "does not do anything in the city since it has become so unsafe". This observation calls to mind that a city may not be such an attractive metaphor for women and elderly people[13].

The design of the interface of DDS did not offer any help to the first-time users in re-interpreting their understanding of the metaphor. On the contrary, it only reinforced their interpretation of DDS as a representation of their own everyday life city, by the use of metaphors such as tourist, inhabitant and the logo on top of the home-page[14]. Even sixty six-year-old Stella, who was the only participant who did not expect to see anything from Amsterdam, changed her mind as soon as she saw the home-page of DDS. From then on, she expected "information about public transportation or districts in Amsterdam" if she entered DDS.

The ambivalent grounded and not-grounded use of the metaphor by the designers caused a lot of confusion and frustration amongst my first-time users. The problems they had in dealing with the home-page offers a good example of this. All except Judith[15] thought that 'inhabitant' meant 'inhabitant of Amsterdam'. As they clicked on the text 'enter the city as inhabitant'[16], a pop-up screen appeared, stating 'user-name' and 'password'. They could not understand what they had to fill in. To some of the first-time users it was hard to understand why they, as citizens of Amsterdam, could not enter DDS as an inhabitant. Others thought it 'fun' to visit Amsterdam as a tourist, because they hoped to be shown 'places you not normally encounter as an inhabitant of Amsterdam', as experienced Internet-user Jan stated. The fact that they were not shown around parts of Amsterdam was felt as a disappointment.

---

borhood information and communication services have special appeal to participants in the trial." [12: 59]

[13] This can be seen as the unintentional transference of values attached to the concept 'city' to DDS. See Van Oost for a similar transference of gender-values to computers because of the 'brain'-metaphor. [28: 11]

[14] Though this logo is fairly small, several of the first-time users noticed it and made a remark about it, typically remarking that they recognized it and that it meant something to them. This shows how much first-time users were looking for parts in the interface which were familiar to them.

[15] She had seen an 'electronic village' a few days before the interview and remembered the virtual community explanations which were given in this village.

[16] For users without any internet-experience, it was even unclear that they could point and click on the texts in the picture. The buttons on the left were much clearer in that sense.

One of the participants thought she could order a cab by using the button 'zijwegen' ('side-streets', which links to a page with related websites), which shows the graphical symbol of a cab and several others expected to get a list with café's if they would press the 'café'-button. The things that did show up when they pressed these buttons, were so different from what they expected that they could not make sense out of them. The confusion of some participants was particularly clear in the use of the 'map'. Though the designers had made it as a navigational tool, all first-time users expected to be shown a map of Amsterdam. As 62-year-old seamstress Ine said: "This is a map of Amsterdam, shall I look at it? (She clicks on the button) No! I really can not see anything on this! (laughs) I do not like this at all, not at all! Because if you click on a map of Amsterdam, naturally I want to see it! (….) You expect to see a map and then you see all those different colors mixed confusedly. No, that is very disappointing." As this quotation shows, for Ine this use of the metaphor was confusing and she did not like it. Although some of the other participants discovered they could click on parts of the map and use it as a navigational tool, all of them expressed similar feelings of frustration as they tried to make sense of it. For Ine, the framework of action of DDS was too far apart from her technological frame and required too many adjustments from her part, so she gave up.

The attempts of the first-time users to understand and use the metaphor of DDS show many more instances of the work they faced, such as clicking on the wrong links, adjusting their views on what DDS was about and handling the frustration, anger and confusion this caused. The script of DDS was not flexible, as it did not allow for the first-time users' interpretation of the metaphor. In this way, the framework of action of DDS excluded several potential users. Because even the two first-time users with a lot of experience with the Internet struggled with the metaphor, it can be assumed that this exclusion was not caused by inexperience with the Internet. This barrier seems to be based on the social-cultural background of potential users, which gave them a different technological frame to interpret the metaphor with than the designers had.

4.2   The Learning-Process

The confusion, which the use of the metaphor caused, could have been less if the designers would have chosen to explain more to potential users[17]. They did not do this because they wanted the users to learn how to use DDS by 'playing around'. Moreover, they did not realize that people might misunderstand their use of the metaphor, as it was based on their own unconscious technological frame and this was the way the metaphor had been used since the conception of DDS. Thus, they thought the use of the metaphor was self-explanatory and they wrote hardly any explanatory texts in DDS. Considering the problems the first-time users had with the interpretation of the metaphor, DDS was all but self-explanatory to first-time users.

So what kind of work did the first-time users have to perform to learn how to use DDS? Experienced Internet-user and highly educated Judith spent a lot of time looking for clues on what DDS was about. She did this in the way the designers had

---

[17] Nielsen draws a similar conclusion: "Specifically, discussions of interface metaphors in manuals should be supplemented with explanations of the differences between the real-world reference system and the computer system." [13: 128]

envisioned: by pressing different buttons and 'playing around'. She, however, expressed several times how frustrated she became because it took her so much time and still she could not get clear what DDS was about. The playing-around learning style was not attractive nor effective for her. Had she been surfing on her own, she told me, she would have given up very quickly, because "it was not easy enough for me to get inside". After almost an hour of trying, she still was unsure whether DDS was intended as a way to search certain information or for social reasons[18]. She had to perform too much work to get adjusted to the script, so she gave up.

Not only did DDS give no clues about what DDS was to be used for, inside DDS there were also not enough or not clear enough clues about how to navigate or what certain things would connect to. For the first-time users without previous Internet-experience, this was particularly problematic. Faced with the home-page of DDS, all of them were looking for a 'start-button', or a way to 'enter' DDS. Presumably because of their button-like character, the four advertisements at the bottom of the entrance-screen were most similar to what they were looking for. Especially the one with a cross, which means that it is an outdated connection, drew a lot of attention. Almost all first-time Internet-users pressed one of the advertisements to 'start DDS'. They did not understand that these advertisements took them away from DDS, as they did not know yet what DDS would look like. Without the help of the researcher, they 'got lost' and would not have seen more of DDS than the home-page.

The index was the only navigational method that all first-time users recognized as a navigational tool and which they could actually use. The index was, however, made with the internal logic of DDS in mind: only names of customers can be found in this alphabetical list. Because the first time users of DDS were looking for words in the index like 'nature', 'health', 'gardening' or 'areas within Amsterdam' they could not find what they wanted by using the index. Some of them drew the (incorrect) conclusion from this attempt that this kind of information was not available in DDS[19] and they gave up looking for it.

A similar kind of use of a 'designers-logic' came to light when the first-time users got confronted with error and failure-messages. This happened many times to the first-time users. These messages were most of the time standard-messages that did not help them to deal with the particular situation with which they had to deal. A striking example of this is the message users get as they press the text 'enter the city as inhabitant', which because of the confusions around the metaphor, many of the first-time users did. A system-message pops up, giving no more information than 'username' and 'password'. Pressing 'ok' at the bottom of the screen without filling in a user-name brought up the same pop-up screen, much to the irritation of the first-time users who did this. Clicking the 'cancel'-button brought out another screen, stating amongst other things: 'oops, no access to this closed building' and 'the owner of this building thinks you should not be here'. When this happened to 48 year old teacher Aram, he said: "Right at the start, you click on something and bang, you are immediately told that you are actually somewhere where you are not allowed to be. That is somewhat discouraging. It is not very hospitable. (...) if you start with that it is not very pleasant."

---

[18] She could not find an easy way to find information and she did not find it suitable for social use because she did not think DDS offered an attractive environment.

[19] Moreover, most of the information they had said they wanted, such as information about shops, restaurants and public transportation, was not available in DDS.

To some of the first-time users, these and similar kinds of messages caused self-consciousness and confusion, as they felt the text meant they had done something wrong and they could not figure out what that could be.

All in all, one can say that the learning methodology in DDS was not attractive to first-time users. In the hour which was used for the interface-experiments, none of the participants could learn what DDS was about, what information could be found in it and how they could navigate through the city. They were not given sufficient help by the system to get to understand the system. The 'playing around' way of learning might be a nice way of learning if the frame of reference of the user is close to that of the designer. If that is the case, it may be easier for the first-time user to predict what will happen if they click on a link.

It seems DDS has been made for a very specific group of people who have the time and who want to spend it on 'playing around'. Several authors suggest that men in general have more spare time than women and are more interested in 'playing around' [7, 9]. Women mostly want to use the Internet if they consider it useful[20] and they do not spend as much time on it [6][21]. Thus, DDS seems to be more attractive for masculine than for feminine users. These data suggest that it was not coincidental that Jan and Ferdi were the only first-time users who considered re-visiting DDS after this research, both men who said they enjoyed the 'playing around' style of learning. For experienced Internet-user Judith, who expressed that she did not like to play around on the Internet because she "lost so much time with it", this part of the script had an excluding effect.

The experiences of the first-time users as they tried to learn how to use DDS suggested that it was somewhat easier to learn how to use DDS for experienced Internet-users. Experienced users could, for example, more easily distinguish advertisements from the DDS-interface and they did not spend so much time looking for the 'start-button'. On the other hand, the designers' choice to make users learn how to use DDS by 'playing around' was more connected to gender than to the amount of experience of the first-time users with the Internet. And although most first-time users said that given enough time, they could probably learn how to use DDS, it seems that DDS did not fit their tastes and preferences. Nor did DDS provide them with a motive to invest the work needed for this.

5   Conclusions

What were the barriers the first-time users of DDS faced? In my study, I found two major aspects in the framework of action of DDS which did not connect with the technological frame of the first-time users I studied. Firstly, the designers assumed that their users would understand the concept of a virtual world by using the metaphor of a digital city. The designers use of the metaphor 'city' did, however, not connect

---

[20] In an extensive overview of literature about gender and ICT, van Zoonen [27] suggests that mostly male preferences for content are met on the Internet, making it more useful for masculine users. Lately, this seems to improve.

[21] In feminist studies, these kinds of differences are often explained by pointing at the importance of technology in giving shape to masculinity and femininity in present society [8, 11, 25].

with the everyday-life experience and the ensuing interpretation of the metaphor by the first-time users I studied. Though the use of the metaphor had originally been a tool to make it easier to use DDS, to the first-time users it has become a barrier. The second major barrier in the script of DDS was that users were expected to learn how to use DDS by 'playing around'. For most of the first-time users, this meant that the work they had to put into adjusting themselves to the script of DDS simply was too much. The frustration, self-doubt and anger they experienced while they got acquainted to the interface were not matched by the attraction DDS offered to them.

What kind of conclusions can be drawn from the methods I used? This and other studies show that testing an interface with the 'least skilled users' seems to be a good way of at least improving the usability of an interface [10, 13, 18]. As these skills are related to overlapping categories such as Internet-experience, professional status and gender, age and ethnic background, this would mean that the interface would be easier to use for 'all' [19]. However, this study also suggests that 'basic computer skills', such as using the mouse or knowing how to use a scroll-bar were not the most important factor in deciding whether a first-time user could use DDS. The difference in technological frame between the first-time users I studied and the designers of DDS, seems to offer a better explanation for the problems of the first-time users I studied. Thus, I would argue to test interfaces with first-time users with a different technological frame than the designers, e.g. on the basis of their ethnical background, their gender or their age[22].

All in all, a script-analysis with the use of first-time users seems to be a promising way to uncover some of the exclusion-processes at work on the Internet. If designers want to take seriously their wish to reach 'everybody', they need to do a lot more work to bridge the gap between their world and the world of the diverse users they try to reach.

References

1.   Akrich, M., *The De-Scription of Technical Objects*, in *Shaping Technology/Building Society: Studies in Sociotechnical Change*, Bijker, W.; Law, J., Editors. 1992, MIT Press: Cambridge. p. 205-224.
2.   Akrich, M., *User Representations: Practices, Methods and Sociology*, in *Managing Technology in Society, The Approach of Constructive Technology Assessment*, Rip, A.; Misa, T.J.; Schot, J., Editors. 1995, Pinter Publishers: London, New York. p. 167-184.
3.   Akrich, M.; Latour, B., *A Summary of a Convenient Vocabulary for the Semiotics of Human and Nonhuman Assemblies*, in *Shaping Technology/Building Society*, W. Bijker; Law, J., Editors. 1992, MIT Press: Cambridge. p. 259-264.
4.   Van Bastelaer, B.; Lobet-Maris, C., *Social Learning regarding Multimedia Developments at a Local Level. The Case of Digital Cities*. 1998, University of Namur: SLIM Research, DG XII.

---

[22] There is a political reason to perform these kinds of tests even when the interface is not 'meant for all'. As Star convincingly argues, non-users of a technology are often influenced by the introduction of that technology [21]. For this reason, Wyatt suggests to involve non-users in the design of technology to take into account the influence of new technology on their world [26].

5. Van den Besselaar, P, I. Melis, D. Beckers, Digital cities: organization, content and use, in *Digital Cities: Experiences, Technologies and Future Perspectives*, T. Ishida & K. Isbister (eds) 2000, Springer-Verlag: Dordrecht. p. 18-32.
6. Bimber, B., *Measuring the Gender Gap on the Internet*. Social Science Quarterly, 2000. **81**(3).
7. Boomen, M.v.d., *Internet ABC voor vrouwen, een inleiding voor D@t@d@mes en modemmeiden*. 1996, Amsterdam: Instituut voor Publiek en Politiek.
8. Cockburn, C.; Ormrod, S., *Gender & technology in the making*. 1993, London: Sage.
9. Ford, N.; Miller, D., *Gender differences in Internet perceptions and use*. Aslib Proceedings, 1996. **48** (7/8): p. 183-192.
10. Goodwin, N.C., *Functionality and Usability*. Communications of the ACM, 1987. **30** (3): p. 229-233.
11. Kleif, T., *I'm no athlete, but i can make this thing dance*. Science, Technology & Human Values, Forthcoming.
12. Kraut, R., Scherlis, W.; Mukhopadhyay, T.; Manning, J.; Kiesler, S., *The HomeNet Field Trial of Residential Internet Services*. Communications of the ACM, 1996. **39** (12): p. 55-63.
13. Nielsen, J., *Usability Engineering*. 1993, San Diego, London: Academic Press. 358.
14. Orlikowski, W.J.; Gash, D.C., *Technological Frames: Making Sense of Information Technology in Organizations*. ACM Transactions on Information Systems, 1994. **12**(2): p. 174-207.
15. Oudshoorn, N.; Rommes, E.; Stienstra, M., *Configuring the User as Everybody. Gender and Design Cultures in Information and Communication Technologies*. Science, Technology & Human Values, Forthcoming.
16. Rommes, E., *Gendered User-Representations*, in *Women, Work and Computerization, Charting a Course to the Future*, Balka, E.; Smith, R., Editors. 2000, Kluwer Academic Publishers: Dordrecht. p. 137-145.
17. Rommes, E., E. van Oost, N. Oudshoorn, *Gender in the design of the digital city of Amsterdam*, in *Virtual Gender; Technology, consumption and identity*, A.A. E. Green, Editor. 2001, Routledge: London and New York. p. 241-261.
18. Rubin, J., *Handbook of Usability Testing, How to plan, design, and conduct effective tests*. 1994, New York: John Wiley & Sons, Inc. 330.
19. SCP, *Digitalisering van de leefwereld, een onderzoek naar informatie- en communicatietechnologie en sociale ongelijkheid*. 2000, Den Haag: Universiteit Utrecht.
20. Shneiderman, B., *Universal Usability, Pushing human-computer interaction research to empower every citizen*. Communications of the ACM, 2000. **43**(5): p. 85-91.
21. Star, S.L., *Power, technology and the phenomenology of conventions: on being allergic to onions*, in *A Sociology of Monsters: Essays on Power, Technology and Domination*, J. Law, Editor. 1991, Routledge: London. p. 26-56.
22. Stephanidis, C.; Savidis, A., *Universal Access in the Information Society: Methods, Tools, and Interaction Technologies*. UAIS, 2001. **1**: p. 40-55.
23. Suchman, L. *Knowing Technologies*. Paper presented at conference *Epistimic Cultures and the Practice of Interdisciplinarity*. 2001. Trondheim.
24. Tyre, M.J.; Orlikowski, W.J., *The episodic process of learning by using*. International Journal of Technology Management, 1996. **11**(7-8): p. 790-798.
25. Wajcman, J., *Feminism confronts Technology*. 1993, Cambridge: Polity Press.
26. Wyatt, S., *Non-users also matter: the construction of users and non-users of the Internet*, in *How Users Matter: The Co-construction of Users and Technology*, in: Oudshoorn, N.; Pinch, T. Editors. forthcoming, MIT Press: Cambridge MA.
27. van Zoonen, L., *Gender en ICT, Literatuuronderzoek ten behoeve van Infodrome*. 2001, Infodrome: Amsterdam.
28. van Oost, E., *Making the computer masculine*, in *Women, Work and Computerization, Charting a course to the future*, Balka, E.; Smith, R. Editors. 2000, Dordrecht, Kluwer Academic Publishers, p.9-16.

Log Analysis of Map-Based Web Page Search on Digital City Kyoto

Kaoru Hiramatsu

NTT Communication Science Laboratories
2-4, Hikaridai, Seika-cho, Soraku-gun, Kyoto 619-0237 Japan
hiramatu@cslab.kecl.ntt.co.jp

Abstract. This paper analyzes how people use map-based user interfaces of regional information systems on the Internet. The analysis is based on the log data of InfoMap, which is supplied on the Web site of the Digital City Kyoto prototype. InfoMap provides a map-based user interface that has useful functions enabling users to choose links to Web pages using digital maps. The log data of InfoMap was recorded automatically on the Web server and enabled us to analyze access frequencies, function usages, and content selections. In this paper, the characteristics of the map-based user interface compared with the characteristics of traditional text-based search engines are explained.

1 Introduction

Online map services are one of the major content providers on the Internet. Some of them provide the digital maps with some content. Such services are convenient for users who wish to find helpful information within specified areas, but no information is available on the significant differences in users' search behaviors and choices of displayed contents between map-based information search and text-based traditional search engines.

To clarify such differences, it is necessary to investigate user-level and content-level log data of online map services. Accordingly, we analyzed the log data of the map-based Web page search on the Digital City Kyoto prototype [1]. The Digital City Kyoto prototype provides an online map service called InfoMap [2], which has useful search functions enabling users to choose links to Web pages in various manners. The search functions are based on the GeoLink system [3], which enables users to perform search with constraints on logical and geographical relationships. Since December 1999, we have been supplying InfoMap as a digital map service on an experimental information portal site, the Digital City Kyoto prototype. For one and a half years, over 20,000 users have used this service and have visited more than 75,000 times. The log data of InfoMap contains three kinds of user operations, i.e., accesses from users' PCs, search requests to InfoMap, and selections of displayed contents. The access frequency and the search request are typical factors of analysis allowing some statistical data of traditional search engines to be compared. On the other hand, the selections of

M. Tanabe, P. van den Besselaar, T. Ishida (Eds.): Digital Cities, LNCS 2362, pp. 233–245, 2002.

displayed contents comprise one of the characteristic operations of a map-based user interface. The log data of the content selections is analyzed as 'the access frequency per unit area' in comparison with the 'content density'. This comparison may show whether areas with dense content (like downtown areas and shopping malls in the physical city) have a stronger attraction for users.

In the following section, we illustrate details of InfoMap. Then, we analyze its log data that was recorded in Digital City Kyoto and discuss it from viewpoints of access frequencies, function usages, and content selections.

2   Map-Based Web Page Search: InfoMap

2.1   Basic Idea

InfoMap is a map-based interface for browsing online city information. We have been supplying InfoMap since about one and a half years ago on the Web site of the Digital City Kyoto prototype. Fig. 1 is a screen image of InfoMap.

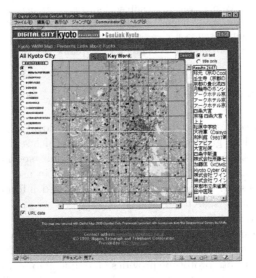

Fig. 1. A screen shot of InfoMap

InfoMap displays a digital map that includes some icons representing geographical positions of Web pages. If the mouse cursor enters an icon image area, then the title of the corresponding Web page pops up as a balloon help. By clicking the icon, the Web page is displayed in a new browser window. In a listbox on the right side of the map image, the titles of displayed Web pages are listed in the order of distance from the cursor point. In this paper, position data and Web page uniform resource locations (URLs) are called points of interest (POI). On

InfoMap, the position data of each POI is precise enough for superimposition on a detailed digital map image with a scale of 1 dot to 1 meter.

For users to efficiently browse a lot of online city information with geographical attributes, we are developing InfoMap as a Java applet with the following extended functions.

1. Incremental data downloading
2. Map scrolling
3. Switching between a wide area map and details

To let users efficiently browse a lot of online city information, InfoMap downloads POI data from its data server on a Web server host via a common gateway interface (CGI) program on demand. While downloading and displaying the data, a user can simultaneously operate InfoMap to browse information and navigate to respective Web pages.

InfoMap uses digital map images in the GIF format because of the processing speed of the Java applet and copyright of the map data. We have prepared a wide area map image that covers the Kyoto metropolitan area and 108 detailed map images for viewing street level information. By clicking a button at the upper left of the map image, the map image switches between the wide area (Fig. 1) and detailed maps (Fig. 2). Map scrolling is also available by dragging the mouse on the map image or using the scroll bars.

Fig. 2. InfoMap with a detailed area map image

2.2   Search Functions

InfoMap has two search functions, i.e., keyword search and category search. The keyword search function enables users to search for Web pages by specifying favorite keywords. The category search function enables users to select information by category. Both search results are displayed on the digital map as icons.

InfoMap has category buttons at the left of the map image for switching superimposed information categories. The categorization of Web pages is based on the categories in the local yellow pages which are coordinated with hierarchies of popular search engines and directory services, and which are specified for online city information with geographical attributes.

Fig. 3 and Fig. 4 are examples of category search on InfoMap. Fig. 3 shows a distribution of dining category information. The map indicates the tendency of many restaurants concentrated in the downtown area of Kyoto. Fig. 4 shows a distribution of public transportation information. The map indicates that this category contains the Web pages of stations and bus stops located along streets.

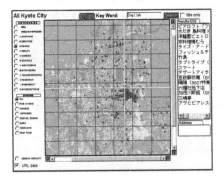 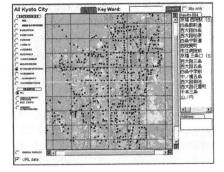

Fig. 3. Dining information   **Fig. 4.** Public transportation information

2.3   Back-End System Architecture

After InfoMap starts on a Web browser, it downloads a digital map image and POI data, and then superimposes them on the map. The search functions of InfoMap are processed with a backend system on the Web server. The backend system utilizes a GeoLink system [3]. Fig. 5 shows the backend system architecture of InfoMap.

Within this architecture, all files and data are transfered via the Hyper-Text Transfer Protocol (HTTP). At the beginning, the Web browser receives an HTML document and class files of InfoMap from the Web server, and then InfoMap starts on the Web browser. Next, InfoMap accesses the GeoLink system for downloading Web page data via a CGI program. Because of security issues with Java applets, the GeoLink system should be on the same host as the Web server.

Search requests from InfoMap are received by the GeoLink system via the CGI program on the Web server. The CGI program translates the requests into queries in GeoLink SQL. For further details of the GeoLink system and GeoLink SQL, see [3].

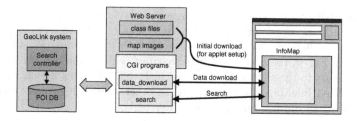

Fig. 5. Backend system architecture

2.4   Contents

The POI data, displayed on the digital maps of InfoMap as icons, comprise sets of the URL information of individual Web pages and the geographical positions indicated by the descriptions in the individual Web pages. For quick response purposes, the POI data are stored on the GeoLink system before being used from InfoMap.

The arrangement of the POI data needs to allow a user to extract information representing geographical positions from Web pages and to find the coordinates of the positions as longitude and latitude using a geographical information system (GIS). There are three methods for Web page retrieval: (1) search for Web pages according to results of exploring stores and buildings on a street of the city; (2) extract Web pages by Web robots; and (3) perform registration by accepting applications from Web page owners in a target area. There are also two methods for extracting positional information from Web pages and finding their geographical coordinates: (1) extract positional information using morphological processing and finding their object attributes in GIS; and (2) check and compare the information manually.

The arranged POI data are added to the the information categories. Before using the POI data on InfoMap, we also obtained the permission to link to each page from the owners of the Web pages. The POI database of the Digital City Kyoto prototype currently has about 5,000 POI and is accessible from InfoMap.

3   Access Frequency Analysis

In this section, we start with analyzing the access frequency of users using cookie data.

The analyzed log data were recorded from December 10, 1999 to April 26, 2001. The log data of InfoMap were classified into URLs consisting of CGI program names and arguments and cookie data including unique codes assigned by the Web server. During this period, InfoMap was accessed 75,004 times by 22,330 users (Tab. 1). The access frequency, that is the average number of accesses per users, was 3.4. From the viewpoint of search function usage, the users could be divided into two groups: a group using the search functions of InfoMap and a group not using them. The access frequency of the former group was 4.7 (48,856 accesses by 10,375 users) and that of the latter was 2.2 (26,148 accesses by 11,955 users). This difference is exhibited more clearly in the cumulative distribution (Fig. 6). In Fig. 6, the first immediate sharp increase of the line for the former group appears to the right of the line for the latter. This means that the former group utilized InfoMap more frequently. In other words, those users who knew search functions did use InfoMap more frequently.

Table 1. Access frequency of InfoMap

	number of users	number of accesses	frequency
Total	22,330	75,004	3.359
search users	10,375	48,856	4.709
search non-users	11,955	26,148	2.187

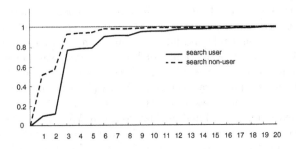

Fig. 6. Cumulative frequency distributions of InfoMap

4   Function Level Log Analysis

The search requests recorded in the log data included the names of search functions and arguments. It was therefore possible to sum up the search function calls and to classify the users' search targets. In this section, we analyze the log data of the category search and the keyword search.

4.1   Category Search

The category search function of InfoMap enables users to select among displayed information categories by radio buttons. The POI data in the GeoLink system are classified into 14 categories according to Web page descriptions. Example results of the category search function are shown in Fig. 3 and Fig. 4.

During the period analyzed, the category search function was used 57,775 times by 8,440 users. The distribution of content over the various content categories is shown in Fig. 7, and the corresponding distribution of use of these content categories is shown in Fig. 8.

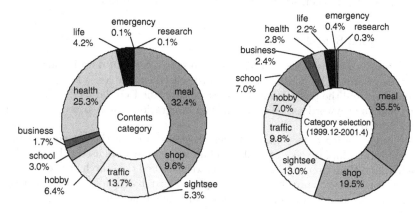

Fig. 7. Total category contents   **Fig. 8.** Total category selections

The first important point of the category selection graph is that the categories of meal, shop, sightsee, and traffic were frequently used by the InfoMap users and the categories of research, emergency, life, and health were infrequently used. Every content category of InfoMap has a unique character, but the categories are similar to other media, such as books, magazines, and other Web pages. Accordingly, this observation reflects that the tastes of the users of InfoMap are equal to the general taste on the Internet. The high correlation between preferences of magazine readers and Internet users was also indicated in the Internet user profile report [4].

Even more important is that the number of category selections did not correspond with the number of category contents. In this log data, the health category was a typical example that had comprehensive contents, but was not accessed frequently. In other words, the categories that had comprehensive contents were not always accessed more frequently than the categories that did not have such contents. As described above, each category of InfoMap has a unique feature so it is natural that the purposes and motivations to use the category were different. However, this analysis led to the finding that the effect of comprehensive contents is less significant than influence of the user groups and public tastes on the Internet.

Yahoo! JAPAN reported the favorite categories on their site through an investigation by Web user questionnaires [5]. The report said the categories of hobby, sports, computer, Internet, and entertainment received comparatively higher scores and the categories of social science, politics, education, and health received comparatively lower score. The log data of InfoMap also indicated similar tendencies: the frequently accessed categories can be compared to casual contents and the infrequently accessed categories can be compared to relatively serious contents. Therefore, both Yahoo! JAPAN's report and the log data of InfoMap are quite similar in that the users had stronger inclinations to use more casual information. This tendency should be one of the strong manifestations of users' expectations when searching for information on the Internet.

4.2 Keyword Search

The keyword search function enables users to search for POI data by specifying favorite keywords. The range of the keyword search encompasses the text parts of Web pages and the postal addresses derived from the POI data with GIS. This means that the keyword search function is an integration of text-based Web page search and GIS.

Although the log data contained every keyword used in the keyword search function of InfoMap, it was impossible to find words that were used substantially more frequent than than others. Therefore, we classified the search keywords into types of words as shown in Fig. 9. The keyword search of InfoMap was invoked 20,217 times and 6,591 words were entered into this function.

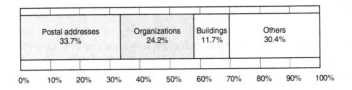

Fig. 9. Utilized words for keyword search

First and foremost, postal addresses were most frequently used in the keyword search of InfoMap. The percentage of this type was 33.7%. This high percentage was partly caused by a unique addressing system in Kyoto which uses street names and administrative district names conjunctively. Next, the second frequently used word type was organization names (24.2%) and the third was building names (11.7%).

It might be appropriate to compare the convergent word types on InfoMap with traditional text-based search engines on the Internet. Lycos provides one of the largest text-based search engines and reports lists of top 50 search keywords on their Web site weekly [6]. The reports have said that Lycos users more frequently use keywords related to entertainers, artists, and digital contents such as video games, music files, and wall papers for PCs and cellular phones. On the other hand, they infrequently use words related to geographical objects in the search engine. Therefore, the keyword usage tendency on Lycos is in contrast to the word type convergences on InfoMap. This contrast might be caused by the Web page design of and the contents included on InfoMap. As mentioned above,

InfoMap uses digital maps for navigating users and displays retrieved results on the maps. In this design, it naturally follows that the digital maps restrict the users' suppositions because the search range of InfoMap is restricted to the displayed map area. It seems reasonable to suppose that the users of InfoMap understand that they should search only for contents related to the displayed map. If this assumption is true, the lack of contents in the displayed area presumably causes user dissatisfaction with the retrieval results. Therefore, contents that are in the range of the digital maps should be included comprehensively.

5   Content Level Log Analysis

Let us turn to an analysis on the selections of displayed contents on InfoMap. The content of InfoMap is distributed as shown in Fig. 10. Each content item that is accessible from InfoMap is marked using a small '+' character. The horizontal axis of this figure means the longitude and the vertical axis means the latitude. Both the longitude and latitude are displayed as decimal numbers. This figure shows that the available content clearly clusters in the Shijokawaramachi area, which is one of the downtown areas in Kyoto (point ⟨135.77, 35.00⟩ on the map). In this area, there are a lot of shops and restaurants and the content density amounts to 599 URLs per square kilometer.

During the period of the analysis, the Web server recorded 29,637 clicks by 6,232 users as content selections on InfoMap. We classified the log data in terms of content and added in Fig. 10 the frequency of visiting the content as the vertical axis. The extended graph is shown in Fig. 11, which is a 3D bar graph of the content access frequencies on InfoMap. In Fig. 11, the content that was most frequently accessed is plotted as the longest vertical line at (135.734047, 35.028279). The content was a link to a Web page of a fruit shop that sells items at both a physical shop and a virtual shop. It was accessed 697 times by 45 users during the analysis period.

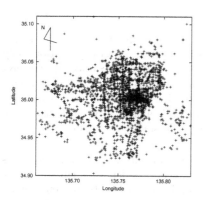

Fig. 10. Content distribution

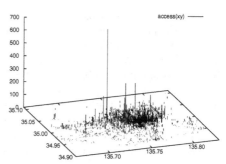

Fig. 11. Access frequency per content

Graphs like this provide raw representations of the log data, but they do not help very much to understand the effects of digital maps on content accessing. To clarify the effects, we applied dissimilarity analysis methods to the log data.

First, we removed the geographical attributes from the log data and sorted them according to their ranks of access frequency. Fig. 12 is a graph that represents access frequencies of Web pages against their ranks using a log-log scale. In this graph, the plot of top 500 Web pages seems to be fitted to a straight line which decreases gently. This graph is similar to the Zipf-like distributions mentioned in [7] and [8]. The original Zipf law [9] provides an explanation of the relation between the word appearance frequency and ranking. While the Internet was growing up, this law has come into common use to explain user behavior of accessing information on the World Wide Web and the caching strategies of Web contents. According to the distribution in Fig. 12, it seems that the content access frequency on InfoMap also follows the above Zipf-like distributions.

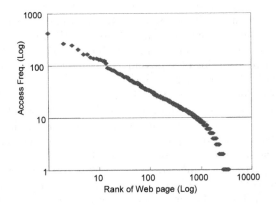

Fig. 12. Web page rank ordered by access frequency

Next, we shift our focus to digital maps and will try to analyze the clustering of access in specific areas. Using Zipf-like distributions as an explanation, only a few contents are able to get frequent accesses. However, InfoMap displays not only normal Web pages but also digital maps, so another kinds of access convergence should be observable. To find such convergence, we divided the targeted area of InfoMap into several grids. In this analysis, two grid sizes were used: the division of the targeted area into 0.005 square degrees each and into 0.02 square degrees each.

The next step was to compute and plot the density of content, as well as the access frequency per grid. Fig. 13 plots the content density results and Fig. 14 shows the access frequency per grid results. Both graphs utilize 0.005 square degree grids. Fig. 15 and Fig. 16 are the same graphs as Fig. 13 and Fig. 14 respectively, except that 0.02 square degree grids are utilized for the plotting.

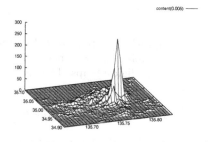

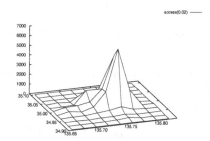

Fig. 13. Density of content distribution (1)

Fig. 14. Access frequency per grid (1)

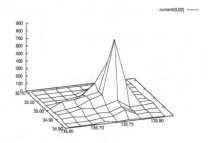

Fig. 15. Density of contents distribution (2)

Fig. 16. Access frequency per grid (2)

In Fig. 13 and Fig. 15, both content distributions have a sharp peak at the same location. These peaks are representations of the clusering of content around the Shijokawaramachi (in Fig. 10). On the other hand, in Fig. 14 and Fig. 16, there are differences between the peaks of the access frequency distributions. In Fig. 14, two access peaks can be discerned: the area containing the most frequently accessed content and the content area at Shijokawaramachi. The former is an effect of one frequently accessed content as shown in Fig. 11 and the latter can be interpreted as a result of gathering of content. The result of gathering content is more significant in Fig. 16. In Fig. 16, the peak at Shijokawaramachi remains, but the other peak gets more blunt.

These differences can be interpreted as one of the effects of introducing the geographical maps into Web page search. They indicate two different strategies to attract users to Web pages. One is to create attractive content on a single page, and the other is to make clusters of pages with content. These strategies are also common in traditional Web page design, but the analysis in this paper makes it clear that they are also effective for Web page retrieval using digital maps.

6   Conclusion

In this paper, we analyzed the log data of InfoMap, which were provided on the Web site of the Digital City Kyoto prototype. We explained users' behaviors on InfoMap and the access frequency of contents on the digital maps. The analysis of the log data can be summarized as follows:

- Frequency of use of the content was related to familiarity with the search functions.
- The category search function of InfoMap results into similar use patterns as the text-based directory services.
- Approximately 70% of the words used in the keyword search function are postal addresses and names of organizations and buildings.
- The relation between the content access frequency and the ranking on InfoMap follows a Zipf-like distribution.
- The accesses of the content converged into one area, accessed with a high frequency.

The above points should be fed back to the user interface design of InfoMap. Moreover, these observations can be used to build Web sites with digital maps, such as virtual malls on the Internet and regional information portal sites like the Digital City Kyoto prototype.

InfoMap covers Kyoto city and the analyzed log data were recorded over 16 months. Therefore, the results reported here are based on data about a very specific period and area. It is of course uncertain whether these results can be generalized. Future analysts will have to answer this question.

Acknowledgement. This paper owes much to the thoughtful and helpful comments of Prof. Toru Ishida of Kyoto University, Kiyoshi Kogure and Jun-ichi Akahani of NTT Communication Science Laboratories, Kenji Kobayashi and Yuji Nagato of NTT Comware corporation, Ben Benjamin, and members of the Digital City Kyoto Experimental Forum. We also wish to thank the content holders for the permission they gave to use their Web pages concerned with Kyoto.

References

1. Digital City Kyoto prototype: http://www.digitalcity.gr.jp/
2. Hiramatsu, K., Kobayashi, K., Benjamin, B., Ishida, T., and Akahani, J.: Map-based User Interface for Digital City Kyoto. INET2000 The Internet Global Summit (in CD-ROM) (2000)
3. Hiramatsu, K., and Ishida, T.: An Augmented Web Space for Digital Cities. SAINT2001, pp.105-112 (2001)
4. Video Research Netcom: Internet user profile report.
   http://www.videor.co.jp/info/010308.html (in Japanese)
5. Yahoo! JAPAN: 6th Web user questionnaires.
   http://www.yahoo.co.jp/docs/result/result6/ (in Japanese)

6. Lycos: Lycos 50.
   http://50.lycos.com/ (in English), http://www.lycos.co.jp/50/ (in Japanese)
7. Huberman, B. A., Pirolli, P. L. T., Pitkow, J. E., and Lukose, R. M.: Strong
   Regularities in World Wide Web Surfing. Science, Vol. 280, pp. 95–97 (1998)
8. Breslau, L., Cao, P., Fan, L., Phillip, G., and Shenker, S.: On the Implications of
   Zipf's Law for Web Caching. 3rd International WWW Caching Workshop (1998)
9. Zipf, G. K.: Human Behavior and the Principle of Least Effort. Addison-Wesley
   (1949)

Connecting Digital and Physical Cities

Toru Ishida[1], Hiroshi Ishiguro[2], and Hideyuki Nakanishi[1]

[1]Department of Social Informatics, Kyoto University
[1]JST CREST Digital City Project
[2] Department of Computer and Communication Sciences, Wakayama University

Abstract. As a platform for community networks, public information spaces that mirror the city metaphor are being developed around the world. The aim of *digital cities* is to pursue a future information space for everyday urban life, unlike the creation of new businesses which is the current obsession of the Internet. We started the basic research project called *"Universal Design of Digital City,"* a five year project established in 2000, a part of the Core Research for Evolutional Science and Technology (CREST) run by the Japan Science and Technology Corporation (JST). The objective of this project is to construct digital cities as the infrastructure that encourages the participation of all people, including the disabled and the aged. We will develop basic technologies for the universal design, focusing on *'sending information,'* *'receiving information,'* and *'participation.'* This paper introduces some of various experiments such as crisis management, environmental learning, and shopping street navigation. Digital cities are not imaginary since they correspond to the physical urban spaces in which we live. Basic technologies including perceptual information infrastructure and social agents are being developed for connecting digital and physical cities.

1. Why Digital Cities

The notion of digital cities can be defined as follows: *digital cities will collect and organize the digital information of the corresponding cities, and provide a public information space for people living in and visiting them* [4]. Digital cities have been developed all over the world, and can be connected to each other via the Internet, just as physical cities are connected by surface and air transport systems.

Why do regional information spaces attract people given that we are in the era of globalization? We realize that the Internet has fostered global businesses, but at the same time, it enables us to create rich information spaces for everyday life. While the Internet makes businesses global, life is inherently local. Business requires homogeneous settings to allow global and fair competition, while daily life can remain heterogeneous reflecting our different cultural backgrounds. If differences exist in business, standard protocols are needed to over come them, but we do not need any standard for social interaction. If the differences are significant, we will turn to the Internet for cross-cultural communication support.

M. Tanabe, P. van den Besselaar, T. Ishida (Eds.): Digital Cities, LNCS 2362, pp. 246-256, 2002.
© Springer-Verlag Berlin Heidelberg 2002

With the development of the Internet, economies of scale have driven business activities to become global. Even small companies can participate in the worldwide business network, since the Internet significantly reduces search and negotiation costs to find partners and markets. The Internet makes commercial transactions much easier in most business areas. On the other hand, globalization is not so frequent in everyday life. Although the Internet has widened the information channels available, it cannot physically move people. Statistics show that people still spend their income for housing, shopping dining and so on where they live. Everyday life substantially remains local even though the Internet offers international reach.

Table 1. Two Extremes in Internet Use

Business	Everyday Life
Global	Local
Market (Competitive)	Community (Collaborative)
Homogeneous	Heterogeneous
Standard Protocol	Cross-Cultural Communication

Table 1 shows two extremes of Internet use. The table does not mean that the two types of usages are always disjoint, various combinations are common in Internet use. The motivation for studying digital cities is to shift our view of Internet use from one side (business) to another (everyday life). Both perspectives should be combined to build a public information space in which people can participate and interact, and to create consensus for the various problems.

2. What Is Real?

Digital cities are for supporting our everyday life. It is natural for people living in a city to create a public information space that corresponds to the physical city. The question is, however, whether or not it represents an efficient usage of the Internet. The Internet is often viewed as a new continent. For example, the Internet yields the possibility of building a virtual mall comprising a huge number of shops that cannot exist in any physical city. The locality of digital cities might constrain the possibilities inherent in the Internet.

To discuss this issue, we examine an interesting example found in the shopping street community in Kyoto. The community is formed by 3,000 shops in Kyoto. They jointly started a site that enables customers to make electronic account settlements by debit and credit cards. Purchasing requests from within or beyond the local community are processed electronically and goods are delivered by logistics companies. As a result, all shopping streets in Kyoto now appear on the Internet. Thousands of shops are already offering services under this framework. At first glance, this seems to be just another form of global virtual mall like Yahoo. However, its business model is totally different.

Global virtual malls are often called platform businesses. Providers of the platform offer reliable and trustful places, and invite suppliers as well as customers. It does not matter whether or not the suppliers have a presence in the physical world. The Kyoto shop alliance, on the other hand, represents real world entities. Credibility has been established through the long history of physical Kyoto. The question is how this local mall can compete with huge existing global virtual malls. Economies of scale are often observed in the Internet. It must be hard for small malls to achieve success because fewer services are offered. It seems that local malls, which are hard to scale up, cannot compete with global malls. This, however, is not the entire story, if consumers are not interested in just buying goods but in the city as a whole. In this case, a digital city, which creates a whole city in the Internet, can be a solution to support local malls.

We tend to think that a city constructed in cyberspace is fictional. But what is a real city? Is a physical city real? Let us take a modern company as an example. A physical company is composed of buildings and staff. However, it is almost impossible to understand its activities by observing only its physical space. Without reading e-mails or checking project WEB pages, activities of the company are hard to grasp. The company's real activities are lie in both digital and physical space. We think "digital" and "physical" make things "real." We think digital cities are not imaginary cities existing only in cyberspace, but complement the corresponding physical cities, and provide an information center for actual urban communities. As in modern companies, digital activities will become an essential part of urban life in the near future.

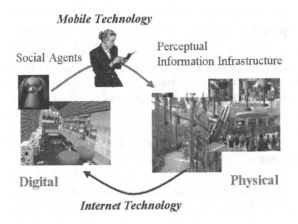

Fig. 1. Connecting Digital and Physical Cities

In the rest of this paper, we describe two different types of technologies currently under research to connect digital and physical cities. One is called the *perceptual information infrastructure*, which gives computer networks the ability to selectively obtain information from the physical space. The other is software called *social agents*, which can play a social role in human communities [3]. Figure 1 illustrates one approach to using these two technologies for integrating digital and physical cities.

3. Perceptual Information Infrastructure

The perceptual information infrastructure bridges the digital and physical cities by using computer vision technologies [6]. Omni-directional vision sensors embedded in the environment monitor human activities, build photo-realistic virtual spaces, and recognizing human behaviors. The perceptual information infrastructure offers new vistas to the Internet. Figure 2 shows a newly developed omni-directional vision sensor [5]. This camera takes 360-degree images. The images are reflected from the curved surface mounted just above the upward facing CCD camera. A black needle is mounted in the center of the camera. This needle absorbs all reflections from within the glass and makes it possible to get a clear picture. The entire camera can be downsized to just a few centimeters. As an example, a omni-directional sensor yielded the middle and right images in Figure 2. The omni-directional sensor is convenient for observing a town and communicating with multiple persons. The development of omni-directional sensors triggered the study of the perceptual information infrastructure. Various application systems for supporting people to send and receive information are under development.

Fig. 2. Omni-Directional Vision Sensor [5]

Sending information becomes easier with the omni-directional sensor. With a normal camera, it is necessary to turn the camera to the direction desired when taking a picture. This operation must be performed by users, but is not easy for aged or handicapped people. Otherwise, more expensive and complex machine control is needed. The benefit of the omni-directional sensor is that such control becomes unnecessary. Software has been developed that allows the desired section to be extracted from the 360-degree picture. For example, consider the case in which a handicapped or aged person wants to send their own picture to close relatives. It is not easy for them to adjust the orientation of the camera and speak to it accurately. With the omni-directional sensor, once it has been positioned, all they have to do is to speak to it, the software extracts the proper picture.

The omni-directional sensor also makes receiving information easier, because a virtual space can be created easily from 360-degree photos. When a series of video streams are available, a 3D virtual space that permits walk through can be created automatically. In detail, the system smoothly shifts the pictures to match the user's movements. If we place multiple omni-directional sensors in a physical space, users can walk though the live videos taken by those sensors. This is a new alternative to building 3D computer models. It enables us to create historical and natural objects, such as temples and forests. The methodology, called *Town Digitizing*, forms a real-time virtual space that permits walk-through. The images captured by a series of omni-directional vision sensors are automatically fused based on the visitor's "virtual" location to reproduce what the user would see in a corresponding physical city. Although Town Digitizing requires a high-speed computer network, the rapid progress of the Internet will relax this problem in near future.

Fig. 3. Town Digitizing in Kodaiji

Figure 3 shows a map of Kodaiji (temple) in Kyoto. The photos in Figure 3 are a typical image sequence of users moving in a virtual space. As shown in Figure 3, Town Digitizing is especially suitable for representing environments with many historical or natural objects [7]. Such environments are often far from the city center and are not easy, especially for aged people, to access. People can share a historical or natural environment through the virtual spaces built *by Town Digitizing*.

The omni-directional vision sensor is not only for building virtual spaces but can also be used for recognizing human activities. We develop software to track walking humans, record their trajectories, and recognize their behavior. One merit of this multiple camera system is that the viewing area of the cameras can overlap. That is, the sensor network can cover a wide area with a small number of cameras and offer stereo views. This sensor network can be used in many situations. It can monitor and support the activities of aged people in hospitals and streets. It can realize secure monitoring systems in public places, such as stations and banks.

As described above, the omni-directional sensor and the network remove a barrier between the physical and digital spaces and make sending and receiving information easier, even for the aged and handicapped people.

4. Social Agents

Digital cities have two functions: to collect and reorganize digital information of corresponding cities, and to provide a public information space for people living in /visiting them. The idea of human-like software to support activities in digital cities seems unrealistic. However, research into artificial intelligence and social psychology is bringing us close to realizing this goal.

To connect residents and visitors, one trial for developing social interaction in digital cities uses avatars in the 3D space. Figure 4 shows a view of avatars controlled by humans walking in the 3D virtual space called *FreeWalk* [8]. This technology allows a number of avatars to walk around the digital city in real-time. By making links between the avatars and the people walking in the corresponding physical city, we can realize communication between digital tourists and people walking in the city. As walking motion can be generated by the user's machine via a WEB browser plug-in, only the walking position/velocity and direction need be downloaded. Thus, a large number of avatars can be created rapidly in real-time. Aside from the "known" avatars, adding a virtual population will activate the digital city and make it more attractive. In addition, a scenario description language called Q that can control the behavior of thousands of social agents is currently under development. Agents autonomously behave under the social constraints given by the scenarios, and dynamically respond to other avatars (humans) and agents (software).

We are trying to create a group of social agents that support the various activities of participants in a digital city. We expect social agents to show their ability as coordinators for building and maintaining online communities. The playgrounds of social agents include virtual and mobile environments. In a virtual environment, social agents interact with avatars (humans) visiting the same world. In a mobile environment, social agents appear on PDAs or wearable computers to interact with people living in the physical world. Social agents can enter into communities in both environments. The service industry is a good example. Social agents can troll through vast information repositories of products and services, communicate with customers, and work twenty-four hours a day.

Fig. 4. Avatars and Agents in a 3D Virtual Kyoto

Evacuating people safely in the case of disaster is another example of social agents playing an important role both in digital and physical cities. In evacuation simulation, the possible roles of social agents include pedestrians, station employees, salesclerks and so on. Realistic evacuation simulations can be realized by having pedestrian agents act as people running around to escape. Such simulations would help a crisis management center to accumulate experiences and to make correct decisions, since social agents would exhibit the mistakes typical of people. In real evacuation, social agents would appear on the user's PDA to provide appropriate instructions. For success of simulation, social agents have to be trusted by people. Functional accuracy to make correct decisions is not enough to be trustworthy agents. Technologies to create trustworthy agents is to be explored.

To understand the nature of social agents, we are performing a series of social psychological experiments. Effects of introducing social agents in human communities have not been well investigated. We are currently conducting experiments to see how social agents support human communication and influence human relations. Social agents can act as go-betweens among people who have different social identities such as inhabitants and visitors, young and aged, and so on. In our experiment on cross-cultural communication between Japanese and American students, the agents influenced not only the impressions of agents but also the impressions of conversation partners and the stereotypes of nationalities [2]. For example, if the agent encouraged students to discuss political problems, the Japanese students became as talkative as the Americans.

Another experiment to observe the influence of agents on human-human relations shows that social agents have the ability to affect human relations. We first observed that if an agent agrees/disagrees with a human's opinion, the human develops positive or negative feelings toward the agent. Is balance theory [1] works in this situation? If so, when a human has a positive or negative feeling toward the agent and thinks that the partner has the same feeling to the agent, the human tends to have a positive feeling toward the partner. Contrary, if a human thinks that the partner has a different feeling toward the agent, the human tends to have a negative feeling toward the partner. Figure 5 explains this situation. We observed that the agent that lies, i.e. has exhibits different responses to different people, can create discord between people. On one hand, if there is less communication between the two people, it is easier for the agent to control their relationship: the agents may become unsafe entities if the amount of communication between users is insufficient. On the other hand, we found that people could use agents safely in their community if the communication among people is adequate while using the agents. Results of this experiment demonstrate the ability and the limitations of agents to influence human relations. In future, we may need an ethics law governing the development of agents.

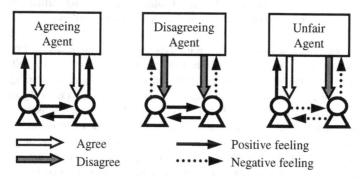

Fig. 5. Balance Theory for Agent and Two People

We are currently studying conversational agents that learn; they improve their social behavior automatically. It is still difficult to develop general-purpose agents that can communicate on all topics with people satisfactorily. However, by carefully selecting the application domains there is a hope that we can create task-specific agents. The Wizard of Oz method has a framework that makes agents learn conversation gradually. In the first stage, agents suggest speech candidates for a wizard (a human) behind them to select the most appropriate one. If no appropriate speech is suggested, the wizard enters dialog directly. Users speaking to those agents do not notice the presence of the wizard behind the agents. The first stage can be implemented easily, but the agents never become intelligent in this stage. In the second stage, a learning capability should be added to the agents. The agents memorize conversations, create finite state automata, and generalize them to keep the automata tractable. By narrowing down tasks, the agents would offer quite good speech candidates to the wizard after training. They would finally converse without help of the wizard. Such conversational agents can be applied to various tasks. The agents will be useful for shopping, navigation, and supporting the aged and handicapped.

5. Applications

Connecting digital and physical cities will stimulate the creation of various applications. As part of our digital city project, we advanced three pilot applications.

The first application involves evacuation simulations in a three dimensional virtual Kyoto station; this pilot application project links computer scientists, architects, and social psychologists. The simulation is planned to be performed with 100 people connected via the Internet, and 1000 social agents controlled by a given scenario. In previous research into simulating human behavior in crisis situations, people were displayed as small circles in two-dimensional flows, a technique common in hydrodynamic simulations. In a real crisis situation, directions from officers and speech among people will greatly influence the result. Unfortunately, the 2D simulation fails to well reproduce the social interaction. The 3D virtual cities now make it possible to recreate this interaction. The scenario is as follows.

> In 200X, an evacuation simulation involving Kyoto railway station will be conducted in 3D virtual Kyoto with 1000 social agents. 100 citizens will participate via the Internet. The data is to be collected and analyzed for planning real evacuations. In 200Y, an earthquake occurs and a fire starts in Kyoto station. The situation in the physical space is captured by omni-directional sensors and sent to the control center through wireless networks. The movement of people as a group is grasped and displayed on the screen in the center. Based on the results of previous evacuation simulations, appropriate directions are sent to the peoples' mobile terminals, and conversational agents start to guide their users.

The evacuation simulation in the virtual Kyoto station brings up the following issues. What can we learn from the simulation results in the virtual space? Even if the simulation indicates heavy casualties, it is not clear what this means. People may think the virtual space simulation is just like a video game. We thus started research from two different aspects. The first aspect is to understand how people behave differently in the physical space from the virtual space. People are given the same task in both spaces (for instance, leave via a given exit) and all behaviors recorded by eye cameras are analyzed. We are interested in how difficult it is to move in a virtual space without peripheral vision, which is inherent in the physical space. The second aspect is to understand the difference between human-human and human-software interaction. People's reactions must be different according to whether the directions were given by humans or software officers, but different in what way? These issues must be analyzed carefully in controlled experiments before conducting a large-scale simulation.

The second application involves navigating aged people through shopping streets using the perceptual information infrastructure and social agents.

An aged person is looking for a shop on Shijo Street. There is a map, however, it does not well correspond to the real town. The omni-directional sensors detect the person's position, orientation, and behavior. All information is sent to the control center through wireless networks. The information is combined to understand the situation of the street including that of the aged person. His view is reproduced using the virtual street, and landmarks appropriate for him are extracted. A conversational agent then directs him by using the extracted landmarks. An image extracted from the virtual street is displayed on his portable terminal to indicate the landmarks.

For the third application, the same technologies are applied to environmental learning in a university forest.

Parents and children are provided with studies on the environment in a forest of Kyoto University. Live videos, taken by pre-installed omni-directional sensors, are sent to the education center via a broadband fiber network. A virtual space is reproduced from the live videos. An instructor (or a social agent) of environmental learning in the center can know what is going on in the forest in real time. A participant may send photos of plants to the center to ask the instructor for information. The instructor then moves to the participant's location in the virtual forest, talks to the participant, and sends the requested information to the participant's portable terminal.

What is common in these three experiments is that the perceptual information infrastructure and social agents combine physical and digital cities to support people not only when they sit in front of their PCs but also when they move in the physical world.

6. Cross-Cultural Communication in Digital Cities

Unlike the conventional telephone network, there is no centralized control mechanism in the Internet. Even the power of governments cannot stop the flow of information. Anyone such as a politician, scholar, businessperson, and student has equal access to the enormous store of information. Instead of huge hierarchical organizations, a knowledge network of small organizations or individuals covers the world.

Unlike conventional mass media, the Internet allows us to directly contact thousands of vivid instances. While mass media filters collected information, refines and edit them, the Internet is a huge depository simply accumulating original instances. For example, children who want to be music conductors can find plenty of information not only about famous conductors but also about other children in foreign countries with the same dreams.

There are two reasons for discussing cross-cultural communication in the context of digital cities. The first is that, in any city in the world, the citizens are becoming more diverse. A public information space can play a major part in bridging the cultures. The second reason is that a digital city will represent the real city on the Internet. We have 40,000,000 visitors per year in Kyoto, but we expect more people will visit Kyoto via the Internet. Therefore, cross-cultural communication must be supported, even though the main purpose of digital cities is to support the everyday life of local residents. A local information space and a platform for cross-cultural communication are two sides of the same coin.

We should be aware that the ratio of English web pages worldwide has been decreasing rapidly. As the Internet will be applied to everyday life more and more, the ratio of English web pages will keep on decreasing. It is obvious that the need for cross-cultural communication will increase significantly. Without linguistic and cultural support tools, it is not possible for people to create productive interaction. Connecting digital and physical cities will, together with the latest machine translation technologies, increase the opportunity to participate in cross-cultural communication.

Acknowledgement. The author wishes to thank, Scott Brave, Satoshi Koizumi, Clifford Nass, Satoshi Nakazawa, Katsuya Takanashi, Mohan Trivedi, and Ken Tsutsuguchi for their collaborative work, and many other colleagues for helpful discussions.

References

1. F. Heider, The Psychology of Interpersonal Relations, Wiley, 1958.
2. K. Isbister, H. Nakanishi, T. Ishida and C. Nass, "Helper Agent: Designing an Assistant for Human-Human Interaction in a Virtual Meeting Space," *CHI-2000*, pp. 57-64, 2000.
3. K. Isbister, "A Warm Cyber-Welcome: Using an Agent-led Group Tour to Introduce Visitors to Kyoto," *Digital Cities: Experiences, Technologies and Future Perspectives*, Springer-Verlag, pp. 391-400, 2000.
4. T. Ishida and K. Isbister Eds., *Digital Cities: Experiences, Technologies and Future Perspectives*, Lecture Notes in Computer Science, 1765, Springer-Verlag, 2000.
5. H. Ishiguro, "Development Low-Cost and Compact Omnidirectional Vision Sensors," In Ryad Benosman and Sing Bing Kang Eds., *Panoramic Vision: Sensors, Theory and Applications*, Springer-Verlag, Berlin, 2001.
6. H. Ishiguro, "Distributed Vision System: A Perceptual Information Infrastructure for Robot Navigation," *IJCAI-97*, pp. 36-41, 1997.
7. S. Koizumi, G. Dai and H. Ishiguro, "Town Digitizing for Building an Image-Based Cyber Space," *Digital Cities II*, Springer-Verlag, 2002.
8. H. Nakanishi, C. Yoshida, T. Nishimura and T. Ishida, "FreeWalk: A 3D Virtual Space for Casual Meetings," *IEEE Multimedia*, Vol.6, No.2, pp.20-28, 1999. H. Rheingold, *The Virtual Community*, Addison-Wesley, 1993.

Twin Worlds: Augmenting, Evaluating, and Studying Three-Dimensional Digital Cities and Their Evolving Communities

Katy Börner

School of Library and Information Science, Indiana University
10th Street & Jordan Avenue, Bloomington, IN 47405, USA
katy@indiana.edu
http://ella.slis.indiana.edu/~katy

Abstract. New approaches and tools are required to inform the design and implementation of 3-dimensional (3-D) digital cities and to steer the growth of their virtual communities. This paper argues to apply information visualization techniques and to utilize *Twin Worlds* – pairs of virtual worlds in which one world is devoted to visualize user interaction data collected in the other world – to augment, evaluate, and research the digital cities of tomorrow. The approach is exemplified by means of an abstract scholarly digital city: A 3-D collaborative *Memory Palace* – a shared resource of online documents (web pages, papers, images, videos, software demos) for faculty and students at the School of Library and Information Science at Indiana University – and its twin, *Mirror Garden* – a second 3-D world that visualizes user interaction data collected in the *Memory Palace*.

1 Introduction

Today, digital cities (DCs) and community networks are developed all over the world (Ishida & Isbister, 2000). They are used for orientation, education, job hunting, urban planning, disaster management, and social welfare etc.. They can be seen as a local social information structure, a communication medium, a tool to improve local democracy and participation, a practical resource to organize every day life, or a space in which to experience and experiment with cyberspace (van den Besselaar et al., 2000).

Most DCs utilize the World Wide Web – an elaborate, connected network of documents – and augment it with diverse synchronous and asynchronous communication facilities such as chat, email, message boards, etc. However, in this environment, people have to chat constantly to be visible to others. Elements like word choice, text format and layout, and timing replace nonverbal aspects of communication such as gestures, facial expressions, proximity, etc. commonly found in face-to-face interaction. Still, despite these "replacement" methods, web surfing remains a lonely activity – one is unaware of other users since they and their "digital footsteps" remain mostly invisible over the web.

M. Tanabe, P. van den Besselaar, T. Ishida (Eds.): Digital Cities, LNCS 2362, pp. 257-269, 2002.

However, what people attract most are people. Advances in computer and networking technologies fueled the rapid growth of 3-D browser systems that enable the creation of compelling, multi-modal, multi-user, navigable, collaborative virtual environments in 3-D that are inhabited by avatars (graphical icons acting as placeholders for human users in a cyberspace system), and provide means for interacting with the objects in the environment, with embedded information sources and services, or with other users and visitors of the environment. Several DCs, e.g., *Virtual Helsinki, Digital City Kyoto, Virtual Los Angeles*, and *Virtual Bremen* make extensive use of 3-D virtual real estate, and others have experimented with it, e.g., *The Digital City Amsterdam*. (URL's are in the references list)

Today's DCs have very diverse goals and serve the similarly wide-ranging needs of their communities. Surprisingly little is known for most of them. Research on virtual cities (or virtual worlds or virtual environments)[1] and their communities is just beginning to emerge (Kim, 2000; Preece, 2000). Often, techniques are borrowed from various disciplines like sociology, psychology, anthropology, ethnography, groupware, communication science, and geography (mapping, organizing spatial data), to name just a few. However, 3-D virtual worlds have unique features such as 3-D user interaction, multi-modality, usage of avatars, etc. that are hard to address with combinations of existing techniques. Novel approaches and tools are required to inform the design and implementation of 3-D digital cities and to steer the growth of their virtual communities.

Heim (1997) and Jakobsson (1999) argue that virtual worlds (VWs) are fundamentally different from our real world and that the underlying principle for VWs – the interaction among its users – should become the foundation for a new theoretical perspective on VW design (Holmström & Jakobsson, 2001). We argue that tracking and visualization of user interaction data collected in 3-D can be seen as an enabling tool to guide users, to evaluate and optimize user interactions in 3-D, and to research VWs.

The paper starts with an introduction and discussion of 3-D collaborative information visualizations that utilize 3-D online browser technology. Subsequently, we introduce the approach of twin worlds and instantiate it in terms of a scholarly digital city – a shared resource of online documents for faculty and students at the School of Library and Information Science (SLIS) at Indiana University and its twin world, which visualizes user interaction data. We conclude with a discussion of the approach.

2   Collaborative Information Visualizations & Twin Worlds

Information visualization techniques (Card et al., 1999; Chen, 1999; Ware, 1999; Spence, 2000; Dodge & Kitchin, 2000) can be used to map virtual worlds as well as user actions enabling us to guide visitors of VWs and to research the development and usage of 3-D virtual worlds, as well as the evolution of their communities.

---

[1] We see a digital city as a special kind of virtual world or virtual environment and will use the terms interchangeably throughout the paper.

While the majority of today's information visualizations are designed for single users, we propose to create 3-D information visualizations that can be collaboratively explored by groups of people to discover important patterns and information hidden in data or to better find, filter, and manage data.

These collaborative information visualizations (CIVs) can be constructed using commercially available 3-D *Online Browser Systems*. Frequently used systems are Blaxxun's online community client-server architecture, Microsoft's Virtual Worlds Platform, Active Worlds technology by Activeworlds Inc., or the new Adobe Atmosphere browser, to name just a few. (URL's are in the references list)

Each of the 3-D browser systems facilitates the creation of multi-modal, multi-user, navigable, and collaborative virtual worlds in 3-D that are interconnected with standard web pages, and that are accessible from standard computer platforms via the Internet, 24 hours and 7 days a week. Damer (1997) provides an excellent review of different systems and existing virtual communities. To appreciate the potential of 3-D browser systems one has to try them out for oneself.

Collaborative 3-D VWs differ from single user systems in that they equip their users with sophisticated self-representations called avatars that wave, dance, and share space. Avatars provide a means of interacting with objects in the VW, embedded information sources and services, or other users. In all these systems, users can communicate synchronously via a chat facility. In addition, VWs facilitate natural, multi-perceptual interaction using spatial sound, animation, and video.

The selection of an appropriate browser system is critical since the technology that mediates user interaction has a great impact on the forms that interaction will take (Jakobsson, 1999; Preece, 2000). Active Worlds (AW) is one of the most popular VW systems. It hosts over six hundred different worlds in the main, entertainment-oriented universe, and more than one hundred worlds in EduVerse, a special universe with an educational focus. AW is based on Render Ware, an interactive 3-D Graphics API. It differs from VRML-based systems in the ease with which participants can build within the world. A user simply selects an existing object, makes a copy of it, and renames it as a different object. Multiple users can work and design artifacts together in a 3-D space without stopping or leaving the world.

Fig. 1 (left panel) shows the AW interface. In contains three main windows: a 3-D graphics panel populated by avatars, a web browser window, and a chat window. At the top are a menu bar and a toolbar for avatar actions. Users can collaboratively navigate in 3-D, move their mouse pointer over an object to bring up its description (see Fig. 2 and 3), click on 3-D objects to display the corresponding web page in the right window of the AW browser, or teleport to more fruitful information patches. The web browser maintains a history of visited places and web pages so that the user can return to previous locations.

Fig. 1 (right panel) shows a sample overview map with area labels of a 3-D virtual world named *iUni* which hosts different learning environments (Börner, 2001a). The map was rendered in 2-D, based on the list of objects that made up the world on Dec 6th, 2000.

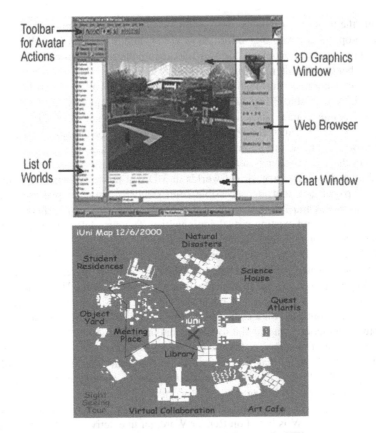

Fig. 1. 3-D AW interface and a 2-D map of a VW

Collaborative information visualizations utilize the 3-D space to connect information to places. In addition, the 3-D space acts as a shared meeting place. The 2-D overview map supports searching and filtering of information and eases navigation. It can be customized to match specific user needs and interests.

Twin Worlds are pairs of CIVs in which one world is used to visualize user interaction data collected in the other world. Subsequently, we exemplify CIVs in terms of a collaborative *Memory Palace* and *Mirror Garden*.

3 Collaborative Memory Palaces

The exponential growth of digital documents makes it increasingly difficult for users to locate relevant resources. Focused digital libraries and repositories help their user communities to contribute and share documents, but necessitate new interfaces for the collaborative contribution, exploration, modification, and management of information. Today, search engines are users' first choice for retrieving documents. However, search engines provide no way to examine the volume and composition of a certain data set or to find out who else is currently interested in the same topic, document, or question. Web search is a very lonely activity. Your friend could query your favorite search engine with the exact term at the very same moment and you both are starring at the endless list of matching documents. However, you have no way to connect or communicate.

Visual interfaces to digital libraries (DLs) aim to visualize the structure of documents or the composition of a database. In addition, they facilitate interactive browsing of large document sets (Börner & Chen, 2001). Typically, they are designed for a single user.

CIVs can be applied to create interfaces to digital libraries and repositories that are highly interactive, visual, and collaborative. The resulting virtual 2-D/3-D places can be seen as abstract digital cities of knowledge tailored for scholars belonging to a certain department, research field, etc.. City districts resemble topic areas and the city map conveys the general composition of a research field.

Like real world libraries, 3-D visual interfaces to DLs provide not only access to information, but also serve as informal meeting places for people with common interests, and are instrumental in the formation of special interest groups.

The concept of 3-D visualizations of documents is not new. Pioneering work by Steve Benford aimed at the organization of document collections either according to hand selected desired mappings or semantic "closeness" based on statistical methods or explicit relations and links between documents. The implemented system, VR-VIBE, enables users to interact with 3-D visualizations of bibliographies. Users can specify keywords that they wish to use and place them in 3-D space. Representations of retrieved documents are then displayed in the 3-D space according to how relevant a document is to each of the specified keywords.

The *Data Mountain* system by (Robertson et al., 1998) exploits spatial memory for document management. It arranges small screen grabs of documents, called thumbnails, on an incline plane textured with passive landmarks. Simple 3-D depth cues such as perspective views and occlusion are used to ease access and management of a large number of web page thumbnails. User studies report reduced storage and retrieval time as well as higher task accuracy for this interface. Similar studies and results for interfaces that exploit spatial memory for information access are reported in (Czerwinski et al., 1999; Woodruff et al., 2001; Cockburn and McKenzie, 2001). However, all these systems are designed for a single user.

The *Knowledge Garden* (Crossley et al., 1999) is one of the very first collaborative information visualizations. It uses VRML to provide a 3-D environment where people can meet colleagues and share relevant information among a community of interest. Agents provide access to shared information resources and facilitate the generation of group or personalized searches and customized knowledge representations. To our knowledge, users can't contribute new documents to this space and there is no 3-D to 2-D web space connection.

Robertson (2000) describes a web-based digital library that places knowledge sharing and community building at the core of its design. The system supports personal web sites, personal topic profiles for library research services, information service choices, and collaborative research requests that provide people with views of each others' activities and interests and support the formation of special interest groups. He identified four factors essential for community building: place, the ability to see what others are doing, communication and interaction facilities, and individuals acting as facilitators. We fully agree and are interested to design digital cities for scholarly communities that are highly usable, sociable, and pleasurable.

We started to create a collaborative *Memory Palace* for a specific interest group, e.g., students, faculty, and staff in a certain university department (Börner, 2001b). The term *Memory Palace* refers to highly evolved mnemonic structures developed in classical Greek culture to manage and recite great quantities of information. Basically, a *Memory Palace* resembles a non-linear storage system or random access memory that is responsive to the user's position in an imagined space. The more elaborate the palaces, the more information that can be stored, and the more paths lead to the same kind of information.

Anders (1998, p. 34) argues that *"The memory palace could resurface as a model for future collective memory allowing users to navigate stored information in an intuitive spatial manner"* and that *"... cyberspace will evolve to be an important extension of our mental processes"* allowing us to *"... create interactive mnemonic structures to be shared and passed from one generation to the next."* The proposed *Memory Palaces* could serve as an ever-evolving repository of a user community's knowledge that members can discuss, learn from, contribute to, and collectively build upon. Section 5 provides a sample scenario that describes what users experience in this space as well as basic technical details.

4 Mirror Gardens

A large number of diverse social visualizations have been developed to show data about a person, illuminate relationships among people, or to visualize user group activity. Börner & Lin (2001) provide an extensive review of existing approaches and systems.[2]

Owners of virtual worlds or digital cities are most likely interested in answers to questions such as: "Who is using it?", "What do people do?", "What resources do they access?" among many others (van den Besselaar et al, 2000). At the same time, there is a need for more sophisticated navigation support for users as well as awareness tools[3] to find out "What places to see, what to do?", "What are the most popular

---

[2] Not covered in this review is the eRENA project (http://www.nada.kth.se/erena/) which developed tools for 3-D recording and playback that can be utilized in post-production or for the creation of new kinds of animation and virtual experiences.

[3] TOWER is the name of a recent project (http://orgwis.gmd.de/projects/tower/) that aims to support cooperation and awareness in co-located teams (Prinz et al., 2000). It augments existing systems through sensors which detect user operations in the respective systems and discloses them in a 3-D *Theatre of Work* world.

places/documents?", "What is new?", "Who is online?", "Whom can I ask for which information?", "When is xx typically available and where?", etc.

To answer these questions, we suggest collecting user interaction data such as navigation, manipulation, chatting, and web access activity, and visualizing these data sets in a second twin world which we call *Mirror Garden*. The term *Mirror Garden* was derived by merging the term *Mirror World* as envisioned by Gelernter (1992) and *PeopleGarden* coined by Xiong & Donath (1999).[4]

The *Mirror Garden* world utilizes a 2-D overview map and a 3-D CIV space to visualize usage patterns of interest such as:

- **General usage patterns:** Where do users login from? Who are they? How long do they stay? Do they login regularly or irregularly? How many people are in the world at which time? Are there general bursts of activity?
- **Navigation patterns:** Which general routes do users take? What are the most popular places? How do people move and place themselves in urban space? Are there well-traveled paths that may indicate a particular problem solving strategy? Which places are multi-way branching places, pass through places, or (final) destination areas?
- **Manipulation patterns:** Who manipulates (creates, modifies, deletes) which objects, and when?
- **Conversation patterns:** Where do people talk? Which places in 3-D are used for long, intricate discussions, and which are sites of quick exchanges? How long, what about, and to whom do people talk? What is the size of conversational groups? How do conversational topics evolve? How does the environment influence conversational topics?
- **Web access patterns:** Which web pages are accessed by whom, when, from where, and how often?

In this way, the *Mirror Garden* provides navigation support for visitors of virtual worlds and helps designers with the organization and layout of world content and the tuning of interaction possibilities. In addition, it can serve as a research tool to study virtual worlds and their evolving communities.

5 Twin Worlds in Action – The SLIS Document Space

To demonstrate the twin world approach we began to implement two worlds – iPalace and iGarden – in Active World's Educational Universe.

The iPalace – *Memory Palace* – world aims to support collaborative information access and management. It consists of semantically organized online documents laid

---

[4] Xiong & Donath's (1999) system uses a particularly apt flower metaphor to create individual data portraits of chat participants and a garden metaphor for combining these portraits to present a visualization of conversation activity.

out in a 3-D space. About 530 people – including about 300 students in Bloomington and 200 students in Indianapolis - will have access to this space.

It is seeded with about 8,000 links to online documents such as text, images, video, software demonstrations, etc. collected from personal favorites or bookmark lists created by SLIS faculty. The full text of all documents was retrieved and semantically analyzed using data mining techniques such as *Latent Semantic Analysis* (Landauer et al., 1998). The resulting document-by-document similarity matrix was used to group semantically similar documents. The explanation of these techniques would go beyond the scope of this paper. The reader may consult the author's work on the *LVis – Digital Library Visualizer* project (Börner, 2000a; Börner, 2000b; Börner et al., 2000) for details.

Subsequently, data layout algorithms such as Treemaps (Shneiderman, 1992) were used to spatially organize topic areas – each representing a set of semantically similar documents – in 2-D space. The resulting 2-D layout is used to position web page links in the 3-D iPalace world. In 3-D, each document is represented by a square panel textured by the corresponding web page's thumbnail image and augmented by a short description such as the web page title (similar to Robertson et al's, [1998] *Data Mountain* interface). The objects that make up the 3-D world are rendered in a Java applet as a 2-D topic map that is displayed in the web interface for navigation purposes. Users are able to click on the map in order to teleport into the corresponding topic area in the 3-D space. Users can enter particular search terms, which results in highlighted web pages containing those terms in the 2-D map. This way, areas containing documents of interest can be easily identified. In addition, users can collaboratively examine, discuss, and modify (add/delete resources, annotate) documents, thereby converting this document space into an ever-evolving repository of the user community's collective knowledge that members can access, learn from, contribute to, and build upon. The space becomes a shared *Memory Palace* representing the knowledge of the community.

The iGarden – *Mirror Garden* – world visualizes user interaction data such as navigation, manipulation, chatting, and web access activity (Börner & Lin, 2001) utilizing a 3-D world and corresponding 2-D map. It is created based on mined logs that have been collected in the *Memory Palace*. It can be used to guide users, to evaluate the effectiveness and usability of the world and to optimize design properties, or to examine the evolving user community. The explanation of the user interaction data analysis and visualization techniques are beyond the scope of this paper.

Below are two scenarios that aim to convey the appearance and functionality of both worlds.

Scenario#1 – The iPalace world: Imagine you are a student who is taking the Human-Computer Interaction course and you are interested in documents on usability. You launch the 3-D online browser and login to the iPalace world using your self-selected virtual nickname and avatar.

Your avatar is placed in the middle of a square world; the sky is filled with photos of influential people in the fields of Human Computer Interaction, Usability Studies, Human Factors, Interface Design, etc. guiding your navigation. In front of you are different teleports. You click on the one that says "Usability Studies" and your avatar is instantly teleported to an area filled with 3-D objects that link to documents on this topic. The objects are textured with thumbnail images of corresponding documents. You quickly recognize some new objects. Objects at higher elevations link to documents that other users found particularly relevant. Moving the mouse pointer over an object brings up a short description of the document and its number. Clicking on objects brings up the corresponding document in the 2-D web interface for reading, printing, etc. (see Fig. 2). Alternatively, you can enter a search term "Usability" in the 2-D web interface which highlights relevant documents on the 2-D map. Clicking on a document displayed in the 2-D map instantly teleports you to the corresponding 3-D space so that similar references can be explored. You might also see other users in this space whom you can ask for relevant documents and advice. Lonely web searching and browsing can thus be converted into a collaborative examination and discussion of documents.

In addition, you can modify this world. For example, you can change the relevance of a document by communicating with a helpful bot (machine program) named HelpMe. The corresponding chat messages would read "HelpMe document#:=relevance#." The relevance value can be set between 0 and 99 and its average number will be reflected by the height of the document's object. Alternatively, you can add documents via the web interface. The new documents will be accessible in the 3-D world after the next update.

You may also want to find users that are interested in similar topics. You teleport into the iGarden world (see scenario #2) to find chat or document access activity that matches certain topics.

Fig. 2. Still of the iPalace – *Memory Palace* – world

Scenario #2 – The iGarden world: Imagine you are part of the iPalace Wizard group and interested in examining the usage patterns of the world. You enter the iGarden - a magic world of glass and flowers (see Fig. 3). All objects you remember from the iPalace world are replaced by transparent objects of similar shapes. Some of these objects carry abstract symbols to indicate that they link to web pages, function as teleports, activate sound sources, etc. Another set of abstract symbols, e.g., flowers, is used to visualize user interaction data.

You are especially interested in web access patterns during the last two months. Utilizing the 2-D map, you filter out user activity in this time span and quickly identify the most often accessed web links. Also, you are curious to see if the new design of the entrance area improves communication. You click on the corresponding 2-D map to teleport into the 3-D entrance area. Happily, you see that there are many new flower patches in this area indicating that many discussions have taken place. Additionally, you would like to know if the latest teleport to the meeting area was used. At this point, you consult the 2-D map again and notice that so far it has only been used twice. In order to find out where people talk about usability issues, you enter the term into the "search for semantically similar chat text" window and the 2-D map shows dots at all the places in which users discussed usability. At any time, you can hit a button on the 2-D web interface, and you will be transported into the corresponding place in the iPalace world.

Fig. 3. Still of the iGarden – *Mirror Garden* – world

Note that both worlds are automatically (re)created in fixed cycles to ensure incorporation of new documents into the iPalace world and an up-to-date status of the iGarden. Both worlds are adaptive, collaborative information visualizations that provide access to either online documents or user interaction data. Both support all three major navigation paradigms (Dourish and Chalmers, 1994): spatial navigation – mimicking our experiences in the physical world; semantic navigation – driven by semantic relationships or underlying logic; and social navigation – taking advantage of the behavior of like-minded people.

User participation and collaboration is encouraged by organization of regular events such as reading groups that discuss influential documents, specific research topics, etc.

Please feel free to visit our virtual worlds via http://vw.indiana.edu/.

6 Discussion

Computers are evolving from a mathematical engine, a data/information engine in administrative systems, a personalized tool to support the competence of a skilled worker, and an autonomous agent capable of learning, helping and giving advice, into a *mediator of human-to-human interaction* (Holmström & Jakobsson, 2001, p.1). Similarly, the real transformative power of the Internet seems to come from the new and varied forms of communication that it enables among people (Dodge, 2001). The high interest in collaborative digital cities and virtual worlds reflects this trend.

However, the design and evaluation of collaborative spaces and the steering and nourishment of their evolving communities requires new approaches and techniques to monitor and optimize them.

This paper proposed collaborative information visualizations and the utilization of twin worlds to:

- Assist users in making sense of the world and its information resources as well as to increase awareness of collaboration possibilities.
- Aid designers of user-centered 3-D VWs in the evaluation and optimization of world content and layout as well as the selection of interaction possibilities
- Enable researchers to monitor, study, and research VWs and their evolving communities.

We believe that CIVs and the approach of twin worlds can help to match a DC to the interests and interactions of its inhabitants and to avoid its degeneration into a public database, a glossy brochure promoting a real town, an elaborate 3-D model, or a communication facility that fails to promote and nourish a community.

Acknowledgements. We acknowledge ActiveWorld's generous support in providing free hosting of 3-virtual worlds and an active research environment in EduVerse, a special universe with an educational focus. Several students are involved in the design and evaluation of *Twin Worlds*. Among them are Sy-Miaw Lin, Yu-Chen Lin, Tamara McMahon and Min Xiao. We would like to thank the anonymous reviewers for insightful comments on an earlier version of this paper. Makato Tanabe, Toru Ishida, Peter van den Besselaar, Kyoshi Kogure, and their colleagues did an outstanding job in the organization of the 2nd Kyoto Meeting on Digital Cities. It was a real pleasure to participate in this intellectually highly inspiring event.

This research is supported by Indiana University's High Performance Network Applications Program and an academic equipment grant by Sun Microsystems.

References

Anders, P. (1998) Envisioning Cyberspace: Designing 3-D Electronic Spaces, McGraw-Hill Professional Publishing.

van den Besselaar, P., Melis, I. & Beckers, D. (2000) Digital Cities: Organization, Content, and Use. In T. Ishida & K. Isbister (Eds.), Digital cities: Technologies, experiences, and future perspectives. Lecture Notes in Computer Science (vol 1765), Berlin: Springer-Verlag, 18-32.

Börner, K. (2001a) Using Active Worlds Technology to build an iUniverse of 3-D collaborative learning environments. IEEE Learning Technology newsletter. January.

Börner, K. (2001b) iScape: A collaborative memory palace for digital library search results. Proceedings of the International Conference on Human-Computer Interaction, New Orleans, LA, August 5-10, M. J. Smith, G. Salvendy, D. Harris, R. J. Koubek (Eds) Usability Evaluation and Interface Design, Volume 1, Lawrence Erlbaum Associates, London, pp. 1160-1164, 2001.

Börner, K. & Chen, C. (2001) Visual Interfaces to Digital Libraries – Its Past, Present, and Future. Proceedings of the First ACM+IEEE Joint Conference on Digital Libraries, Roanoke, VA, USA, p. 482, 2001.

Börner, K. & Lin, Y-C. (2001) Visualizing Chat Log Data Collected in 3-D Virtual Worlds. Information Visualisation Conference, London, England, July 25-27, pp. 141-146, 2001.

Börner, K. (2000a) Searching for the perfect match: A comparison of free sorting results for images by human subjects and by Latent Semantic Analysis, Information Visualisation 000, Symposium on Digital Libraries, London, England, 19 -21July, pp. 192-197.

Börner, K. (2000b) Extracting and visualizing semantic structures in retrieval results for browsing. ACM Digital Libraries, San Antonio, Texas, June 2-7, pp. 234-235.

Börner, K., Dillon, A. & Dolinsky, M. (2000) LVis - Digital Library Visualizer. Information Visualisation 2000, Symposium on Digital Libraries, London, England, 19 -21 July, pp. 77-81.

Card, S. K., MacKinlay, J. D. & Shneiderman B. (Editors) (1999) Readings in Information Visualization: Using Vision to Think, Morgan Kaufmann Publishers.

Chen, C. (1999) Information Visualisation and Virtual Environments. Springer Verlag.

Cockburn, A., & McKenzie, B. (2001) 3D or not 3D? Evaluating the effect of the third dimension in a document management system. In Proceedings of CHI 2001 (Seattle WA, February 2001), ACM Press, 434-441.

Crossley, M., Davies, N.J., McGrath, A. J. & Rejman-Greene, M. A. Z. (1999) The Knowledge Garden. BT Technology Journal, Vol. 17, No. 1, January 1999. Available online at http://www.bt.com/bttj/vol17no1/08.pdf.

Czerwinski, M., Dumais, S., Robertson, G., Dziadosz, S., Tiernan, S., & van Dantzich, M. (1999) Visualizing implicit queries for information management and retrieval. In Proceedings of CHI'99 (Pittsburgh PA, May 1999), ACM Press, 560-567.

Damer, B. (1997) Avatars!: Exploring and Building Virtual Worlds on the Internet. Peachpit Press.

Dodge, M. & Kitchin, R. (2000) Mapping Cyberspace. Routledge.

Dourish, P. & Chalmers, M. (1994) Running Out of Space: Models of Information Navigation. Short paper presented at HCI'94 (Glasgow, UK, 1994). http://www.dourish.com/papers/

Gelernter D. H. (1992) Mirror Worlds: Or the Day Software Puts the Universe in a Shoebox...How It Will Happen and What It Will Mean. Oxford University Press.

Heim, M. (1997) Virtual Realism, Oxford University Press, Oxford.

Holmström, H. & Jakobsson, M. (2001). Using models in virtual worlds design. Proceedings of the 34th Annual Hawaii International Conference on Systems Sciences, Los Alamitos, CA: Institute of Electrical and Electronics Engineers (IEEE) Computer Society.

Ishida, T. & Isbister K. (Editors) (2000) Digital Cities: Technologies, Experiences, and Future Perspectives. Lecture Notes in Computer Science (vol 1765), Berlin: Springer-Verlag, 246-260.

Jakobsson, M. (1999). Why Bill was killed - understanding social interaction in virtual worlds. In Nijholt, A. et al. (Eds.), Interactions in virtual worlds. Proceedings of the fifteenth Twente workshop on language technology. Enschede, The Netherlands: Twente University.

Kim, A. J. (2000) Community Building on the Web: Secret Strategies for Successful Online Communities, Peachpit Press.

Landauer, T. K., Foltz, P. W. & Laham, D. (1998) Introduction to Latent Semantic Analysis. Discourse Processes, 25, 259-284.

Preece, J. (2000) Online Communities: Designing Usability and Supporting Sociability. John Wiley & Sons.

Prinz, W., A. McGrath, A. Penn, P. Schickel & F. Wilhelmsen (2000) TOWER - Theatre of Work Enabling Relationships. Proceedings of eBusiness and eWork, Madrid, 2000.

Rheingold, H. (1993) Virtual Communities, Secker & Warburg, London

Robertson, G., Czerwinski, M., Larson, K., Robbins, D. C., Thiel D. & van Dantzich, M. (1998) Data mountain: Using spatial memory for document management. Proceedings of the 11th annual ACM Symposium on User Interface Software and Technology, pp. 153 – 162.

Robertson, S. (2000). The digital city's public library: Support for community building and knowledge sharing. In T. Ishida & K. Isbister (Eds.), Digital cities: Technologies, experiences, and future perspectives. Lecture Notes in Computer Science (vol 1765), Berlin: Springer-Verlag, 246-260.

Shneiderman, B. (1992) Tree visualization with tree-maps: 2-d space-filling approach. ACM Transactions on Graphics 11, 1 (Jan. 1992), pp 92 - 99.

Spence, R. (2000) Information Visualization. Addison-Wesley.

Ware, C. (1999) Information Visualization: Perception for Design, Morgan Kaufmann Publishers.

Woodruff, A., Faulring, A., Rosenholtz, R., Morrison, J., & Pirolli, P. (2001) Using thumbnails to search the Web. In Proceedings of CHI 2001 (Seattle WA, February 2001), ACM Press, 198-205.

Xiong, R. & Donath, J. (1999) PeopleGarden: Creating data portraits for users. Proceedings of the 12th annual ACM Symposium on User Interface Software and Technology, pp. 37 – 44.

Virtual Helsinki	http://www.arenanet.fi/helsinki
Digital City Kyoto	http://www.digitalcity.gr.jp
Virtual Los Angeles	http://www.aud.ucla.edu/~bill/ACM97.html
Virtual Bremen	http://www.vc.org/deutschland/bremen/bremen/
Digital City Amsterdam	http://www.dds.nl

Blaxxun's online community client-server architecture http://www.blaxxun.com/community
Microsoft's Virtual Worlds Platform   http://www.vworlds.org/
Active Worlds technology   http://www.activeworlds.com/
Adobe Atmosphere browser   http://www.adobe.com/products/atmosphere/
VIBE   http://www.crg.cs.nott.ac.uk/research/technologies/visualisation/vrvibe/

Creating City Community Consanguinity: Use of Public Opinion Channel in Digital Cities

Tomohiro Fukuhara[1], Ken'ichi Matsumura[1], Shintaro Azechi[2],
Nobuhiko Fujihara[3], Kazunori Terada[1], Koji Yamashita[1], and
Toyoaki Nishida[4]

[1] Synsophy Project, Communications Research Laboratory,
2-2-2 Hikaridai, Seika-cho, Kyoto 619-0289, Japan
{tomohi-f,matsu,kazuno-t,yamasita}@synsophy.go.jp
[2] School of International Cultural Relations, Hokkaido Tokai University,
5-1-1-1 Minamisawa, Minami-ku, Sapporo, Hokkaido 005-8601, Japan
s_azechi@di.htokai.ac.jp
[3] Research Center for School Education, Naruto University of Education,
Takashima, Naruto, Tokushima 772-8502 Japan
fujihara@naruto-u.ac.jp
[4] School of Engineering, The University of Tokyo,
7-3-1 Hongo, Tokyo 113-8656, Japan
nishida@kc.t.u-tokyo.ac.jp

Abstract. People moving into cities have trouble acquiring informal information because it is not easy for them to join discussions of the people already living there. We therefore developed an automatic community broadcasting system helping city residents share informal information. This Public Opinion Channel (POC) collects opinions from city residents and broadcasts them continuously. Here we describe the conceptual framework of the POC, a prototype POC system, and the evaluation of that prototype system. The results from a social psychological experiment show that the prototype system helps newcomers express their opinions to a community easily.

1 Introduction

Community support systems in digital cities should help newcomers get informal information about their cities. Many people who move into large cities know little about those cities and have few local interests. It is not easy for them to join in the discussions of their new neighbors because they have few opportunities to talk with them. Residents with Web access can use municipal bulletin board systems (BBS) to talk with each other, but many are reluctant to post messages on these systems because others often respond by posting angry and inflammatory messages. Furthermore, it is hard for newcomers to follow discussions on the BBS. A communication support system should help newcomers join their neighbors' discussions by making it easier for them to follow those discussions and post messages.

We have therefore developed an automatic community broadcasting system called a *Public Opinion Channel (POC)*, that collects and broadcasts the opinions of city

M. Tanabe, P. van den Besselaar, T. Ishida (Eds.): Digital Cities, LNCS 2362, pp. 270–282, 2002.

residents continuously, making it easy for newcomers to join discussions and get informal information about their new city.

We made a prototype POC system that consists of a *POCViewer*, which is a tool for browsing opinions and stories, and a *community broadcasting server* that generates and broadcasts stories on the Internet as TV and radio programs. The results of a social psychological experiment using the prototype POC system show that this prototype system enables newcomers to easily express their opinions to the community.

This paper is organized as follows. Section 2 describes the conceptual framework of our POC, Section 3 gives an overview of the prototype system, Section 4 describes the results of an experiment with this prototype system, and Section 5 discusses the accessibility of the POC system and also discusses related work.

2   Public Opinion Channel

The POC is an automatic community broadcasting system that elicits opinions from community members, generates a story from them, and broadcasts the story within the community[1][2]. Figure 1 shows an overview of the POC. The input is the opinions of community members, and the output is a story, which is a set of opinions relevant to each other. Some stories include information from an encyclopedia on a CD-ROM or a DVD-ROM, related Web pages, and discussion logs such as the archives of a BBS.

The POC and community members interact in the following stages.

1. Call-for-opinions stage
2. Broadcasting stage I
3. Feedback stage
4. Broadcasting stage II

Call-for-Opinions Stage

In this stage the POC calls for opinions from community members. After it announces the topics of upcoming stories, members send the POC their opinions on those topics. It also allows members to suggest other topics. Various communication tools can be used. People walking down the street can send their opinions from their mobile phones or PDAs, and people in offices and schools can send their opinions from PCs.

The posted opinions are anonymous because anonymity is necessary for discussions among city residents. According to Azechi [3], anonymity facilitates the discussion of serious subjects themes because the absence of the name and e-mail address of the person posting an opinion protects that person from attack by authorities and opponents.

Broadcasting Stage I

In this stage the POC generates and broadcasts a story to the community. After eliminating messages that contain malicious words or repeat the same pattern of strings, it classifies the remaining opinions and summarizes them in a short text by using text clustering.

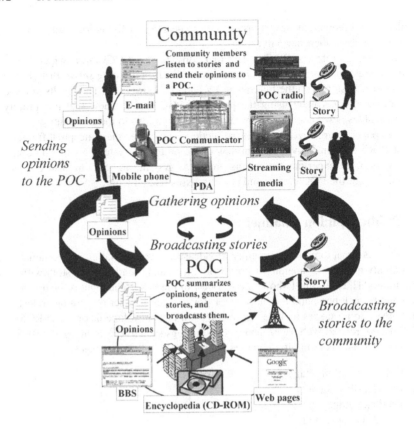

Fig. 1. Concept of a POC. The POC gathers opinions from community members, generates stories (sets of related opinions), and broadcasts those stories within the community.

Then it puts into the story related information retrieved from Web pages, encyclopedias, and the archives of BBS.

People can listen to or watch the stories via various media players including Internet streaming video and audio players. Some stories are narrated by agent newscasters or disc jockeys who can tell stories by using Text-to-Speech (TTS) systems. Others are broadcasted as text messages.

Feedback Stage

In this stage the community members send their comments or other opinions to the POC. Some might send corrections or additional information, and others might suggest new topics. This feedback is used when updating the stories.

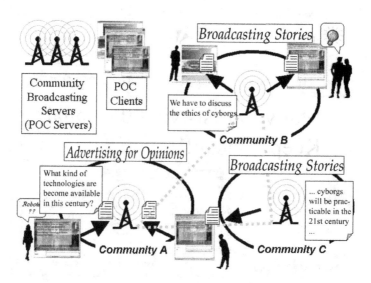

Fig. 2. Overview of the prototype POC system. The community broadcasting servers generate stories and broadcasts them to POC clients that display them automatically.

Broadcasting Stage II

In this stage the POC broadcasts the updated stories to the community and accepts members ratings of the stories. According to these ratings, some stories are rebroadcasted frequently and others are eliminated.

3   Prototype POC System

3.1   Overview of the Prototype POC System

Our prototype POC system consists of a *community broadcasting servers (POC servers)* that broadcast opinions and stories to *POC clients* that automatically display them. Figure 2 shows an overview of the prototype system. Each community broadcasting server collects and broadcasts opinions and stories on a specific theme and community members interested in that theme (e.g., museums in the city) can post their opinions to the appropriate server.

3.2   POCViewer

The *POCViewer* is a passive message viewer. That is, it automatically displays opinions and stories one by one. Users can browse opinions and stories just as they watch TV. Figure 3 shows a screen image of the POCViewer. On the screen is shown an opinion consisting of a title, a body, and a URL referring to a Web page. In the POCViewer

Fig. 3. Screen image of the POCViewer. The POCViewer shows opinions and displays stories automatically. Users can watch opinions and stories just as they watch TV.

all messages are treated as anonymous ones. Although the Name field is shown in the figure, the information in that field is used only for authentication and is never displayed on the screen.

The POCViewer creates *a chain of messages* and displays messages corresponding to the chain (Figure 4). Users can create a chain of messages by specifying keywords. When a user specifies keywords, the POCViewer retrieves opinions and stories based on those keywords and creates a new chain of messages consisting of retrieval results. When new opinions or stories that include the keywords are posted to the community broadcasting server, the POCViewer puts those messages into the chain. Messages are retrieved by using the n-gram search method[4]. Although the retrieval results include messages not relevant to the query, this method is suitable for retrieving diverse messages including the query.

The POCViewer displays messages repeatedly so that newcomers can easily find past messages and join in the discussion. In mailing lists and BBSs, only new messages are displayed and referred to by people, old messages are hardly ever referred to. Although messages valuable to newcomers are posted to mailing lists and BBSs, they are stored in messages logs and hardly referred to by newcomers. The POCViewer, though, continuously and repeatedly displays messages corresponding to a chain of messages. By displaying messages continuously, it makes it easy for newcomers to find valuable messages in past discussions. This might encourage them to post their own opinions.

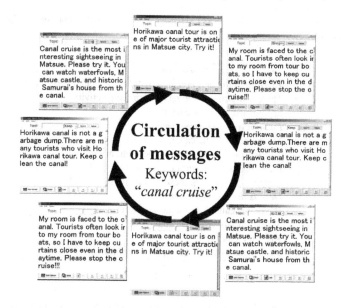

Fig. 4. A chain of messages. The POCViewer continuously displays messages corresponding to the chain. When it reaches the last one in the chain, the POCViewer displays the top message in that chain again.

Thus the POCViewer enables community members to find past messages and easily join the discussions in a community.

3.3 Community Broadcasting Server

The community broadcasting server generates stories based on opinions posted by community members, and it broadcasts those stories within a community.

Generating Stories

A story consists of several opinions related to a keyword and an example of a story is shown in Table 1. There, three opinions relevant to the keywords "canal cruise" are introduced in the story. Opinions are retrieved from an opinion database on the community broadcasting server, and the retrieved opinions are ordered chronologically. When the story is broadcasted as a radio program, a disc jockey (DJ) agent introduces each opinion.

The community broadcasting server generates a story that has a *context* which here means a semantic relationship between sentences. The context is necessary for a story, which is hard to understand without a context. The context is generated as follows.

1. Pick up an opinion (source opinion) from an opinion database.
2. Retrieve opinions from the opinion database by using the title of the first opinion.

Table 1. Example of a story. A disc jockey (DJ) agent introduces three opinions (Op.1 to Op.3) related to the keywords "canal cruise".

DJ	*Let's talk about "canal cruise".*
	The title of the first message is "Matsue canal cruise".
Op.1	The canal cruise is the most interesting activity in Matsue city. Please try it!
DJ	*I will introduce this message.*
Op.2	My room faces the canal. Tourists on tour boats often look into my room. I have to keep my curtains closed even in the daytime. Please stop these cruises immediately!
DJ	*Here is the last message.*
Op.3	Horikawa canal is not a garbage dump. Many tourists visit the canal. Keep it clean!
DJ	*Thank you. We are waiting for your opinions.*

3. Sort retrieval results chronological order and add the first n opinions to the source opinion. (n is a specified threshold)

The server generates a story consisting of a source opinion and n opinions retrieved from the opinion database. The server first picks up an opinion that becomes first opinion (source opinion) of the story. Our prototype system picks up a source opinion randomly from the opinion database. Then a community broadcasting server retrieves related opinions based on title of the source opinion. Retrieval results are sorted chronologically, and the first n opinions are added to the source opinion.

Broadcasting Messages

The community broadcasting server broadcasts opinions and stories to POC clients as TV and radio programs. Users can watch a TV-program-style story by using the POCViewer, which plays the stories while narrating the messages by using a TTS system. Users can also listen to the radio-program-type programs by using MP3 players such as Winamp[1]. The server generates an MP3 audio file of a story and broadcasts it by using an MP3 audio streaming server such as icecast[2].

4   How Effective Is the POC?: Social Psychological Findings

Messages that one member posts on the POC system should encourage other members to post messages, and we had an experiment to find out how well our prototype system actually stimulates the circulation of messages by helping newcomers find information and post opinions.

---

[1] http://www.winamp.com/

[2] http://www.icecast.org/

Table 2. Gender and age of participants.

	Male	Female	Age (average)
SMs	5	2	28.0
NCs	5	1	25.3
Total	10	3	26.8

4.1 The Summary of the Experiment

The seven starting members (SMs) of our experimental community spent two weeks using the POCViewer to talk about domestic topics in the Kansai area of Japan before they were joined by six newcomers (NCs). To find out how well the prototype POC system supports SMs and NCs, we evaluated the members' impressions of the community as well as their thoughts about how hard it was to find information and post information. We also measured the number of messages by the each of the two subsets of members (SMs and NCs).

4.2 Method

Participants

The 13 participants were 10 males and 3 females. Most of the SMs were from a graduate school of social psychology and most of the NCs are from a school of computer science. Their genders, average age, and group assignments are listed in Table 2.

Starting Members

The starting members were recruited through mailing lists. We emailed questionnaires to 12 applicants and issued them IDs for the POCViewer. Five of the applicants were excluded from the experiment because they could not install the POCViewer because of operating systems or network troubles, so only seven actually participated.

Newcomers

The newcomers, also recruited through mailing lists, were recruited two weeks after the experiment. We sent questionnaires to seven applicants and issued them IDs for the POCViewer. One never actually participated and was therefore excluded from analysis.

Experiment Execution Period

The experiment execution period is summarized in Figure 5.

Task

Participants were required to find and post information related to the daily life in their area. The topics were about spots that can be recommended but are not well known.

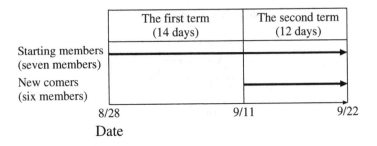

Fig. 5. Periods during which the SMs and NCs participated in the POC community.

Table 3. The experimental groups' impressions of the community.

No.	Evaluation items	SM		NC		All members	
		Mean	SD	Mean	SD	Mean	SD
Q1	The atmosphere of the community was good.	4.43	0.53	4.00	0.63	4.23	0.60
Q2	We had many exchanges of information with one another.	2.71	1.50	2.83	1.17	2.77	1.30
Q3	I could know what other members know.	4.29	0.49	3.83	0.41	4.08	0.49
Q4	It was easy for me to join the community.	4.00	1.00	3.67	0.82	3.85	0.90
Q5	I could not keep up with topics of conversation.	3.43	0.98	3.67	1.03	3.54	0.97
Q6	Members were behaving maliciously to me.	5.00	0.00	5.00	0.00	5.00	0.00
Q7	I could know the thoughts of other members.	2.86	0.90	3.17	0.75	3.00	0.82
Q8	The community was exclusive.	4.86	0.38	4.50	1.22	4.69	0.85

4.3   Results

Participants' Impressions of the Community

The participants' impressions of community were evaluated by questionnaire after the experimental period and are listed in Table 3. Each item was rated on a 5-points scale (i.e., ranging from 1 to 5), with a rating of 3.00 corresponding to indifference. The mean scores for seven items were greater than 3.00 in the column of all members in the Table 3, so we concluded that the participants' impressions of the Kansai community were generally positive.

The lowest scores were for the evaluation items "We had many exchanges of information with one another (Q2)" (2.77) and "I could know the thoughts of other members (Q7)" (3.00). One possible reason for this is that the members could not exchange information directly. People accustomed to direct communication might wonder about how to connect message with the people sending those messages. In the POC community, in which anonymity is assured, it is difficult to exchange information while relating clearly to other members.

Table 4. Numbers of messages posted by the two experimental groups.

	SMs	NCs	All members
Total messages	151	201	352
Average per day	5.81	7.73	13.54

Table 5. Estimated costs of finding and posting information.

Evaluation items	SMs		NCs		total	
	Mean	SD	Mean	SD	Mean	SD
Finding information was easy.	3.29	1.38	2.67	1.03	3.00	1.22
Posting information was easy.	3.86	1.46	3.50	1.64	3.69	1.49

Information Posting Behavior

The numbers of messages posted by the SMs and NCs (total number posted during the experiment as well as daily means) are listed in Table 4. The SMs posted an average of 5.81 messages per day, 3.85 per day during the first part of the experiment and 8.42 per day during the second part. Although the participation period of the NCs (12 days) was shorter than the SMs' (26 days), the NCs posted more messages than SMs (201 vs. 151).

One SM said that the large number of messages posted by NCs encouraged him to post messages, and the SMs as a group actually posted messages more frequently after the NCs joined the group.

To confirm that the NCs change the posting behavior of the SMs, we compared the actual cumulative contribution of the SMs with their cumulative contribution predicted from their posting behavior before the NCs arrived. Figure 6 shows that the number of messages posted by the SMs increased sharply and shortly after the NCs joined the community. Thus we found not only that NCs posted messages more frequently than SMs but also that the participation of the NCs activated the community, stimulating the SMs to send more messages.

The Cost of Finding and Posting Information

Participants answered questions about the cost of finding and posting in the POC community. The results, listed in Table 5, indicate that the POCViewer is a better tool for posting information than finding information. The table also indicates that the cost of finding and posting information is lower for SMs who have been in the community longer.

4.4 Summary

NCs posted messages to the Kansai community more frequently than SMs. The posting of messages by NCs postings stimulate postings by SMs and increased the circulation

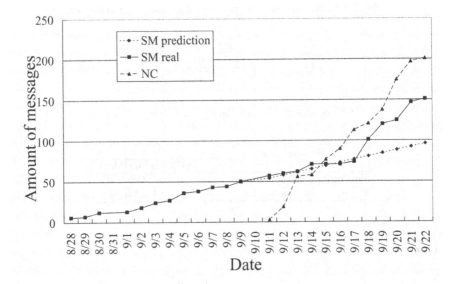

Fig. 6. The cumulative contribution of each groups and the cumulative contribution of the SMs predicted from their contribution before the NCs participated.

of information. Though other communication tools might support a community as well as the prototype POC system including the POCViewer, we conclude the POC system can support members posting information.

NCs thought the cost of finding information was rather high. Although we think this is largely a result of the relatively short time they were part of the POC community, we also think that the POCViewer did not adequately support the information finding behavior of the NCs. The effectiveness of the POCViewer must be further evaluated experimentally. We should also compare the POCViewer with other communication tools with regard to the ease of finding and posting information.

5   Discussion

5.1   Accessibility of a POC

There are two accessibility issues relevant to a POC: its physical accessibility and its cognitive accessibility. The physical accessibility of a POC can easily be improved by broadcasting stories on the regional or cable TV stations and community radio stations in a city. City residents can easily listen to the stories and watch them. They can also easily post their opinions by using a PC connected to the Internet. Community members who do not have a PC connected to the Internet can post their opinions with the help of telephone operators. Because an implementation system of the POC clients such as the POCViewer is quite simple, it can easily be ported to PDAs and Java enabled mobile phones.

For the second issue, the prototype POC system facilitates the cognitive accessibility of newcomers in a community. The experiment with the prototype POC system showed that newcomers were able to post messages to the community easily. Because the POCViewer displays messages continuously, newcomers were able to find past messages and reply to them. The experiment also showed, however, that POCViewer users have difficulties finding information. This is because the current implementation of the POCViewer is not suitable for browsing a large amount of messages. Creating a chain of messages in the POCViewer is not intuitive, and the chains that are created by a user are not used by different users. Furthermore, users are forced to browse messages along the course of the chain. The POCViewer must be improved in ways that make it easier for users to find information.

5.2 Related Work

Tanaka and his colleagues proposed information visualization tools using a TV metaphor[5]. Someone using these visualization tools can view Web documents or results retrieved from a database passively, as when watching a TV program. One of the major differences between our prototype POC system and these information visualization tools is that it displays messages continuously. The information visualization tools focus on the visualization of Web pages and database retrieval results, whereas the POC system focuses on circulating various messages in a community. By circulating messages, community members can find old messages and be reminded of their content. The POC system thus helps newcomers join the communities in the city.

Nakata proposed a framework for facilitating a process of reaching a community consensus on serious issues such as environmental problems[6]. He proposed a multi-modal communication system and a visualization tool facilitating the process of reaching a consensus. One of the major differences between the POC system and the system and tools he proposes is the approach to support the discussion of a serious issue. A POC introduces the opinions of community members by way of disinterested parties; that is, newscaster agents or DJ agents. We think this facilitates content-oriented discussions in a city.

6   Conclusion

We have built a prototype POC system that helps city residents share informal information and exchange their opinions. It consists of a community broadcasting server that generates and broadcasts stories within a community and of the POCViewer that shows opinions and stories continuously. Experimental results show that the system helps newcomers communities. In the future we will improve the POCViewer so that messages can be found more easily and will evaluate the system by comparing it with other communication tools.

References

1. Azechi, S., Fujihara, N., Kaoru, S., Hirata, T., Yano, H., and Nishida, T.: "Public Opinion Channel: A challenge for interactive community broadcasting," In: Ishida, T., and Isbister, K. (eds.), *Digital Cities: Experiences, Technologies and Future Perspectives*, Lecture Notes in Computer Science, 1765, Springer-Verlag, pp. 427-441(2000).
2. Nishida, T., Fujihara, N., Azechi, S., Sumi, K., and Hirata, T.: "Public Opinion Channel for Communities in the Information Age," *New Generation Computing*, Vol. 14, No. 4, pp. 417-427(1999).
3. Azechi, S.: "Social psychological approach to knowledge-creating community"; In: Nishida, T. (ed.): *Dynamic Knowledge Interaction*, CRC Press,pp.15-57(2000).
4. Sato, S., and Kawase, T.: "A high-speed best match retrieval method for Japanese text"; *Japan Advanced Institute of Science and Technology (JAIST) Research Report*, IS-RR-94-9I (1994). (Available from JAIST library.) (http://www.jaist.ac.jp/library/ENG/)
5. Tanaka, K., Nadamoto, A., Kusahara, M., Hattori, T., Kondo, H., and Sumiya, K.: "Back to the TV: Information visualization interfaces based on TV-program metaphors," *IEEE International Conference on Multimedia and Expo2000 (ICME 2000)*, New York (2000).
6. Nakata, K.: "Enabling public discourse," *Workshop notes of the JSAI-Synsophy International Conference on Social Intelligence Design*, pp.47-54(2001). (http://www.synsophy.go.jp/sid2001/papers/)

Agent-Based Coordination of Regional Information Services

Jun-ichi Akahani[1], Kaoru Hiramatsu[1], Yoshikazu Furukawa[2], and
Kiyoshi Kogure[1]

[1] NTT Communication Science Laboratories, NTT Corporation
2-4 Hikaridai, Seika-cho, Soraku-gun, Kyoto 619-0237, Japan
{akahani, hiramatu, kogure}@cslab.kecl.ntt.co.jp
[2] NTT Comware Corporation
2-4 Hikaridai, Seika-cho, Soraku-gun, Kyoto 619-0237, Japan
furukawa.yoshikazu@nttcom.co.jp

Abstract. This paper proposes an agent-based framework for coordinating heterogeneous regional information services. It is necessary to deal with distributed and heterogeneous information services since regional information sources are geographically distributed and the characteristics of regions vary the required regional information according to regions. It is also necessary to integrate information user-adaptively since users of regional information services have specific characteristics, such as knowledge about the region. In this paper, we propose an agent-based framework that consists of server and user agents. Some server agents wrap distributed regional information servers to provide flexible communication. Some server agents provide certain mediation services, such as ontology translation, to enable the coordination of heterogeneous information servers. Each user agent integrates information received from other agents according to a user model to enable the provision of user-adapted information. A prototype system, called the *GeoLinkAgent* system, has been implemented based on the framework.

1 Introduction

Information spaces, the Internet in particular, continue to grow explosively. In the real world, on the other hand, the ongoing globalization has been diversifying the way we live. Accordingly, it is now necessary to integrate heterogeneous information and adapt it to each individual user to provide adequate information.

Regional information is essentially distributed and heterogeneous since regional information sources are geographically distributed and the characteristics of regions vary the required regional information according to regions. For example, users will want information about public transportation in regions with well-developed public transportation services. In contrast, people will want road traffic information in regions without public transportation services.

On the other hand, as today's ongoing globalization diversifies the way we live, more and more users are finding homogeneous information unsatisfactory.

M. Tanabe, P. van den Besselaar, T. Ishida (Eds.): Digital Cities, LNCS 2362, pp. 283–291, 2002.

Users of regional information services have specific characteristics, such as knowledge about the region in question. For example, travelers may have access to local regional information servers. In order to provide adequate information to these users, user-adaptive information integration is required.

We therefore propose an agent-based framework for coordinating heterogeneous regional information services. This framework consists of server and user agents. Some server agents wrap distributed regional information servers to provide flexible communication. Some server agents provide certain mediation services [10], such as ontology translation. Mediation services that translate regional ontologies enable the coordination of heterogeneous information servers. Each user agent communicates with server agents and integrates information from other agents according to a user model, which represents the characteristics and preferences of its user. Information integration based on this user model enables the provision of user-adapted information.

Based on this framework, we have been implementing a prototype system, called the *GeoLinkAgent* system. This prototype system adopts the GeoLink system [5,6], which is used in the Digital City Kyoto [7] prototype, as a regional information server. From the viewpoint of interoperability, we adopt the Agent Communication Language (ACL) standardized by the Foundation for Intelligent Physical Agents (FIPA) [3] for inter-agent communication.

In this paper, we first discuss issues related to regional information services. We then present an agent-based framework that enables the flexible coordination of regional information services. Finally, we demonstrate the GeoLinkAgent prototype system based on the framework.

2   Issues in Regional Information Services

In this section, we discuss issues related to regional information services.

2.1   Distributed Information Sources

Regional information servers are distributed at both the logical and implementation levels. Regional information sources are geographically distributed, and many of them generate real-time information, such as road traffic, weather, and so on. Considering the reliability and freshness of the information, it is better to maintain information in the neighborhood of the information sources. For example, it is better to maintain traffic information in Tokyo with a regional information server in Tokyo rather than in another area, such as New York. From the viewpoint of the credibility of information, it is better to maintain regional information with information servers responsible for that information. This is why regional information servers are distributed at the logical level.

Furthermore, it is impossible to provide worldwide information with one concentrated information server because of the limitations of network traffic and computational load. This is why regional information servers are distributed at the implementation level.

This geographical distribution of information sources implies a horizontal distribution of information sources, as shown in Fig. 1.

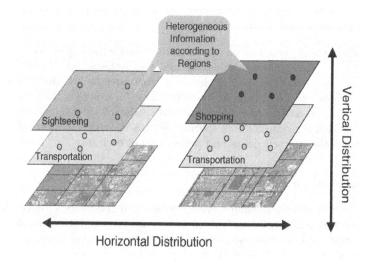

Fig. 1. Distributed and Heterogeneous Information Sources

2.2 Heterogeneous Information

The characteristics of regions, such as the regional scales and industrial structures, vary the required regional information according to regions. For example, people will want information about the public transportation, such as train schedules, in regions with well-developed public transportation services. In contrast, people will want road traffic information in regions without public transportation services.

Even in the same region, different kinds of information may be required in sub-regions. For example, people in a downtown area of the region will more often require shopping information than sightseeing information. In a suburb area, on the other hand, people will more often require sightseeing information than shopping information.

These regional characteristic differences affect, for example, the categorization of information. Cultural differences also make the categorization of information vary according to the region. For example, the detailed categorization of Japanese restaurants, such as traditional Japanese, Japanese noodles, and so on, may be required in Japan. On the other hand, one category, e.g., Japanese restaurant, may be sufficient in the United States. Therefore, it is necessary to translate information categories in one region to those in other regions.

This heterogeneity of information sources implies a vertical distribution of information sources, as shown in Fig. 1. Accordingly, we must deal with both the horizontal and vertical distribution of regional information sources.

2.3   Adaptation to Various Users

As today's ongoing globalization continues to diversify the way we live, more and more users are finding homogeneous information unsatisfactory. Users of regional information services have specific characteristics, such as knowledge about the region in question. For example, travelers may have access to local regional information servers. In order to provide adequate information to these users, user adaptation is required. More specifically, it is necessary to filter information according to the characteristics and preferences of each user.

2.4   Information Integration

As the world becomes more and more borderless, our spheres of activities become more and more heterogeneous. This makes it necessary to integrate information from multiple regional servers, especially at the borders of multiple regions. For example, a traveler at Niagara Falls may want information about restaurants in Canada and accommodations in the United States. This problem becomes more serious for commuters, as they need information for both the business areas where they work and the residential areas where they live. Therefore, user-adaptive information integration is required.

3   An Agent-Based Framework for Coordinating Regional Information Services

In this section, we propose an agent-based framework for coordinating regional information services. This framework consists of server and user agents as shown in Fig. 2.

3.1   Basic Architecture

To deal with distributed and heterogeneous information services, we introduce server agents that wrap regional information servers and provide mediation services, such as ontology translation. We also introduce user agents each with a user model to integrate information according to its individual user.

Based on the request of the user, the user agent formulates a query message wrapped by an agent communication language and sends the query message to a server agent. The server agent may then forward the query to other agents using mediation services. The server agent that wraps regional information servers replies to the query message. The user agent integrates information from other agents according to the user model.

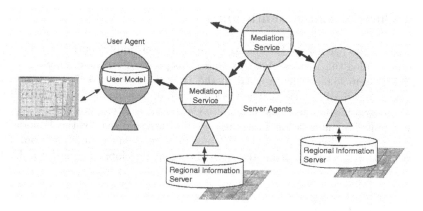

Fig. 2. Agent-Based Framework for Coordinating Regional Information Services

3.2   Adaptation to Information Source by Mediation Services

A server agent communicates with user agents and other server agents. Some server agents wrap distributed regional information servers to provide flexible communication. Some server agents provide certain mediation services, such as ontology translation. Server agents may have both of these functions (See Fig. 2).

Mediation services that translate regional ontologies enable the coordination of heterogeneous information servers. Consider, for example, the case where a user agent asks a server agent representing the Kyoto region about restaurants in New York. As previously explained, classification in Japan differs from that in the United States. By viewing such classification as ontologies, the user can obtain information without concern about differences in regional characteristics. In the above example, if the server agent for Kyoto translates a Japanese ontology to an American ontology, the user can obtain information without considering any classification differences between Japan and the United States.

3.3   Adaptation to User Based on User Model

Each user agent communicates with server agents and integrates information from other agents according to a user model, which represents the characteristics and preferences of the individual user. Information integration based on this user model enables the provision of user-adapted information.

Consider, for example, a user who prefers good restaurants closer to a certain station even if they are expensive. We assume that there is a server agent that provides a list of restaurants according to their distance from the station and another server agent that provides a list of restaurants based on reputation. After the user agent integrates the information from these server agents based on the user model, it can provide the user with information about restaurants matching the user's preferences.

4 Current Implementation

Based on the agent-based framework, we have been implementing a prototype system, called the *GeoLinkAgent* system. This prototype system adopts the Ge-oLink system [5,6], which is used in the Digital City Kyoto [7] prototype, as regional information servers. The GeoLink system provides Web search facilities with geographical conditions. From the viewpoint of interoperability, we adopt the Agent Communication Language (ACL) standardized by the Foundation for Intelligent Physical Agents (FIPA) [3] for inter-agent communication. This prototype system is implemented with the agent development platform JADE [2].

4.1 User Agent

Each user agent provides search facilities for Web pages with geographical conditions such as region, category, and keyword. Based on the input from its user, the user agent asks a server agent to search for Web pages matching the specific category and keyword in the specified region. Agents communicate with each other through FIPA ACL as explained below. The server agent (or another server agent) provides Web search results each consisting of a URL (Universal Resource Locator) with a corresponding physical location and a digital map for the specified region. The Web search results are displayed as icons on the digital map, as shown in Fig. 3. The user can browse each Web page by clicking its representative icon.

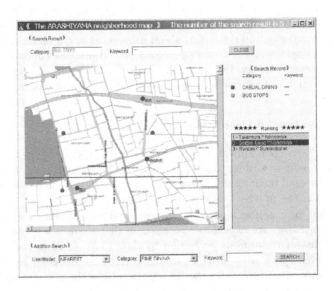

Fig. 3. Search Results of a User Agent

The user agent allows for a sequence of Web searches in the same region. For example, after searching for Web pages of restaurants in a region, it can then search for bus stops in that region.

Currently, a simple user model in which the user prefers the closest location is implemented. For the above example, pairs of a restaurant and the nearest bus stop are listed in the order of distance between the restaurant and the bus stop, as shown in Fig. 3. To calculate the distance, we use the physical locations associated with the URLs.

4.2   Server Agent

Each server agent communicates with user agents and other server agents. In our prototype system, agents communicate with each other using FIPA ACL messages. An example of an agent message is shown in Fig. 4. In this example, a server agent "server1" forwards a query about "restaurants" with the keyword "Tofu" in the "Arashiyama" region to a server agent "server2."

```
(query-ref
   :sender server1
   :receiver server2
   :content ((all ?x
                  (geolink-search-result
                      :region "Arashiyama"
                      :category restaurant
                      :keyword "Tofu"
                      :geoURL ?x ) ) )
   :language FIPA-SL
   :ontology agent-cooperate-server
   :protocol FIPA-Query )
```

Fig. 4. Example of Agent Message

We have implemented a simple mediation service that forwards queries based on a server agent's knowledge about other server agents. In our prototype system, a server agent that wraps regional information servers maintains a list of categories and regions for which the server agent can answer. Suppose that a server agent A is asked about a category C in a region R. If C and R are in A's list of categories and regions, then agent A asks the regional information server. Otherwise, agent A forwards the query to other server agents.

5   Related Work

There has been a lot of research on information integration in the fields of database and artificial intelligence [8,9,10]. The Information Manifold system [9] exploits information source descriptions to integrate information from heterogeneous information sources. However, these source descriptions must be given manually. Automatic methods for obtaining source descriptions are necessary. The Ariadne system [8] provides a wrapper mechanism to integrate information from heterogeneous information sources. This system enables vertical information integration, such as information integration from restaurant review sites and maps. However, it is not clear if it can also provide horizontal information integration. In contrast to these systems, our system introduces user agents with user models for user adaptation.

Recently, several ontology languages of the Semantic Web have been proposed [4]. It is possible to describe ontologies for regional information with ontology languages such as DAML+OIL.

The Agentcities project [1] has just started to connect cities based on agent technologies. This project also provides agent-based mediation services, but it is not clear what kind of information integration is available. Fortunately, as the Agentcities project adopts FIPA ACL for inter-agent communication, it will be possible for our agents to communicate with AgentCities' agents.

6   Conclusions

We have proposed an agent-based framework for coordinating heterogeneous regional information services. This framework consists of server and user agents. Server agents that provide certain mediation services, such as ontology translation, enable the coordination of heterogeneous information servers. User agents, which integrate information according to user models, enable the provision of user-adapted information.

A prototype system has been implemented based on the agent-based framework. Currently, we have implemented a simple mediation service that forwards queries based on a server agent's knowledge about other server agents. We are also implementing an ontology translation mechanism.

References

1. Agentcities. http://www.agentcities.org/.
2. F. Bellifemine, A. Poggi, and G. Rimassa. JADE–a FIPA-compliant agent framework. In *Proc. of the Fourth International Conference and Exhibition on The Practical Application of Intelligent Agents and Multi-Agents*, pages 97–108, 1999.
3. Foundation for Intelligent Physical Agents (FIPA). http://www.fipa.org/.
4. J. Hendler. Agents and the semantic web. *IEEE Intelligent Systems*, 16(2):30–36, 2001.
5. K. Hiramatsu and T. Ishida. An augmented web space for digital cities. In *Proc. of the 2001 Symposium on Applications and the Internet*, pages 105–112, 2001.
6. K. Hiramatsu, K. Kobayashi, B. Benjamin, T. Ishida, and J. Akahani. Map-based user interface for Digital City Kyoto. In *Proc. of INET2000 The Internet Global Summit*, 2000.

7. T. Ishida, J. Akahani, K. Hiramatsu, K. Isbister, S. Lisowski, H. Nakanishi, M. Okamoto, Y. Miyazaki, and K. Tsutsuguchi. Digital City Kyoto: Towards a social information infrastructure. In *Proc. of International Workshop on Cooperative Information Agents (CIA-99)*, pages 23–35, 1999.

8. C. A. Knoblock and S. Minton. The ariadne approach to web-based information integration. *IEEE Intelligent Systems*, 13(5):17–20, 1998.

9. A. Y. Levy, A. Rajaraman, and J. J. Ordille. Querying heterogeneous information sources using source descriptions. In *Proc. of the 22nd International Conference on Very Large Databases (VLDB-96)*, pages 251–262, 1996.

10. G. Wiederhold and M. Genesereth. The conceptual basis for mediation services. *IEEE Expert*, 12(5):38–47, May 1997.

Realization of Digital Environmental Education — A Future Style of Environmental Education in Dynamically Changing Virtual Environment —

Masaya Okada[1], Hiroyuki Tarumi[2], Tetsuhiko Yoshimura[1], Kazuyuki Moriya[1], and Tetsuro Sakai[1]

[1] Graduate School of Informatics, Kyoto University,
Yoshida Honmachi, Kyoto 606-8501 Japan.
okada@bre.soc.i.kyoto-u.ac.jp
{yoshimu,moriya,sakai}@i.kyoto-u.ac.jp
[2] Faculty of Engineering, Kagawa University,
2217-20, Hayashi-Cho, Takamatsu, Kagawa 761-0396 Japan.
tarumi@eng.kagawa-u.ac.jp

Abstract. The important key to success of environmental education is to realize space and situation where people of diverse backgrounds can universally participate in environmental education and can mutually exchange their candid opinions and practical experiences. Our system, DigitalEE, is designed and implemented to pursue universality of participation in environmental education with the concepts of digital cities. Learners in real forest, environmental specialists in laboratories, and virtual tourists at homes or hospitals can make interactive real-time communication via online 3D virtual nature generated by DigitalEE. Information available via the 3D virtual nature is continuously updated at participants' own free will, and is used as communication contexts at participants' discussion on environmental issues. DigitalEE creates an original form of public participation in digital cities such as collaborative interaction between real and virtual worlds, and makes realization of digital environmental education: a future style of environmental education in dynamically changing virtual environment.

1 Introduction

Recently, environmental education has been steadily getting one of the most important educational areas against the background of diverse and global environmental issues that are increasingly becoming significant social concern. This research regards activities of people practicing environmental education as social activities and actively tries to change them with the concepts of digital cities.

One of the main concepts of digital cities [1] is to support social activities of people living in real cities by accumulating information on the cities with city metaphors. However, even if digital cities represent real cities in the physical world, people who actually exist in the real cities cannot participate in the digital cities. Therefore, participation in conventional digital cities is "virtual", and this is thought to be a problem that should be solved for realization of digital cities based on universal participation of all people.

M. Tanabe, P. van den Besselaar, T. Ishida (Eds.): Digital Cities, LNCS 2362, pp. 292–304, 2002.

Fig. 1. Digital environmental education based on universal participation from real and virtual worlds.

This paper introduces digital environmental education conducted with "DigitalEE" [2,3], which is an information system for interactive and collaborative environmental education (Figure 1). DigitalEE supports interaction among learners in real natural forest, environmental specialists in laboratories, and virtual tourists at homes or hospitals by means of "3D virtual nature", which is a VRML (Virtual Reality Modeling Language) world representing the natural forest. All participants interactively communicate with each other and make various discussion while virtually sharing the same time and space between real and virtual worlds. Practical experiences in environmental education are constantly accumulated in 3D virtual nature, and practitioners of environmental education can conduct the education while making good use of the accumulated experiences. Similarly, not only empirical knowledge of people really suffering from environmental pollution but also observations and achievements of learners are recorded in the shared 3D virtual nature.

3D virtual nature is not a metaphor of a real "city" but a metaphor of real "forest". However, the 3D virtual nature is thought to fall under the category of digital cities because it is a metaphor of really existing space in the real world, and is well suited to the concepts of digital cities. This research makes a proposal for a future style of environmental education conducted in a dynamically changing digital city on the Internet, and tries to change both activities of people practicing environmental education and educational styles of conventional environmental education. Application of the concepts of digital cities to environmental education indicates a new direction of digital cities.

2   Environmental Education through Communication

Several requirements should be satisfied to conduct successful environmental education [2,3]. For example, effective environmental education should be based on mutual
supplementation of both direct and indirect experiences [4]. Valuable environmental
knowledge is requisite for effective environmental education because increase of learners' environmental knowledge desirably changes their environmental attitude [5]. Successful environmental education requires support by competent educators who have
comprehensive and sufficient knowledge on ecology and sociopolitics as well as diverse
pedagogical skills [6]. As demonstrated in our past papers [2,3], DigitalEE sufficiently
satisfies these essential requirements. In addition to the requirements, this paper places
special emphasis on importance of practicing environmental education through communication because active communication of environmental information with various
people significantly contributes to improvement of learners' environmental attitude and
environmental values.

2.1   Local Activities with Global Viewpoints

So far, environmental education has been often practiced through recycling, off-campus
activities, street sweeping, and natural experiences as approaches trying to practice environmental education through learners' local activities. Even if learners perform such
activities as a part of environmental education, achievement of sufficient educational
effects cannot be expected unless learners understand the contribution of local activities
to global environmental issues. Teaching global environmental issues with educational
materials such as books and video tapes has learners think globally, but in many cases,
learners cannot feel given information as reality [7]. If learners grasp global environmental issues as events occurring in other distant areas, environmental education cannot
have enough educational effects. Adding global viewpoints to learners' local activities
is essentially important, and it is indispensable to introduce devices that help learners
grasp the environment globally into present environmental education. It is never expected that learners can acquire their own senses of values on the environment through
only local activities such as recycling and street sweeping. The local activities must be
supplemented with information enough to help learners grasp meanings of the activities
and to have learners consider relationships between the local activities and preservation
of the global environment.

2.2   Critical Thinking through Communication

Environmental problems are complicated social issues including contradicted concepts
such as development and preservation. Not denying either development or preservation,
but searching for the best way balanced between the two concepts is important for solution of environmental issues and sustainable development, and it is undesirable to force
educators' or environmentalists' absolute senses of values on learners [8]. Processes that
learners critically think about environmental issues from global viewpoints should be
regarded as vitally important to make learners have opinions and senses of values that
are not implanted by educators but created by themselves. One of the most important

Fig. 2. A learner exploring real nature (Kamigamo Experimental Forest, Graduate School of Agriculture, Kyoto University) with a mobile computer.

factors for the processes is communication of environmental information with various people who have diverse backgrounds, experiences, knowledge, and opinions. Living people can be considered as "knowledge sources", and recognition of unknown activities, different opinions, and diverse experiences of others through communication can stimulate intellectual interests of learners, and can give learners various thinking and orientation towards environmental actions [8]. Exchange of opinions and achievements with others who have different thinking requires learners' reconsideration of learning achievement, critical thinking about environmental issues, and logical expression of opinions. Communication refines and improves environmental values, and integrates physical senses obtained through direct natural experiences with spiritual knowledge. Education mainly adopting communication and discussion is absolutely appropriate for environmental education, and for success of environmental education, it is crucial to realize space and situation where learners can know candid opinions of various people through communication and can consider global environmental issues with the people.

3   Realization of Digital Environmental Education

Detailed explanation for system structure of DigitalEE has been already described in another papers [2,3], and we would like you to find the description in them. In this section, while indicating an outline of the system, we give introduction of a future style of environmental education realized by DigitalEE and consider possibility of environmental education adopting the concepts of digital cities.

3.1   An Overview of DigitalEE

DigitalEE is a support system for collaborative environmental education that has been developed against the background of diverse requirements and potential in environmental education such as needs for virtual tours to the natural environment [9], potential of environmental education with Internet technologies [10], importance of environmental

Distributed Virtual Environment Representing Real Nature.
(Kamigamo Experimental Forest, Kyoto University)

A Sphere Object Linked to a Panoramic Photograph.

Participants' Avatars Based on Their Portrait Photographs.
- People in the Real World: Control by GPS Information.
- People in Virtual Worlds: Control by Users' Direct Input.

Pasted Objects Linked to Created Web Pages.

Fig. 3. 3D virtual nature, a 3D spatial metaphor of real nature.

education supported by knowledgeable educators in the distance [6], and necessity of supplementation of real experiences in visited nature [9]. DigitalEE realizes environmental education through worldwide communication via distributed virtual environment that participants in real forest and participants in other distant locations can universally access. Each of the former participants takes part in DigitalEE with a mobile computer equipped with a GPS (Global Positioning System) receiver, a PHS (Personal Handyphone System) card, and a digital camera (Figure 2). Each of the latter participants takes part in the system with a personal computer connected to the Internet. All participants can make discussion on environmental issues while virtually sharing the same time and space between real and virtual worlds via 3D virtual nature, which is a 3D spatial metaphor of real forest (Figure 3). At the present time, a part of Kamigamo Experimental Forest, Graduate School of Agriculture, Kyoto University is constructed as 3D virtual nature.

DigitalEE is designed with a client-server model, and all participants share 3D virtual nature without inconsistency by exchanging information necessary for controlling distributed virtual environment via the server with TCP/IP. All participants are expressed as avatars based on their portrait photographs in 3D virtual nature (Figure 3). The avatar of each participant in real forest is drawn at the corresponding position in the 3D virtual nature according to positional information obtained by the GPS receiver. On the other hand, the avatar of each participant in a distant location is drawn in the shared virtual world according to movement of participant's view from a VRML browser by his or her direct input with a mouse or a keyboard. All participants make interactive communication while viewing 3D virtual nature, a 2D vegetation map, a frame for text-based communication, and web contents in addition to panoramic photographs that can be seen in all directions (Figure 4). Web contents, which are linked from the 3D virtual nature, include names, features, botanical values, ecological meaning, and seasonal changes of plants in addition to information on environmental issues. The web contents and educational quizzes have been being created in cooperation with environmental specialists at Kyoto University.

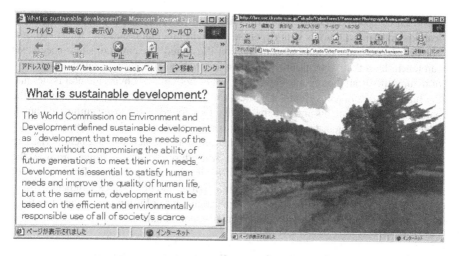

Fig. 4. A web page (left) and a panoramic photograph (right).

3.2   Collaborative Interaction via Changing 3D Virtual Nature

The DigitalEE program (an environmental education program with DigitalEE) is carried out after online announcement of the date and time of the program and a call for the following participant:

- Learners learning about the environment by actual exploration of nature.
- Virtual tourists getting environmental information by virtual visits to nature.
- Environmental specialists in environmental issues and forest ecology.
- People performing practical activities in environmental preservation.
- People suffering from environmental pollution.

DigitalEE is designed to achieve educational effects by support of independent environmental learning through interaction among various participants via 3D virtual nature. 3D virtual nature is being dynamically updated along the time axis according to participants' continuous accumulation of the following diverse environmental knowledge:

- Observations and achievements derived from learners' natural experiences.
- Expertise of specialists in environmental issues and forest ecology.
- Practical experiences of practitioners of environmental education.
- Empirical knowledge of people suffering from environmental pollution.

The above environmental knowledge is accumulated as both VRML objects in the shared 3D virtual nature and web pages on the server. All participants can make mutual communication in the dynamically changing virtual environment while sharing the knowledge in semi-real time and using it as communication contexts. Learners and virtual tourists can learn ecology of plants while finding and viewing new information that is constantly updated in shared 3D virtual nature. Environmental specialists can provide learners and virtual tourists with expertise on environmental issues and forest ecology. For instance, as an example of conversation illustrated [3], environmental specialists can teach them that recognition of local environmental condition through observation of natural life around us enables consideration of both global environmental issues and the future of natural ecosystems. Learners can ask environmental specialists about the names of unknown plants and rare insects that they found, and convey empirical knowledge derived from their direct experiences to other participants. Virtual tourists can get learners' vivid and realistic information that are not obtained without actual visits to the environment such as beauties of nature, warmth of the sun, and murmuring of the winds in trees in addition to knowledge of environmental specialists. Practitioners of environmental education can introduce their activities and practical experiences to other participants, and people suffering from environmental pollution can appeal to others against damage caused by destruction of environmental balance.

3.3   Environmental Education through Worldwide Communication

DigitalEE generates 3D virtual nature on the Internet, digital and virtual communities where people involved in environmental education can simultaneously gather and can freely exchange diverse environmental information. Via shared 3D virtual nature, participants throughout the world can make interactive discussion on environmental issues from global viewpoints while sharing learners' real physical experiences and other participants' spiritual knowledge. At the discussion, learners can obtain not secondhand knowledge derived from teaching materials but firsthand knowledge of the parties concerned. The DigitalEE program is conducted in the open world, not in the closed world. DigitalEE realizes global environmental education through worldwide communication among people who have diverse backgrounds, empirical knowledge, practical experiences, and various expertise.

3.4   Practical Experiences Accumulated in 3D Virtual Nature

Know-how and practical experiences of practitioners of environmental education are treasure houses of knowledge, and accumulating them is essential to promote success of environmental education, but there has been no adequate device for accumulation of the know-how and the practical experiences. DigitalEE proposes ideas that accumulate various environmental knowledge, e.g., empirical knowledge of people suffering from environmental pollution and practical experiences of people actually trying to solve environmental issues, as common knowledge sources available to the public in all over the world. The accumulated knowledge sources are records reflecting opinions and thinking of various people in diverse positions differently from conventional educational materials created by educators' absolute senses of values. The knowledge sources increase in proportion to the number of participants and practice times of the DigitalEE program. Practitioners of environmental education can conduct the education while making good use of practical knowledge obtained by past succeeded and failed environmental education programs that were conducted throughout the world.

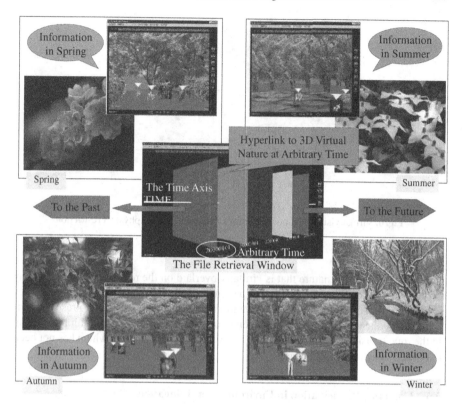

Fig. 5. Interactive virtual visits to 3D virtual nature changing in the time transition.

3.5   Interactive Virtual Visits to the Past Natural Environment

The natural environment is the space dynamically changing in the time transition, and various aspects of the environment are shown through seasonal changes. Most flowers in natural forest usually bloom in only particular seasons, and we cannot observe plants that bloom in another season. It is significant in environmental education to have learners make consideration of changes of the natural environment with the passage of time [11].

3D virtual nature is information space that is changing with the passage of time according to accumulation of various information, and changes of the 3D virtual nature synchronize with changes of the real natural environment (Figure 5). Through the DigitalEE programs practiced in four seasons, various information in every season is added to 3D virtual nature. Participants can enter 3D virtual nature at arbitrary time by clicking a board object in a file retrieval window, and can achieve communication with other participants while virtually existing in the past environment. This function realizes virtual visits to the past natural environment, and people can observe growth of plants while comparing present environmental condition with past environmental condition. Learners in real nature can find plants living at present, which did not live in the past,

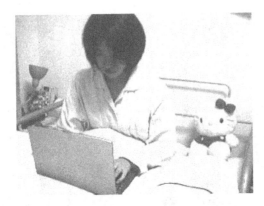

Fig. 6. Virtual visits to real nature from a bedroom without physical restriction.

by viewing 3D virtual nature that is virtually overlaid on the real world via the display of their mobile computers. Through experience of the past natural environment, they can also find plants living in the past environment, which do not live at present. Environmental education through environmental observation of natural condition changing in the time transition is one of the unique advantages of DigitalEE, which has not been realized by any other systems.

3.6   Universal Participation in Environmental Education

People suffering from a long illness or physical handicaps cannot freely obtain and transmit various information because of diverse restriction on daily life such as long-term constraint of going out and long-period stay in a hospital. Patients and the handicapped can often have only limited communication with particular persons such as doctors, nurses, and their family, and they remarkably lack opportunities of communication with various unknown people. On the other hand, school excursions to natural parks are often made as a part of environmental education, but most of patients and handicapped people often have difficulties in participating in the excursions, and they severely lack chances of obtainment of natural experiences and empirical knowledge. If they are children in a stage of development, lack of chances of contact with outside people and shortage of opportunities of obtaining real natural experiences are expected to cause harmful influences on their mental and intellectual growth. It is essentially required to provide such patients and the handicapped with information and experiences similarly to healthy people who can freely obtain diverse physical and spiritual experiences.

With DigitalEE, people in good health, the handicapped, patients under medical treatment at homes, and long-term hospitalized people can universally participate in the same virtual space representing real forest without restriction of physical distance and physical handicaps (Figure 6), and can learn the environment together while sharing real physical experiences. It is well known that the natural environment contributes to healing of mental and physical stress by bringing out our ability for spontaneous cure. VRML, which is used for representation of nature in this research, does not have expression ability enough to bring out healing ability of natural space. However, DigitalEE makes real-time provision of information of people actually existing in real nature for patients and the handicapped, and enables their virtual existence in the forest. DigitalEE offers them opportunities of communication with people that they cannot usually contact. The system stimulates their imagination with a metaphor of real forest, and allows their mind to travel all over the world freely from homes or hospitals. Enabling patients and the handicapped, who are under limitation of going out, to make contact and communication with outside people means that their closed living space becomes open to the outside. Healing effects achieved by the contact and the communication have not been verified in this research, but at least it is expected that the contact and the communication will improve quality of life of the patients and the handicapped who have heavy physical and mental stress in limited living space. Moreover, this system provides them with opportunities to learn the environment through free virtual exploration of real nature with participants from all over the world such as environmental specialists, practitioners of environmental education, people suffering from environmental pollution, and learners actually exploring real nature. Creation of environmental education based on universal participation of various people has vital importance for further activation and improvement of environmental education.

4 Original Concepts as Research on Digital Cities

4.1 Exploration of Digital Environmental Education Communities

AOL Digital Cities [12], Digital City Amsterdam [13], Virtual Helsinki [14], and Digital City Kyoto [15] are four main digital cities that characterize present research on digital cities. Each digital city has a different goal such as a vertical market, public communication space, a next generation metropolitan network, and a social information infrastructure [1]. Our digital city, i.e., 3D virtual nature, has a clearly distinct goal such as creation of digital communities for global environmental education through worldwide communication. Digital cities having the same or a similar goal have not been proposed so far.

4.2 The 3D Spatial Metaphor of Attractive Real Forest

Differently from conventional digital cities, 3D virtual nature is an unexampled digital city representing real forest with a 3D spatial metaphor. Nowadays, natural forest in good conditions is extremely rare against the background of highly urbanized society, and its value is steadily increasing. Natural space has many functions that urban space does not have, and most people are usually deeply impressed by approaching nature. Natural space is so attractive that it can awake peoples' motivation for visits, as Taylor showed needs for virtual tours to the natural environment [9]. Our research is not research that simply applies the concepts of digital cities to natural space. The research indicates a new direction of digital cities by utilization of the concepts of digital cities for enabling services that can be realized only in attractive natural space.

4.3   A Digital City Adopting Seasonal Changes of the Real World

3D virtual nature is a digital city adopting seasonal changes of the real world. Seasonal changes of the natural environment are more remarkable and drastic than those of cities. The digital city links to the real world, and it changes with the passage of time. Information obtained from the digital city is constantly updated while synchronizing with changes of the physical world. This is an interesting feature of this system.

4.4   Universal Participation of People in Real and Virtual Worlds

Technologies for public participation, information integration, social agents, and information security are unique technologies in digital cities [1]. DigitalEE is designed to pursue universality of public participation in digital cities, and the system generates an original form of the public participation such as collaboration and communication between real and virtual worlds. Technologies enabling such collaboration and communication have not been proposed so far, and this is a unique advantage of DigitalEE.

On the other hand, although competent educators do not usually exist near learners, and their direct instruction is not easily available [16], support by such educators is important for successful environmental education [6]. DigitalEE realizes environmental education conducted in a digital city where various environmental specialists can universally participate. Utilization of the concepts of digital cities for provision of services that have never been realized, e.g., our environmental education supported by competent worldwide environmental specialists who are usually unavailable, is expected to substantially enhance peoples' motivation for participation in digital cities.

4.5   Real-Time Information Integration at Participants' Requests

In addition to the technologies for public participation, DigitalEE proposes original technologies for information integration such as constant accumulation of realistic environmental information at participants' free requests. 3D virtual nature is designed to pursue reality of information space that is being constructed in processes of participation of various people in the DigitalEE programs. Processes of real-time information integration ceaselessly increase information available from the 3D virtual nature and attractiveness of the 3D virtual nature.

Conventional digital cities are essentially static information space, which do not dynamically change in real time at participants' requests. Static virtual worlds that never change after creators' construction enable virtual walkthrough in the worlds, but they are not expected to have possibilities beyond creators' intention or expectation even if the virtual worlds look quite realistic. Both continuous reflection of new information in digital cities and visible changes of digital cities are keys to make digital cities more appealing, and it is anticipated that updating digital cities of participants' own free will gives the participants more acute interests in the digital cities. Dynamic changes of 3D virtual nature are expected to generate unexpected human interaction that cannot be encouraged by conventional static digital cities.

5 Conclusions and Future Work

We have introduced digital environmental education: a future style of environmental education in a dynamically changing digital city that is accessible from real and virtual worlds. DigitalEE generates online virtual communication space in which learners, environmental specialists, and practitioners of environmental education can make various discussions on global environmental issues. The system enables environmental education through learners' local activities that are supplemented by diverse environmental information with global viewpoints. DigitalEE also enables environmental education through interactive virtual visits to the natural environment that is dynamically changing in the time transition. Practical and empirical experiences in environmental education are accumulated in 3D virtual nature as common knowledge sources available to the public, and practitioners of environmental education can conduct the education with the accumulated experiences. Our proposal realizes global environmental education that various people in different positions can universally participate in without restriction of time, space, and physical handicaps, and the proposal is vitally important for further activation and improvement of environmental education.

As research on digital cities, this research has proposed a digital city having a unique and unexampled objective. The digital city, i.e., 3D virtual nature, synchronizes with seasonal changes of the real world, and creates an original form of public participation in digital cities: universal participation in a digital city from real and virtual worlds. This research has actively tried to change social activities of people involved in environmental education by using the concepts of digital cities. DigitalEE contributes to equal provision of opportunities of receiving the same education for all people, thus application of the concepts of digital cities to educational areas enhances possibilities of digital cities, and indicates a new direction of digital cities.

As future work, we are supposed to conduct experiments in cooperation with environmental specialists in forest ecology at Kyoto University to verify not only educational effects achieved by interaction between learners and distant environmental specialists but also educational effects achieved with prepared web contents and environmental quizzes. The following will be investigated with tests and questionnaires given after the experiments: changes of closeness to nature, changes of environmental awareness, increase of environmental knowledge, betterment of environmental values, and improvement of attitude on environmental preservation. Detailed procedure for the experiments and targeted experimental subjects are now being examined during preliminary experiments with careful deliberation.

Acknowledgements. The authors would like to express sincere gratitude to Professor Toru Ishida at Department of Social Informatics, Graduate School of Informatics, Kyoto University for his valuable advice. The authors would also like to extend deepest thanks to members of Division of Biosphere Informatics, Department of Social Informatics, Graduate School of Informatics, Kyoto University for their generous cooperation. This research has been partly supported by Core Research for Evolutional Science and Technology of Japan Science and Technology Corporation.

References

1. Ishida, T. and Isbister, K.: Digital Cities: Experiences, Technologies and Future Perspectives, LNCS1765, Springer-Verlag (2000)
2. Okada, M., Tarumi, H., Yoshimura, T., and Moriya, K.: Distributed Virtual Environment Realizing Collaborative Environmental Education, Proceedings of the 16th ACM SAC2001 Symposium, ACM (2001) 83-88
3. Okada, M., Yoshimura, T., Tarumi, H., Moriya, K. and Sakai, T.: DigitalEE: A Support System for Collaborative Environmental Education Using Distributed Virtual Space (Written in Japanese), The Transactions of the Institute of Electronics, Information and Communication Engineers, Vol. J84-D-I, No. 6 (2001) 936-946
4. Oh, S. and Muto, T.: The Effects of Views of Nature and Experience of Nature on One's Environmental Values (Written in Japanese), Environmental Education, Vol. 7, No. 2 (1998) 2–13
5. Bradley, J. C., Waliczek, T. M. and Zajicek, J. M.: Relationship between Environmental Knowledge and Environmental Attitude of High School Students, The Journal of Environmental Education, Vol. 30, No. 3 (1999) 17–21
6. May, T. S.: Elements of Success in Environmental Education through Practitioner Eyes, The Journal of Environmental Education, Vol. 31, No. 3 (2000) 4–11
7. Kouyama, K.: Wisdom Obtained from the British Disease, Reversal of Reality and Fiction (Written in Japanese), PHP INTERFACE (1978) 113-117
8. Mizukoshi, T. and Kihara, T.: Creation of New Environmental Education (Written in Japanese), Minerva Syobou (1995)
9. Taylor, G. L.: Disinger, J. F.: The Potential Role of Virtual Reality in Environmental Education, The Journal of Environmental Education, Vol. 28, No. 3 (1997) 38-43
10. Yamada, A. and Tadokoro, C.: A Survey on Internet Use among Japanese GLOBE Teachers (Written in Japanese). Environmental Education, Vol. 9, No. 2 (1999) 45-50
11. T. Oosawa.: The Present Situation of Garden Trees in Kindergartens and the Problems of Their Practical Use (Written in Japanese). Environmental Education, Vol. 8, No. 2 (1999) 55-63
12. AOL Digital Cities, http://www.digitalcity.com/
13. Digital City Amsterdam, http://www.dds.nl/
14. Virtual Helsinki, http://www.hel.fi/infocities/
15. Digital City Kyoto, http://www.digitalcity.gr.jp/
16. Simmons, D.: Using Natural Settings for Environmental Education: Perceived Benefits and Barriers, The Journal of Environmental Education, Vol. 29, No. 3 (1998) 23–31

A 3-D Photo Collage System for Spatial Navigations

Hiroya Tanaka, Masatoshi Arikawa, and Ryosuke Shibasaki

Center for Spatial Information Science, the University of Tokyo
4-6-1, Komaba, Meguro-ku, Tokyo 153-8904, JAPAN
http://www.csis.u-tokyo.ac.jp/
{tanaka,arikawa,shiba}@csis.u-tokyo.ac.jp

Abstract. This paper proposes a new style tool, a 3-D photo collage system, to manage new style of digital cities. This system allows ordinary people to create, publish, share and navigate pseudo 3-D spaces using perspective photos on the Web. We present a framework of the 3-D photo collage system and characteristics of a prototype system based on it. Finally, some experiments using it are shown.

1 Introduction

Digital cameras have become popular recently. Photos produced by the digital camera are *spatial contents* that mean the data with *spatial keys* [1]. Examples of spatial keys are geographic coordinates, addresses, telephone numbers and zip codes. Most of spatial contents, especially photos, include richer information about spaces or places in the real world (Fig. 1).

Spatial Contents

Real World

Fig. 1. Associations between the real world and spatial contents

Photos are useful materials for creating realistic digital cities on the Web. In fact, most of digital cities have been constructed by using photo-texture mapping on 3-D geometric models. However, their contents are difficult for ordinary people to produce. It is almost impossible for ordinary people to make 3-D geometric models.

M. Tanabe, P. van den Besselaar, T. Ishida (Eds.): Digital Cities, LNCS 2362, pp. 305-316, 2002.
© Springer-Verlag Berlin Heidelberg 2002

There are some *Image-Based Rendering* approaches for creating pseudo 3-D spaces with photos [2]. QuickTime VR[3] is widely used for publishing photo-based pseudo 3-D spaces with particularly panoramic representation. (Fig. 2).

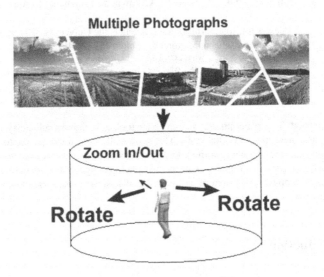

Fig. 2. Functions of QuickTime VR

QuickTime VR tools enable graphic creators to merge photos that were precisely taken and create a rich panoramic scene from one static viewpoint. On the other hand, ordinary people usually do not take panoramic series of photos. Therefore, Quick-Time VR contents are not difficult for experts to produce, but difficult for ordinary people. Regarding control functions of QuickTime VR, it does not cover spatial navigations with multiple photos. For example, it is impossible for users to walk through in QuickTime VR spaces. Furthermore, QuickTime VR does not allow users to add new photos to pseudo 3-D spaces and to extend the spaces incrementally. Except for QuickTime VR, there are few tools for ordinary people to create pseudo 3-D spaces with photos. However, many people want to apply their ordinary perspective photos to publish spatial representations or spatial navigations. It might be useful to associate many photos taken at different places and to create various meaningful routes for navigations.

A new style tool called *Image-Based Non-Rendering (IBNR)* was innovated for constructing pseudo 3-D spaces based on photos taken by digital cameras at low cost [4,5,6]. In IBNR, a photo taken in the real space is used as the background of a Web page, and a picture of a person is pasted on the background picture to serve as an avatar. By scaling and moving the picture of the avatar, IBNR allows users to experience walkthrough in the static background image. By linking such scenes as a hypermedia, users can appreciate a large-scaled pseudo 3-D space on the Web. IBNR also provides more useful functions such as multi-user environment and a script language for describing behaviour of avatars. However, one of the shortcomings of IBNR is that background images are not changed continuously while users walk through in IBNR space. It is often difficult for users to recognize direction and position in a pseudo 3-D space.

Sect. 2 gives an overview of a 3-D photo collage system. Then, we discuss basic mechanisms of creating and navigating pseudo 3-D spaces in Sect. 3 and 4, respectively. Sect. 5 shows the results of experiments with a prototype system. Sect. 6 concludes with some remarks.

2 Overview of a 3-D Photo Collage System STAMP

This paper proposes a new framework of creating digital cities based on a photo collage technique in 3-D spaces. Our basic idea comes from an artistic representation *"photo collage"* on 2-D canvases, that is, a general method of scanning and arranging original photos. It provides a reminder of memorable sights or events in the real world. Photo collage is originally 2-D and static graphic representation, while our proposed representation is pseudo 3-D and interactive one. Our 3-D photo collage system is called STAMP (Spatio-Temporal Associations with Multiple Photographs). STAMP enables users to publish and navigate public pseudo 3-D spaces comprised of multiple photos on the Web. This system makes much use of human's spatial cognition of perspective scenes. Users can create not only intensive panoramic scenes but also extensive 3-D scenes easily to navigate interactively and continuously. 2-D and 3-D geometric models are not adopted for these pseudo 3-D spaces. Users apply only their own photos and make spatial associations with photos by easy operations. A 3-D photo collage space is a kind of hypermedia, because making an association between two different photos is similar to attaching a start anchor and an end anchor to two HTML pages in order to create a hyperlink between them.

STAMP is a new tool for ordinary people to create spatially-linked multimedia contents using photos on the Web. In addition, photos can be easily connected to existing 3-D photo collage spaces made by this tool. STAMP may have the capability of self-organization for digital cities and digital earth. It is different from any conventional methods for creating digital cities.

STAMP is not intended as a mathematical and physical analysis tool, but it may be useful for spatial navigations and spatial presentations on the Web. Users can navigate pseudo 3-D spaces naturally and easily only by selecting one photo among multiple linked photos overlaid on the present focused photo. Users can share or relive their own or others' experiences sequentially. STAMP may be useful for creating and navigating image-based digital cities. Fig. 3 shows basic two components: STAMP-Maker and STAMP-Navigator, for creating and navigating pseudo 3-D spaces.

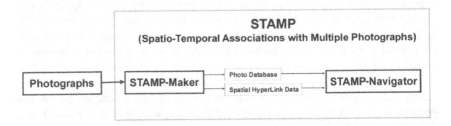

Fig. 3. Two basic components of STAMP: STAMP-Maker and STAMP-Navigator

3 Methods of Creating Pseudo 3-D Spaces

3.1 Basic Associations

This section discusses basic mechanisms of creating pseudo 3-D spaces using STAMP-Maker, one of the components of STAMP. Operations for associating photos are very simple. A user specifies the same feature or area for two photos by drawing one rectangle or polygon on each of the two photos. For example, there is the same tobacco shop on two photos, and a user draws one rectangle enclosing the tobacco shop on each of the two photos (Fig. 4(a)). After drawing two corresponding rectangles on the two photos, the two photos are superposed by matching the corresponding rectangles (Fig. 4(b) and Fig. 5). Specifying two rectangles on two photos means attaching a start anchor and an end anchor for creating spatial hyperlink between two photos. Thus, users can associate any photos even if photos are taken by different people or taken on different days (Fig. 6). Users can also create additional spatial hyperlinks on photos. Therefore, users can create many different routes for spatial navigations (Fig. 7).

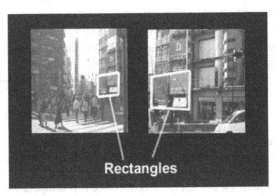

Fig. 4(a). Two corresponding rectangles drawn by users on two photos

Fig. 4(b). Two photos matched by corresponding rectangles

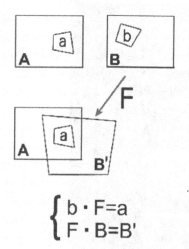

A, B: original shapes of photos

B': a transformed shape of a photo

a, b: rectangles specified by a user

F: transformation matrix

$$\begin{cases} b \cdot F = a \\ F \cdot B = B' \end{cases}$$

Fig. 5. Matching rule for superposing two photos

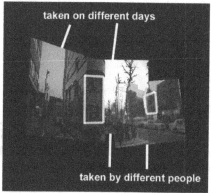

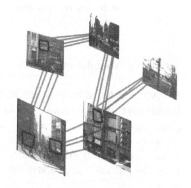

Fig. 6. Pieces of associations between photos taken by different users on different days

Fig. 7. Multiple routes for spatial navigations defined by users

3.2 Manually Reducing Shape Distortions

Sect. 3.1 has described the way of matching two photos manually. However, there is a weak point that some extreme distortions occur in the transformed photos in some cases. The upper photo in Fig. 8 shows one of such examples. To solve this problem, STAMP offers a function for users to reduce distortions of photos by hands. Users can drag and move vertices representing the boundary of the current photo to set a new transformed shape (Fig. 8). Users can adjust photos to new positions that may be the best aesthetically. In the lower photo in Fig. 8, distortions have been reduced.

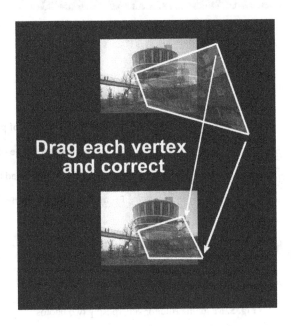

Fig. 8. Interactive adjusting operation for matching vertices to correct shapes

3.3 Adding Metadata to Photos

STAMP enables users to attach metadata to each photo. The metadata of photos are usually text data such as information about a name of a photographer, a name of a place, date and so on. Sound data can also be a kind of metadata of photos. By adding metadata to photos, users are able to publish a pseudo 3-D space as multimedia content. Using STAMP-Maker, users can associate photos and attach metadata. Finally users can publish a large and detailed pseudo 3-D space on the Web.

4 Methods of Navigating Pseudo 3-D Spaces

4.1 Walkthrough

STAMP offers a navigating tool in addition to a creating tool. People can navigate Web-published pseudo 3-D spaces through a simple interface. This navigation system displays one focused photo and several linked photos that are translucent and overlaid on the focused photo (Fig. 9). People can select a next photo from linked photos by direct clicking. The navigation system displays a short animation that represents a smooth movement from one photo to another. It is realized by changing values of transparency for each photo and by deforming photos using affine transformation (Fig. 10). Thus, users can freely step forward, step backward, step sideward, rotate, and zoom in/out in the pseudo 3-D spaces by selecting one from candidate photos. STAMP allows people to experience like walking through the real world.

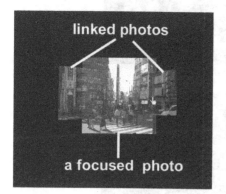

Fig. 9. Navigation interface

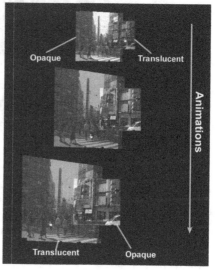

Fig. 10. Walkthrough with animation

4.2 Link-Levels

This navigation interface has a property of "Link-Levels". The navigation interface can display multiple photos in pseudo 3-D spaces. The property "Link-Levels" represents the number of levels from the focused photo. The number of levels means the depth in the graph composed of spatial-links among photos. For example, if a user specifies "3" for "Link-Levels", STAMP displays one focused photo, the first level linked photos, and the second level linked photos that are linked to the first level photos (Fig. 11(a)). STAMP is considered to provide consistent spatial information for small areas, but inconsistent one for wide areas. Therefore, as "Link-Levels" increases, the pseudo 3-D space becomes inaccurate and warped (Fig. 11(b)). However, it will work well for human beings because we have excellent visual perceptions to understand spatial relationships between many distorted and associated photos that are linked indirectly one another.

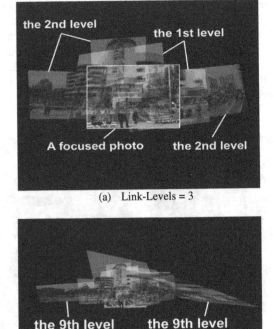

(a) Link-Levels = 3

(b) Link-Levels = 9

Fig. 11. Superposed representation

4.3 Transcoding from Space to Time

In order to make people experience relations between distance and time, STAMP changes the traversing time of one photo to another photo. For instance, we can appreciate the next photo instantly if the position where the next photo was taken is near the current viewpoint in the real world. On the other hand, it takes more time to move to the next photo if the position is far. This constraint makes users feel distance in pseudo 3-D spaces.

STAMP compares areas of two photos which are scaled by matching parts of them. If the difference of the areas is large, the distance between the two positions where the photos were taken may be far. If it is small, the positions may be near. Thus, the area ratio of matched photos is a value concerning *time* to navigate photos. STAMP changes duration of walkthrough animations (Sect. 4.1) depending on the proportion (Fig.12). This function makes user's navigations more realistic in *time*.

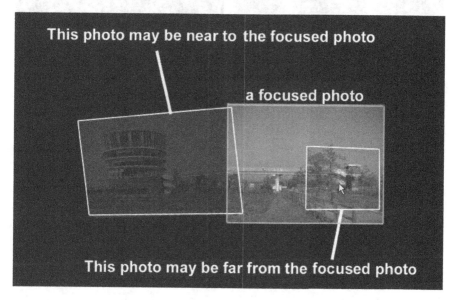

Fig. 12. STAMP changes duration of walkthrough

5 Implementation and Experiment

We have developed a prototype system including STAMP-Maker (Sect. 3) and STAMP-Navigator (Sect. 4) using a scripting language 'LINGO' with a dynamic multimedia contents authoring software 'Macromedia DIRECTOR (©macromedia)'. STAMP-Navigator is a *ShockWave* application that works on most Web browsers.

In order to evaluate our prototype system, we asked three persons to take photos by digital cameras, to use our tools and to create pseudo 3-D spaces. We chose the area around the intersection of Meiji Street and Omotesando Street in Tokyo as our focused area for this experiment. The participants took photos in this area, both outside and inside of buildings. It took only one hour to create one experimental pseudo 3-D space by STAMP (Fig. 13). The number of photos and spatial-links were 52 and 34, respectively in the pseudo 3-D space. We were convinced that STAMP is easy and effective enough for ordinary people to construct pseudo 3-D spaces using digital cameras.

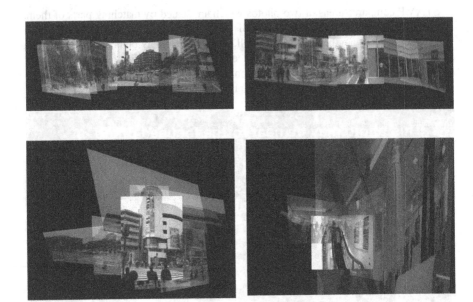

Fig. 13. Several scenes of a pseudo 3-D space created by participants

6 Conclusions

These days many people want to create and publish spatial contents about their own areas and regions on the Web, and therefore easy and useful tools are necessary. STAMP can be expected as a versatile tool for ordinary people to make much use of their photos in a new spatio-temporal style. There are five characteristics of STAMP:

- STAMP-Maker can produce pseudo 3-D spaces from users' own 2-D perspective photos. Users can easily create a large and detailed pseudo 3-D space by associating their photos.

- STAMP-Navigator allows users to move naturally in the pseudo 3-D spaces like 3-D continuous spaces. Users can step forward, step backward, step sideward, rotate, and zoom in/out in the spaces. It is realized by changing values of transparency for each of two photos and by deforming photos using affine transformation.

- The pseudo 3-D spaces are open to public. People can easily add their own photos to the pseudo 3-D spaces created by another person. People can also add new photos to the pseudo 3-D spaces later. As a result, the extent of the 3-D spaces become larger, and the levels of detail of the 3-D spaces increase with the progress of time.

- By attaching more information to photos such as a message, time, location and direction, the pseudo 3-D spaces made by STAMP can become incrementally richer in a semantic sense. Moreover, visitors can add texts and contribute various multimedia contents to the pseudo 3-D spaces, and they can also share these contents in the same way they do in BBS.

- Most of 3-D spaces produced by STAMP have some distortions that may not be neglected in some purposes, especially in physical analysis.

Our future work will focus on the following five points:

- Function of importing, exporting and managing various multimedia files. This function would enable a user to use an extensive pseudo 3-D space as a desktop. *Extended Desktop System* [7] was innovated for managing a desktop with camera images. It was mainly designed to deal with intensive scenes. We will try to develop a new desktop environment which can manage larger and more extensive scenes in the real world.

- Adding a software component for integrating pseudo 3-D spaces with ordinary 2-D geometric maps.

- Transforming pseudo 3-D spaces into sketch maps and cognitive maps. These maps are different from ordinary geometric maps and are more topological and interactive ones.

- Evaluating the accuracy of a pseudo 3-D space and designing the general logical data schema of contents.

- Functions of automatic calibration and photo-matching using image processing technology.

Acknowledgments. We would like to thank Prof. Masahiko Tsukamoto and Mr. Takeshi Sagara for their valuable comments to our research. This work is supported in part by Research for the Future Program of Japan Society for the Promotion of Science under the Project "Researches on Advanced Multimedia Contents Processing (JSPS-RFTF97P00501)."

References

1. Arikawa, M., Sagara, T., Okamura, K.: Spatial Media Fusion Project. Proceedings of 2000 Kyoto Int'l Conf. on Digital Libraries: Research and Practice, Organized by Kyoto University, British Library and National Science Foundation (U.S.A.), Kyoto University, Kyoto, Japan (2000) 75-82
2. Go, J.: Epipolar Geometry in Stereo, Motion and Object Recognition: A Unified Approach. Kluwer Academic Publishers (1996)
3. QuickTime VR: http://www.apple.com/quicktime

4. Tsukamoto, M.: Image Based Pseudo 3-D Visualization of Real Space on WWW. Digital Cities: Technologies, Experiences, and Future Perspectives, Lecture Notes in Computer Science, Springer-Verlag, Vol. 1765 (2000) 288-302
5. Ogawa, T., Tsukamoto, M.: Tools for Constructing Pseudo 3-D Space on the WWW Using Images. New Generation Computing, Vol.18, No. 4 (2000)
6. IBNR (Image Based Non-Rendering): http://www-nishio.ise.eng.osaka-u.ac.jp/IBNR
7. Sakane, Y., Tsukamoto, M., Nishio, S.: The Extended Desktop System for Real World Computing using Camera Images. Proc. of the 2001 Symposium on Applications and the Internet, SAINT-2001, San Diego, California (2001) 195-204

Study on Mobile Passenger Support Systems for Public Transportation Using Multi-channel Data Dissemination

Koichi Goto[1] and Yahiko Kambayashi[2]

[1] Railway Technical Research Institute and Kyoto University, School of Informatics
2-8-38, Hikari-cho, Kokubunji-shi, Tokyo 185-8540 Japan
goto@rtri.or.jp
[2] Kyoto University, School of Informatics
Yoshida-Honmachi, Sakyo-ku, Kyoto 606-8501 Japan
yahiko@i.kyoto-u.ac.jp

Abstract. We have been developing mobile passenger support systems for the public transportation. In this application field, various kinds of data must be handled and integrated. Examples of such data are route information, fare information, area map, station map, planned operation schedule, real-time operation schedule, vehicle facilities and so on. Depending on the user situation, different information should be supplied and personalized. In this paper we propose the human support system used in the multi-channel data dissemination environments. On the other hand, the transportation systems can gather information about situations and demands of users and modify their services for users. In this paper we will discuss efficient methods to handle dynamic integration, personalization and filtering using multiple data dissemination channels and on-demand data channels. Current prototype system developed to be used visually handicapped passengers is also shown.

1 Introduction

The mobile computing technologies are rapidly growing and spreading their application fields [1,2,3]. Especially supporting human activities in the outdoor environment is one of the important applications of mobile computing. The researches on Digital Cities reflect this fact. We have been developing mobile passenger support systems for the public transportation to be used at railway stations and bus stations. Major requirements are as follows. (1) Various kinds of data must be handled and integrated. Examples of such data are route information, fare information, area map, station map, planned operation schedule, real-time operation schedule, vehicle facilities, congestion information etc. Some of them are dynamically changing. (2) Depending on the user situation such as destination, current location, time etc., different information should be supplied. (3) Personalized user interface for handicapped and old people is especially required. (4) There are two kinds of data sources, fixed and moving. We must handle data from moving sources such as trains and buses. The data from the moving sources are temporarily supplied. (5) Although most of user requests are processed by means of integrating transmitted data, on-demand process should be also required. (6) The system must be used in the case of emergency when the system load is expected to be very high.

M. Tanabe, P. van den Besselaar, T. Ishida (Eds.): Digital Cities, LNCS 2362, pp. 317–330, 2002.

Because of the last requirement we will not use a centralized system. Various kinds of data are transmitted to mobile terminals. Integration, personalization and filtering are performed at each terminal. In this paper we will discuss efficient methods to handle dynamic integration, personalization and filtering using multiple data dissemination channels and on-demand data channels. Current prototype system to be used by visually handicapped passengers is also shown.

2   Digital Cities and Public Transportation

One of the important purposes of the research on Digital Cities is to support the activities of people moving in cities [4]. In outdoor fields, people can access Digital Cities corresponding to the real cities and get useful information from the digital world. And the users begin the next activities using that information. In case that the city has a large area, people may utilize some transport facilities. Actually in the central areas of large cities, public transportation systems execute important roles. To support the users of Digital Cities, information about the public transportation systems is indispensable. In this paper we show a new concept of passenger support system for public transportation. When users enter a control area of a public transportation system, such as a railway station, the user can get guide information from the multiple data channels installed in the area. The information is filtered, personalized and integrated according to the personal situations of the user, such as the location, favorite things and physical conditions.

On the other hand, the public transportation systems can get useful information about users using mobile communications, such as numbers of the users, their destinations, future plans etc. The services of the transportation can be changed according to the real-time demands of users. This scheme is not possible in the current operation systems of public transportation. Acquiring the real-time demands of the users is very difficult. The bi-directional relation between users and systems is a very important research theme of Digital Cities. If the transportation systems have abilities to change their services according to the demands, the system can offer more convenient environments for the users. Using the new passenger support system, the information from the users can be gathered by the system. Although services may be adaptively changed according to the user demand, the public transportation systems are not able to offer an individual service for each user. It is difficult to satisfy all the users sufficiently, because the services have tendency to answer to the average requests. So it is very important to inform users of situations of current services and offer useful guide information, such as "what to do next", "how to do that" and "where to go next" to satisfy his/her own demand personally. The objective of our research is to realize such user services.

3   Mobile Passenger Support Systems for Public Transportation

To utilize the public transportation, passengers need various kinds of information. They must know transportation service networks and what kinds of services are offered. Additionally there are many other kinds of information, such as fares, how to buy tickets, station map, operation schedule, vehicle facilities, congestion information etc. The most desirable support method is that a human agent guides the passenger from the origin to the destination of the travel. However providing such services to all the passengers is impossible. Passengers must gather necessary information by themselves and decide their next actions. The left side of Fig. 1 shows this situation.

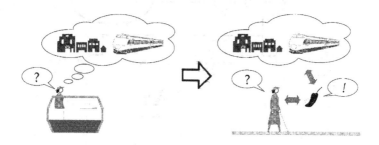

Fig. 1. Current user situation and new user situation

Our solution is to develop a personalized support system using mobile terminals. The mobile terminal should have functions to collect information, make travel plans according to the user's requests, purchase necessary tickets and guide the passenger on the all the way of the travel. Although on-demand communications are suitable for making plans, broadcast communications are necessary for real-time guiding in service fields. The reason is that there are a vast number of passengers in the same area and the system must be used even in the case of emergency when the system load is expected to be very high. So we have adopted the decentralized system in which the mobile terminals act a main role for supporting passengers. In this environment a user can ask a question to the mobile terminal at any time and any place, and he/she can get an appropriate answer from the mobile terminal. The right side of Fig. 1 shows this new situation.

Integration, personalization and filtering are performed at each mobile terminal. Depending on the user situation such as destination, current location, time etc., different data should be supplied and personalized user interface for handicapped and old people is especially required. Although most of user requests are processed by means of integrating disseminated data, on-demand process should be required for purchasing tickets on site or other transaction based requests. It is necessary to provide multiple communication channels, some for data dissemination and others for on-demand processing.

4   System Configuration

The basic system configuration of the proposed passenger support system is shown in Fig. 2. There are basically three components in the system, namely central server, local servers and mobile terminals of users. The mobile terminals can communicate by both on-demand mode (mainly with the central server) and broadcast mode (mainly with local servers and moving data sources).

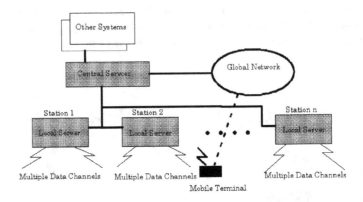

Fig. 2. System Configuration

4.1 Central Server

A passenger can communicate with the central server directly using on-demand channel including Internet. The central server has its own databases containing information about the transportation services such as transportation network, fares, station map, operation schedules etc. The central server is connected to other systems such as seat reservation system for supporting passengers in several aspects. Generally the information given by the central server is not so detailed, but of enough level to make a plan. The detailed information can be given in service fields. The central server also gives the following information concerning local data channels: Types (broadcast or on-demand), frequencies, contents, data organization structures, service locations, timing and conditions, etc.

4.2 Local Servers

Local servers are placed at service fields such as stations. The central server can deliver common information of the transportation system to the users in the fields via local servers. A local server sends these common data to passengers with the following location dependent information using several dissemination channels.

- Detailed station map
- Operation schedules of trains departing from and arriving at the station
- Platforms related to trains
- Real-time operation information
- Information of stores and restaurants
- Other facilities in the station.

4.3 Mobile Terminals

Each passenger has a mobile terminal. There is a software agent having abilities to integrate and personalize information for the passenger in it. The agent can use personal data of the user and the past travel records. The agent supports the user activities using the central server and local servers according to the user's requests and personal data. For handicapped passengers, mobile terminal should have suitable user interface for them. Namely for visually handicapped passengers, mobile terminals should communicate by means of voice.

5   Data Delivery and Personalized Supports to Passengers

The data of local servers are transmitted via wireless channels. There are two types of data sources, one is a fixed data source and another is a moving data source (Fig. 3).

Fig. 3. Image of data sources

5.1   Fixed Data Sources

A fixed data source broadcasts data from a fixed place. If the contents of a channel are geographical data of a station, the transmission area is within the station. If the contents are data about a shop, the transmission area is the neighborhood of the shop and the data are provided during the time when the shop is open. If the contents are the total operation schedule of trains, the transmission area may cover all the regions of the railway. Same radio frequencies are shared by different data sources geographically and timely.

Some channels are used for on-demand information retrieval. By connecting with the central server or local servers, terminals can retrieve information and execute some transaction type processes. The number of channels, however, is smaller than the number of the passengers of the site, so some connection requests may be rejected.

5.2   Moving Data Source

Trains and buses also broadcast data about their operations (time table, stopping station list etc., accommodation and facilities etc.) as moving data sources. Passengers can get accurate information about the train operations. Even if trains of different destinations will come at the same platform, the mobile terminal can receive the data from the current train and tell the user to ride it or not according to the destination of the user. Moreover, if necessary, the mobile terminal can make or remake the schedule of the passenger on site. This function is very useful for visually or aurally handicapped passengers because the guide information is given by visual or voice messages in the public transportation and these passengers cannot use some of them.

5.3 Channel Organization

There is a directory channel in every local area. The mobile terminal can check the channel and know how to get necessary data using data channels. As for the access method to each channel, we can use the results of the researches for channel efficiency and saving of the battery of mobile terminal [5,6,7].

The user may get data of the same attribute from the different sources in different fineness. Generally a user wants to see which station are the starting station and the ending station in the planning phase and need not know the detailed structure of the stations. If the user wants to get details in the planning phase, the central server can search the location of the information and retrieve it. The fineness of data of the same item changes according to the following channels.

– Global information network (Internet level)
– Local area channels (Station level)
– Small area channels (Facilities or utilities level)
– Moving channels (Vehicle level)

5.4 Functions of Mobile Terminal

The functions of mobile terminals are divided into four categories. These are User Interface, Data Management, Communication Control and Machine Control.

1. User Interface
   Functions of this category are for the communication with the user. Though normally the mobile terminal has buttons for input of data or commands and some display for information output. Voice communication method is important because of the restriction of the size of the mobile terminal. As we will show in the discussion of the prototype system, oral communication is especially useful for visually handicapped users. Functions for conversation control and user requests management are necessary for the high level communication with the user.

2. Data Management
   Functions of this category are for data management of the mobile terminal. Various data are stored in the mobile terminal. Personal data are used for personalization of data acquisition and presentation. Some data such as transportation service status, station maps are temporarily stored. Current location data are updated along with the movement of the user. Action schedule is set by the user or generated by the mobile terminal according to the destination indicated by the user.

3. Communication Control
   Functions of this category are for channel communications. The mobile terminal monitors the data channels and stores the status of channels. According to the situations or the requests of the user, the mobile terminal gets data from the adequate data channel. The mobile terminal must have the functions for on-demand communication too. The function for acquisition of location data is included in this category.

4. Machine Control

Functions of this category are for hardware monitoring and control. The monitored components are such as battery, memory space, input / output devices. The alarm message shall be offered to the user if there is an irregular situation in the mobile terminal.

5.5   Procedures for Information Integration and Dynamic Personalization

The integration method of information is a very important issue of the support system. The mobile terminal should present personalized information in a consistent manner in spite of the change of channels and their contents according to the movement of the user and the situation of the transportation services dynamically. As passengers don't want to know the details of the system structure, information must be seen as if it is given from a one large database reflecting the environments. The support procedures in the normal situation and the emergency situation are shown below.

1. Normal Procedure The outline of a supporting procedure in the normal situation of railway is as follows. The user has already made a plan before arriving at the station. The plan is to go to BBB station from AAA station via the route CCC until time DDD.

   a) At the entrance of the AAA station, the mobile terminal checks the directory channel of AAA station.

   b) The mobile terminal gets station map and train operation data from the corresponding channels.

   c) The mobile terminal selects the train to ride for going to BBB station via the route CCC until time DDD.

   d) If necessary, the mobile terminal reserves a seat using on-demand channel. It is possible that the mobile terminal itself works as a ticket.

   e) Using the station map the mobile terminal tells the direction to go to the platform. If the user can use a display, the guide message is shown on the display.

   f) If the user wants to go to other places such as toilets or restaurants. The mobile terminal checks the map and guides the user. During the walk, the mobile terminal can get more detailed information about the route and destination.

   g) After arriving of a train at the platform, the mobile terminal gets the data from the train and checks whether the user should get on it or not.

   h) In the train, the mobile terminal gets the schedule of the train and tells the user if there is an irregular situation or not.

   i) Just before arriving at BBB station, the mobile terminal tells the user to get off.

   j) After getting off the train, the mobile terminal gets the map of BBB station and guides the user to the exit.

2. Emergency Procedure

   In the real environments, services may change according to the accidental events. In an emergency situation, it is necessary to inform all the passengers of the current service status and alternative ways. As there are a huge number of passenger in the same service area and their objectives are different one another, it is impossible to communicate them through on-demand communication network.

Our solution is that the directory channel gives an irregular signal and how to get the details of the current situation (mobile terminals check the channel periodically). Each mobile terminal checks data channels and examines whether it is necessary to change the plan of the user. If it is necessary, the mobile terminal starts to make a new plan. It is possible that a data channel sends software to improve the functions of mobile terminals.

Various kinds of local problems may happen in the public transportation system, so it is impossible to gather all the data into the central system in real time. The central system records the actual behavior of the transportation system including the local irregular events. Important events are also recorded in the mobile terminals. If any adjustment processes are necessary, they shall be executed afterwards according to the records.

6   Data Acquisition from Passengers and Demand-Oriented Services

The data flow is not restricted only the direction from the system to users. When the users enter an area supported by the system, the mobile terminal can communicate with the system and register the existence and demands (destination, desired arrival time etc.) of the user. If the user need execute some specific process, he/she also executes it using the mobile terminal. An example of such a specific process is reservation of train seats. By communicating with the users, the transportation system can get the following information:

- The number of the users existing in the service area
- The distribution of destinations of the users
- The user flows of the transportation network
- The possible users of other facilities in the service area, such as shops in the station
- The existence of users who need specific services, such as physically handicapped people

As for the railway, to change the operation schedules of trains is not easy because resources of cars and crews for trains are restricted and the frequent changes of work schedules may bring confusions. However the small changes are possible. For example the departing period between one train and the next train can be changed. In case that many passengers miss a train if the train keeps on the original departing time, the time should be delayed according to the information about the passenger flow. This kind of on-demand service can be adopted more easily for the operation of buses. Even for the railway, if the automatic operation system is adopted, the train operation re-scheduling can be executed is more easily. In case that the frequency of train operations is high, the train services may be offered as if they were elevators moving horizontally according to user demands.

Even if it is impossible to change the operation of trains, the support system can advise users to avoid the unbalance concentration. Namely the system can tell some of users which car they should choose.

The one of the procedures to acquire the user data and is as follows;

- When a user enters into the some supporting area, the user communicates with the system to register his/her existence in it and tell his/her demands. This process is executed automatically by the mobile terminal.
- The system gives some number (or identifier) to the user to be classified for getting information afterwards. Namely the user belongs to the some groups of which users have the same objectives.
- The user can get information by filtering the broadcast data according to the given group number.

This mechanism can make reduction of communication loads. In the public transportation system, generally destinations of users can be classified into a small number of groups. For example, at a station users can be classified into two groups, one for riding trains bound for Tokyo, and the other for riding trains bound for the reverse side of Tokyo. Trains may be divided into more classes, such as express train and ordinary train and the each group may be divided into more sub-groups. But the number of groups is considered to be not big. The group number has time restriction. If the number of becomes timeout and the user remains in the same area, the user must re-register for getting new group number.

The system can utilize this scheme to control users for improving environmental conditions of the area. For example, to distribute the flow of users in the station, the system can advise some groups to go through one way and for other groups to go through the other way. Of course users have liberty to choose any route. One-to-one communication is not suitable in case that a huge number of users exist in the same area. The system we proposed here is a solution for such an environment.

7   Prototype System for Visually Disabled Passengers

There are many handicapped passengers in transport environments such as disabled people (visually disabled, auditory or physically disabled persons, etc.), aged persons, pregnant women, small children, foreign persons who can not speak Japanese and ordinary people who are not familiar with using transport facilities. The system proposed in this paper is very suitable to support these handicapped passengers and it can make public transportation systems friendly to use. We are now developing a prototype system for visually handicapped passengers as the first target [8]. Fig. 4 shows the basic configuration of the system. To support visually handicapped passengers, we need location data of the accuracy of at least 30cm because there are many dangerous places in the station, such as platforms. We have adopted the technique to embed RF/ID data tags recording location data under guide blocks for blind persons on the station floor (Fig. 5). The mobile terminal can read location data through a cane in which a small reader is installed. The communication distance between the cane and data carriers is about 20 cm. The size of the mobile terminal is 145mm x 80mm x 20mm and the weight is about 240g including battery. Fig. 6 shows a cane and a mobile terminal. The system may use other location system such as GPS additionally.

All operations of the mobile terminal can be done by voice and messages are given by voice too. Every time the mobile terminal gets a location datum from a data carrier, it

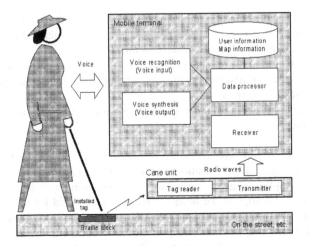

Fig. 4. Configuration of Prototype System

Fig. 5. RF-ID tags embedded under the guide tiles on the station floor

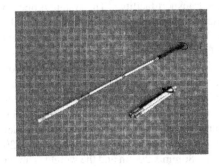 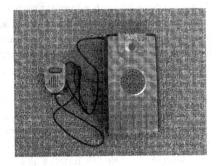

Fig. 6. Prototype mobile system

generates a message about the current situation by mapping the location datum with the station map. If the user misses a message, it is possible to repeat the message by saying 'repeat'. So visually handicapped passengers can know where they are now and which direction they should go by using the mobile terminal. The examples of these messages are as follows.

- At the stairs: Here are downward stairs of 20 steps. - At the concourse: Here is a ticket vending machine in front of you. You are in front of a rest room.
- At the platform: This is the platform No.3 or the platform for XXX-line. This is the Hikari super express No.51.
- In the coach: This is the coach No.5.

It is also possible to make a more adaptive message by setting a destination. The mobile terminal guides the user to the destination by voice. If the user is on the wrong way, the mobile terminal makes an alarm such as "Return to the last informed position and turn to the right". If a passenger is in a dangerous situation (for example, the user is walking on the edge of a platform), the mobile terminal gives a beep sound alarm or vibration alarm of the cane. The scheme of our system can be adapted to other kinds of disabled persons. If the user is a person disabled to move, for example, he/she can get information about equipment to support him/her to move in the station, such as elevators, escalators and slopes through his/her portable computer attached to his/her wheelchairs.

8   Field Test in an Actual Station at Tokyo

The participants in the field test for estimating the system were 10 real visually disabled people. We did not change or control the conditions of the environment of the station, such as train schedules, broadcasting voice messages and passenger flows. However, in the case where there was a dangerous situation such that another passenger may hit the disabled person, we intervened in to guard the disabled person. Before starting an examination, the participants were given the information about the improved points of the new system and used it in the concourse of the station for getting accustomed with the usage of the system.

Fig. 7. Field test in an actual station

Then, we gave them three subjects to:

(a) Walk from a place outside the station to another place which is positioned in front of a train door on a platform (there are steps in the route),

(b) Walk using two kinds of guidance levels which differ in their details of guide messages and compare them, and

(c) Use the function by which the system gives the users the information where they are now.

During their test walks using the system, we took videos with two video cameras, and recorded the guide messages and the reactions of users on notebooks by walking with them. Scenes of the test are shown in Figure 7. By examining the results of the field test, we have confirmed that the functions of the system work effectively in actual stations too.

The considerations about the results of the test are as follows.

1. Move by voice guidance and navigation

   The subject (a) is to walk from a point before ticket vending machines to the point in front of a specific train door on a platform. This route is about 100m long and there are ticket checking gates and descending steps on the way. We have confirmed that the user can arrive at the destination by following the guide messages of the system. The mean time required to the destination is 3 minutes and 58 seconds. The mean speed is 0.57 m/sec when walking in the concourse. We asked the participants who have the mental map of the test area beforehand to walk along the same route in the concourse without using the system. The mean speed in this case is 0.60 m/sec. In the hearing session after the test, they said that the move by the guide of the system is satisfactory. However, examining the video recorded in the test, five of ten participants sometimes went past the turning point one or two steps. We expect that this phenomenon will disappear if they become more familiarized with the usage of the system.

2. Installation of the Braille blocks

   There is an expansion joint — joint position of buildings — in the concourse and it often confused the participants because they misunderstood that it was a line of Braille blocks. The complicated installation of blocks such as those near a toilet entrance perplexed their walks. In order to use this system more effectively, it is required to consider the optimum installation method of the Braille block.

3. Arrangement of radio tags

   The radio tags are embedded in intervals of less than 5 m along the straight line of Braille blocks. On the turning point, in order to guide them quickly, tags are embedded in the blocks adjacent to the turning point. Consequently, it was sometimes observed that detecting the tag at the center of turning point is difficult for the user who has stopped at the turning point. So it is considered that tags should be embedded in the Braille block positioned at the center of the turning point.

4. Size and weight of portable system

   Nine of ten participants desired that a portable terminal would be smaller and lighter. Five participants commented that the cane is heavy. As the current system is a trial product, it is designed with a margin in the size and weight. So many of the participants were not satisfied with the current system contrary to our expected.

5. Guidance level

The system has two guidance levels, the detailed level and the simple level. At the detailed level, the system tells the user the distance to the destination and the distance to the next right- or left-turning point. At the simple level, the system omits the distance information, etc. We asked the participants to compare the two guidance levels considering the user-friendliness. Although the opinion on which level they prefer differs from person to person, most comments can be summarized as "I want to select either of them depending on the situation whether I am familiar with the station or not." Moreover, all participants estimated the function as "it is very good for users to be able to select the guidance level according to their will, like with this system."

6. Human interface

In order to evaluate the human interface of the system, we asked participants to operate the system by themselves. The operations they performed are setting destinations, selection of a guidance level and setup of a voice pitch of messages offered by the system. As a consequence, we have confirmed that even aged participants can use the system without special training. In the hearing session after the test, they answered that the operation by using collar unit is satisfactory. As for the operation by voice, eight persons answered "it is easy," but two persons commented that the performance of voice recognition is poor. In addition, a few persons commented that it is necessary to be able to sense more clearly how it works when he/she operates the small volume dial attached to the portable terminal.

7. Mental stress and resource for attention

In the test at the actual station, noise from the environment, such as announcement, voice of other passengers and noise generated by trains, differs from that of the test field at the institute. In addition, visually disabled persons get more stresses caused by the interference of other passengers and the fear of the fall from a platform, etc. Since visually disabled persons cannot depend on visual information like other passengers, they need to pay attention to the aural information and the contact information from their feet or canes to detect the difference in level or obstacles. We asked the participants about their mental stresses and resource for attention. All of them answered that it is possible to pay attention to the surroundings and sense dangerous points. They also said that they could get information from this system easily even when a train was approaching.

8. Others

The points that many participants estimated as good about the functions are as follows;

a) Although there is a restriction that they must use it only on Braille blocks, they can get the current location whenever they want.

b) The system offers proper information to guide to the train door or stairs even on platforms. Moreover, if he/she misses the route, the system offers a message to correct the route.

c) The system gives the opportunity for them to use various equipment and utilities at large stations effectively as they can receive appropriate information.

A past research, which investigated the difficult tasks when a visually disabled person uses a railway without a care worker, reported the difficult tasks at a railway station are "purchase of tickets," "move to a platform" and "move on a platform." Orientation — knowing the relative position between him/herself and surroundings — is indispensable to the task about moving. The reason why the task about "moving" is considered so difficult is that it is very difficult to get information about "orientation" if they cannot utilize visual information. We think that the participants evaluated the system as (a) and (b) above, because the information about orientation is given by the system easily. As a common opinion, they told that "I want to carry this system and use large stations alone even if I am not familiar with the stations."

9   Concluding Remarks

In this paper we have introduced a new concept of passenger support system for the public transportation system based on information integration and dynamic personalization in multi-channel data dissemination environments. The prototype system for visually handicapped passengers has been presented. There are many research issues to be resolved in future. These are radio communication method for multi-channel data dissemination, data organization of each channel, efficiency and reliability analysis, effective personalization technique, improvement and evaluation of the prototype system, implementation of intelligent software agents, good human interface and cost analysis etc. We will continue to research on these issues for implementing the system in the real world. This work has been supported in part by CREST of JST (Japan Science and Technology Corporation).

References

1. D. Barbara, D.: Mobile Computing and Databases - A Survey. IEEE Transactions on Knowledge and Data Engineering, 11(1) January/February (1999) 108–117
2. Dunham, M., et al.: Mobile Computing and Databases: Anything New? SIGMOD Record, Special Section on Data Management Issues in Mobile Computing, 24(4): December (1995) 5–9
3. Imielinski, T. and Badrinath, B.: Mobile Wireless Computing - Challenge in Data Management. Communications of the ACM, 37(10) (1994) 18–28
4. Ishida T., et al. Digital City Kyoto: Towards A Social Information Infrastructure. International Workshop on Cooperative Information Agents (CIA99), Cooperative Information Agents III, Lecture Note in Artificial Intelligence, Vol. 1652, (1999) 23–35
5. Imielinski, T., Viswanatham, S. and Badrinath, B.: Data on Air: Organization and Access. IEEE Transactions of Knowledge and Data Engineering, 9(3) May/June (1997) 353-372
6. Imielinski, T., Viswanathan, S. and Bardrinath., B.: Power Efficiency Filtering of Data on Air. Proceedings of the International Conference on Extending Database Technology (ETDB) (1994) 245–258
7. Hu, Q., Lee, D. and Lee., W.: Optimal Channel Allocation for Data Dissemination in Mobile Computing Environments. Proceedings of the 18th International Conference on Distributed Computing Systems (ICDCS98) (1998) 480–487
8. Goto, K., Matsubara, H. and Myojo, S.: A Mobile Guide System for Visually Disabled Persons. Proceedings of 4th International Symposium on Autonomous Decentralized Systems (ISADS99) (1999) 12–17

Spatial Information Sharing for Mobile Phones

Hiroshi Tsuji[1], Masato Terada, Yuki Kadowaki, Masaaki Tanizaki,
and Shigeru Shimada

Hitachi, Ltd.
2-4-1 Hamamatsucho, Minato, Tokyo, Japan, 215-0013
tsussy@hkg.odn.ne.jp

Abstract. We presented an environment for spatial information sharing in the previous notes. The basic concept is that contents holders can submit up-to-date information on their under-sheet map and others can view them on their favorite map. In Japan, more than 63 million mobile phones are in use and most of them called KEITAI. Many such phones have internet access capabilities. Then, there are chances to get up-to-date information by KEITAI. This paper describes the concept of the spatial information sharing for mobile phones, and discusses its potential applications.

1 Introduction

We presented the concept of a spatial information sharing environment [1]. Our presentation included a forecast that predicts the following:

(1) Using Internet technology, many consumers will use non-expensive GIS (Geographical Information System) service once a week or once a month. Most of them will accept less precise information because they use the service for fun or merely for convenience's sake, while traditional professional users are projected to make frequent use of the precise and expensive GIS.

(2) Push services (information delivery service) will be the preferred type. A GIS application will provide a route map that will navigate users to their points of interest.

(3) In order to make community, users will exchange information and discuss on mutual topics of interest by using map.

Today mobile phone is not an analog but a digital tool. Mobile phones called KEITAI allow users to exchange mail message and access to Web sites. Most people carry their KEITAI with them whenever they are away from their home. They do not only communicate verbally using the voice mode but also exchange information using digital data.

---

[1] His current address is : Department of Industrial Engineering, Osaka Prefecture University, 1-1 Gakuen-cho, Sakai, Osaka 599-8531, Japan.

M. Tanabe, P. van den Besselaar, T. Ishida (Eds.): Digital Cities, LNCS 2362, pp. 331-342, 2002.
© Springer-Verlag Berlin Heidelberg 2002

Thus, KEITAI has become established in the Internet technology infrastructure as the foremost device for making communities. As described elsewhere [2], community computing is a new and important issue. Because current-generation KEITAI has a small display to see, simple button for inputting, and a few interfaces for peripheral devices, it is good idea to use PC in order to complement the features of their KEITAI. It is reasonable that we use a PC with a large display and keyboard at home or in our office. It is also reasonable that we use PC for lengthy tasks and KEITAI for those tasks that can be accomplished quickly.

In accord with this trend, spatial information will be shared among people by using KEITAI and PC. This paper describes our experience and the perspective of spatial information sharing for digital cities.

2 Requirements for Walking Navigation Using Spatial Information Sharing

We refer to the application of spatial information for use with KEITAI as walking navigation.

2.1 Walking Navigation

Let us first analyze the requirements for spatial information sharing on KEITAI. A KEITAI can be used at home, office, and school, and in a moving motor vehicle. Imagine a user who would like to get both location-oriented and up-to-date information. For example, a user may want to find the location of the nearest bank or that of a shop that offers time sales service on road. Our basic premise is that spatial information sharing on KEITAI allows people to be navigated to a specific location. Let us focus on the walking navigation concept.

The task of navigation of a person requires a KEITAI to know the users current position and their destination. There are alternatives how to identify a user's current position. If KEITAI has GPS (Global Positioning System) feature, it can automatically determine its current position. In the case that KEITAI does not have this positioning feature, the user must indicate directly express to KEITAI his position. The most convenient way to do this is to use the name of the nearest railway or subway station.

There are several different ways for a user to express their destination. The user may specify the name, address, or the phone number of the destination explicitly. To express them implicitly, there should be database which transforms a desire such as "I want to eat" or "I want to enjoy" to the name of destination.

It is not feasible for KEITAI to display a complex map because of the smallness of the screen. We think that route map and route guidance are useful as well as an area map.

Examples of these three kinds of maps are shown in Figure 1. Let us define the three kinds of maps as follows:

1) Area map is the bird's eye view that includes both the current position and the destination,
2) route map shows how to reach the destination from the current position,
3) route guidance shows which cross-section the user makes turn.

Landmark is a map symbol for an object such as a bank and restaurant. In general, a map that includes as many landmarks as possible is useful. However, note that this rule does not apply to KEITAI because of its small screen. Therefore, only landmarks indispensable to walking navigation should be plotted. Note that which landmarks are useful and necessary for the man navigation depends on user's status, current position, and destination.

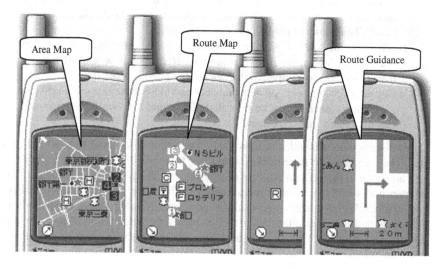

Fig. 1. Man Navigation Map for Mobile Phones.

Note that there are also alternative routes provided. In general, the shortest path is desirable for a user. However, there is an exception; the route should not include steps but slope for those users whose mobility is impaired, such as a handicapped person.

The route guidance should show in which direction the destination is and how to reach it. Sometimes text message or voice messages such as "walk along Midosuji-street to the north and turn right at the second block" supplement what the map provides.

Although the area map, the route map, and the route guidance complement each other for walking navigation, some applications may require the use of one or more of them.

2.2 Contents Layers and Access Control

Let us consider the contents of spatial information sharing. In general, there are layers in spatial information. The basic layer includes information about natural objects such as the topography of the land, the borders of a river, or lake, etc. The next layer includes information about artificial objects such as road, railway, and so on. Public facilities, such as schools and police stations are included in the upper layer. Note that the landmarks for these public facilities are generally included in most maps. For each specific application, we have to abide by guidelines below.

The strategic planner of bank supplies us with comments on their branch propagation. He would like to deliver a unique map for their potential as well as current customers.

(1) There should not be any landmarks for branches of competitor banks on their guidance map for their branch. However, they would like to use the existed landmarks of public facilities if possible.

(2) They would like to grant permission to other companies to use their branches as landmarks if they request so. Rather, they would offer use of their landmarks to companies that are not their competitors.

(3) Day after day, banks open new branches and close those that are inefficient. And some branches may be relocated. Therefore, they would like to maintain map easily and on demand.

Let us discuss other examples of up-to-date information that would be available on a map. The manager of a supermarket would like to deliver the time sales information with area map to the persons who are near his tenant. The person who schedules road maintenance would like to offer the up-to-date information such as location and period. Time sales information and road maintenance information have valid deadline. Then, it is desirable that after valid deadline passes the information disappears from the map automatically. Further, it is also desirable that there is property on author's information [1].

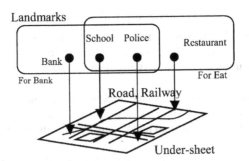

Fig. 2. Under-sheet and Landmarks.

The requirement discussed implies that there should be complex access control for the spatial information layers. This means that a simple geographical information system with landmark maintenance function is insufficient for spatial information sharing in digital cities. This is our prime point.

2.3 Contents Sources for Spatial Information

Next, let us consider how to get and update contents for implementation. Simply considered, the spatial content consists of the followings items that are shown in Figure 2:

(1) an under-sheet map that includes time-invariant geographical shape, roads, bridges and so on,

(2) time-variant landmarks for banks, schools, police and other such facilities.

Table 1 shows alternative ways to get these contents. The related topics are discussed elsewhere [3][4].

Table 1. Alternative for Sources of Spatial Contents.

	Under-sheet	Landmarks	Notes
(1)	GCP²	GCP	Expensive
(2)	GCP	Original	Our Approach
(3)	Original	Original	Time Consuming

If we use both of the above from a geographical contents provider (GCP), our load is reduced. However, in general, contents provided by a GCP are very expensive. Only specific organizations such as police headquarters, the gas and electrical energy providers, and telephone companies have built excellent GIS [5]. Furthermore, GCP does not always continually update their landmarks. In general they update them once a year.

Moreover, contents provided by a GCP are not always useful for KEITAI users because they want to get not only locative information but also up-to-date information. Most information holder would like to provide up-to-date information on their own, such as "today's special" by a restaurant, and "under construction" by a road maintenance company.

On the other hand, if we decide to purchase neither of them, it is a time-consuming task to develop contents. The under-sheet is independent from the applications. It is general-purpose contents.

Based on the analysis, we would use a commercial under-sheet map and outsource its modification if necessary. We decided to adopt the Digital Map 2500 (spatial data

---

² GCP : Geographical Contents Provider

framework: See [6]) developed by "The Geographical Survey Institute". Digital Map 2500 covers most major cities of Japan and encompasses about 70 CD-ROMs.

Digital Map 2500 can be used just for the under-sheet map because there are few time-invariant landmarks. It includes roads in the vector data format and therefore, it can be used for the route search algorithm. However, there are some nuisances, for example, there are no distinctions between the subway and the surface railway.

Then, we need a type of software that allows users to specify landmarks on Digital Map 2500. This software must provide a flexible access control mechanism for the landmarks.

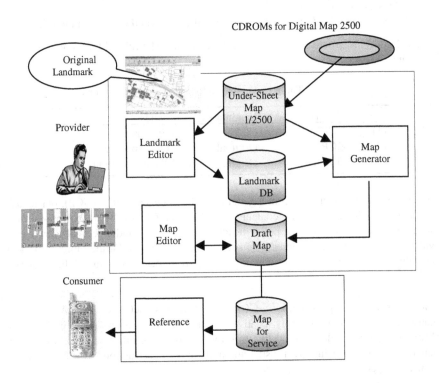

Fig. 3. System Components for Spatial Information Sharing.

3 System Configuration and Functions

This chapter discusses the system configuration and the functions of the presented spatial information sharing system that is shown in Figure 3. As mentioned before, we decided to use the Digital Map 2500 as the under-sheet map. We extract road, railway, and other pertinent information from the CD-ROM version contents and store them in under-sheet map DB. There are functions in our landmark editor that allows users to add, delete, and update landmarks.

Figure 4 shows an example of a landmark editing operation by PC [9]. The landmark has the property that defines name, location, icon, access control, and so on. Access control includes information such as who specifies the landmark, how long it is valid, and which type of category the landmark belongs to. Thus, we should use a database management system that has the function of high-speed spatial indexing [10].

The map generator in Figure 4 makes the area map, the route map, and the route guidance from the under-sheet map and landmarks. Three kinds of map shown in Figure 1 are stored in an image format specified by KEITAI devices.

Under the restriction of screen size and font size for KEITAI, the map generation algorithm tries to insert as many landmarks as possible. The route map generation algorithm uses the shortest path finding method. Route guidance shows the corner on the way to a destination. It is important that there are some significant landmarks at the corner.

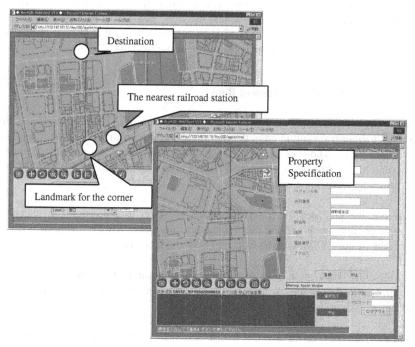

Fig. 4. An Example of Landmark Registration Operation.

There are two alternatives for map generation timing: offline generation and real-time generation. We developed prototypes of both and evaluated them for about two thousands examples. Then, we find that there is room for manual enhancement in a machine-generated map. Furthermore, map generation component consumes computing time. Therefore, we prefer offline generation to real-time generation at this time. Manual enhancement allows operators to not only correct errors but also improve readability.

Which area of the map is appropriate for a user depends on the destination and current position. For KEITAI not equipped with GPS feature, the following is a sample operation flow for the map reference shown in Figure 1:

(1) Select destination,
(2) Select the nearest station,
(3) Select one from area map, route map or route guidance.

4 Applications for Walking Navigation

The target of our research is to share spatial information between PC and KEITAI. The basic idea is that content holders who use a PC put the landmarks on the undersheet map and users who have KEITAI have access to the spatial information. Using three examples, let us consider the applications of the basic idea.

4.1 Guidance for ATM Location of Bank

The purpose of this application is to show the location of ATM. When we are in a business trip, or traveling in an unfamiliar area, we often want to find the location of the nearest ATM. Those persons, who spend the evening drinking and end up missing final train home, thus being compelled to take a taxi home, call their bank's 24-hour call center for the nearest location of an ATM.

Therefore, the guidance to an ATM location is a typical application for our spatial information sharing. When the users inputs s bank name, KEITAI with GPS feature shows the nearest ATM with the map, and business hours of operation.

To realize this application, a bank operator puts landmarks for their ATMs. To save operation time, he often uses the public landmarks that were registered by other companies.

From the viewpoint of the users, it is desirable that the nearest branch they have accounts are shown on KEITAI screen when they express "I would like to deposit money". To implement such a requirement, the service provider will have to aggregate the personal accounts of the users.

4.2 Hotel Reservation and Confirmation

One of the killer business applications for the Internet is hotel reservation. Internet reservation saves brokers margin, is easy to check vacant room and rate, and allows users to post notices commenting on the quality of a hotel's services.

Traditionally, when we reserve a hotel, the hotel gives us a confirmation number, the hotel's telephone number, and directions to the hotel, which we usually write down. However, KEITAI changes our routine.

When we make a hotel reservation, the hotel sends the confirmation mail to our KEITAI. The mail message includes the confirmation number, the telephone number, and URL for the map to hotel. Therefore, those who have KEITAI need not take down any information in writing. The application image is shown in Figure 5.

Fig. 5. Display Image for Hotel Reservation and Confirmation.

The mail message to KEITAI may include the URL for a bulletin board. In such case, it is not load for users to inform the hotel quality for community. Then, information sharing is promoted.

4.3 Push Delivery for One-to-One Marketing

Because KEITAI has an e-mail exchange function and a WEB access function, it is available not only for a PULL type service but also for a PUSH type service. It is possible for the service providers to deliver the information on bargains to persons who are in a specific area, for example, in the Shinjuku shopping district.

For push delivery service, users supply service providers with their profile. Sometimes it is called permission-based marketing. To push the information effectively, the service providers retain records of a user's reaction and distinguish the campaign sensitive persons from others. There should be a user profile that specifies a user's demographics and particular interests. The basic idea can be borrowed from elsewhere [7] .

Thus, a service provider has the chance to announce up-to-date information to previously segmented people, as shown in Figure 6. The bargain sale information should include the location. The sample communication is shown in Figure 7. Note that using KEITAI, the user can be advised easily of information on bargains in their community. Thus, information sharing is also promoted.

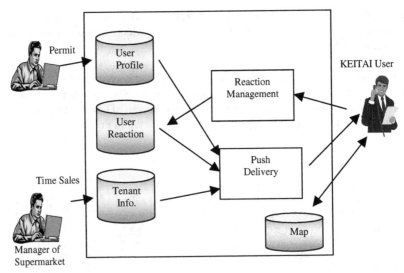

Fig. 6. System components for One-to-One Marketing.

Fig. 7. Display Image for PUSH Information Delivery Service.

5 Experiences

We are authorized to copy and use the Digital Map 2500 provided by The Geographical Survey Institute [8]. We have the database that includes all data published through December of 2000. Currently, database size is 20 GB, and it includes 1.5 million records and 8.8 GB spatial indexes for fast access. The experience is expressed as follows:

(1) The presentation of rivers, railways and streets is important. Subways usually run beneath the surface while most railways run on the surface. Unfortunately, the Digital Map 2500 does not distinguish between two. To solve this problem, we use railway name: if the subway is shown, we regard it should be erased from the map. However, some subways run partially on the surface, while some general railway run below under the street. Therefore, a human operator has to check the map.

(2) Unskilled operator spent 15-30 minutes to register landmarks for a screen size map while a skilled operator spent 10-15 minutes. To reuse the effort for registration, landmark sharing is an important issue.

(3) When we register landmarks, we also specify which street the object for the landmark face. Without this specification, a computer program might miss and navigate the users to the wrong entrance.

(4) The Digital Map 2500 is a general-purpose under-sheet map. It was not developed only for walking navigation. Therefore, it is difficult to find the shortest path in areas where there are a lot of underground facilities. There are cases that needed whether there are crosswalks or not. Thus, for practical use, authorized persons should check the generated the area map, the route map, and the route guidance by performing a walk-around inspection of the area. That means that there are issues for real-time map generation.

(5) The size of a map Gif file for an I-mode terminal is 3 KB. This is reasonable for practical use.

(6) Access statistics will be collected and analyzed in the future. For each application, the Internet business marketers are interested in knowing what kind of people are interested in what kind of landmarks from which web sites. Such marketing information including advertising will have an impact on Internet business strategies.

6 Conclusion

In the previous workshop, we proposed the concept for spatial information sharing. KEITAI promoted the realization of the concept. Our perspective are 1) inexpensive spatial contents are delivered via the Internet, 2) push type contents delivery is useful, 3) the discussion on spatial information will be reactivated.

To verify our concept, we have developed an environment for spatial information sharing where the under-sheet map is the Digital Map 2500 provided by "The Geographical Survey Institute" of Japan. The environment allows PC users to add, delete, and update landmarks on the under-sheet map. The landmarks have a property that includes the access control for spatial information sharing.

We have discussed three kinds of applications that are based on our environment for spatial information sharing. We also described the experience of building applications for spatial information sharing.

Currently, KEITAI promotes communication among a variety of communities. By building applications for spatial information sharing, we would like to regard our environment as the infrastructure of digital cities.

Acknowledgement. The authors would like to express sincere thanks to Mr. Masahiro Sugawara and Dr. Taizo Kinoshita for his useful advice and encouragement.

References

1.   H. Tsuji, et al: Environment for Spatial Information Sharing, in Digital Cities, (Ed. by Toru Ishida and Katherine Isbister), Springer, (2000) 314-325.
2.   Ishida (Ed.)(1999): Community Computing and Support Systems, Springer.
3.   Tokuda, T., K. Tazaki, T. Yamada, H. Mizuno, and S. Kitazawa: On Extraction of WWW Pages with Spatial Information for Mediating their Distribution, Proc. of IEEE/SMC'99. (1999)
4.   Yamada, T., H. Mizuno, and S. Kitazawa, Map-based information mediation on the Web with float coordinate system, Proc. of IEEE/SMC'99. (1999)
5.   Star, J. and J. Estes: Geographic Information Systems, Prentice Hall. (1990)
6.   The Geographical Survey Institute: http://www.gsi-mc.go.jp/
7.   Yamada, T and H. Tsuji: Browsing Local Community "What's New" in Spatial Context, In Proc. of First International Workshop on Practical Information Mediation and Brokering and the Commerce of Information on the Internet (I'MEDIAT'98). (1998)
8.   Hitachi, Ltd.: http://wtc1.e-transformation.hitachi.net/w-navi/
9.   Hitachi Software, Ltd.:
      http://www.hitachi-sk.co.jp/Products/GIS/GEOMATION/pages/top.html
10.   Hitachi, Ltd.: http://www.hitachi.co.jp/Prod/comp/soft1/hirdb/

Agents in the World of Active Web-Services

Bernard Burg

Hewlett-Packard Laboratories, 1501 Page Mill Road, MS 1U-16,
Palo-Alto, CA 94304
Bernard_Burg@hp.com

Abstract. Agents, as well as many other technologies around the semantic web, have shown an increased maturity through standards and open-source. These improvements have been very self-centered and led to the creation of silos. Time has come to integrate these improvements into an ecosystem, bringing a larger picture towards active web-services, that is capable of serving each individual user personally. This article presents these evolutions, positions agents, and introduces the open testbed of this ecosystem currently in construction under the auspices of Agentcities.

1 Introduction

The world of services is evolving towards 'web-services', a simple concept where applications advertise their own capabilities, search for other applications on the web and invoke their services without prior design. These web-services can reason about their capabilities to combine services and negotiate. Although the ideal world of web-services looks far-fetched, this article gathers some of the pieces of technology representing first steps towards this vision, in particular standards and open-source projects. However, due to the complexity of the web-services, there is a flurry of standards and software in competition and deployment becomes a key issue. This article describes an effort in deploying a freely accessible and open experimental environment for global web-services.

In the first section, we describe several pieces of technology fitting into this environment and in particular, the communication stack of the semantic web. In the second section we position agents in this environment and describe their added value in proactively accessing and processing services on our behalf. The third section describes the Agentcities initiative, which aims to deploy globally these environments into a freely open testbed accessible from anywhere. Agentcities is a new generation tool going a step beyond the open source concept by leveraging experience on shared testbeds in a shared environment.

2 Evolution of E-services towards Web-Services

We view web-services and their provision as containing the following key aspects:

2.1 Web-Services

Web-services are flexible, Internet-based applications that allow companies to create new products and services faster than existing methods which consist of dynamic assembly of loosely coupled components (e-services, legacy data...). This is very

M. Tanabe, P. van den Besselaar, T. Ishida (Eds.): Digital Cities, LNCS 2362, pp. 343-356, 2002.

different from the traditional hard-wired approach for developing applications. Fixed applications tend to resist change, whereas web-services assume that change is ever present. Web-services require research in: explicit representations of e-services and their capabilities; their re-use in different contexts to form new and dynamic services; the creation of a heterogeneous and competitive environment; reputation networks, negotiation, contracts …

Some benefits of web-services include faster time-to-market, convergence of disparate e-business initiatives, significant reduction in total cost of ownership, easy-to-use software tailored for business people rather then IT staff.

2.2 Peer-to-Peer Computing

Peer-to-peer computing can be defined as *"sharing of computer resources and services by direct exchange"*. Current popular applications of peer-to-peer computing include distributed file sharing and distributed processing. However, these systems are just examples of what peer-to-peer computing can aspire to. As commercial peer-to-peer systems become developed and deployed, they will address applications such as dynamic integration and coordination of systems residing on arbitrary nodes of a network (ranging from wireless devices to server-class computers) in areas such as enterprise application integration, e-commerce, and network management. Agent-based peer-to-peer applications require research in: a new deployment and execution paradigm of pervasive computing; delegation of tasks and pro-active behavior; high level communication incorporating flexible interaction protocols, ontology and semantic models for communication; a virtual and pro-active representation of the user.

The area of multi-agent systems has addressed and provided answers to these questions for many years. Agents are effectively autonomous entities that coordinate their actions.

2.3 Mobile and Personal

The trend for personal information tools is towards small devices carried in the pocket or worn by users and connected nomadically through a wireless link. User interfaces predicated on browsing capabilities are no longer sufficient. Direct manipulation interfaces, as promoted by HTML and HTTP in their current forms, are not powerful enough to answer advanced user queries, nor do they lend themselves easily to helping build new Internet-based business models. Research is looking into a higher level of personalization and delegation of tasks, in aiming to provide a restricted but pertinent choice of services to the end-user. Awareness of the user's context becomes one of the key elements to the success of these new interfaces. Services based around mobile wireless devices require research in: An explicit representation of the user, their preferences, and other personal information; individually customized services; An explicit representation of the context, including location, task and user goals; A safe repository for the user data.

These three drivers are bringing a new set of requirements for the engineering of the web-services and place a premium on the ability of software components to exhibit a certain degree of autonomous goal-seeking behavior in dealing with the task they have been engineered to perform. The nature of this autonomous goal-seeking behavior has been studied for a long time in the agent technology community, therefore the research in the area of web-services would benefit from leveraging the concepts and models that have been developed in that context. In next section we describe the semantic stack allowing to reason over web-services, the section after focuses on agents, their autonomy and proactive behavior leading towards an active web.

3 The Semantic Layers of Web-Services Communications

3.1 Description

Web-services require more infrastructure to realize all of their potential benefits than their existing static counterparts. There is a clear trend towards an explicit representation of web-services and the addition of semantic communications to the existing syntactic ones. We give below a short description of the extension of communication technologies towards semantics (see Figure 1).

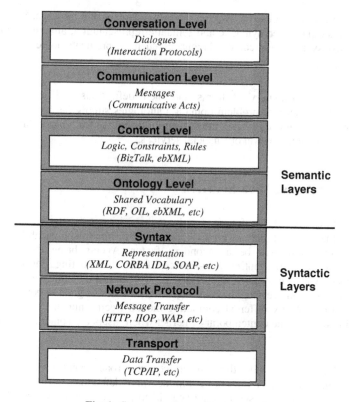

Fig. 1. *Communication technology stack*

3.2 Semantic Layers

Dialogs and Interaction protocols define message interactions between agents at the conversation level, that is, when two or more agents agree to exchange messages using a specific interaction protocol. The interaction protocol shows the messages that each agent can send and receive at each stage of the conversation. Interaction protocols can be simple, such as requesting an agent to complete an action and the agent agreeing or refusing; or complex, such as an auction or a call for proposals;

Communicative acts define standard, application-independent methods for passing semantic messages between agents. A communicative act is a verb-utterance providing context for the contents of a message, for example, request, inform, etc. Communicative acts are application-independent, as opposed to services or actions which are application-dependent and can be reused across a wide range of application environments. Technically, an *Agent Communication Language* (ACL) provides a standard way of representing meta-information that can be associated with a message, such as the sender, receiver, the ontology used to express the message content, etc.;

Content languages are used to express the actual content of a message. Some services may use a simple, fixed syntactic and semantic representation, although a number of agent-based systems use content languages such as predicate logic and constraint choice languages;

Ontology is a vocabulary of terms and their definitions and relations that are applicable in the current problem domain. Ontologies supply the basis of semantics, by describing in a formal system the domain of discourse for a particular application, such as information retrieval or financial services.

4 Towards Active Web-Services

When looking towards the future of web-services, we predict the breakthrough will come in the form of access to services. Added intelligent capabilities through semantic reasoning will be a secondary factor. Agents bring the most crucial capability to turn the entire web-services from the existing dormant mass of information where users need to surf and browse, into a dynamic set of capabilities deployed around and serving the user. Agents represent this great opportunity towards a new and completely different computing model, freeing humans from numbers of chores imposed by the contemporary Internet where users are sometimes enslaved by computers.

In particular, agents will turn the web-services into proactive entities working as peers to serve the end-user, representing him/her and defending his/her interests in a competitive world where services are negotiated and composed dynamically. Agents introduce an unparalleled level of autonomy into future systems so that users can delegate high-level tasks in a generic manner. Therefore Agents need to get: mission statements, the definition of domains of competence, and a definition of autonomy through policies to be applied in these domains. These domains and policies need to support reasoning as they might be overlapped in real life, for example, the policies of multi-national companies have to comply with the policies of the nations in which these companies operate. These domain and policies mechanisms permit deployment and dynamic adaptation to any situation. In particular, they allow web-services to combine without prior design, negotiate end-to-end contracts to insure the final result of composed web-services, and monitor their execution on behalf of the user. Some initial experimentation on automatic generation of contracts show encouraging results towards contractual web-services [Rodrigez98].

Agents will become the trusted intelligent interface between man and machine, allowing communications through speech acts and representing the interest of the user in any web transaction at any time, like a trusted friend or lawyer. Hence agent interfaces need to evolve towards ease of use, ease of delegation and monitoring of tasks, increased privacy, personalization and security, and user habits being acquired through learning. See overview on subject in [Dickinson01]

Agents can now migrate to slim wireless appliances, and evolve in a multitude of micro worlds, typically the cells of wireless phones, malls, schools, a community of friends; and discover the resources and represent their user. This technology needs to be rolled out on a large scale to test the deployment capabilities as well as the usability of the technology in a mass market.

4.1 What Has Fundamentally Changed in Agents since 20 Years?

The key property of agents is to communicate with others, whoever and wherever they are. This communication problem was overlooked in the past as initial agent technology was entrenched in incompatible proprietary technology, where most of the agents were unable to interoperate and were therefore defeating their very purpose of existence. Today the only viable solution is to deploy agents on a global scale.

Progress in Agent Technology

Agents needed a standard allowing them to communicate and interoperate. The FIPA standard was created in 1997 and brings this much needed interoperation model to agents. The next step was to provide freely accessible implementations of standard agent environments to develop a critical mass around the technology, and prepare a market and future deployment. We present in the following, 7 open source implementations operating in various environments running from servers to small appliances; as well as a Java Community Process on Agent Services. The most important step to success becomes then a large-scale deployment of an open freely accessible testbed to share the technology, gather feedback and generate the critical mass of users. This was the initial charter of Agentcities, a global initiative started in Europe and spreading to other countries such as Australia, New Zealand, Japan, Canada and the US, presented in last section.

From an Agent-Centric to an Agent-Integrated World

Now that agents have a foundation for interoperability, are getting deployed, the agent community has to reassess its position with regards to other initiatives, such as UDDI, SOAP, DAML, OIL and the semantic web, each of which is bringing answers to problems initially addressed by the agent community. It is clear that these questions were not specific to agent technology and needed generic solutions of their own. Therefore the agent community needs to evolve from its insular agent-centric vision towards an agent-integrated ecosystem of technologies, embracing all relevant standards into an operational and deployable world. This evolution defines the charter for the Agentcities Task Force, an organization leveraging the efforts of the Agentcities around the world towards this freely accessible ecosystem for experimentation on the future active web-services.

At the end of this section, we will describe an architecture under development at HP Labs targeting all the constraints of these future integrated systems spanning over the complete web-service ecosystem.

4.2 The Agent Standard FIPA [FIPA00]

The Foundation for Intelligent Physical Agents (FIPA) is the leading body in agent standardization. There are currently about 65 member companies, almost equally represented in Asia, Europe and America with a strong representation of telecommunication and software companies.

The FIPA standards follow an open process. FIPA meets quarterly for a one-week period in which Technical Committees and Work Groups develop the specifications. Members are invited to participate as well as anybody who wants to contribute to the technical progress of the work. Anybody can send technical proposals, comments or even submit work-plans to FIPA. In between meetings, the work progresses via email reflectors and sometimes through ad-hoc meetings.

Information on FIPA specifications, proposals, meetings, registrations, activities.... and the standards themselves are accessible from the web-site.

4.3 Open Source Implementations: 1st Generation

Several FIPA platforms have been developed, tested, and are distributed under Open source license (see Table 1). These platforms are running on servers and laptops and are all interoperating according to the FIPA2000 standard. FIPA dedicated a bake-off session in April 2001 to test, promote and facilitate the end-to-end interoperability between these platforms. A list of minor issues were identified and reported back to FIPA where ambiguity and effectiveness might be improved, and a workplan for producing a set of conformance tests was submitted to FIPA. Let us mention that ZEUS is actually more than an agent platform as it is an Agent development environment dedicated to the rapid prototyping of collaborative agent applications. All these platforms are currently interoperating in the Agentcities project.

Table 1. *Open source platforms for servers and laptops*

Company	Agent Platform	URL
BTexact Technologies (UK)	ZEUS	http://www.labs.bt.com/projects/agents/zeus/
Comtec (Jp)	Comtec Agent Platform	http://fipa.comtec.co.jp/glointe.htm
CSELT (It)	JADE	http://sharon.cselt.it/projects/jade
Fujitsu Labs (USA)	AAP	http://www.sourceforge.net/
Nortel Networks (UK)	FIPA-OS	www.nortelnetworks.com/fipa-os

4.4 Open Source Implementations: 2ⁿᵈ Generation

After the success of this first generation of platforms, two evolution paths were pursued towards industrial strength and deployment. The first of them led to the development of platforms for small appliances. Project LEAP[LEAP00] (Lightweight Extensible Agent Platform) started from JADE and redefined its kernel so that it could run on as small profiles as phones or watches (J2ME CLDC MIDP), while remaining scaleable to the complete JADE environment and provides the same API. Project CRUMPET [CRUMPET99] (CReation of User-friendly Mobile services for PErsonal Tourism) started from FIPA-OS and developed the MicroFIPA-OS which is capable of running on PDA profiles (J2ME CDC) using the same API as FIPA-OS. (See Table 2).

Table 2. *Open source platforms for PDA and phones*

Company	Agent Platform	URL
LEAP consortium	LEAP	http://leap.crm-paris.com
CRUMPET consortium	MicroFIPA-OS	http://fipa-os.sourceforge.net/

In parallel to the evolution of the FIPA2000 specification and the platforms, FIPA started an effort towards the design of an Abstract Architecture in 1999 which reached a level of experimental specification in April 2001. The Abstract Architecture focuses on core agent interoperability -- message transport and agent discovery; with a specific intention of allowing the deployment of agent systems in commercial and industrial contexts. Some FIPA members (Fujitsu, Sun, IBM, and HP) led the effort to create the Java Agent Services project, a Sun Java Community Process standard for interoperability amongst Java agents. The reference implementation of this effort should be available in November 2001, and includes in particular conformance tests. For further details see http://www.java-agent.org

4.5 HP's Blueprint for Future Active Web-Services

The key to success of future systems is the ability of hosting an ecosystem of technologies that is capable of evolving with time and of welcoming new bricks of technology into an integrated world, of being deployed in decentralized networks like the internet, or centralized ones like the telecommunications, or in spontaneously created ad-hoc networks. In each case, the management and configuration of these services will change, but the global functional structure remains the same. Figure 2 gives a functional view of future web-services.

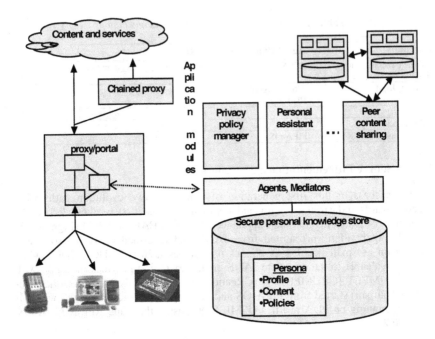

Fig. 2. *Functional view of future web services*

The user accesses web-services through any existing appliance: PDA, phone, laptop, voice mail, or pager and communicates either with proxies and portals (current static manner), or through agents or mediators as part of a middleware transforming the web-services into an active environment. These agents reach both:

- Applications, such as:
  - Privacy policy managers that allow the definition of policies and domains of competence to delegate and monitor high-level tasks;
  - Personal assistants, accessing calendars, agendas, meeting schedulers, presence managers to organize life more efficiently, and balance life between work and leisure;
  - Peer content sharing, organizing, integrating and discovering sources of knowledge, vocabulary and communities;
  - …

- Private information to the user in a secure and trusted environment, allowing a control of access and a selective disclosure of content in a variable manner according to personal policies and profiles. This needs to have the full reasoning capabilities of the semantic web to reason over profiles, interests and skills in a given context.

4.6 HP's Implementation Effort on Active Web-Services Based on Bluestone

The Java™ 2 Platform, Enterprise Edition (J2EE) (http://java.sun.com/j2ee/) defines the standard for developing multitier enterprise applications. Bluestone's Total-e-Server is a J2EE-compliant application server that provides a scaleable and robust solution for application development, deployment, integration and management. Among its components is the Universal Listener Framework (ULF) which supports the ability to accept data in numerous different protocols, process the data, and then communicate with the application server, thereby gaining access to various data and services, typically through Enterprise Java Beans. A Load Balance Broker (LBB) can be interposed as a way to share the load among multiple instances of the application server. (See Figure 3).

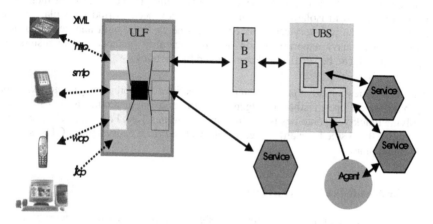

Fig. 3. *Structure of Bluestone*

As a first step, HP implemented agents into Bluestone. In the future we aim to develop a complete web-services environment, including UDDI, DAML, OIL, SOAP, ontologies, location awareness, etc into Bluestone. This leads to the definition of capability sets of future web-servers. This Bluestone environment answers the quest for reusability and evolution of the web-services. However, there is a need for experimentation to determine the configurations and the mode of use of all these components in the future. Agentcities provide the ideal test environment where these integrated capability sets can be used by large numbers of users and web-services.

Current Implementation
At HP Labs, we have started to prototype this environment and are evaluating a new industrial strength multi-agent platform. This platform combines the J2EE-based HP Bluestone with the JADE multi-agent platform. The combination offers unique robustness, scaleability, manageability and flexibility. In addition, the core of the agent platform called LEAP can run in the J2ME MIDP environment, providing a seamless interaction between servers and appliances.

Our application system uses JADE agents to implement personal assistants, team assistants, calendar assistants, room brokers and teleconference bookers. We use Apache, JSP's and Bluestone ULF to provide uniform access to and from multiple appliances and communication modes including browsers, phones, wireless PDA's, speech, email, etc. We have encapsulated a number of existing real world services using Bluestone J2EE or http capabilities: Microsoft Exchange, HPL RoomBooker/ HP reserve, and MeetingPlace teleconference line service.

5 Deployment of Active Web-Services

The technologies for active web-services are blooming. However, most of them have been constructed in isolation of each other and they need to find their place in the ecosystem of the web-services. This ecosystem needs to be built and deployed on a large scale to carry experimentation out in a scientific manner, where results are openly shared, can be verified and commented by anybody.

The Agentcities initiative is a first step into this direction spreading around the globe by building an open testbed for agents. As the ecosystem around agents has been evolving quickly, Agentcities is creating an Agentcities Task Force (ACTF) in aiming to extend the testbed toward the complete web-services ecosystem. ACTF is in its formation phase.

5.1 The Agentcities Project [AC00]

Agentcities is an initiative, originally designed to create a worldwide network of agents that is permanently available 24/7, open to anyone who wants to deploy - agents, applications and services – in an heterogeneous environment.

The Agentcities project aims to create a network where agents that are running on different platforms, owned by different organizations, implemented in different ways and providing diverse services, can interact. Although standards such as DAML+OIL, ebXML, XML, RDF and others are relevant, the basis for this interoperability will be the FIPA standard for software agents [FIPA00].

The nodes in the Agentcities network (see Figure 4) are agent platforms. Agents running on a particular platform are able to connect to other publicly available platforms and communicate directly with their agents. Applications involving agents on multiple different network nodes can be created through the flexible use of this inter-agent communication model and the semantic frameworks, shared ontologies, content languages and interaction protocols that support it.

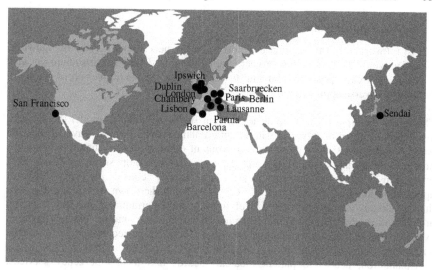

Fig. 4. *Deployed Agentcities Platforms in Agentcities.RTD*

Some nodes in the network will further provide useful services such as directory services (white and yellow pages), ontology services (simple repositories or more complex services for sharing ontology definitions), gateways (to perform translations between, for example, different transport protocols, languages, security domains and the like), testing and bootstrapping (automated systems to test the interoperability of platforms and to enable simple debugging and monitoring).

Towards a Global Network

- Two projects Agentcities.RTD [ACRTD00] and Agentcities.NET [ACNET00] have been funded by the European Commission's 5th Framework IST program (14 and over 50 partners respectively).
- Related project funding proposals have been submitted in Canada (19 partners), France (7 partners), Finland (2 partners) and Hungary (4 partners).
- Projects are planned in Japan (8 partners), the United States (12 partners), Australia, New Zealand and Switzerland.

Figure 4 shows the deployed platforms in Agentcities.RTD, as well as the countries in the process of submitting an Agentcities project, in color. Please consult the website for updated information.

Although these projects each have their own funds and aims (deployment of services, distributed holonic manufacturing, user interface and learning, ontologies, domain and policies, and wireless deployment ...), they are unified in the objective of creating a global interoperability infrastructure based on common standards.

Agentcities Applications

Whilst infrastructure (messaging, directories, etc) is necessary to create the network, the objective of the Agentcities project is not simply to deploy infrastructure but also to create a rich, open environment to explore the semantic-web ecosystem by supporting diverse applications.

The initial example of developing a platform in the network to model the services available in a town or city: tourism, entertainment, events, history, travel (hence the name *Agentcities*) simply provides a convenient domain focus to begin tackling the problems of semantics, ontology and dynamic service composition in manageable proportions. Other Agentcities projects are already considering very different application domains and how to exploit Agentcities in their own way. Interest groups that are already forming include: Travel, tourism and entertainment services, centered around cities and major events; Business services, like market places, payment systems, transactions and catalogue services; Coordination technologies, for media streaming and synchronization; Medical and healthcare services, for organ transplantation, access to patient medical records and local emergency services; Manufacturing and supply chain integration, for coordinating distributed manufacturing processes and supply chain integration; Security services, for analyzing and addressing the security needs of such open, heterogeneous environments; eLearning, for distributed tutoring systems; Personalization of user services to suit individual tastes; and seamless deployment over any kind of network.

5.2 Agentcities Task Force

With the progress of the Agentcities deployment around the world the need of a forum for coordination appeared to leverage efforts in the Agentcities network, and also to generalize it towards the complete ecosystem of web-services. This effort is called Agentcities Task Force (ACTF). It will act in the following capacity:

- Coordination: Facilitate coordination between different projects and activities contributing to and using the Agentcities network.
- Network support: Encourage and support joint resources such as directories, ontology repositories and the like.
- Promotion, dissemination and liaison: Raise awareness of work being carried out in the network to effectively contribute to existing standards bodies and to encourage increased interest, participation and development.

The ACTF will need to act as a coordinating body between different Agentcities projects, and will also have to liaise with relevant standard bodies where the Agentcities community might bring valuable experimental feedback on agent platforms, content representation, ontologies, content manipulation, agent communication and interaction protocols. At the time of writing, the ACTF is still being formed and a consultation process is underway.

6 Conclusion

Different bricks of future web-services are reaching maturity mainly through standard efforts in various domains and open-source implementations. Web-services now need some landscaping to allow each of these initiatives to reassess its position in this new ecosystem.

Agentcities marks a new step in this evolution by deploying and opening a freely accessible testbed at planetary scale. Therefore anybody can participate, share ideas and test them in this environment. The initial scope of Agentcities was to test agent technology. However, as it grows, the scope gets more generic to become, with the ACTF initiative, a testbed for the complete ecosystem of web-service technologies. This is a great opportunity to compare and measure the added value of each technology in several environments, like different types of networks. We believe agents will find their niche in the access to this ecosystem where they provide unique delegation and representation capabilities, so that you do not have to work for the web, but the web works for you.

Thanks

The author would like to thank Hewlett-Packard Laboratories for the support to his group, all members of the Agent Mobility Department and the Bluestone team, in particular Tony Wasserman, for their excellent collaboration. In addition, special mention goes to Steven Willmott (EPFL) and Jonathan Dale (Fujitsu Labs of America) for our joint work on the Agentcities concept, and in particular, for authoring several papers on Agentcities and Agentcities Task Force [AC01], out of which the last section was highly inspired.

References

[AC00]   Agentcities web site http://www.agentcities.org/
[AC01]   *Agentcities: a Worldwide Open Agent Network.* Steven Willmott, Jonathan Dale, Bernard Burg, Patricia Charlton, Paul O'Brien. AgentLink review, in review.
[ACRTD00]   *Agentcities.RTD: Testbed for a Worldwide Agent Network-Research and Deployment.* European Union Project Number IST-2000-28385, 2000. http://www.agentcities.org/EURTD/
[ACNET00]   *Agentcities.NET: Testbed for a Worldwide Agent Network-Take Up Measure: Trial/Testbed.* European Union Project Number IST-2000-28386, 2000. http://www.agentcities.org/EUNET/
[ACTF01]   *Agentcities Task Force Proposal*, Willmott, S., Dale, J., Burg, B., Charlton, P and O'Brien, P., 2001. http://www.agentcities.org/
[CRUMPET99] *The Creation of User-Friendly Mobile Services Personalised for Tourism.* European Union Project Number IST 1999-20147, 1999.
[Dickinson01] The Interface as agent: a comparative review of human-agent interaction. In review.

[FIPA00]   *The FIPA Standard for Interoperating Software Agents.* The Foundation for Intelligent Physical Agents, 2000.
`http://www.fipa.org/`

[LEAP00]   *Lightweight Extensible Agent Platform.* European Union Project Number IST-1999-10211, 2000. `http://leap.crm-paris.com/`

[Rodrigez98]   *A system for document telenegotiation (negotiator agents).* Rodrigez J.M and J. Sallantin.   COOP'98: 3rd International Conference on the Design of Cooperative Systems, Cannes, France, May 26-29, 1998, pp. 61-66.

Town Digitizing for Building an Image-Based Cyber Space

Satoshi Koizumi[1], Guiming Dai[2], and Hiroshi Ishiguro[2]

[1] CREST, Japan Science and Technology Corporation
[2] Wakayama University
Sakaedani 930, Wakayama 640-8510, Japan

Abstract. This paper proposes a town digitizing for building an image-based cyber space. The cyber space consists of omnidirectional cameras and a large number of omnidirectional images connecting them. We discuss on details of the town digitizing technique and possibilities of the cyber space in this paper. The technique is divided into three steps: omnidirectional image acquisition, parameter estimation among omnidirectional images, and smooth interpolation among them. The omnidirectional images are taken using the powerwheel or the tripod with the omnidirectional camera. Then the parameters among omnidirectional images are estimated by Hough transform and template matching. Based on the estimated parameters, the system smoothly interpolates the omnidirectional images and generates continuous virtual views. That is, the system allows users to move in the virtual space like a previous 3-D graphics system. This paper also shows the validity of the town digitizing by building a model of Kyoto city.

1 Introduction

One of the important issue of a virtual space is the quality of the views. Better quality of the views brings better reality to the virtual space. Almost all of previous works build the virtual space based on 3-D geometrical models of the environment. Therefore, it takes costs for measuring the environment and building the 3-D models [2]. For example, it takes a couple of years to build a city model. In addition to the cost for building 3-D models, the previous works [1,3, 4] need to render images to the 3-D models in order to obtain the photo-quality views. That is, they take three steps: measuring the environmental structure, acquiring 3-D CAD models and rendering photos taken in the real world.

On the other hand, this paper proposes a new image-based method to build a virtual space. Our technique, called town digitizing, uses an omnidirectional camera developed by [7]. By taking omnidirectional images in the real world with the camera, we get visual information that is sufficient for building the virtual space. The omnidirectional images are smoothly interpolated and generate view sequences for exploring in the virtual space. Figure 1 shows a comparison between the 3-D model-based method and the omnidirectional image-based method.

A demerit of the image-based method is the high memory cost. However, recent progress of computer hardware provides us sufficient capacity in the hard

M. Tanabe, P. van den Besselaar, T. Ishida (Eds.): Digital Cities, LNCS 2362, pp. 357–370, 2002.
© Springer-Verlag Berlin Heidelberg 2002

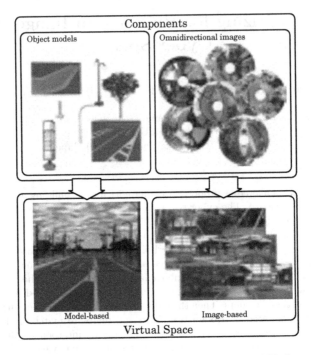

Fig. 1. 3-D model-based V. S. and Image-based V. S.

drive and onboard memory. We consider the image-based method will be one of the solutions for building the virtual space.

The town digitizing technique allows us to build a photo-realistic city model quickly. It consists of the following three steps.

(1) Image data acquisition with an omnidirectional camera
(2) Parameter estimation among the omnidirectional images
(3) Virtual view generation by smoothly interpreting the images based on the estimated parameters.

Especially, the parameter estimation is important in this technique. This paper proposes automatic methods using visual properties of omnidirectional images. In addition to the town digitizing technique, we have built a Kyoto city model by the technique. This paper shows the impressive experimental results in Kyoto city.

2   Image-Based Cyber Space

A town digitizing technology is an important fundamental one that influences the reality of a virtual space. The conventional method to build town models needs much computational power to measure the geometry. On the other hand, the digital image with high resolution can provide rich information which enables us to feel the reality of objects in the environment. Based on the digital images, we build a virtual space. Figure 2 shows the conceptual design of the virtual space. This virtual space has connections to the real world by the omnidirectional cameras. Our purpose is to build a platform that connects networked-virtual worlds and the real worlds. Therefore, we call it "cyber space platform".

The platform consists of three components. The first one is a digital omnidirectional image. The image is able to get the environmental information around of a place where the image is taken. In Figure 2, the omnidirectional image represents as a black sphere. The next component is a technique to connect two omnidirectional images that are taken in an interval. This technique smoothly interpolates them and generate white pipe between black spheres in Figure 2. Finally, the third component is an omnidirectional camera to acquire the real-time information. The camera links to the real world and it is represents as the blue sphere in Figure 2. We call the camera Town Camera.

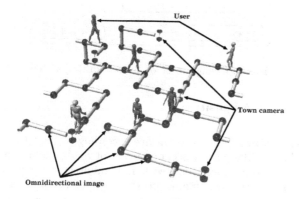

Fig. 2. Conceptual figure for the cyber space

3   Town Digitizing Technique

The town digitizing technique needs several software components. Figure 3 shows the configuration of a software system for the town digitizing. The system is divided into three parts: omnidirectional image acquisition, parameter estimation among omnidirectional images, and smooth interpolation among them. An important thing when we take the image is to acquire them with the same quality. To maintain the same conditions for taking an omnidirectional image, we have developed two input devices, a powerwheel-type device and a tripod-type device. The next thing that we need to do is to interpolate among omnidirectional images. For this purpose, we estimate the parameters among them by using Hough transform and template matching. By smoothly interpolating among them based on the parameters, users can move in the virtual space like a previous 3-D graphics system. This section describes the detail of the system.

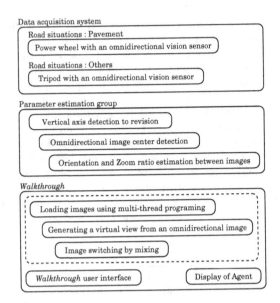

Data acquisition system
Road situations : Pavement
Power wheel with an omnidirectional vision sensor
Road situations : Others
Tripod with an omnidirectional vision sensor

Parameter estimation group
Vertical axis detection to revision
Omnidirectional image center detection
Orientation and Zoom ratio estimation between images

Walkthrough
Loading images using multi-thread programing
Generating a virtual view from an omnidirectional image
Image switching by mixing

Walkthrough user interface   Display of Agent

Fig. 3. Configuration of Town digitizing system

3.1   Image Data Acquisition

We have prepared two types of the device according to the situations as shown in Figure 4. We use the powerwheel on pavement roads and a tripod for others. The powerwheel has a 2-meter pole with an omnidirectional camera on the top. Figure 5 shows the attached omnidirectional camera. The user can take omnidirectional images with a cable release while sitting on the powerwheel. Further, by using a notebook computer, the user can always verify whether omnidirectional images keep the same quality. If it is difficult to use the powerwheel, the user uses the tripod.

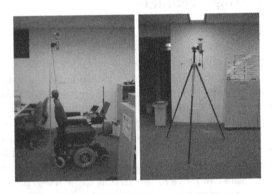

Fig. 4. Image acquisition device of the powerwheel and the tripod type

Fig. 5. Attached omnidirectional camera

3.2   Parameter Estimation

For building an image-based virtual space using omnidirectional images, the following six parameters are necessary.

- Parameters depending on an omnidirectional image.
    1. Tilting angle of the vertical axis of the omnidirectional camera.
    2. Position of the center point of the omnidirectional camera on the image.
- Parameters between two omnidirectional images.
    1. Direction between the observation points.
    2. Angle of elevation between the observation points.
    3. Zoom ratio which is in proportion to the distance.

The parameters depending on an omnidirectional image are necessary for generating virtual views from the omnidirectional image and for smoothly interpolating among them. The generated virtual view is distorted if these parameters are not precisely estimated. In the following sections, we introduce automatic methods for the parameter estimation based on visual properties of omnidirectional images.

Parameters depending on an omnidirectional image. The algorithm[8,9] transforming an omnidirectional image into a rectilinear images are sensitive to the tilt angle of the rotation axis of the omnidirectional camera and the position of the projection on the image plane. To decrease the distortion of the virtual view, the proposed system automatically estimates them.

The automatic method is divided to three steps: edge detection by Sobel filter, line-segment detection by Hough transform, and estimation of an intersection of the detected lines. First of all, we extract the omnidirectional edge-image by using Sobel filter. By discriminant analysis of the histogram of the edge image, the omnidirectional binary edge image is obtained. The source image and the binary image are shown in Figure 6-(a) and -(b), respectively. The reasons why we pay attention to the edge image are: vertical components of the object, like a pillar, around the omnidirectional camera represent the direction of the

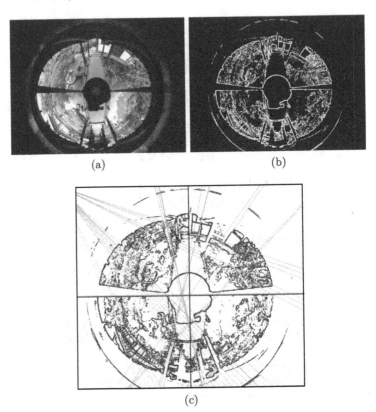

(a)

(b)

(c)

Fig. 6. (a): Omnidirectional source image, (b): omnidirectional binary edge image, and (c): detected lines by using conventional Hough transform

gravity in almost all environments, and their projection radiate from the center of the omnidirectional image. If the rotation axis is tilted, the center of those radial edges is shifted.

Here, we detect those radial edges as lines by conventional Hough transform. Figure 6-(c) shows the result of the detection for the binary edge image (Figure 6-(b)). We transform a pixel on the detected lines with Gaussian Distribution into the parameter space. By computing the summation of the pixel value, we obtain the intersection of them. That is, the position of the pixel that has the maximum pixel value represents the tilt angle of the rotation center.

Since the shape of the projections of the black needle and the hyperboloidal mirror of the omnidirectional camera is circle on the omnidirectional image, the center point at the omnidirectional image estimates by extracting their positions. Using generalized Hough transform for the omnidirectional binary edge image, we detect those circles. Figure 7 shows the parameter space of generalized Hough transform, where the parameters are the position of the center. In the image, the point of the pixel which has the maximum value is the position of the center point

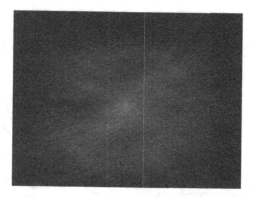

Fig. 7. Detected center point at the omnidirectional image by generalized Hough transform

on the omnidirectional image. Based on these estimated parameters, the system revises the omnidirectional image by geometric operations. As the result, the system can generate virtual views without distortion from the omnidirectional image.

Parameters between two omnidirectional images. Parameters between two omnidirectional images are also important in the smooth interpolation of them. There are three parameters: direction, angle of elevation, and zoom ratio. Figure 8 shows the geometrical relationship between two omnidirectional images. $X_iY_iZ_i$ and $X_jY_jZ_j$ -coordinates mean the coordinate in the omnidirectional camera at the each observation point (i-th place and j-th place) where a user takes i and j -th image. $Z_i(Z_j)$ is on the optical axis of the omnidirectional camera. θ_{ij} and ϕ_{ij} show the direction and the angle of elevation between the i-th point to the j-th point. Another parameter, the zoom ratio, depends on the view angle ψ_{ij}. Assuming that a distance from the focal point in the hyperboloidal mirror to the projection window and the pixel size of the projection window are constant, we can compute the zoom ratio R_{ij} as,

$$R_{ij} = \frac{1}{\tan \psi_{ij}} \tan \frac{\psi_0}{2} \qquad (1)$$

where ψ_0 is an initial view angle, i.e. the zoom ratio is 1.

In Figure 8, there is only one straight line which links a focal point C_i at the i-th point to a focal point C_j at the j-th point. Both of omnidirectional images always take same scene which is on the straight line. Then the view projected by the window $A_i(B_i)$ and the view projected by the window $A_j(B_j)$ take the same scene roughly, where the angle between A_i and B_i is 180 degree. However, the size of the object in the view is different because of the distant observation points each other. By adjusting the zoom ratio, their size can be adjusted.

Based on the constraint, the proposed system computes cross-correlation between the projection window A_i and A_j and between B_i and B_j. By detecting

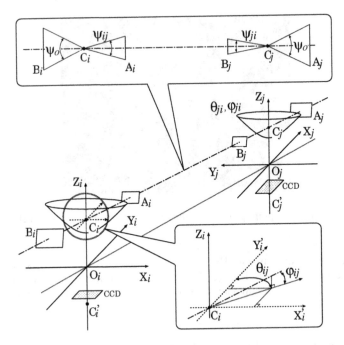

Fig. 8. Relationship between two omnidirectional images (vision sensors)

the maximum value of the cross-correlation, the system can estimate the parameters.

Figure 9 shows the system window of the software for automatic parameter estimation. This software displays four views by window A_i, B_i, A_j, and B_j with the estimated parameters. We can check the result of the estimation from these views.

3.3   Smooth Interpolation

To allow users to move in the image-based virtual space, the system displays virtual view sequences interpolated smoothly. We have developed a viewer system that users can operate simply and understand their positions in the virtual space. The viewer system consists of three routines (shown in Figure 3). The first routine generates virtual views. The second one is the user interface to explore the virtual space. The third one displays the agent as the user to show the user's position in the virtual space.

The first routine is divided into three processes: the image loading process by using multi-thread programming, the virtual view generation process, and the mixing process to switch images. The resolution of an omnidirectional image is low around the image center. Therefore, a high-resolution camera is needed. However, according to the resolution of image, the data size becomes larger and the cost for loading is higher. The multi-thread programming solves this problem.

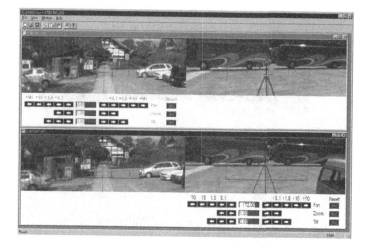

Fig. 9. System window of the software for parameters estimation

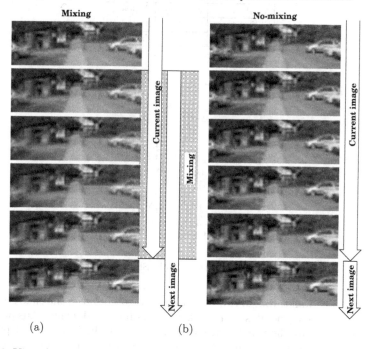

(a)   (b)

Fig. 10. Virtual view sequence with the mixing process and without the mixing process

The second process generates virtual view sequences by increasing the zoom ratio. By increasing the zoom ratio, the system can allow users to move in the virtual space like a previous 3-D graphics system. Figure 10-(a) shows a generated virtual view sequence, as an example. We can find that it is sufficient

Fig. 11. System window of Walkthrough

Table 1. Number of images and mileage

Area	# Images	Mileage
Shijou-town	8,611	16.21[km]
Arashi-yama	1,785	5.41[km]

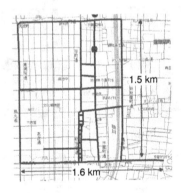

Fig. 12. Routes on the map in Shijou-town area

for realizing the walkthrough. However, there is a gap between the enlarged view and the view which generates from the next omnidirectional image. This problem cannot be solved by the simple switching. To decrease the gap, the last process in the first routine mixes two virtual views. Figure 10 shows the comparison of the simple switching and the mixing. By using this mixing process, we can decrease the gap as shown in the figure.

In order to realize the exploration in the virtual space by the users, we have divided all of omnidirectional images into sets of four/five neighbor images. The set represents a short route. At the end of the short route, it is connected to other routes and the users can choose a direction for the exploration. As an user

Fig. 13. Example of a virtual view sequence in Shijou-town area

interface, the second routine has a dialog-based controller. The users can choose the direction of the movement in the eight directions by using this controller. The walkthrough window is shown in Figure 11. The controller is at the upper-right in Figure 11.

The system displays a birdview map in the lower region of the system window. The last routine displays an icon as a user on the map. The system can compute

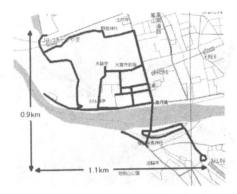

Fig. 14. Routes on the map in Arashi-yama area

the user's position from the utilized omnidirectional image and the zoom ratio. On the map, the direction of the view is represented as an arrow.

4   Virtual City Models

To verify the town digitizing techniques, we have built virtual spaces of Kyoto city, which is a historical city in Japan. As experimental environments, we have selected two areas in Kyoto, Shijou area and Arashi-yama area. Shijou-town is a downtown where the traffic is always heavy. Arashi-yama area which is a scenic spot is a complex environment that includes many natural objects like trees. Figure 12 and Figure 14 show all of routes where we have taken the omnidirectional images in Shijou-town area and Arashi-yama area, respectively. Table 1 lists the number of image and the mileage in each area. An example of view sequence that is generated by the proposed technologies for each area is shown in Figure 13 and Figure 15, respectively.

In this experimentation, we have found the following problem. The problem is that a gap when switching images occurs in the situation where the surrounding objects are anti-symmetry along the route, for example, a sidewalk between a building and a large road. The mixing process decreases the gap, but it still remains. To solve this problem, we need to take omnidirectional images with a shorter interval. However, in other situations, we could confirm that the mixing process shows a sufficient effect. In the case of the natural environment, it is possible to handle them. In the case of the previous 3-D graphics system, representation of the complicated surface is difficult. However, the proposed method works better since it is image-based method.

There are similar works to ours. In Movie-Map system [5], the user can walk along the virtual street based on images that have been captured before. However, the user can view the images only from the original viewpoint of the camera. Another similar system based on the image-based rendering is "QuickTime VR" [6]. In the system, users can look around a scene from fixed points. This system, however, does not allow users to walk around in the virtual space. The proposed method allows the user to view from the arbitrary viewpoint of the camera and

Fig. 15. Example of a virtual view sequence in Arashi-yama area

to walk along the street in the virtual space. That is, we can consider that the proposed method will be a general modeling method for the real world.

In the section 2, we have proposed a concept of cyber space. We believe the cyber space realized by the town digitizing technique and the town cameras will be a next-generation information infrastructure that connects between the computer network and the real world.

References

1. R. Raskar, G. Welch, M. Cutts, A. Lake, L. Stesin, and H. Fuchs, The Office of the Future: A Unified Approach to Image-Based Modeling and Spatially Immersive Displays, *SIGGRAPH '98*, 1998
2. H. Gouraud, Continuous shading of curved surfaces, *IEEE Trans. on Computers*, vol. 20, pp. 623-628, 1971
3. S. B. Kang and R. Szeliski, 3-D scene data recovery using omnidirectional multibaseline stereo, *Proc. Computational Vision and Pattern Recognition Conf.*, pp. 364-370, 1996
4. T. Takahashi, H. Kawasaki, K. Ikeuchi, and M. Sakauchi, Arbitrary view position and direction rendering for large-scale scenes, *Proc. Computational Vision and Pattern Recognition Conf.*, pp. 296-303, 2000
5. A. Lippman, Movie-Maps. An application of the optical videodisc to computer graphics, *SIGGRAPH '90*, pp. 32-43, 1990
6. S. E. Chen, QuickTime VR - An image-based approach to virtual environment navigation, *SIGGRAPH '95*, pp. 29-38, 1995
7. H. Ishiguro, Development of low-cost and compact omnidirectional vision sensors and their applications, *Proc. Int. Conf. Information systems, analysis and synthesis*, pp. 433-439, 1998
8. K. Yamazawa, Y. Yagi, and M. Yachida, Omnidirectional imaging with hyperboloidal projection, *Proc. Int. Conf. Robots and Systems*, 1993
9. Y. Onoe, K. Yamazawa, H. Takemura, and N. Yokoya, Telepresence by real-time view-dependent image genreration from omnidirectional video streams, *Computer Vision and Image Understanding*, Vol. 71, No. 2, pp 154-165, 1998

Language Design for Rescue Agents

Itsuki Noda[1,2], Tomoichi Takahashi[3], Shuji Morita[4], Tetsuhiko Koto[5], and
Satoshi Tadokoro[6]

[1] CARC, AIST
[2] PREST, JST
[3] Chubu Univ.
[4] Kobe Univ.
[5] Univ. of Electro-Communications
[6] Kobe Univ.

Abstract. We are proposing a model of communication and a specification of a language for civilian agents in RoboCup Rescue Simulation System.

Robust information systems are critical infrastructures for rescue activities in huge disasters. In order to simulate (and evaluate) a certain rescue information system, we need to design abstract model of agents' communication, which is an important factor to affect the performance of the rescue activities. Especially communication among civilians, who are the majority in damaged area, will be the primary information source for rescue agents.

In order to build the abstract model, we design "four layers model of communication", which consists of knowledge, attention, device, and transmission layers. Using the model, we can discuss and implement uncertainty and effectiveness of various communication method including mobile phones, broadcasts, blackboards and so on.

Then, we design specification languages for civilian agents behave in the simulated disaster world, which can reflect natural language features like uncertainty and lack of words.

Keywords: Location-based, Multi-Agent, Rescue, Communication, Distributed Simulation

1 Introduction

Huge disasters and rescue activities in them are so complex systems that it is difficult to predict damages and to make a plan for the rescue. Especially, there are few efficient methods to analyze effects of human activities. As [1] pointed out, *simulation* is a key method to analyze such kind of complex systems in which intelligent agents like human act. Rescue simulation is also required from the social viewpoint as follows:

- The simulation can be used to evaluate city and rescue planning.
- The simulation will be effective for training rescue teams, especially central commanders.

M. Tanabe, P. van den Besselaar, T. Ishida (Eds.): Digital Cities, LNCS 2362, pp. 371–383, 2002.
© Springer-Verlag Berlin Heidelberg 2002

- The simulation will be utilized for real-time damage estimation and rescue planning.

Because the huge disasters and rescue activities include very wide phenomena, the simulation requires huge computation power. Fortunately, as mentioned by [1], we can get such huge computation power by distributed simulations over computer networks. In addition to it, distributed simulation have advantages in the following three aspects:

- The system should have a capability to extend parallelism over distributed computers, so that it can simulate as wide area as necessary. Because huge disasters like earthquake are open phenomena, it is better to simulate as wide area as possible. Parallel simulations of segmented area over distributed computers will be an effective solution for the problem.
- The system needs to accept plug-in sub-simulation modules. Huge disasters includes various phenomena, each of which needs a special model and a theory for the simulation. It is difficult to develop an unified model to handle the whole phenomena. Therefore, the simulation system should have a capability to plug modules in it to extend domains incrementally. This also helps an incremental and open-sourced development style.
- The system needs to handle agents' activities. Especially, communication between agents is important, because the communication is a key factor for agents to decide their behavior. A main problem on the simulation of communication is that it is still hard to develop a concrete model of the communication.

Based on these aspects, we have been designing a simulator system of huge disasters with rescue activities. The rest of this article, we show a brief plan for the system design of the distributed simulation system in Section 2, and propose a framework for agent simulation module for it in Section 3.

2   Distributed Rescue Simulation System

2.1   Overview

Purposes of the design of our rescue simulation system are:

- To provide a facility to plug-in simulation modules each of which is an expert to handle a certain phenomena like fire, traffic or building collapse.
- To provide a facility to execute simulation in parallel for each sub-region of a damaged area.
- To provide a standard set of simulation modules that enable for researchers to investigate and improve the simulation of a certain phenomenon in huge disasters.
- To provide a way to show a result and a process of the simulation and to interrupt the simulation in real time.

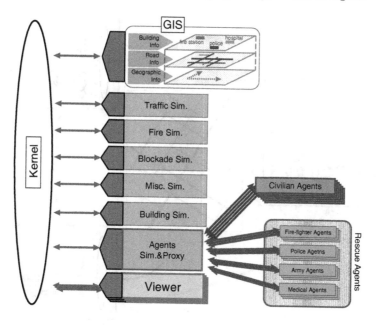

Fig. 1. Rescue Simulation System

- To provide a framework to introduce intelligent agents easily into the simulation.

For this purpose, we, RoboCup Rescue Project Team, have been designing a distributed rescue simulation system as shown in Figure 1. The system consists four parts:

- kernel and basic libraries
- expert simulation modules
- human interface modules
- agent simulation modules

2.2 Kernel and Basic Libraries

In the case to develop a total simulation system for disaster and rescue, the system should have a capability to integrate expert simulation systems for various fields. In addition to it, the system should be able to simulate divided areas in parallel and integrate the results. For this purpose, we are designing a kernel and basic libraries for distributed simulation system, which provides the following facilities:

- to synchronize distributed modules:
  The synchronization mechanism is a key in the distributed simulation system. Especially, the mechanism must be able to handle various dependency

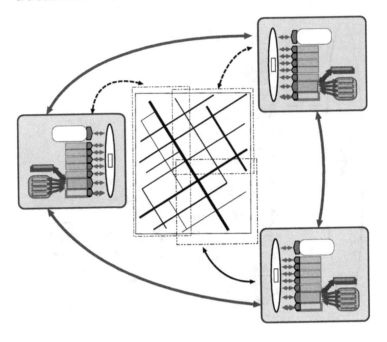

Fig. 2. Parallel Simulation with Overlapping

among modules in a flexible way. In order to do this, we use tree representation of logical orders of execution [8] and waiting mechanism based on
data-gram.
In addition to it, we will introduce to adjust results of parallel simulation of
geographically divided areas.

– plug-in:
Because huge disaster and rescue are a complex of various phenomena, it is
necessary to be able to extend the simulation systems incrementally. This
means the simulation system should have a facility to plug-in a new simulation module with minimum modifications. In order to solve conflicts among
modules, the system will provide a basic facility to manage conflicted data
and mechanism for users to define a way of conflict resolution.

2.3   Expert Simulator Modules

As mentioned above, huge disasters include various types of phenomena, for example, fire, collapse, traffic, and so on. In order to cover such major phenomena,
we will provide the following expert simulator modules.

– **Fire Simulator**:
estimates expansion and reduction of fire with taking degrees of building
collapses and effects of fire fighting into account.

- **Building Simulator**:
  estimates how much buildings collapse by quakes.
- **Blockade Simulator**:
  estimates how much roads are blocked by the damage of quakes and building collapse.
- **Traffic Simulator**:
  simulates movements of peoples and cars and estimate the degree of traffic jams.

Note again that the system has a capability to plug-in new modules. So, we can expand the system by adding new modules. Moreover, these simulators are the same as other modules, so that we can replace the modules to other implementations.

2.4   Agent Simulation Modules

Including agents' activities is the most significant feature of our system. However, developing the agent simulator is still a hard problem. Especially, decision making process is an open issue in researches on artificial intelligence and multi-agents systems. So, compared with other simulation modules, we treat the agent simulation modules differently.

First of all, we separate an agent into a body and a brain; the body part is simulated in the agent simulation module, and the brain part is open to researchers of agents. The researchers of agents can develop a program for the brain to make the decision, which connect to the body-part module. In other words, the agent simulation module becomes a server and brain programs connect with it as clients. As shown by RoboCup Soccer Simulation league, this style makes it easy for agent researchers to join the rescue simulation.

Secondly, we formalize communication among agents, and define the communication model. We discuss this point in Section 3.

3   Agent's Activity and Communication Simulation

3.1   Layered Commutation Model

In the rescue simulation, modeling agents' activities are key issue. Especially, communications among agents are an important factor to decide the agents' physical performance.

In order to model the communication for the simulation, we design "four layers model of communication". The four layers are:

- **Knowledge Layer**
  to process syntax and semantics of communication. This layer is open for agent programmers.

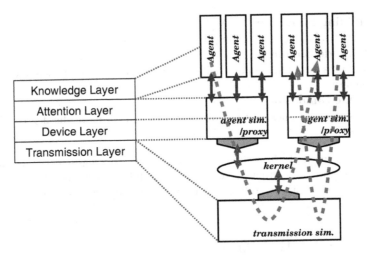

Fig. 3. Four Layers Model of Communication and Mapping to the Simulation System

- **Attention Layer**
  to simulate responsibility of human communication ability. For example, reading bulletin boards require human active attention. If information is on a bulletin board, human can not know the information without giving attention to the bulletin board. On the other hand, a siren attracts attention of most of human even if the human does not pay attention to the sound. This layer also simulates the communication capacity of human.
- **Device Layer**
  to simulate availability and functionality of devices like telephone, PDA, PC, and so on.
- **Transmission Layer**
  to simulate transmission of physical signals like sound, electric wave, telephone line, and so on.

Figure 3 shows a mapping from the four layers to the simulation systems. The knowledge layer correspond to agent clients, in which original messages are generated and interpreted. The attention layer is in the agent simulator/proxy modules, which filter received information according to status of agents' attention and resources of agents' body. For example, when an agent is not paying attention to a bulletin board, it can not get information from the memo on the board. When an agent is listening a message, it can not listen another message in the same time.

The device layer is also in the agent simulator/proxy modules, which filter information according to devices required in a specified communication method. For example, the agent need to have a mobile phone or find a wired phone to call a fire department office. The transmission layer corresponds to an expert simulator for the transmission. In the case of mobile phone, the simulator checks resource for the connection. When agents communicate by direct conversation, the simulator calculates the area the voice can reach.

The separation to the four layers helps for researchers to introduce new method of communication into the simulation system. When researchers want to introduce their new PDA devices with mobile phones into the simulator to test their facility for rescue domain, they should only develop their own device layer and combine it into the agent simulator/proxy modules. If they want to introduce new transmission method (like bluetooth) with PDA, it is possible by implementing both of device and transmission layers.

Basically, specification of language used in the knowledge layer is open in the rescue simulation system. Agents can transfer information by any kind of formats with each other. However, it will be required to provide interoperability among heterogeneous types of agents that are developed separately. Therefore, we need a specification of the rescue agent language. For the first step, we are designing a language for civilian.

FIPA already specify several languages for applications similar to our domain. For example, FIPA KIF [6] and FIPA CCL [4,11] are designed respectively for interchange of knowledge and for information gathering. But all proposed specifications in FIPA do not fit for our purpose in rescue simulation, because the language needs to reflect natural language features. Especially, civilian agents should behave as standard human civilians in the virtual world, so that civilian's conversation will be incomplete and ambiguous.

The natural language itself, on the other hand, is too wide and complex to handle in the rescue simulation. There are many unsolved issues in the natural language processing. Fortunately, we can limit variation of utterances for the rescue domain, where there are few complicated language phenomena.

Based on these consideration, we design a formal language.

3.2   Basic Syntax

Basically we use the similar syntax as S-expression of FIPA's communication language, that is:

```
(SpeechAct :sender Agent
           :receiver Agent
           :content Content
           ...)
```

Currently, the variations of *SpeechAct* are inform, query-if, query-ref, request, commit, acknowledge, and not-understood. An inform clause tells that the sender believe the content is true. A query-if clause asks the receiver whether the content is true or not. A query-ref clause asks the receiver to fill the information denoted by ':wh'. A request clause asks the receiver to do the content. A commit clause tells the sender will do the content in future. An acknowledge clause tells that the sender receives a message. In contrast to it, a not-understood clause informs that the sender can not understand the content. We also permit to use say speech act for the general purpose, because sometimes it may be difficult to determine a speech act of uttered sentences. A say clause can have an optional :acttype slot to specify the speech act. For example, (query-if ...) is equivalent to (say :acttype query-if ...).

3.3 Syntax for Content

In order to reflect flexibility of natural language, we use an S-expression of frame representation for the content. The syntax of the representation is

> (*FrameName* :*SlotName1* *SlotValue1*
> :*SlotName2* *SlotValue2*
> ...)

SlotNames should be *Symbols*, and *SlotValues* should be an S-expression of a *Data*, where *Data* is one of *Frame*, *Symbol* or *SpecialForm*. For example, "building (id=300) is in fire" and "agent (id=100) carries agent (id=200) to the building (id=300)" are respectively represented as:

```
(is :subject (building :id 300)
    :state in-fire)
(do :action carry
    :subject (agent :id 100)
    :object (agent :id 200)
    :destination (building :id 300))
```

SpecialForm includes the following expressions:

```
(:set Data*)
(:list Data*)
(:not Data)
(:wh [Data])
```

:set and :list forms denote collections of *Data*. :not form denotes negation of *Data*. :wh is used in query-ref clause to specify which information is queried.

Table 1 and Table 2 shows whole definition of the civilian language.

3.4 Location Based Communication

Robust information systems are critical infrastructure for rescue in huge disasters. An important feature of information for rescue is that the information is tightly related with 'location' with regard both to its contents and to its certainty.

Consider a case that a civilian reports fire information to a rescue office by telephone. In this case, the information about the location must be included in the report explicitly. However, the civilian may not be able to express accurate location. Moreover, if the civilian got the information not by watching the fire directly but by hearing it from another civilian, accuracy of location information will decrease.

Table 1. Definition of Civilian's Communication Language

$$
\begin{aligned}
Clause &::= \text{'('} \ ActType \ Role\_Vale\_Pair* \ \text{')'} \\
ActType &::= \text{'inform'} \mid \text{'query-if'} \mid \text{'query-ref'} \mid \text{'request'} \mid \text{'commit'} \\
&\quad \mid \text{'acknowledge'} \mid \text{'not-understood'} \mid \text{'say'} \\
Role\_Value\_Pair &::= Role \ Value \\
Role &::= Keyword \\
Keyword &::= \text{':'}RoleName \quad\quad ; \text{symbols that begin with ':'.} \\
RoleName &::= Symbol \\
Value &::= Data \\
Data &::= AtomData \mid Frame \mid SpecialForm \\
AtomData &::= Symbol \mid Number \\
Frame &::= \text{'('} \ Tag \ Role\_Value\_Pair* \ \text{')'} \\
SpecialForm &::= Collection \mid LogicalForm \\
Collection &::= Set \mid List \\
Tag &::= Symbol \quad\quad ; \text{symbols that begin with ":" are reserved.} \\
Set &::= \text{'('} \ \text{':set'} \ Data* \ \text{')'} \quad ; \text{non-ordered list} \\
List &::= \text{'('} \ \text{':list'} \ Data* \ \text{)} \quad ; \text{ordered list} \\
LogicalForm &::= Negation \\
Negation &::= \text{'('} \ \text{':not'} \ Data \ \text{)}
\end{aligned}
$$

In such case, if communication devices like PDA and mobile phone can get the location information and add it to the report automatically, it will help the rescue office to process the information. This kind of features can be implemented in the device layer of communication model shown in Section 3.1. For example, suppose that a civilian reports "a building is in fire" and the device add the location information. The original message of the civilian

```
(is :subject (building) :state (fire))
```

will be translated into

```
(inform :location (at :x 100 :y 200)
        :content (is :subject (building)
                     :state (fire)))
```

by the device layer.

In this way, researchers can easily test new devices and new methods to help rescue activities using the total rescue simulation system.

4 Concluding Remark

4.1 Comparison with HLA

Researches on distributed simulation systems are done mainly for military simulation and training [9,10]. DIS (Distributed Interactive Simulation) [2] and HLA

Table 2. Examples of Communication

(1) Agent(ID=100) say to agent(ID=200) "person(ID=150) is buried at a building(ID=250)".
```
(inform :sender (agent :id 100)
        :receiver (agent :id 200)
        :content (is :subject (agent :id 150)
                     :state (buried) :place (building :id 250)))
```
We also can be denote ":state buried" instead of ":state (buried)". A symbol is equivalent to a frame its tag is the symbol and has no slots.

(2) Agent(ID=100) say to agent(ID=200) "person(ID is unknown) is buried at place(100,200)".
```
(inform :sender (agent :id 100)
        :receiver (agent :id 200)
        :content (is :subject (agent)
                     :state (buried) :place (position :x 100 :y 200)))
```
We can omit :id slot in the agent frame when it is unknown. Generally, any kind of slots can be omitted.

(3) Agent(ID=100) ask to agent(ID=200) "which building is broken, how much, and when?". Then Agent(ID=200) answer to agent(ID=100) "at time 15, building(ID=150) is broken in degree 100."
```
(query-ref :sender (agent :id 100)
           :receiver (agent :id 200)
           :content (is :subject (building :id (:wh))
                        :time (:wh) :state (broken :degree (:wh))))
(inform :sender (agent :id 200)
        :receiver (agent :id 100)
        :content (is :subject (building :id 150)
                     :time 15 :state (broken :degree 50)))
```

(4) Agent(ID=100) say to someone "help!".
```
(request :sender (agent :id 100)
         :receiver (agent :tid T1)
         :content (do :subject (agent :tid T1)
                      :action (help) :object (agent :id 100)))
```
When the same agent (or building) occurs twice in the expression, we can assign temporal id (:tid) to denote the identity in the expression.

(5) Agent(ID=100) say to agent(ID=200) and agent(ID=300) "move away!".
```
(request :sender (agent :id 100)
         :receiver (:set (agent :id 200) (agent :id 300))
         :content (do :action (move)))
```

(6) Agent(ID=100) say to agent(ID=200) "please say to person(ID=300) to move away".
```
(request :sender (agent :id 100)
         :receiver (agent :id 200)
         :content (do :action (request :receiver (agent :id 300)
                                       :content (do :action (move)))))
```
We can embed a clause in any part of content.

(High-Level Architecture) [3] have been developed for this purpose. These works focuses on connecting stand-alone simulators like flight simulators over networks. In such simulation, accuracy of simulation of behaviors of each planes and vehicles is more important than interaction between them. Therefore, DIS and HLA is designed mainly for synchronizing relatively independent object simulators.

In the rescue simulation, on the other hand, interactions among agents occur more frequently. Therefore, execution of each simulation module should be controlled more carefully. Moreover, the rescue simulation includes so various physical phenomena each of which requires specialized simulation model, that it is difficult to make an integrated single model of whole phenomena. From these points of view, the phenomena-based distributed simulation style is suitable for rescue simulation rather than object-based distributed simulation style like HLA.

In addition to it, the proposed model is focusing flexibility of model of agent's communication. Unlike military systems, rescue activities and communication in it are not well organized, because activities of civilians, who are majority of agents in damaged area, are not negligible. Therefore, the simulation system is required to have an ability to implement new communication model, method, and devices.

4.2 Situated Communication

A benefit of using frame is that it is easy to add or omit slots from a frame. The benefit enables to reflect an important feature of natural language conversation, *situated communication*. In human communication, we tend to omit words when they are well known for both of sender and receiver, or when they are not so important. As shown in example (6), we can omit slots when they can be filled by receiver. In this example, :subject slots in the do frames and :sender slot in the embedded request frame are omitted.

One of open issues in the situated communication is how to solve references like pronouns. We can avoid this by assigning temporal id for referenced information as shown in example (4). But this method is not applicable easily in the case the reference points outside of a clause, because we need to define a scope of the temporal id over discourses.

Another issue of situated communication is how to control contexts. In order to fill omitted information, we need to select a right context as a pool of information. Fortunately, flows of contexts seem to be straight-forward in conversation in the rescue domain. In this case, we can control contexts by introducing :in-reply-to slots into the *Clause*.

4.3 Complex Logical Forms

We suppose that all civilian's utterances are simple sentences. Therefore, we introduce only negation (:not form) as logical forms. This has the following merit:

- It is easy to control the amount of communication transfered. We can treat a simple sentence as a unit of communication, so that we may be able to limit the number of sentences for an agent to say or hear.
- It is easy to define the civilian's behavior as a response to listened messages.

In future, however, we will need to introduce complex or compound sentences, which require more complicated logical forms like 'and', 'or' 'if' and so on.

4.4 Languages for Rescue Agents

While we define a civilian's language to reflect features of natural language, we are thinking that rescue agents will use more formal and well formed language between themselves. Compared with civilians, rescue specialists will be trained to use unambiguous and clear expressions. It is also required that the language can be specify complex combination of conditions and actions, which is similar to a kind of programming language. For this purpose, we can use more formal languages specification like FIPA's Content Language Library [5].

4.5 Link to the Real World

As mentioned in Section 1, the rescue simulation has the following social requirements:

- to evaluate city and rescue plans
- to train rescue teams
- to estimate damages and to plan rescue actions in real-time

Especially, the second and the third requirements are strongly related with the real world. In future, the simulation system needs to have capabilities to include real phenomena into the simulation as follows:

- In the training situation, the system must provide realistic information to trainees, and recognize responses of trainees in a natural way.
- In the real-time estimation and planning situation, the system need to integrate real value sensed in the real world and the simulation.

The proposed system and communication design only provides a fundamental framework for these requirements. To satisfy them, we need tackle the following open issues:

- effective human interface:
  In order to communicate with trainees or civilians, we need to have more effective interface for human. Especially, natural language processing is most important. [7] is also trying to use natural languages to control unmanned aerial vehicles. We may be able to use such a system for the simulation system.
- framework of agent's behavior:
  In the rescue simulation, agents must behave as human. Although it is impossible to realize human complex behavior completely by the current technologies, we may be able to restrict the behaviors into simple cases, because we need to take care of emergency situations in the rescue simulation. Behaviors in the emergency situations are still complex. But we can provide a framework to define agent's behaviors, by which social psychologists can use easily to investigate the human behavior.

— sensor-fusion and roll-back mechanism:
When real-time sensed data in the real world are available in the simulation, the system should have a mechanism to fuse the data into the simulation. The fusion is not so simple, because the sensor data will come with delay. In this case, the system needs to have a role-back mechanism to re-calculate the simulation. The fusion also requires a way to determine how long time the system needs to roll-back.

References

1. J. L. Casti. *Would-be Worlds: how simulation is changing the frontiers of science.* John Wiley and Sons, Inc., 1997.
2. Thomas L. Clarke, editor. *Distributed Interactive Simulation Systems for Simulation and Training in the Aero Space Environment,* volume CR58 of *Critical Reviews Series.* SPIE Optical Engineering Press, April 1995.
3. Judith S. Dahmann. High level architecture for simulation: An update. In Azzedine Bourkerche and Paul Reynolds, editors, *Distributed Interactive Simulation and Real-time Applications,* pages 32–40. IEEE Computer Society Technical Committee on Pattern Analysis and Machine Intelligence, IEEE Computer Society, July 1998.
4. FIPA, Geneva, Switzerland. *FIPA CCL Content Language Specification,* Aug. 2000. Document number XC00009A (http://www.fipa.org/).
5. FIPA, Geneva, Switzerland. *FIPA Content Language Library Specification,* Jul. 2000. Document number XC00007A (http://www.fipa.org/).
6. FIPA, Geneva, Switzerland. *FIPA KIF Content Language Specification,* Aug. 2000. Document number XC00010A (http://www.fipa.org/).
7. Oliver Lemon, Anne Bracy, Alexander Gruenstein, and Stanley Peters. Information states in a multi-modal dialogue system for human-robot conversation. In *Proc. of Bi-Dialog, 5th Workshop on Formal Semantics and Pragmatics of Dialogue,* pages 57–67, 2001.
8. Itsuki NODA. Framework of distributed simulation system for multi-agent environment. In *Proc. of The Fourth International Workshop on RoboCup,* pages 12–21, Aug. 2000.
9. Stow 97 - documentation and software. WWW home page http://web1.stricom.army.mil/STRICOM/DRSTRICOM/T3FG/SOFTWARE_LIBRARY/ST% OW97.html.
10. Warfighters' simulation (warsim) directorate national simulation center. WWW home page http://www-leav.army.mil/nsc/warsim/index.htm.
11. Steven Willmott, Monique Calisti, Boi Faltings, Santiago Macho-Gonzalez, Omar Belakhdar, and Marc Torrens. CCL: Expressions of choice in agent commnication. In *The Fourth International Conference on MultiAgent Systems (ICMAS-2000).* IEEE, July 2000.

Urban Pilot
A Handheld City Guide That Maps Personal and Collective Experiences through Social Networks

Aradhana Goel

Masters of Science in Architecture (1999-2001), Design Technology Group
Massachusetts Institute of Technology, Cambridge, MA 02139, US
a_goel@alum.mit.edu

Abstract. This paper investigates the use of handheld mobile devices as personalized tools for city navigation that go beyond cartographic limitations and directory services. The volatile, unpredictable randomness of the city life and its ever-changing patterns need dynamic navigational means. Unfortunately, existing devices and their applications do not fully address the impelling potential of real-time interactivity generated by Wireless and Global Positioning Systems (GPS). This study proposes a tool, which encourages personal perceptions and collective experience of cities by providing a dynamic information space that overlaps the city with individual users. The tool is characterized by a three-tier structure of Personal Filtering, Social Networking and Information Layering. It filters the information through personalization, shares the personal perception through social networks and layers the information with collective experience. Hence it is designed as a regenerative information system based on social networks that allows for the creation of new patterns and interpretations.

1   Context

Exploration of cities is a three-way process of communication between the user who has particular needs and characteristics, the information that is a representation of a set of spatial and temporal relationships and the physical place around the user. Looking at a very broad categorization, the information is accessed in 3 forms; the traditional paper medium, the digital medium and the current mobile initiatives in this field.

It is interesting to note that there exists a wide range of cartographic maps and paper guidebooks; from highly specialized guides like 'Native's guide to New York' to the objective catalogues like 'Official Guide to New York'. These are static representations but offer dynamic perceptions since they are relevant in particular context and time. It has inherent in itself the concept of versatile audiences and customization of information for the target audience.

The digital guides (like http://www.digitalcity.com), on the other hand, provide large amounts of up-to-date information with retrieval based on a hierarchical system or keyword search. It solves the problem of scale and redundancy of information, but not of information anxiety [1] caused by excessive information and irrelevancy to the

M. Tanabe, P. van den Besselaar, T. Ishida (Eds.): Digital Cities, LNCS 2362, pp. 384-397, 2002.
© Springer-Verlag Berlin Heidelberg 2002

user. Dynamism is limited to updates and customizing this information is a difficult task. This is a static representation of a dynamic phenomenon in a medium that has inherent in itself properties of time and mutability. Digital information in this form is not portable like a simple paper guidebook and the information needs to be assimilated, downloaded and printed, to eventually become an updated guidebook.

Current Mobile handheld technology and applications are addressing this issue of portability of digital information. Cities are repositories of knowledge and sometimes being in the right place, at the right time, with access to right kind of information becomes a key factor in experiencing the physical space meaningfully. The unprecedented connectivity generated by the wireless and GPS technology, has led to research initiatives in location-based, context specific application. But the existing roadmap of technology, device industry, applications and services is still disintegrated. The challenge this paper addresses is to tap the potential of this real-time interface to generate a dynamic information structure for urban explorations that can not only reveal hidden patterns and but also create new patterns.

2   Hypothesis

City is a dynamic and regenerative phenomenon. It is comprised of ever-changing people, patterns and connections. These attributes make the relationship between the individual and the city highly volatile. This dynamic perception of the city contains in it the hidden information patterns. Our mind engages the city at various levels and is constantly trying to decipher these hidden patterns.

This paper claims that an individual's engagement with the city can be heightened and hidden patterns can be revealed by the appropriate use of technology. Since the experience of the body in space is the most vital phenomenon, and it is equally important to be in the right place at right time, this paper advocates the use of mobile handheld device technology. But the paper also proposes a shift in perception. The city is neither about information accessed, nor about the technology. It is about the people, their experiences and their connection with the city. The proposed tool (Urban Pilot) aims to encompass both individual perception and collective experience of people through a regenerative system of information based on social networks.

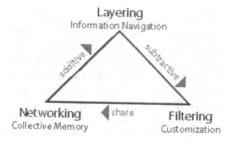

Fig. 1. Three-tier cyclic structure of Filtering, Networking and Layering

Urban Pilot is designed as a three-tier cyclic structure of Filtering, Networking and Layering. It would, Filter the information through personalization; Share the personal perception through social networks, And Layers the information with collective memory. This cycle adds an interpretive and regenerative layer to the whole system and is the key element that characterizes the ecological property of the city.

3   Design Theory

Urban Pilot is a handheld city guide that can be downloaded and customized to most handheld devices. This section lays down its design theory based on the three-tier structure of Filtering, Networking and Layering.

3.1   Filtering

One of the most important factors responsible for the volatility of city information is the diversity of its people. This would mean that the Urban Pilot audience is a heterogeneous mix of people and one type of information would not fit all. Hence the system allows the users to input their user-profiles at different stages of use. As the information is retrieved, the tool outputs the relevant information that matches the user-profile data. This system of sieving the information layers is referred to as 'Filtering' and the input mechanisms are referred to as 'Filters'.

The tool has three levels of filtration - pre-screen filters, contextual temporal filters and collaborative filters. Pre-screen filters gauge the interest pattern and familiarity level of the person, Variable persona filters capture his context and the Collaborative filters enhances the system's recommendation over a period of time based on peer usage.

Hence, the information retrieval is based on a system of gradual filtering of data that progressively updates the information and personalization becomes more powerful over time. It requires a basic framework for understanding the audience, deciphering key differences and usage patterns, categorizing them in user profiles and developing an appropriate information language for each profile [2].

Pre-Screen filters. This initial level of customization of the tool sets the backdrop for all exploration. The user input is done at the time of application download. Input parameters are basic profiles involving 'Context' (time and familiarity with the place) and 'Audience Characteristics' (demographic details of age and gender, interests).

These rule-based filters also alter the thematic information landscape, and may change the mode of delivery. At the most basic level, users get categorized into travelers and the residents. The system also begins to customize information by the interest and objective of the user. There are various secondary references where an attempt has been made to categorize users and their behavior patterns [3,4].

When the user downloads this application, he is automatically registered into the system as a member of the network. These people are connected directly to each other, any time, and any location. The system categorizes them into three categories. Friends are Urban Pilot users that match with the user's address book. The user has established 'close-ties' with these people. Peers are like-minded people matched by the system using their profiling data. These links depict the weak ties between them where relationships are based on homogeneity, reputation and trust. Strangers are the broad networks of people with seemingly no common ground. This concept of generating social networks has been elaborated later.

Fig. 2. Urban Pilot users are connected directly to each other, any time, and any location

Temporal filters. Temporal filters are time-bound, contextual variables that give information about the user's spatial, temporal and psychological context. At first, the user chooses an "Urban Lens". The design demonstration shows four categories, The-Works (comprehensive detailed view of the city), Hot-Picks (popular view), Off-Beat (off the beaten track, unique view) and Get-Active (adventurous and activity based exploration). Depending on the current time and context of the user, the individual can choose their persona and vary it as needed. The choice of these four categories by the author is not important. What is important is that the system is providing an opportunity to input your personality in a particular time and context. Each of these personas has its own appropriate way of interacting with the city and has a unique sub-set of themes that are filtered from the overall information system.

The next level of filtering is in the form of time and context-sensitive urban variables. These filters are visualized in the form of four sliders (time, mobility, sociability and price sensitivity) that enable a degree of variability. 'Time' slider would determine whether the tool would "allow chances to occur (more time) or deliver a programmed experience" [5].

The 'Mobility and Time' sliders affect the navigation layer and accessibility maps. Together they change the scale of the information represented in order to maintain its relevancy to the user. The third slider depicts the 'Sociability Factor'. This would impact the collaborative networking between the user and his peers using the system.

A low scale of sociability would let each person feel the presence of his peers but would not allow real-time interaction. The last filter records the 'Price Sensitivity'.

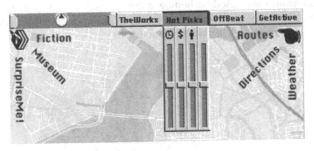

Fig. 3. Filtering is in the form of time and context-sensitive urban variables

Collaborative Filters. This is based upon simultaneous group-use over a period of time. As each person uses the tool and makes choices, a matrix is created that matches the user-profiles with probable individual behaviors. This probability can be captured in a rule-based filtering system.

Personalization means crafting different experiences for different people. Typically the existing personalization engines match user-profiles with content information to produce custom content that is little more than targeted ads and recommendations. This paper is proposing a personalized experience that involves re-shaping Urban-Pilot's structure & content.

3.2   Layering

The information of the city is represented in thematic layers that are organized by its degree of volatility. Volatility of information refers to the degree of change in perception, vis-à-vis time. There is a core information base that represents the periodically monitored data such as the history of a particular place. The next level is the services where the information is accessed from the server in real-time, like the traffic and weather. One's own diary (Notes-to-Myself) represents the most versatile and personal information. The community-based information (Notes-to-Share) data represents the highest level of volatility because this data is regenerative - constantly formed and reformed by social networking. Each layer is represented as an information wheel.

Core. The core represents information that is permanent in nature but is updated regularly. These are urban cartographic maps that are interpretive maps (representational in character).

"The best Visualizations are not static images to be printed in books, but fluid, dynamic artifacts that respond to the need for a different view..." [6]. These visualizations are arranged thematically to reveal different spatial and temporal patterns of the city. Some of the generic themes in this core layer could be Timelines, Historic Maps, Fictional Narratives, Topography, Flora and Fauna.

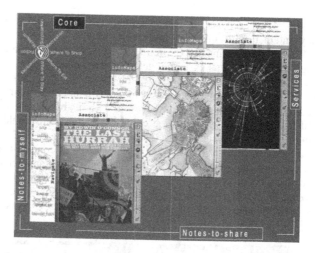

Fig. 4. Core Layer with Timelines, Historic Maps, Fictional Narratives

Services. These are information layers that represent the volatile information that can be collected real-time from a central server. This layer links the objects of reference to the related services. For example, if a user chooses a restaurant, then this service layer could lead to booking a table through the wireless network.

On the other hand, it could give time-sensitive information like traffic and weather, or it could compute directions from point-A to point-B taking into account the user's position coordinates. It can also present an accessibility map to the user by computing the multi-variate data of traffic, weather and available mode of transport.

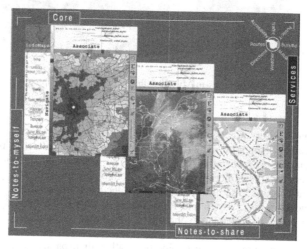

Fig. 5. Services Layer with time-sensitive information like traffic, directions and weather

Notes-to-Myself. The proposed system accumulates the personal memoirs of the users as they interact with the tool and each other to retrieve, edit and add information. When a user begins to explore the space, he/she is given a base map. At the beginning, the system makes some general recommendations. As the user chooses a path, the system records his travel data. The user has a choice of personalizing this data and maintaining a travelogue by annotating this map with text, graphic or audio input. These notes can be accessed by time, by themes or by place.

It is useful here to speculate that some cognitive image maps could result from such a system that can be of various types (Node and Landmark map, Cartoons, Photo Montage, Pictorial, Graphical or Illustrative). These maps are "concept maps or (mind maps, as they are sometimes called) ... Usually such maps are constructed informally by simply sketching them on paper ... An individual can use a concept map as a tool for re-organizing his or her own personal structure, and it may reveal patterns of relationships between ideas that were not evident when the concepts were stored internally" [7].

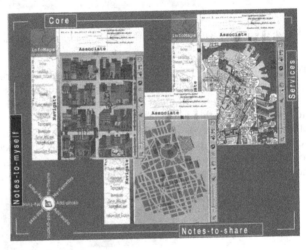

Fig. 6. Notes-to-Myself with cognitive image maps

Notes-to-Share. Users always have a choice of keeping their personal perceptions private, or sharing them with the Urban Pilot community as a collective memoirs. The personal memoirs are accessible to the user only and can be downloaded onto a remote server, but the collective memoirs go into the information system. These annotations are grouped as either Reflections, Anecdotes, Information, Travel Tips or Short-term postings like Gossip and Pin-up-Boards. This is the most dynamic layer, since it is a result of constant evolution of ideas that occur as a result of social networking.

These layers encourage active exploration rather than passive consumption, like "...a guide that can provide the specifics if the person knows what he has in mind; or that can be open-ended but supportive references which encourage the reader to explore" [8].

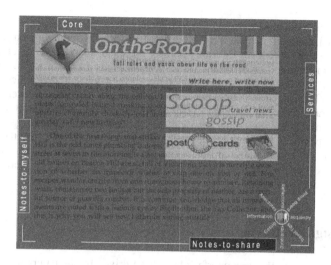

Fig. 7. Notes to Share with Reflections, Anecdotes by people

3.3   Networking

The core information base needs to be layered with the volatile memory of people in order to present the city as an interpretation, rather data. 'Peer-to-Peer' social networking [9] captures spontaneous interactions and use people as knowledge repositories to develop a collective memory of a place.

Fig. 8. Regenerative Cycle of Collective Memory

The urban Pilot creates a system of synchronous and asynchronous networking where the personal notes of people are shared with the larger community on a voluntary basis. When a user retrieves information from 'Notes-to-Share', he is given the option to rate the information on a 'Rating Slider'. This slider is a kind of a 'Trust Filter' that attempts to develop a peer reputation system. 'In a system that relies on strong interpersonal connections, branding, in the form of reputation, accrues to the individual rather than the product.' [10] As the referenced information accumulates points, it progresses from being 'Personal', to 'Sharable' and finally being 'Reputable'. While the personal information degenerates over a period of time, the reputable information finds its place in the core information system. This generates a collaborative system where social networks created and the information shared is characterized by spontaneity.

4   Design Prototype

The technology and the user-interface have been driven by the nature of services and content. The device is based on the convergence of the mobile device technology, Voice recognition system, Wireless and GPS capability and improved Graffiti

Fig. 9. The proposed tool is an application designed for the existing Palm

technology. The functions identified in the designed prototype are filtering & retrieving the information, exploring & annotating to personalize information, sharing & rating of information from social networks.

The prototype has a toolbar, a personality bar and four wheels that represent the information system. The toolbar provides tools for orientation, networking and search by people, place or purpose. The personality filter lets one choose an urban lens to view the city and then input data for personalization of information. The four wheels represent the four information layers and are accessed through a rotary button. The design iterations was done by building user scenarios that have been categorized as:

4.1   Careful Exploration of a Place

The audience addressed is people who have the commodity "Time" and intent to "Explore" the cityscape (travelers and by residents). The level of familiarity with or knowledge about the place is limited and one wants to assimilate most of the relevant information in the given time. The intent of this user-scenario is:
- ☐ Customizing the information through personal filters
- ☐ The cycle of collective memory

Story Board #1 (Part #1) The character is a historian who has recently shifted to Boston, Beacon Hill area from New York and has been using this system to maintain a travelogue of Boston. He has been using the Timeline and Fictional Narratives of the CORE to update his view. He records and shares his experiences as Reflections of the streets of Beacon Hill and Anecdotes about the weather.

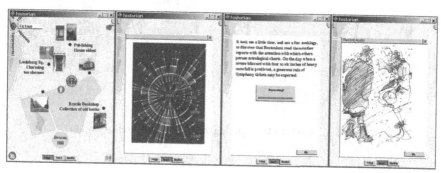

Fig. 10. A new resident (historian) exploring Boston

Story Board #1 (Part #2) This character is a 40-year-old Italian woman writer is in Boston on a conference. She is traveling with her 5-year-old child. The conference ends on Friday and she wants to explore Boston over the weekend before she leaves. The system would thus need to cater to both the personality types, of a writer and of a mother. She uses the 'Urban Lens' to customize her city view.

She then wanders around the Beacon Hill Area; reaches one of the streets where some coachmen used to live and wonders what it is like to live here now. Uses NOTES-TO-SHARE and accesses the information shared by historian. She wants to find out about the system's recommendation for the Boston Common; Finds that it might be good for her child and plans to go there. It is a show featuring authors and illustrators of children books. Her child loves the show and gets busy there.

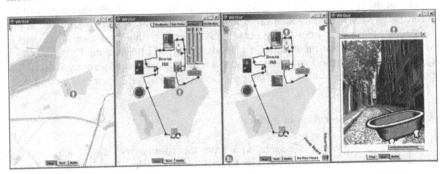

Fig. 11. Writer/Traveler looking for a customized itinerary

In the meantime, she uses Urban Pilot to find more information on Beacon Hill and decides to check anecdotes by famous people. When its time to wrap up, she uses the 'surprise-me' in the CORE layer to check out the system's recommendations.

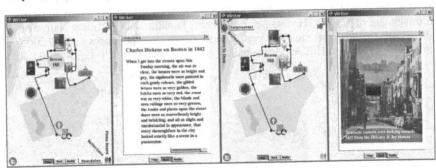

Fig. 12. Writer/Traveler exploring the Beacon Hill Area of Boston

4.2   Day-to-Day Relaxed Navigation of the Place

Here the tool is used to find quick solutions to a query. This would usually apply for the residents or people who are highly familiar with the place. The intent of this user-scenario is:

☐ Synchronous and asynchronous networking between close-ties and weak-ties
☐ Annotating the information and maintaining personal notes
☐ Voluntary sharing of personal notes with the social community

Story Board #2. The character is a 28-year-old Boston college student who has gone to the Fenway stadium in Boston to watch a Red Sox game. He uses the Urban Pilot to network with his friends and peers.

He opens the application and the system shows him his last annotated map of Fenway area of Boston. He uses the 'Hot-pick' urban lens and inputs: an 8-hour time window, a medium mobility level, a high level of sociability and very low money value. He could use the CORE to get information and SERVICES to buy tickets.

He instant messages to his friend Tom. They both plan to go to Avalon after the game and decide to put this information on the pin-up-board for others to join. The game continues and the Pete checks the board at the end of the game. There is message posting on the pin-up-board by Avalon that suggests a last minute change! This reflects the ability of such a system to account for dynamic updates.

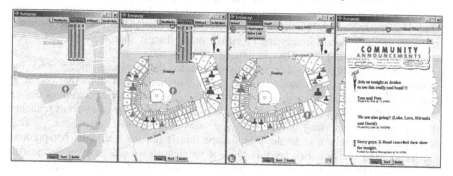

Fig. 13. A Boston student planning an evening while watching a Baseball game

One of the peers would like to chat with Pete. Pete accepts his chat request and answers his question. To make the point more clear, he accesses his NOTES-TO-MYSELF and sends a synchronize request to the peer. This is an example of networking and knowledge exchange between people linked by homogeneity. Pete might want to know other people's opinions about the current game. He decides to access the NOTES-TO-SHARE and take a look at the reflections posted.

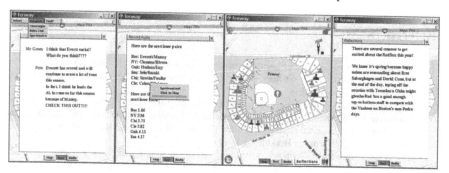

Fig. 14. Networking / Information sharing among Peers

5   Conclusions

The proposed tool - Urban Pilot - is a city-guide for a handheld device where the focus is on the shift in perception from 'information and technology' to the 'city, its connection with people and their experiences'. The tool captures the individual perceptions and collective experiences. It not only updates the information, but also creates an ecological system that allows for the creation of new patterns and interpretations. The Urban Pilot tool acts as a mediator between the individual and the physical, emotional and collective space around him. The focus is on this concept of connection rather than the isolated design of a particular prototype.

Though this paper focuses on a system of exploration the tool offers the potential of being an analytical system. While personal memory could generate a self-analyzing tool, it is collective memory that can be seen as a social mirror reflecting the ever-changing patterns of urban life. It is interesting to speculate that these personal memoirs could generate interesting cognitive maps that, if shared, could add a rich layer of information to the collective experience of the city.

Future work might involve investigation into the business model and the infrastructure needed to maintain such a system. Another area of study that is crucial to this work is user-interface design. A thorough research into the spectrum of device and application design needs to be researched. The present is far away from realizing the dream of 'accessing information by anyone, anytime, anywhere'. This investigation assumes a technology landscape that is not yet available, but predicts that supporting technologies for this kind of application would be very successful. Though the author has carried out some design iterations (both device and application design), this information system could open various possibilities. The author would like to carry out some usability tests on the design proposal and further iterate based on the user- feedback.

Acknowledgments. This paper is a part of thesis presented in partial fulfillment of the author's graduate research program at MIT. The author would like to acknowledge the thesis committee (William J. Mitchell, William Porter, David Rose, Carol Strohecker) for their help and guidance in this research.

References

1.   Wurman, Richard Saul. Information Anxiety 2. (Indianapolis, Ind., Que, 2001)
2.   Viant Innovation Center Project, Experience Architecture: The strategy and design of ecommerce personalization,
     http://viant2-ecdc-3.digisle.net/pages/frame_thought_traffic.html, 2001.
3.   Southworth, Michael. Smart Maps for advanced traveler information systems based on user characteristics: final report. (Berkeley: Institute of Urban and Regional Development, University of California at Berkeley, c1994)
4.   The Viant Innovation Center is a research group at Viant, which is a leading Internet consulting firm that helps clients in a broad range of industries plan, build, and launch digital businesses. http:///www.viant.com
5.   Hack, Gary and Hollister Rob, Cashing in on the Guidebook Boom: It's a long, long way to 76, Landscape Architecture, January 1974

6. Ware, Colin, Information Visualization: Perception for Design, (Morgan Kaufman Publishers 2000)
7. Ibid.
8. Hack, Gary and Hollister Rob, Cashing in on the   Guidebook Boom: It's a long, long way to 76, Landscape Architecture, January 1974
9. Viant Innovation Center Project, The Human Side of Peer to Peer: where technology and people come together, http://viant2-ecdc-3.digisle.net/pages/frame_thought_traffic.html, 2001. "Peer to peer, or P2P, is a network technology where all the nodes have equal access to its peers... that results in a decentralized design which is a powerful tool."
10. Ibid.

Author Index

Lecture Notes in Computer Science

For information about Vols. 1–2306
please contact your bookseller or Springer-Verlag

Vol. 2347: P. De Bra, P. Brusilovsky, R. Conejo (Eds.), Adaptive Hypermedia and Adaptive Web-Based Systems. Proceedings, 2002. XV, 615 pages. 2002.

Vol. 2348: A. Banks Pidduck, J. Mylopoulos, C.C. Woo, M. Tamer Ozsu (Eds.), Advanced Information Systems Engineering. Proceedings, 2002. XIV, 799 pages. 2002.

Vol. 2349: J. Kontio, R. Conradi (Eds.), Software Quality – ECSQ 2002. Proceedings, 2002. XIV, 363 pages. 2002.

Vol. 2350: A. Heyden, G. Sparr, M. Nielsen, P. Johansen (Eds.), Computer Vision – ECCV 2002. Proceedings, Part I. XXVIII, 817 pages. 2002.

Vol. 2351: A. Heyden, G. Sparr, M. Nielsen, P. Johansen (Eds.), Computer Vision – ECCV 2002. Proceedings, Part II. XXVIII, 903 pages. 2002.

Vol. 2352: A. Heyden, G. Sparr, M. Nielsen, P. Johansen (Eds.), Computer Vision – ECCV 2002. Proceedings, Part III. XXVIII, 919 pages. 2002.

Vol. 2353: A. Heyden, G. Sparr, M. Nielsen, P. Johansen (Eds.), Computer Vision – ECCV 2002. Proceedings, Part IV. XXVIII, 841 pages. 2002.

Vol. 2355: M. Matsui (Ed.), Fast Software Encryption. Proceedings, 2001. VIII, 169 pages. 2001.

Vol. 2358: T. Hendtlass, M. Ali (Eds.), Developments in Applied Artificial Intelligence. Proceedings, 2002 XIII, 833 pages. 2002. (Subseries LNAI).

Vol. 2359: M. Tistarelli, J. Bigun, A.K. Jain (Eds.), Biometric Authentication. Proceedings, 2002. X, 197 pages. 2002.

Vol. 2360: J. Esparza, C. Lakos (Eds.), Application and Theory of Petri Nets 2002. Proceedings, 2002. X, 445 pages. 2002.

Vol. 2361: J. Blieberger, A. Strohmeier (Eds.), Reliable Software Technologies – Ada-Europe 2002. Proceedings, 2002 XIII, 367 pages. 2002.

Vol. 2362: M. Tanabe, P. van den Besselaar, T. Ishida (Eds.), Digital Cities II. Proceedings, 2001. XI, 399 pages. 2002.

Vol. 2363: S.A. Cerri, G. Gouardères, F. Paraguaçu (Eds.), Intelligent Tutoring Systems. Proceedings, 2002. XXVIII, 1016 pages. 2002.

Vol. 2364: F. Roli, J. Kittler (Eds.), Multiple Classifier Systems. Proceedings, 2002. XI, 337 pages. 2002.

Vol. 2366: M.-S. Hacid, Z.W. Raś, D.A. Zighed, Y. Kodratoff (Eds.), Foundations of Intelligent Systems. Proceedings, 2002. XII, 614 pages. 2002. (Subseries LNAI).

Vol. 2367: J. Fagerholm, J. Haataja, J. Järvinen, M. Lyly. P. Råback, V. Savolainen (Eds.), Applied Parallel Computing. Proceedings, 2002. XIV, 612 pages. 2002.

Vol. 2368: M. Penttonen, E. Meineche Schmidt (Eds.), Algorithm Theory – SWAT 2002. Proceedings, 2002. XIV, 450 pages. 2002.

Vol. 2369: C. Fieker, D.R. Kohel (Eds.), Algebraic Number Theory. Proceedings, 2002. IX, 517 pages. 2002.

Vol. 2370: J. Bishop (Ed.), Component Deployment. Proceedings, 2002. XII, 269 pages. 2002.

Vol. 2372: A. Pettorossi (Ed.), Logic Based Program Synthesis and Transformation. Proceedings, 2001. VIII, 267 pages. 2002.

Vol. 2373: A. Apostolico, M. Takeda (Eds.), Combinatorial Pattern Matching. Proceedings, 2002. VIII, 289 pages. 2002.

Vol. 2374: B. Magnusson (Ed.), ECOOP 2002 – Object-Oriented Programming. XI, 637 pages. 2002.

Vol. 2375: J. Kivinen, R.H. Sloan (Eds.), Computational Learning Theory. Proceedings, 2002. XI, 397 pages. 2002. (Subseries LNAI).

Vol. 2378: S. Tison (Ed.), Rewriting Techniques and Applications. Proceedings, 2002. XI, 387 pages. 2002.

Vol. 2380: P. Widmayer, F. Triguero, R. Morales, M. Hennessy, S. Eidenbenz, R. Conejo (Eds.), Automata, Languages and Programming. Proceedings, 2002. XXI, 1069 pages. 2002.

Vol. 2381: U. Egly, C.G. Fernmüller (Eds.), Automated Reasoning with Analytic Tableaux and Related Methods. Proceedings, 2002. X, 341 pages. 2002 .(Subseries LNAI).

Vol. 2382: A. Halevy, A. Gal (Eds.), Next Generation Information Technologies and Systems. Proceedings, 2002. VIII, 169 pages. 2002.

Vol. 2383: M.S. Lew, N. Sebe, J.P. Eakins (Eds.), Image and Video Retrieval. Proceedings, 2002. XII, 388 pages. 2002.

Vol. 2384: L. Batten, J. Seberry (Eds.), Information Security and Privacy. Proceedings, 2002. XII, 514 pages. 2002.

Vol. 2385: J. Calmet, B. Benhamou, O. Caprotti, L. Henocque, V. Sorge (Eds.), Artificial Intelligence, Automated Reasoning, and Symbolic Computation. Proceedings, 2002. XI, 343 pages. 2002. (Subseries LNAI).

Vol. 2386: E.A. Boiten, B. Möller (Eds.), Mathematics of Program Construction. Proceedings, 2002. X, 263 pages. 2002.

Vol. 2389: E. Ranchhod, N.J. Mamede (Eds.), Advances in Natural Language Processing. Proceedings, 2002. XII, 275 pages. 2002. (Subseries LNAI).

Vol. 2391: L.-H. Eriksson, P.A. Lindsay (Eds.), FME 2002: Formal Methods – Getting IT Right. Proceedings, 2002. XI, 625 pages. 2002.

Vol. 2392: A. Voronkov (Ed.), Automated Deduction – CADE-18. Proceedings, 2002. XII, 534 pages. 2002. (Subseries LNAI).

Vol. 2393: U. Priss, D. Corbett, G. Angelova (Eds.), Conceptual Structures: Integration and Interfaces. Proceedings, 2002. XI, 397 pages. 2002. (Subseries LNAI).

Vol. 2398: K. Miesenberger, J. Klaus, W. Zagler (Eds.), Computers Helping People with Special Needs. Proceedings, 2002. XXII, 794 pages. 2002.

Vol. 2399: H. Hermanns, R. Segala (Eds.), Process Algebra and Probabilistic Methods. Proceedings, 2002. X, 215 pages. 2002.

Vol. 2401: P.J. Stuckey (Ed.), Logic Programming. Proceedings, 2002. XI, 486 pages. 2002.

Vol. 2403: Mark d'Inverno, M. Luck, M. Fisher, C. Preist (Eds.), Foundations and Applications of Multi-Agent Systems. Proceedings, 1996-2000. X, 261 pages. 2002. (Subseries LNAI).

Vol. 2405: B. Eaglestone, S. North, A. Poulovassilis (Eds.), Advances in Databases. Proceedings, 2002. XII, 199 pages. 2002.